Advanced
Ancient India's Vedic Culture

The Planet's Earliest Civilization and How it Influenced the World

Stephen Knapp

May this be an inspiration for you
to take a closer look at what Vedic culture has given to humanity,
and take a stand for helping preserve, protect
and share this culture with others.

Copyright © 2012, by Stephen Knapp

Cover photo: The highly ornate and architecturally amazing *gopurams* (towers) of the Meenakshi temple in Madurai, India.

All interior photographs by Stephen Knapp. Thousands more of his color photos of India are available online through his websites, blogs, or elsewhere.

ISBN-13: 978-1477607893
ISBN-10: 1477607897

Published by
The World Relief Network
Detroit, Michigan, USA

You can find out more about
Stephen Knapp
and his books, free ebooks, research,
and numerous articles and photos,
along with many other spiritual resources at:
www.stephen-knapp.com
www.stephenknapp.info
http://stephenknapp.wordpress.com

Other books by the author:

Contents

CHAPTER ONE

Introduction to Vedic Culture's Advancements

When we talk about the planet's earliest civilization, we are talking about the world's earliest sophisticated society after the last ice age. This means that according to the Vedic time tables, various forms of civilization have been existing for millions of years. But the first record of an organized and developed society was the Vedic culture that arose in ancient India with the Indus Sarasvati civilization, and then spread out from there in all directions around the world.

Often times we see that students, even in India's academic system, have not studied or encountered the contributions that were made by early civilization in the area of ancient India. Not only are they not aware of such developments that had been given from India, but there is often a lack of such knowledge to be studied. Therefore, this book is to help fill that gap of information and to show how this area of the world, indeed, had a most advanced civilization, but was also where many of society's advancements originated.

It can be found that what became the area of India and its Vedic culture was way ahead of its time. This can be noticed in such things as industry, metallurgy, science, textiles, medicine, surgery, mathematics, and, of course, philosophy and spirituality. In fact, we can see the roots of these sciences and metaphysics in many areas of the world that can be traced back to its Indian or Vedic origins.

Furthermore, we often do not know of all the progress that had been made during the ancient times of India, which used to be called Bharatvarsha or Aryavrata. Nor do most people know all that ancient India gave to the world. So let us take a serious look at this.

From the Preface of *Indian Tradition of Chemistry and Chemical Technology*, the authors relate most accurately: "Hindus are a race who

1

have dwelled on the most fundamental questions about life (& death), about nature and its origins. The bold questioning by Hindus gave birth to theories, axioms, principles and a unique approach to and a way of life. The approach to life and the way of life led to the evolution of one of the most ancient and grand cultures on the face of the earth. The spiritual aspects of Hindu culture are more commonly known, the fact that science, technology and industry were a part of their culture is little known.

"For historical reasons, the achievements of ancient Hindus in various fields of science and technology are not popularly known to Indians. The recent research by Sri Dharmpal and others has shown that the colonial invaders and the rulers had a vested interest in distorting and destroying the information regarding all positive aspects of Hindu culture. The conventional understanding today is that Hindus were more concerned about rituals, about spirituality, and the world above or the world after death. That Hindus were an equally materialistic people, that India was the industrial workshop of the world till the end of 18ᵗʰ century, that Hindus had taken up basic questions of the principles of astronomy, fundamental particles, origins of the universe, applied psychiatry and so on, are not well documented and not popularly known. That ancient Hindus had highly evolved technologies in textile engineering, ceramics, printing, weaponry, climatology and meteorology, architecture, medicine and surgery, metallurgy, agriculture and agricultural engineering, civil engineering, town planning, and similar other fields is known only to a few scholars even today. There are about 44 known ancient and medieval Sanskrit texts on a technical subject such as chemistry alone. The information about the science and technological heritage of India is embedded in the scriptures, the epics and in several of the technical texts. The information needs to be taken out of these and presented.

"Facts like Hindus had the knowledge that the sun is the center of the solar system, about the geography of the earth, the way the plants produce food, the way blood circulates in the body, the science of abstract mathematics and numbers, the principles of health, medicine and surgery and so on at a time in history when the rest of the world did not know how to think, talk and write has to be exposed to people. This can draw the attention of these communities, especially the future generation towards 'ideas' that are essentially Indian.

"There are several published works on the history of India. Such works are written by Indian scholars as well as western researchers in oriental and Indological studies. Many of these works are highly scholastic and are not amenable to the common man. There is a need to make the knowledge of science heritage of India known to one and all. Further, there is need for studying scriptures, epics, and other ancient literature (in Sanskrit as well as other regional languages) to unearth the wealth of knowledge of our ancestors. Reports of such studies also need to be published continuously." [1]

This is the goal of the present volume, to easily and simply convey this knowledge for the benefit of everyone, for the correct view of history, and to give credit where credit is due.

THE ADVANCED NATURE OF
ANCIENT INDIAN SCIENCES

Achievements in the sciences of ancient India were known all over the world, even in Arabia, China, Spain, and Greece, countries in which medieval scholars acknowledged their indebtedness to India. For example, the Arab scholar Sa'id ibn Ahmad al-Andalusi (1029–1070) wrote in his history on science, called *Tabaqat-al'umam*:

"The first nation to have cultivated science in India... India is known for the wisdom of its people. Over many centuries, all the kings of the past have recognized the ability of the Indians in all the branches of knowledge. The kings of China have stated that the kings of the world are five in number and all the people of the world are their subjects. They mentioned the king of China, the king of India, the king of the Turks, the king of the Persians, and the king of the Romans. ...they referred to the king of India as the 'king of wisdom' because of the Indians' careful treatment of '*ulum* [sciences] and all the branches of knowledge.

"The Indians, known to all nations for many centuries, are the metal [essence] of wisdom, the source of fairness and objectivity. They are people of sublime pensiveness, universal apologues, and useful and rare inventions. ...To their credit the Indians have made great strides in the study of numbers and of geometry. They have acquired immense information and reached the zenith in their knowledge of the movements of the stars [astronomy]. ...After all that they have surpassed all other people in their knowledge of medical sciences..."

Furthermore, "Whether it was astronomy, mathematics (specially geometry), medicine or metallurgy, each was a pragmatic contribution to the general Hindu ethos, viz., Man in Nature, Man in harmony with Nature, and not Man and Nature or Man Against Nature, that characterizes modern science. The Hindu approach to nature was holistic, often alluding to the terrestrial-celestial correspondence and human-divine relationship. Hindu and scientific and technological developments were an integral part of this attitude that was assiduously fostered in the ancient period." [2]

In his article, *Indic Mathematics: India and the Scientific Revolution*, Dr. David Grey lists some of the most important developments in the history of mathematics that took place in India, summarizing the contributions of luminaries such as Aryabhata, Brahmagupta, Mahavira, Bhaskara, and Madhava. He concludes by asserting, "the role played by India in the development (of the scientific revolution in Europe) is no mere footnote, easily and inconsequentially swept under the rug of Eurocentric bias. To do so is to distort history, and to deny India one of its greatest contributions to world civilizations."

Lin Yutang, Chinese scholar and author, also wrote that: "India was China's teacher in trigonometry, quadratic equations, grammar, phonetics..." and so forth. Francois Voltaire also stated: "... everything has come down to us from the banks of the Ganges."

Referring to the above quotes, David Osborn concludes thus: "From these statements we see that many renowned intellectuals believed that the *Vedas* provided the origin of scientific thought."

The Syrian astronomer / monk Severus Sebokhy (writing CE 662), as expressed by A. L. Basham in his book *The Wonder That Was India* (p. 6), explained, "I shall now speak of the knowledge of the Hindus... Of their subtle discoveries in the science of astronomy – discoveries even more ingenious than those of the Greeks and Babylonians – of their rational system of mathematics, or of their method of calculation which no words can praise strongly enough – I mean the system using nine symbols. If these things were known by the people who think that they alone have mastered the sciences because they speak Greek, they would perhaps be convinced, though a little late in the day, that other folk, not only Greeks, but men of a different tongue, know something as well as they."

There have been many scholars, both old and new, who readily agree and point out the progressive nature of the early advancements found in ancient India's Vedic tradition. So let us take a quick overview of some of what was known and developed in earlier times in the Vedic culture of the East.

American professor Jabez T. Sunderland (1842-1936), President of the India Information Bureau of America, spent many years in India. He was the author of *India in Bondage*, wherein he wrote, "India created the beginnings of all sciences and she carried some of them to a remarkable degree of development, thereby leading the world. India has produced great literature, great arts, great philosophical systems, great religions, and great men in every department of life–rulers, statesmen, financiers, scholars, poets, generals, colonizers, skilled artisans and craftsmen of every kind, agriculturalists, industrial organizers, and leaders in far reaching trade and commerce by land and sea."

Sunderland went on to say, "India was a far greater industrial and manufacturing nation than any in Europe or than any other in Asia. Her textile goods–the fine products of her loom, in cotton, wool, linen, and silk–were famous over the civilized world; so were her exquisite jewelry and her precious stones, cut in every lovely form; so were her pottery, porcelains, ceramics of every kind, quality, color and beautiful shape; so were her fine works in metal iron, steel, silver, and gold. She had great architecture–equal in beauty to any in the world. She had great engineering works... Not only was she the greatest ship-building nation, but she had great commerce and trade by land and sea which extended to all known civilized countries." [3]

In *India in Bondage*, Sunderland also quotes Lord Curzon, the British statesman who was viceroy in India from 1899 to 1905, as saying in his address delivered at the great Delhi Durbar in 1901: "Powerful empires existed and flourished here [in India] while Englishmen were still wandering, painted in the woods, while the English colonies were a wilderness and a jungle. India has left a deeper mark upon the history, the philosophy, and the religion of mankind, than any other terrestrial unit in the universe."

Lord Curzon had also stated: "While we [the British] hold onto India, we are a first rate power. If we lose India, we will decline to a third rate power. This is the value of India."

Similar to this, Beatrice Pitney Lamb, former editor of the *United Nations News*, first visited India in 1949 on an assignment for the Carnegie Endowment for International Peace, writes in her book, *India: A World in Transition*: "In addition to the still visible past glories of art and architecture, the wonderful ancient literature, and other cultural achievements of which educated Indians are justly proud, the Indian past includes another type of glory most tantalizing to the Indians of today–prolonged material prosperity. For well over a millennium and a half, the Indian subcontinent may have been the richest area in the world." [4]

Many other writers and scholars had commented on their high regard for what had been developed in India. For example, to recognize a few, General Joseph Davey Cunningham (1812-1851) author of *A History of the Sikhs*, writes: "Mathematical science was so perfect and astronomical observations so complete that the paths of the sun and moon were accurately measured."

There was much admiration even of the language of India. William Cooke Taylor (1800-1849), author of *A Popular History of British India*, stated in *Journal of the Royal Asiatic Society, Vol. II*: "It was an astonishing discovery that Hindusthan possessed, in spite of the changes of the realms and changes of time, a language of unrivaled richness and variety; a language, the parent of all those dialects that Europe has fondly called classical–the source alike of Greek flexibility and Roman strength." [5]

French scholar Buffon presented a coherent theory that scholars of ancient India had preserved the old learning from the creators of its sciences, arts, and all useful institutions. Voltaire had also suggested that sciences were more ancient in India than in Egypt. Russian born philosopher Immanuel Kant placed the origin of mankind in the Himalayas and stated that our arts like agriculture, numbers, even the game of chess, came from India.

German scholar Friedrich Schlegel also had a high regard for India, stating that everything of high philosophy or science is of Indian origin. French scholar and judge Louis Jacolliot, in his *Bible in India*, writes: "Astonishing fact! The Hindu Revelation (*Vedas*) is of all revelations the only one whose ideas are in perfect harmony with modern science, as it proclaims the slow and gradual formation of the world." Of course, we can see the videos in which the astrophysicist Carl Sagan says, "The Hindu religion is the only one of the world's great faiths, dedicated to the idea that the cosmos itself undergoes an immense, indeed, an infinite number of deaths and births. It is the only religion in which the time scales correspond to those of modern cosmology."

The point is that all science of the Vedic tradition was developed with or in continuation of the ancient Vedic or spiritual knowledge that was a central point in understanding life. It was part of the Absolute Truth, or

Sanatana-dharma, by which we could understand how to function in this world, and what is the purpose of both this world and our life in it. From this point, so many other developments took place, not as a means to control the environment, but as a means to know how to work holistically with nature for our material and spiritual progress and growth.

People like the Nobel Prize winner Maurice Maeterlinck wrote in *The Great Secret*: "...This tradition attributes the vast reservoir of wisdom that somewhere took shape simultaneously with the origin of man, or even if we are to credit it, before his advent upon this earth, to move spiritual entities, to beings less entangled in matter."

The popular American author Mark Twain also had a high opinion of India, and wrote in *Following the Equator*: "This is India... cradle of the human race, birth place of human speech, mother of history, grandmother of legend, great-grandmother of tradition, whose yesterdays bear date with the moldering antiquities of the rest of the nations... India had the start of the whole world at the beginning of things. She had the first civilization; she had the first accumulation of material wealth; she was populous with deep thinkers and the subtle intellects; she had mines, and woods, and a fruitful soil." [6]

Even in scientific discoveries, there are those who acknowledge the knowing that has taken the rest of the world ages with which to catch up. For example, Fredric Spielberg writes in *Spiritual Practices of India*, with an introduction by Alan Watts: "To the philosophers of India, however, relativity is no new discovery, just as the concept of light years is no matter for astonishment to people used to thinking of time in millions of *kalpas* [days of Brahma]. The fact that the wise men of India have not been concerned with technological applications of this knowledge arises from the circumstance that technology is but one of innumerable ways of applying it. It is, indeed, a remarkable circumstance that when Western civilization discovers relativity, it applies it to the manufacture of atom bombs, whereas, Oriental (Vedic) civilization applies it to the development of new states of consciousness."

Another simpler example is when Dick Teresi, author of *The God Particle* and co-founder of *Omni* magazine, writes in *Ancient Roots of Modern Science*, "In India, we see the beginnings of theoretical speculations of the size and nature of the earth. Some 1,000 years before Aristotle, the Vedic Aryans asserted that the earth was round and circled the sun."

Dick Teresi also acknowledges how much of the knowledge we understand today did not necessarily come from the Greek civilization, but actually existed much earlier in the Vedic traditions of India. He again writes in *Ancient Roots of Modern Science*: "Two thousand years before Pythagorus, philosophers in northern India had understood that gravitation held the solar system together, and that therefore the sun, the most massive object, had to be at its center. Our Western mathematical heritage and pride are critically dependent on the triumphs of ancient Greece. These accomplishments have been so greatly exaggerated that it often becomes difficult to sort out how much of modern math is derived from Greece and how much from ...the Indians and so on. Our modern numerals 0 through 9 were developed in India. Mathematics existed long before the Greeks constructed their first right angle." [7]

THE ANTIQUITY OF VEDIC CULTURE

Many are those who have mentioned the antiquity of the Vedic tradition, but how far back does it go? Traditionally, it was there since the beginning of time. However, even archeologically we can ascertain its very early dates.

For example, archeologists have found 7000-year-old rock paintings in the Aravalli mountain range near Benari dam in the Kotputli area of Jaipur district in Rajasthan in 1991. These paintings are adjacent to the site of the famous Indus Valley Civilization. Such 7000-year-old (5000 BCE) paintings were also found in Braham Kund Ki Dungari and Budhi Jeengore in Rajasthan. This discovery makes the Vedic civilization more ancient than the Egyptian and Greek and Mesopotamian civilizations. This also negates the Aryan Invasion Theory, the hypothesis that the Vedic Aryans were not indigenous, but established themselves after invading the area, which is completely wrong as we will show later in the book. [8]

Along these same line, further verification was also supplied by the *Times of India* (May 30th, 1992, New Delhi edition) wherein it was reported that the department of Archeology and Museums in the city of Jaipur, Rajasthan discovered as many as 300 prehistoric paintings on Kanera rocks in an area of 400 square miles near the town of Nimbahera in Chittorgarh district. These paintings are dated between 50,000 to 60,000 years old. That pushes the earliest reaches of Vedic civilization to at least 50,000 years back.

Additional finds such as these are discovered on a regular basis. Another one is reported in the publication called *Science* (February 23, 2010). It was reported therein that newly discovered archaeological sites in southern and northern India have revealed how people lived before and after the colossal Toba volcanic eruption 74,000 years ago.

The international, multi-disciplinary research team, led by Oxford University in collaboration with Indian institutions, unveiled to a conference in Oxford what it calls "Pompeii-like excavations" beneath the Toba ash.

According to the team, a potentially ground-breaking implication of the new work is that the species responsible for making the stone tools in India was Homo sapiens. Stone tool analysis has revealed that the artefacts consist of cores and flakes, which are classified in India as Middle Palaeolithic and are similar to those made by modern humans in Africa. "Though we are still searching for human fossils to definitively prove the case, we are encouraged by the technological similarities. This suggests that human populations were present in India prior to 74,000 years ago, or about 15,000 years earlier than expected based on some genetic clocks," said project director Dr Michael Petraglia, Senior Research Fellow in the School of Archaeology at the University of Oxford. This exciting new information questions the idea that the Toba super-eruption caused a worldwide environmental catastrophe.

An area of widespread speculation about the Toba super-eruption is that it nearly drove humanity to extinction. The fact that the Middle Palaeolithic tools of similar styles are found right before and after the Toba super-eruption, suggests that the people who survived the eruption were the same populations, using the same kinds of tools, says Dr Petraglia. The research agrees with evidence that other human ancestors, such as the Neanderthals in Europe and the small brained Hobbits in Southeastern Asia, continued to survive well after Toba.

The team has not discovered much bone in Toba ash sites, but in the Billasurgam cave complex in Kurnool, Andhra Pradesh, the researchers have found deposits which they believe range from at least 100,000 years ago to the present. They contain a wealth of animal bones such as wild cattle, carnivores and monkeys. They have also identified plant materials in the Toba ash sites and caves, yielding important information about the impact of the Toba super-eruption on the ecological settings.

Dr Petraglia said: "This exciting new information questions the idea that the Toba super-eruption caused a worldwide environmental catastrophe. That is not to say that there were no ecological effects. We do have evidence that the ash temporarily disrupted vegetative communities and it certainly choked and polluted some fresh water sources, probably causing harm to wildlife and maybe even humans." [9]

In this way, recent discoveries show that the area of ancient India was one of the locations for the oldest civilizations the world has known.

CONCLUSION
THE GREATNESS OF INDIA AND VEDIC CULTURE

History certainly proves that India was also one of the wealthiest countries on the planet in its earlier days. Not only did she have vast treasures of knowledge and developments, but ancient India also had great wealth, such as sapphires, rubies, emeralds, pearls, and other gems, along with sunny climate, great fertility, and much more that was exported to various parts of the world, but the deep levels of knowledge and development was another of her greatest assets. For this reason, the ambition of all conquerors was to possess the area of India.

The pearl presented by Julius Caesar to Servilia, the mother of Brutus, as well as the famous pearl ear-ring of Cleopatra, were obtained from India. The Koh-i-noor diamond, weighing at 106.5 carats, one of the most fabled of diamonds, was taken to England from India. In fact, when Alexander left Persia, he told his troops that they were now going to "Golden India" where there was endless wealth, which made the beauty and riches of Persia look puny.

When the Sultan Mahmud of Ghazni destroyed the famous Somnath temple, he found astonishing wealth in diamonds and jewels. He also sacked Mathura and gathered numerous Deities in gold and silver. Thereafter he went to Kanauj which astonished the tyrant and his followers to such a degree in its wealth and beauty at the time that they declared that Kanauj was only rivaled in magnificence by heaven itself.

Ultimately, it was the wealth of India that drew the barbaric Arabs to the country, and then let the half-civilized Tartars to overrun it. It was the wealth of India that attracted Nadir Shah to ancient India, and from where he captured immense booty, which motivated the Abdali chiefs to renew their attacks on the country.

The people of India were actually not so barbaric as the invaders that forced their way into the country, but rather some of the most civilized in the world, primarily because of their sophisticated level of consciousness and gentleness towards one another caused by their training in the principles of the Vedic spiritual culture.

The character of the Hindus of the day had been described by some of those Europeans who had traveled there back in the 19th century, such as Max Muller, wherein he said: "Warren Hastings thus speaks of the Hindus in general: 'They are gentle and benevolent, more susceptible of gratitude for kindness shown them, and less prompted to vengeance for wrongs inflicted than any people on the face of the earth; faithful, affectionate, submissive to legal authority.'

"Bishop Heber said: 'The Hindus are brave, courteous, intelligent, most eager for knowledge and improvement; sober, industrious, dutiful parents, affectionate to their children, uniformly gentle and patient, and more easily affected by kindness and attention to their wants and feelings than any people I ever met with.'

"Sir Thomas Munro bears even stronger testimony. He writes: 'If a good system of agriculture, unrivaled manufacturing skill, a capacity to produce whatever can contribute to either convenience or luxury, schools established in every village for teaching reading, writing, and arithmetic, the general practice of hospitality and charity amongst each other, and above all, a treatment of the female sex full of confidence, respect, and delicacy, are among the signs which denote a civilized people–then the Hindus are not inferior to the nations of Europe, and if civilization is to become an article of trade between England and India, I am convinced that England will gain by the import cargo.'" [10]

Besides all these considerations, Max Muller also once related: "I wished to point out that there was another sphere of intellectual activity in which the Hindu excelled–the meditative and transcendent–and that here we might learn from them some lessons of life which we ourselves are but too apt to ignore or to despise." [11]

Finally, in what could be a conclusive statement made by a European who had spent many years living and studying the Vedic culture and Sanskrit literature of early India, Max Muller said, "If I were to look over the whole world to find out the country most richly endowed with all the wealth, power and beauty that nature can bestow–in some parts a very paradise on earth–I should point to India. If I were asked under what sky the human mind has most fully developed some of its choicest gifts, has most deeply pondered on the greatest problems of life, and has found solutions of some of them which well deserve the attention even of those who have studied Plato and Kant–I should point to India. And if I were to ask myself from what literature we, here in Europe, we who have been nurtured almost exclusively on the thoughts of Greeks and Romans, and of one Semitic race, the Jewish, may draw that corrective which is most wanted in order to make our inner life more perfect, more comprehensive, more universal, in fact more truly human, a life not for this life only, but a transfigured and eternal life–again I should point to India." [12]

CHAPTER NOTES
1. Prof. A. R. Vasudeva Murthy and Prasun Kumar Mishra, *Indian Tradition of Chemistry and Chemical Technology*, Samskrita Bharati, Bangalore, India, August, 1999, pp. i-v.
2. *Science and Technology in Ancient India*, by Editorial Board of Vijnan Bharati, Mumbai, August, 2002, Foreword by B. V. Subbarayappa.
3. Niranjan Shah, *Indian Tribune* Newspaper, December 8, 2007.
4. Ibid.
5. Ibid.
6. Niranjan Shah, *Indian Tribune* Newspaper, December 1, 2007.
7. Niranjan Shah, *Indian Tribune* Newspaper, December 9, 2005.
8. *India Tribune*, June 1, 1991, Atlanta edition.
9. http://www.ox.ac.uk/images/maincolumn/9440
10. Max Muller, *India: What can it teach us?*, first published in 1883, published by Rupa & Co., New Delhi, 2002, pp. 46-47)
11. Max Muller, *India: What can it teach us?*, Longmans, Funk & Wagnalls, London, 1999, p. 22)
12. Max Muller, *India: What can it teach us?*, first published in 1883, published by Rupa & Co., New Delhi, 2002, p. 5)

CHAPTER TWO

Genealogy of the Solar and Lunar Dynasties

We briefly mentioned in the previous chapter some of the archeological evidence that helps determine the antiquity of the Vedic society. Here we will outline some of the more traditional views such as the genealogy of the main Vedic dynasties that take this civilization even farther back in time and show how these lineages spread throughout the lands. However, remember what we are providing is only a brief summary of the description of what took place over the course of millions of years. So these lists of lineages are not complete. But they can give an indication of how far back in time this tradition goes.

According to the ancient Vedic texts, both the Solar and Lunar dynasties start with the Supreme Creator of the cosmic creation, which is Lord Vishnu, and then goes to the secondary creator, which is Lord Brahma.

Lord Brahma generated several mind-born sons, which include Svayambhu, Pulastya, Angira, Vashishtha, Pulaha, Atreya, Bhrigu, Kratu, Shiva, the four Kumaras, Narada Muni, Atri, and Marichi. However, in this case we are concerned mostly with Marichi and Atri.

First from Marichi descends his son Kashyapa, whose wife Aditi had their son Vivasvan (the start of the Surya-vansha, or Solar Dynasty), and from whom came Vaivasvata Manu. The early dynasties are also described in the *Puranas*. From those records we learn that Vaivasvata Manu had Ila, a daughter, and many sons, the most prominent of which were Ikshvaku, who is considered the patriarch of the Solar Race, as well as Yama, Yami, Ashvini-kumaras, Revanta, Nriga, Sharyati, Dishta, Dhrishta, Karusha, Narishyanta, Nabhoga, Prisadhra, and Kavi.

Now from Atri and his wife Anusuya, they have the sons Chandra, Durvas, and Dattatreya. From Chandra, who is also called Soma and the patriarch of the Lunar Race, descended Budh, from whom came Pururava (with wife Urvashi), and then Ayu, then Nahush, and then Yayati.

Yayati had two wives, namely Devayani (who was the daughter of Shukracharya, guru of the Asuras), and Sharmishtha (an Asura princess). From Devayani came the sons named Turvasu and Yadu. From Turvasu came the Yavanas, later considered to be the Greeks. From Yadu came the Yadu clan known as the Yadavas. It is this dynasty from which Lord Krishna appeared many years later.

From Sharmishtha, the daughter of the Asura king Vrishaparvan, was born the sons named Puru, Druhya and Anu. From Puru came the continuation of the Chandra-vansha or Lunar Dynasty, from Druhya came the Bhoja clan, and from Anu came the Mleccha clan, or those who became the inferior races, considered later to be the Turks and others.

In the *Mahabharata*, Pururava is considered an ancestor of Dushyanta, who is an early king of the Lunar dynasty, later to be known as the Kurus. Arjuna was a descendant of the Pururavas, while Lord Krishna was a descendant of the Yadus. This was also the Suryavamsi or Solar dynasty, considered to have been started by Manu through King Iksvaku. King Sagar, Bhagirathi and Lord Rama were other much earlier kings from this dynasty.

These two main dynasties of the early Vedic empire, who were the sons of Yayati and descendants of Vaivasvata Manu, spread throughout the Asian subcontinent, also known as Aryavrata, as follows: the Druhyus (who later became the Druze) went west of Afghanistan, the Purus settled between the Indus and Ravi rivers, the Anus were in the northern regions of the subcontinent up to the Himalayas, the Yadus were in Gujarat and the Sindh, and the Turvashas ruled the central plains and eastern areas, from the southern regions from Gujarat to Bihar and Orissa. [1]

The Anus were the ancestors of the Persians, offshoots that became known later as the Mlecchas. Thus, the Persians were originally a Vedic people that came out of the Punjab. They still continued with variations of the Vedic traditions, but then the appearance of Zoroaster brought about a new religion. The *Mahabharata* (Adi Parva 85.34) refers to the Mlecchas as offshoots of the Anus, but later the term was generalized to include many people living outside the Vedic principles. The *Brahmanas* (*Shatapatha Brahmana* 3.2.1.24) also used the term for those who lived in the west of ancient India, like the Mid-East and further. [2]

The Druhyus and Anus were often labeled as non-Vedic people, or as unorthodox in their practices. They originally belonged to west India, but migrated farther west into Gandhara or northeast Afghanistan and into Iran and even Central Asia. This may also be why the names of some of the rivers there are closely linked with the Sanskrit names, such as Haraquiti with Sarasvati, or Harirud with Sarayu.

Many scholars consider the Druhyus to have migrated after the wars of Mandhata and Sudas to Lebanon, where they become known as the Druze. Those who have studied the philosophy of the Druze can recognize that their scripture, the *Kutub al-hikma*, which is a collection of epistles and letters, one of which is also called *Epistles of India*, indicates their connection with India. This scripture contains many of the same concepts as found in the Vedic philosophy, such as reincarnation, the nature of the soul, and a transcendent God that is beyond human understanding.

Additionally, the Gulf of Cambay and the city of Baruch (Bhrigu-kachch) was said to be the region of the Bhrigus, the gurus of Manu. While they were considered to be the descendants of Varuna, the deity of the sea, and were also known for their maritime abilities and talents as astronomers, and related to the planet Venus. [3]

LOCATIONS OF THE EARLY VEDIC DYNASTIES

As we can begin to see, the early Vedic dynasties were spread throughout the area of ancient India, but the different clans were centered in particular areas. As explained in *The Rig Veda and the History of India*: The Vedic land "is clearly the Sarasvati-Drishadvati region, as we have shown many times (*Rig Veda* 3.23.3-4). The Druhyus in the west in Afghanistan, the Anus in the north in Punjab, the Purus in the center on the Sarasvati, the Yadus in the southwest in Gujarat, and the Turvashas in the southeast in southern Bihar reflect the position of these peoples in the *Puranas*. Manu's land is clearly the Sarasvati region, which Nahusha, Yayati and Puru inherited. Archaeologically speaking, it is also the main site of civilization in ancient India." [4]

We should also mention that many additional sites remain to be found in the eastern areas of India, simply because there have not been much excavation work in that area as yet, but certain sites have been located. Therefore, the full evidence of civilizational development and information is yet to be uncovered.

Furthermore, "According to the *Puranas*, the Yadus seeded most of the peoples of Central and South Central India, including Rajasthan, Gujarat, Madhya Pradesh, and Maharashtra–an area from Mathura in the north to near Hyderabad in the south, and west at least as far as Kachchh. These were the regions of Anarta (or Saurasthtra), the lands of the Satvats, Chedis, Dasharnas, Bhojas, Vrishnis, Madhus, Kuntas, Andhakas, and Vidarbhas." [5]

This second main dynasty of the Vedic kings, the Solar Dynasty, as described in the *Puranas*, also seemed to expand to places in the east and south, such as Koshala, Videha and Vaishali, from the Gomati River up to the Brahmaputra River. It was also this dynasty who spread its influence farther east into regions that included Burma, Thailand and Cambodia as we can see with the huge Angkor Wat temples, as well as Indochina, and Indonesia.

Kashyapa also fits into the dynasties. Svayambhuva Manu and his wife Shatarupa had Priyavrata and Uttanapada as their sons, along with daughters Akuti, Prasuti and Devahuti. From Devahuti and her husband Kardama came Lord Kapiladeva and nine daughters, which included Anasuya and Kala. Kala with husband sage Marichi gave birth to Purnima and sage Kashyapa. Kashyapa had three main wives, namely Aditi, Diti, and Danu. Aditi is the mother of the Adityas, or the gods like Vivasvan, Mitra, Varuna, etc. Diti is the mother of two groups of those who were against Vedic culture, or the demonic, which were the enemies of Indra, such as Hiranyakashipu and Hiranyaksha, and then the Maruts, the gods of the air who became friends of Indra. Danu was the mother of another group of non-Vedic or demonic beings, the Danavas who are also considered to be the offspring of Kashyapa.

Kashyapa is associated with Kashmir, for which it was named after him (Kashyapa Mira or Kashyapa's lake). Similarly, the Caspian Sea may also be associated with Kashyapa in the same way, all of which shows the connection between this area and the Danavas, or Kashyapa's offspring.

Lord Parashurama later defeated all of the Danavas and drove them out of the area of ancient India, thus forcing them all to head to the northwest regions, such as Afghanistan and beyond. Thereafter, tribes known as Danavas, Daityas, Dasyus, etc., who entered the Middle East and traveled into Europe became known as those princes or Kshatriyas who were against or indifferent to the Vedic *Dharma*. [6]

To explain further, the Yadava kingdom became divided among the four sons of Bhima Satvata. From Vrishni, the youngest, descended Vasudeva, the father of Krishna and Balarama and their sister Pritha or Kunti. Kunti married the Yadava prince Pandu, whose descendants became the Pandavas. Kunti became the mother of Yudhisthira, Bhima, and Arjuna (Partha), the three elder Pandavas. The younger Pandavas were Nakula and Sahadeva, born from Pandu's second wife Madri. After moving to the west coast of India, they lived at Dwaraka under the protection of Lord Krishna. Near the time of Krishna's disappearance from earth, a fratricidal war broke out and most of the Pandavas were killed, who had grown to become a huge clan. Those that survived may have gone on to the Indus Valley where they joined or started another part of the advanced Vedic society. Others may have continued farther west into Egypt and some on to Europe, as previously explained.

This is further substantiated in the *Mahabharata* which mentions several provinces of southern Europe and Persia that were once connected with the Vedic culture. The *Adi-parva* (174.38) of the *Mahabharata* describes the province of Pulinda (Greece) as having been conquered by Bhimasena and Sahadeva, two of the Pandava brothers. Thus, the ancient Greeks were once a part of Bharatvarsha (India) and the Vedic civilization. But later the people gave up their affiliation with Vedic society and were, therefore, classified as Mlecchas. However, in the *Vana-parva* section of the *Mahabharata* it is predicted that this non-Vedic society would one day rule much of the world, including India. Alexander the Great invaded northern India for the Pulinda or Greek civilization in 326 BCE, fulfilling the prophecy.

The *Sabha-parva* and *Bhisma-parva* sections of the *Mahabharata* mention the province of Abhira, situated near what once was the Sarasvati River in ancient Sind. The Abhiras are said to have been warriors who had left India out of fear of Lord Parashurama and hid themselves in the Caucasion hills between the Black and Caspian Seas. Later, for a period of time, they were ruled by Maharaja Yudhisthira. However, the sage Markandaya predicted that these Abhiras, after they gave up their link with Vedic society, would one day rule India.

Another province mentioned in *Mahabharata* (*Adi-parva* 85.34) is that of the Yavanas (Turks) who were so named for being descendants of Maharaja Yavana (Turvasu), one of the sons of Maharaja Yayati, as previously explained. They also gave up Vedic culture and became Mlecchas. They fought in the battle of Kuruksetra against the Pandavas on behalf of Duryodhana and lost. However, it was predicted that they would one day return to conquer Bharata-varsa (India) and, indeed, this came to pass. Muhammad Ghori later attacked and conquered parts of India on behalf of Islam from the Abhira and Yavana or Turkish countries. Thus, we can see that these provinces in the area of Greece and Turkey (and the countries in between there and India) were once part of the Vedic civilization and had at one time not only political and cultural ties, but also ancestral connections. This is the Vedic version of the origin of Aryan civilization and how its influence spread in various degrees throughout the world.

THE PREHISTORIC DATE OF VEDIC BEGINNINGS

From the information we have provided so far it should be obvious that the time period of the earliest of Vedic history cannot be placed for certain. It is clearly prehistoric, and even the Vedic tradition places it at the beginning of time from the creation. And the cycles of *yugas* as outlined by the Vedic texts place that millions of years ago.

Along these lines of thought, as written about by B. B. Radhakrishna of the Geological Society of India (1999), he explains that the *Rig Veda* relates how Himalayan glaciers broke up to release the water which flowed out in seven major rivers (Sapta Sindhu). The inhabitants of the regional plains then composed songs to Lord Indra for releasing the water they needed. The description was no poetic endeavor but a natural event that had to happen in the Late Pleistocene era of about 10,000 years ago, which also means that the *Rig Veda* contained compositions that date back 10,000 years. [7]

In further considering the date of the *Rig Veda*, according to Dr. B. M. Sidhartha, Director of the Birla Science Center, "*Rigved*... was a product of a well-settled civilization going back to 8000 B.C. and beyond on the basis of astronomical dating... and supported by archaeological excavations... the more antique date of 10,000 B. C. proposed for *Rigved* or Vedic culture seemed more plausible in view of the epi-paleolithic agricultural and proto-agricultural civilizations going back to the same period." [8]

These datelines were already proposed by B. G. Tilak when he said, "The Vedic hymns were sung in post-glacial times (8000 B.C.) by poets who had inherited their knowledge or contents thereof from their antediluvian forefathers." [9]

Similarly, when we look at more recent recorded history, the Greek historians of Pliny and Arrian place the date of Vedic civilization somewhere near 6676 or 6777 BCE. And they based it on the reports they got from the ambassadors at the Maurya courts which stated that there were 154 kings who ruled over a period of 6,450 years, all of whom were followers of Vedic *Dharma*. [10]

DATE OF LORD RAMA

As we have said, Lord Rama appeared later in the Solar Dynasty, but even the time frame of His appearance may shed more light on the antiquity of Vedic culture. Naturally, scholars have different views on when He may have existed. Some say He was here a few thousand years before Lord Krishna. In fact, in an April 2011 edition of the *Times of India*, Saurabh Kwatra writes that using the zodiac and the recorded *tithis*, days marked according to the phases of the moon, he calculated that the birth of Lord Rama, as related in the Valmiki *Ramayana*, was December 4th, 7323 BCE. While using other forms of planetary computer software, others have come up with other dates.

Though these may be some of the more recent calculations, still the tradition places the era of Lord Rama much earlier than that. For example, the *Vayu Purana* (70.48) says:

tretayuge chaturvinshe ravanastapasah kshayat I
ramam dasharathim prapya saganah kshayamlyavan II

This relates that the misbehaving Ravana was killed with his kiths and kins in a war with Rama in the 24th Treta-yuga. We are presently in the 28th *chaturyuga* (cycle of 1000 *yugas*) of the Vaivasvat *manvantara*. Furthermore, this is corroborated by Rupa Goswami in his *Laghu Bhagavatamrita* that Rama appeared in the Treta-yuga of the 24th yuga cycle. There are 71 cycles of the four *yugas* in a *manvantara* period, which would mean the appearance of Lord Rama would be about 18 million years ago.

Another interesting point is that in the Suderkand section of the

Valmiki *Ramayana* (5.4.27) elephants with four tusks are mentioned as standing at the gates of Ravana's palace. Also in 5.27.12 an ogress named Trijata sees in her dream Lord Rama mounted on a great elephant with four tusks. The fact that they knew of elephants with four tusks is very intriguing since a quick reference to the elephant with four tusks is called a Mastondontoidea, which is calculated to have evolved around 38 million years ago, and is suspected of becoming extinct around 15 million years ago. This would help verify the ancient date of Lord Rama to be around 18 million years ago.

THE GOTRAS

Another important part of Vedic culture that could help show a little of its traditional antiquity is found in the custom of *gotras*. After the universal creation under the guidance of Lord Brahma, it is recorded that he had 27 sons who were also progenitors for mankind, called Prajapatis, who were the seeds of humanity which spread throughout the world. The familial line from each of these Prajapatis is called a *gotra*. So the names of the *gotra* carries the name of each one of these sages. In this way, the 27 sons of Brahma were also the beginnings for the 27 *gotras*. It is considered that every person is a descendant of one of these *gotras*, and one's *gotra* is often requested during the worship or performance of rituals in the temples. This is a tradition that has gone on for many hundreds of years.

These sons of Brahma were also learned sages called rishis. The main seven sages, called the Saptarshis (Seven Rishis), are Kashyapa, Vashistha, Bharadwaj, Kapila, Atri, Vishvamitra, and Gautama. It is also these Saptarshis which help preserve and propagate spiritual knowledge to humanity for everyone's benefit. Additional sons of Brahma include Svayambhuva Manu, Adharma, Praheti, Heti, Aristanemi, Bhrigu, Daksha, Pracetas, Sthanu, Samshraya, Sesha, Vikrita, Kardama, Kratu, Pulaha, Pulastya, and Agiras. These *gotras* have since increased through time to include many others.

Another point about this is that in India, one's *gotra* is important because they help avoid what would be called inbreeding, or families marrying within their own *gotra*. In fact, sometimes they avoid four *gotras*, which are one's own *gotra*, the *gotras* of both one's father and mother, and the *gotra* of one's paternal grandmother. All of this is said to help prevent

birth defects in their children by keeping people from marrying within the
same genetic roots. In any case, this is a traditional that seems to be traced
back to the beginning of creation.

FIRST MISCALCULATION OF VEDIC ORIGINS

In spite of this review of the Vedic traditions that provide some
insights into how ancient the culture is, there have been, nonetheless, many
errors in establishing its antiquity that have had to be overcome or
corrected. This has certainly been an obstacle based primarily on prejudices
against India's Vedic civilization.

For example, William Jones, who is given so much credit for
recognizing the similarities between Sanskrit and Latin and Greek, actually
was the first to refuse to admit the accuracy of the great historical records
of the Indian Vedic texts. As explained in *The Origin and History of
Mathematics*, "William Jones was one of the earliest Sanskrit scholars to
notice remarkable similarities between Sanskrit and European languages
such as Greek and Latin. It was Jones who first laid the foundation in 1774
A. D., for the western history of India. He obtained from Pandit Radhakant,
a Sanskrit scholar in Calcutta, lists of royal dynasties from the *Bhagavata
Purana* beginning with the start of Kali-yuga in 3102 B.C. He could not
fathom the information he saw and did not want to believe that India had
such great antiquity. He refused to recognize the historical accuracy of the
Puranas. Jones, after consulting with the then governor, Warren Hastings,
declared that, 'the first ages of the Hindus are chiefly mythological and thus
the historical age of India cannot be carried further back to two thousand
years before Christ.'" [11]

The list of kings that Jones reviewed listed 153 kings that spanned
over 6000 years. These were all Hindu kings. He was astonished by this and
refused to recognize its validity. So he deliberately created the problem of
reducing the history of India by 1200 years and confused the two
Chandraguptas. He misidentified Chandragupta Maurya (1534-1500 BCE)
with Chandragupta (327-320 BCE) of the Imperial Gupta Dynasty. In this
way, he made Chandragupta Maurya appear in 327 BCE instead of the
proper time of 1534 BCE. This confusion went on for numerous years so
that many others also did not realize the ancient nature of the Vedic
civilization. It has taken much time and work to overcome this mistake and

the miscalculations that followed by such misjudgments, especially in Western academia, that could have been avoided if people honestly looked at the truths that can be found in the Vedic texts.

CHAPTER NOTES

1. David Frawley, *The Rig Veda and the History of India*, Aditya Prakashan, New Delhi, 2001, p.113)

2. Ibid., p.224.

3. Dr. David Frawley and Dr. Navaratna S. Rajaram, *Hidden Horizons, Unearthing 10,000 Years of Indian Culture*, Swaminarayan Aksharpith, Ahmedabad, India, 2006, p55.

4. David Frawley, *The Rig Veda and the History of India*, Aditya Prakashan, New Delhi, 2001, p. 265.

5. Ibid., p.268.

6. Ibid., p.239.

7. Graham Hancock, *Underworld: The Mysterious Civilization*, Crown Publishers, New York, 2002, p. 169.

8. *Times of India*, August 2, 1993.

9. B. G. Tilak, *The Orion or Researches into the Antiquity of the Vedas*, Pune, India, 1987.

10. Georg Feuerstein, Subhash Kak & David Frawley, *In Search of the Cradle of Civilization*, Quest Books, Wheaton, Il. 1995, p. 246.

11. V. Lakshmikantham and J. Vasundhara Devi, *The Origin and History of Mathematics*, Indian Foundation for Vedic Science, Rohtak, Haryana, India, 2004, p. 2.

CHAPTER THREE

Time Line of Lord Krishna and the Mahabharata War

Another aspect that can show us the early nature of Vedic society, and with a little more reliability, is highlighting the time when Lord Krishna was present. This is another point that has generated many opinions but is now much clearer than ever with the more recent research and findings.

Astrophysicist Dr. Narahari Achar, a physicist from the University of Memphis, clearly showed with astronomical analysis that the *Mahabharata* war took place in 3067 BCE. Examining the *Mahabharata*, books 3, 5, and 18, his sky map software showed that all these descriptions converge in the year 3067. Achar also acknowledged that some 30 years earlier, in 1969, S. Raghavan had arrived at the same date.

In determining the date of the *Mahabharata* war at Kurukshetra, astronomical references in the epic can be used, of which there are more than one hundred and fifty. Most of these that pertain to the war, though there are many scattered throughout the texts, is in the Udyoga and Bhisma Parvas. Those in the Bhisma Parva are especially systematic and are also in accordance with the astrological omens described in the *Atharva Veda* and its Parishishtas, referring mostly to comets. When these are put together with the retrograde motion of Mars before reaching Jyestha, this leads to the unique date of 3067 BCE for the date of the war, which was previously proposed by Professor Raghavan. [1]

This corroborates with the view that the age of Kali-yuga started in 3102 BCE, according to Dr. Achar. As stated in the *Puranas*, Kali-yuga had already begun, but its full influence was held back because of the presence of Lord Krishna. Then when Lord Krishna departed from this world, which is said to have occurred 35 years after the war of Kurukshetra in 3067, making it the year of 3032 BCE, then Kali-yuga began to show more of its effects. [2]

In the time line for the passing away of Grandfather Bhisma, for example, it is said that Bhisma passed away on the Magha, (January-February) *shukla ashtami*, after the winter solstice, which leads to the date of January 13, 3066 BCE for the winter solstice. [3]

So, in considering the chronology according Professor Raghavan, we have:

Lord Krishna's departure from Upaplavya nagara on the mission for peace–September 26, 3067 BCE

Krishna reaches Hastinapura–September 28, 3067 BCE

Lunar eclipse–September 29, 3067 BCE

Krishna rides with Karna–October 8, 3067 BCE

Solar eclipse–October 14, 3067 BCE

The war begins–November 22, 3067 BCE

Fourteenth day of the war, continued into the wee hours of the morning–December 8, 3067 BCE

Balarama returns–December 12, 3067 BCE

Winter solstice–January 13, 3066 BCE

Bhisma's passing away–January 17, 3066 BCE [4]

This accounts for 48 days from the time of Bhisma's fall to the time of his passing. However, it is generally accepted that Grandfather Bhisma had 58 sleepless nights between the time of his fall and the time of his passing. Yet, if you count the 10 days that he lead the armies into war in which he may also have not been able to sleep, that would give the full 58 sleepless nights that are described.[5]

The famous astronomical text known as the *Surya Siddhanta* also states that the sun was 54 degrees away from the vernal equinox when Kali-yuga began on a new moon day, which corresponds to February 17/18, 3102 at Ujjain.

From the internal evidence in the *Mahabharata* text, the coronation of Maharaja Yudhisthir can be determined to be 36 years before the beginning of Kali-yuga, or about 3138 BCE. One scholar, Dr. Patnaik, had calculated the date of the starting of the *Mahabharata* war to be October 16, 3138 BCE from references available in the epic itself.

Of course, different scholars may arrive at variations in their calculations, and there have been a few different versions of the *Mahabharata*, and over the many centuries since it was written, additions and accretions are found. For example, verses 2.28.48-9 mention *roma* and

*Deities of Lord Krishna instructing Arjuna at the Birla Krishna Temple
at Kurukshetra*

Banganga at Kurukshetra where Bhishma laid on the bed of arrows meditating on Lord Krishna with the Pandavas before leaving this world

antakhi in Sanskrit, which some scholars interpret to mean Rome and Antioch. This places these mentions not earlier than 300 BCE since Antioch was founded in 301.[6] However, this does not limit the age of the earlier form of the *Mahabharata,* which is known to have been written shortly after the war of Kurukshetra.

Nonetheless, as B. N. Narahari Achar explains, other scholars have proposed varying years for the *Mahabharata* war, from 3102 BCE to 3139 BCE. However, none of these dates can produce the astronomical configurations described in the *Mahabharata.*

Another point of consideration is that it is generally accepted that the age of Kali-yuga began in February 17-18 of 3102 BCE, which also coincides with the astronomical configurations. This also is given credence from the Aryabhatta Tradition in which Aryabhatta, who lived 476-550 CE, explains that when he was 23 years old, 3600 years of Kali-yuga had elapsed. Aryabhatta, one of the great mathematicians and astronomers of India in the 5th century CE, examined the astronomical positions recorded in the *Mahabharata*. In his work, the *Aryabhattiya*, he calculated that the approximate date to be 3100 BCE, justifying the date of the Kurukshetra war to have been fought about 5000 years ago, as the tradition itself and most Hindus have always said.

This again identifies the year of 3102 BCE. However, the *Mahabharata* itself does not describe when Kali-yuga began. All it says is that the war took place some time during the interval of Dvapara and Kali-yugas, and it certainly took place before Lord Krishna left this world. But there is evidence that Kali-yuga had already begun before Lord Krishna disappeared.

In the *Bhagavata Purana* (1.15.36) it is explained, "When the Personality of Godhead Lord Krishna left this earthly planet in His selfsame form, from that very day Kali, who had appeared partially before, became fully manifest to create inauspicious conditions for those who are endowed with a poor fund of knowledge."

Therefore, Kali-yuga had already appeared, but it was only due to the presence of Lord Krishna who was holding back its influence. But after He left this world, Kali's full potency took effect, which is also stated in the *Kali-raja Vrittanta.* Thus, the war is most likely to have been in 3067 BCE and the beginning of Kali-yuga is accepted as 3102 BCE.

Some people, such as Max Muller and others, have had trouble accepting this date as the time of the *Mahabharata,* because they felt that the descriptions of the planetary positions of the Saptarishis (Ursa Major) were not real. However, a similar description is also given in the second chapter of the twelfth canto of the *Bhagavata Purana*, which helps verify the time of the *Mahabharata*.

One particular point to consider is that it has been shown that the positions of the Saptarishis, as explained in the work of Anthony Aveni, noted author of *The Empire of Time: Calendars, Clocks and Cultures*, that in many cultures, even in Africa and American Indian cultures, it is believed that the entire solar system revolves through the galaxy of the Milky Way, around the brightest star of the Pleiades, in the Taurus constellation. These are known as the Seven Sisters or Krittikas in the Vedic tradition. The brightest star in the Pleiades is Alcyone, and the sun completes one revolution around this star in approximately 3000 years. This has made the Pleiades a sacred object in the sky in many cultures. But the point is that it is this periodic revolution that is why the Saptarishis repeat their positions described in the *Bhagavata Purana* every 2700 years. Thus, when calculations are based on the position of these stars, we have to realize that the Vedic texts, including the *Ramayana* and the descriptions therein, could be relating to time periods much earlier than we think.

TIME OF LORD KRISHNA

A little evidence that can help establish the time of Lord Krishna was in Mohenjodaro, where a tablet dated to 2600 BCE was found which depicts Lord Krishna in His childhood days. This shows that Lord Krishna was popular at least prior to this date. [7]

We also have records from Greek travelers who came to India following Alexander's invasion which have left references to Krishna. Authors like Pliny referred to Krishna as Heracles, based on Hari Krishna. They record that Heracles (Krishna) was held in special honor by the Sourseni tribe (Shuraseni, based on Shura the father of Vasudeva and grandfather of Lord Krishna) in such places as the major city of Methora (Mathura).

The Greek records go on to record that Heracles (Krishna) lived 138 generations before the time of Alexander and Sandrocottas, which was about 330 BCE. This then calculates, based on about 20 years per generation, to roughly 3090 BCE, which is about the right time considering

3102 BCE is the date when Kali-yuga began. Thus, Lord Krishna was a genuinely historical figure who lived about the time of 3200-3100 BCE, having lived to 125 years of age.

WHEN LORD KRISHNA LEFT THIS WORLD

This leads us to the approximate date when Lord Krishna left this world. As B. N. Narahari Achar again describes: "According to the epic *Mahabharata*, Krishna first appears [in the epic] at the time of Draupadi's wedding, and His departure is exactly 36 years after the war. No information about His birth is available in the epic itself, although there is information about His departure. Krishna observes omens (*Mahabharata* 14.3.17), similar to the ones seen at the time of the war, now indicating the total destruction of the Yadavas. [Astrological] Simulations show that in the year 3031 BCE, thirty-six years later than 3067 BCE, there was an eclipse season with three eclipses. A lunar eclipse on 20 October was followed by an annular solar eclipse on 5 November, followed by a penumbral lunar eclipse on 19 November, within an interval of 14 days and at an *aparvani* time. Thus the date of departure of Lord Krishna is consistent with the popular tradition that He passed away 36 years after the war. The information about His birth can be gathered from the *Harivamsha* and the *Bhagavata Purana*.... It should be understood, however, that the date of His departure from this world is established on the information in the epic and on the basis of [astronomical] simulations, and it turns out to be 3031 BCE." [8]

TIME OF LORD BUDDHA

Based on the star orientation in sky maps, it has been calculated by Narhari Achar, using planetarium software used by NASA, that the time of Buddha was actually the nineteenth century BCE, which also corresponds with the tradition of Tibetan Buddhism and the king lists in the Vedic *Puranas*. I elaborated more about this in my book *Proof of Vedic Culture's Global Existence*.

So, we have a basic time frame in which the time of the *Mahabharata* war was about 3167 BCE, Buddha lived during 1887 to 1807

BCE, the first famous mathematician Aryabhatta was born in 476 CE, and the *Shulba Sutras* were composed well before that. Adi Shankara lived from 509 to 477 BCE and intellectually overthrew the Buddhist faith from India to re-establish Vedic *Sanatana-dharma*.

From the above information we can draw a basic time line like so:

1,975,325,000 years ago the world came into existence with the beginning of Brahma's day. Furthermore, from other sources the following is figured:

10,000 to 8,000 BCE: was the end of the glacial period or ice age, when the Vedic priests were still chanting the Vedic hymns and passing it along through the generations in an oral tradition.

3102 BCE: was the beginning of Kali-yuga.

3067 BCE: was the *Mahabharata* war.

3031 BCE: departure of Lord Krishna.

3000 BCE: was about when Vedavyasa composed the main Vedic texts.

1900 BCE: was when the Sarasvati had dried up.

1807 BCE: death of Lord Buddha

1534-1218 BCE: Maurya dynasty

509 BCE: birth of Adi Shankara

327-82 BCE: Gupta dynasty

323 BCE to 200 CE: the start of 1000 years of invasions into India by the Greeks, Yavans, Pahlavas, Shakas, Kushans.

638-1193 CE: Muslim invasions into India.

1784: Hindus overthrow most Muslims from India.

1843: the British capture India.

1947: British finally leave India which becomes independent.

PROOF OF THE EXISTENCE OF LORD KRISHNA

Sometimes there are comments and even controversies amongst those who are less informed regarding whether Christianity or Hinduism (Vedic culture) came first. Some people point out that the devotional elements within the Vedic tradition, especially in regard to the *Bhakti* movements, must have come from Christianity first and then appeared in the Vedic Vaishnava tradition, the followers of which exhibit much love and devotion to Lord Krishna and Vishnu and His other *avataras*. But this idea, that Vedic culture came from Christianity, which some Christian preachers still try to use, could not be further from the truth. The fact is that there is archeological proof that the Vaishnava tradition of devotion to Lord Vishnu existed many years prior to the appearance of Christianity.

Not far from the Buddhist site of Sanchi in Central India, we take a 45-minute ride on the very bumpy road to Vidisha or Besnagar where we find the Heliodorus column, locally known as the Khamb Baba pillar. This was erected by Heliodorus, the Greek ambassador to India in 113 BCE. Heliodorus was sent to the court of King Bhagabhadra by Antialkidas, the Greek king of Taxila. The kingdom of Taxila was part of the Bactrian region in northwest India, which had been conquered by Alexander the Great in 325 BCE. By the time of Antialkidas, the area under Greek rule included what is now Afghanistan, Pakistan and the Punjab.

Heliodorus writes on the stone pillar the time it was erected and the fact that he had converted to Vaishnavism, or the worship of Lord Vishnu. The inscription on the column, as published in the Journal of the Royal Asiatic Society, says:

"This Garuda column of Vasudeva (Vishnu), the god of gods, was erected here by Heliodorus, a worshiper of Vishnu, the son of Dion, and an inhabitant of Taxila, who came as Greek ambassador from the Great King Antialkidas to King Kasiputra Bhagabhadra, the Savior, then reigning prosperously in the fourteenth year of his kingship. Three important precepts when practiced lead to heaven: self-restraint, charity, conscientiousness."

This shows that Heliodorus had become a worshiper of Vishnu and was well versed in the texts and ways pertaining to this religion. It can only be guessed how many other Greeks became converted to Vaishnava Hinduism if such a notable ambassador did. This conclusively shows the Greek appreciation for India and its philosophy.

It was General Alexander Cunningham who was doing an archeological survey in 1877 who first took notice of the significance of the column. However, he did not attend to the inscription that was on it because it was covered with vermilion. This was because the pilgrims who worshiped had a custom to smear the column with vermilion.

It was only in January of 1901 when a Mr. Lake uncovered the paint

The Heliodorus Column at Vidisha.

from what he thought was some lettering. Once the ancient Brahmi text was translated, the historical significance of the column became ever more apparent.

The British Sanskritists, due to their superior views of themselves, had developed the idea that much of the Vedic traditions and legends of Lord Krishna had to have been incorporated from the Bible and the stories of Jesus. However, this Heliodorus column was the archeological discovery that proved to the disappointed British that knowledge of Krishna and the Vaishnava tradition predated Christianity by at least 200 years. The column indicated that the Indians did not adopt legends of Christ to put in their *Puranas* to be used for the stories of Krishna as the British had hypothesized since this gave proof that knowledge of Krishna predated Jesus by almost 200 years.

Another point to consider is that if a Greek official was so impressed with the philosophy of Vaishnavism that he converted to it in 200 BCE, then it means that Vaishnavism and the element of spiritual devotion to God, as found in the *Bhakti* tradition, had to have originated several hundred years if not several thousand years earlier in order for it to have developed to a stage wherein the Greeks were so much impressed by it. So this is a serious historical site to see.

The Heliodorus column also indicates that the Vedic tradition accepted converts at that time. Only after the difficulties between Hindus and Muslims was there a hesitancy on the part of Hindus to accept converts to the Vedic tradition. The Vedic religion saw itself as universal and welcomed all people into its embrace. As Raychaudhari writes: "The Beshnagar record testifies to the proselytizing zeal of the Bhagavatas [Vaishnavas] in the pre-Christian centuries, and shows that their religion was excellent enough to capture the hearts of cultured Greeks, and catholic enough to admit them into its fold."

This evidence further shows that Greece was but a part of Vedic culture and repeated what it and its philosophers had learned from the Vedic sages rather than being a source of the higher levels of philosophy as some people think. Furthermore, this evidence bears witness to the fact that the Christian tradition and its main element of devotion or *bhakti* to God was found in Vedic culture long before it appeared within the confines of Christianity. In fact, much of the deeper spiritual philosophy in Christianity is but a repeat of what had been previously established and much more deeply developed in the older Vedic tradition. So to fathom the deeper aspects of the different levels of devotion to God, one can investigate the Vedic and Vaishnava tradition to learn the finer details.

Additional archeological finds include the Mora Well and Ghosundi Inscriptions, which tell us that the rich and complex Vaishnava conception of God and full expansions of the Godhead into the material universes were already well established in the first two centuries before Christ. Seven miles west of Mathura in the small and unimposing village of Mora, General Cunningham made another vital find regarding the historicity of Vaishnavism. In 1882, on the terrace of an ancient well, he discovered a large stone slab filled with inscriptions. Although more than half of the writing had already peeled away on the right side, the remainder was legible. It was transcribed, and a facsimile of the inscription was published in the Archaeological Survey of India's *Annual Report*. The message was clear. Not only was Krishna worshiped in the centuries before Christ, but also His expansions or associates, especially "the five heroes of the Vrishni Clan." Scholarly research makes evident that these five are Krishna (Vasudeva), Balarama (Sankarshana), Pradyumna, Samba, and Aniruddha.

This was the proof that the complex theology, metaphysics, and cosmology of *Sanatana-dharma* and Vaishnavism definitely existed in an advanced state centuries before Christ. The Mora Well inscription is an important archeological proof of this historical fact.

Furthermore, in the village of Ghosundi in the Chitor district of Rajasthan is found the Ghosundi Inscription, which largely duplicates the message of the Mora Well Inscription. Kaviraja Shyamala Dasa first brought this evidence to light in *The Journal of the Bengal Asiatic Society*. Today, the inscription can be inspected in the Victoria Hall Museum in Udaipur.

The surviving part of this inscription relevant to this chapter reads as follows: "*[this] railing of stone for the purposes of worship is [caused to be made] in the Narayana-compound, [dedicated] to the Blessed Ones [bhagavabhyam] Samkarshana and Vasudeva, the gods...*"

The inscription is in a form of Sanskrit script called Northern Brahmi script, which dates the inscription as being from the second century BCE in either the late Maurya or early Sunga periods. An almost identical inscription also was uncovered nearby and is called the Hathi-vada Inscription. According to K. P. Jayaswal of the Archaeological Survey of India, these inscriptions demonstrate that not only the Kshatriyas but also the Brahmanas or priestly and intellectual class worshiped Krishna as the

"Lord of all," and, thus, Vaishnavism was entrenched in the entire Indian society.

The same point is made in the famous Nanaghat Cave Inscription in the state of Maharashtra, where Vasudeva and Sankarshana (or Krishna and Balarama) are included in an invocation of a Brahmana. On epigraphical grounds, this inscription is dated conclusively as coming from the second half of the first century BCE. Additionally, Raychaudhuri reports:

The Nanaghat Inscription shows further that the Bhagavata [Vaishnava] religion was no longer confined to Northern India, but had spread to the south and had captured the hearts of the sturdy people of Maharashtra. From Maharashtra it was destined to spread to the Tamil country and then flow back with renewed vigor to the remotest corners of the Hindu Vedic world.

There is also much numismatic evidence that corroborates the antiquity of Krishna. For instance, excavations at Al-Khanum, along the border of Afghanistan and the Soviet Union, conducted by P. Bernard and a French archeological expedition, unearthed six rectangular bronze coins issued by the Indo-Greek ruler Agathocles (180-165? BCE). The coins had script written in both Greek and Brahmi and, most interestingly, show an image of Vishnu, or Vasudeva, carrying a Chakra and a pear-shaped vase, or conchshell, which are two of the four main sacred symbols of God in Vaishnavism.

ESTABLISHING THE AGE OF THE EARTH
AND SCHEDULED TIMES OF LORD KRISHNA
BY THE MANU AVATARAS

To more clearly understand the divisions of time that the Vedic culture used to deal with, and get another insight into the antiquity of the Vedic civilization, we can take a closer look at the span of time known as a *manvantara*, or the life time of one Manu. First of all, the Manus appear for certain durations within a day of Brahma. Brahma's day is calculated as 4,300,000 years (the time of one cycle of the four yugas) times 1,000, or about 4,320,000,000 human years. Within one day of Brahma there are 14 Manus. The list of the 14 Manus in this universe is as follows: Yajna is Svayambhuva Manu, Vibhu is Svarocisha Manu, Satyasena is Uttama

Manu, Hari is Tamasa Manu, Vaikuntha is Raivata Manu, Ajita is Ckakshusha Manu, Vamana is Vaivasvata Manu (the Manu of the present age), Sarvabhauma is Savarni Manu, Rishabha is Daksha-savarni Manu, Vishvaksena is Brahma-savarni Manu, Dharmasetu is Dharma-savarni Manu, Sudhama is Rudra-savarni Manu, Yogesvara is Deva-savarni Manu, and Brihadbhanu is Indra-savarni Manu. These fourteen Manus cover the 4,320,000,000 solar years of one day of Brahma. [9]

To understand more completely how long these Manus reign we can consider the following information. For example, there are four ages or *yugas*, namely Satya-yuga, Treta-yuga, Dvapara-yuga, and Kali-yuga, which together comprise a *divya-yuga*, which is one set of the four *yugas*, also called a *chaturyuga*. Let us remember that Satya-yuga lasts 1,728,000 years, Treta-yuga 1,296,000 years, Dvapara-yuga 864,000 years, and Kali-yuga 432,000 years. That is a total of 4,320,000 years. A day of Brahma, called a *kalpa*, lasts for 1,000 of these cycles, and is thus 4,320,000,000 solar years. There are 14 Manus in each day of Brahma. Each Manu is said to exist for one *manvantara*, which is a period of time lasting 71 *divya-yugas*. Therefore, each Manu exists for roughly 306,720,000 years. Additionally, Brahma lives for 100 years, composed of 365 of such days in a year. [10]

From further analysis we can also discover the age of the earth from these Vedic calculations. The present Manu is the seventh in line, called Vaivasvata Manu, the son of Vivasvan. Twenty-seven *divya-yugas*, or cycles of the four *yugas*, of his age have now passed. So 27 *divya-yugas* means 116,640,000 years. It is scheduled that at the end of the Dvapara-yuga of the twenty-eighth *divya-yuga* of the seventh Manu, Lord Krishna appears on earth with the full paraphernalia of His eternal spiritual abode, named Vrajadhama or Goloka Vrindavana. Brahma's day consists of 4,320,000,000 years. In this way, six of these Manus appear and disappear before Lord Krishna takes birth. This means that 1,975,320,000 years of the day of Brahma have gone by before the appearance of Lord Krishna. [11]

Therefore, this is also the age of the earth in this particular day of Brahma by these Vedic calculations. Science is sometimes surprised that such lengths of time were part of the ancient Vedic conception of the universe. This also gives some idea of how long ago the Vedic culture existed before any glacial ice age that we are familiar with took place.

CHAPTER NOTES

1. B. N. Narahari Achar, *Origin of Indian Civilization*, Edited by Bal Ram Singh, Center for Indic Studies, Dartmought, USA, 2010, p. 203.
2. Nicholas Kazanas, *Origin of Indian Civilization*, Edited by Bal Ram Singh, Center for Indic Studies, Dartmought, USA, 2010, p. 53.
3. B. N. Narahari Achar, *Origin of Indian Civilization*, Edited by Bal Ram Singh, Center for Indic Studies, Dartmought, USA, 2010, p. 225.
4. Ibid., p. 231.
5. Ibid., p. 244.
6. Nicholas Kazanas, *Origin of Indian Civilization*, Edited by Bal Ram Singh, Center for Indic Studies, Dartmouth, USA, 2010, p. 53.
7. V. S. Agrawal, *India in the Days of Panini*, 1953.
8. B. N. Narahari Achar, *Origin of Indian Civilization*, Edited by Bal Ram Singh, Center for Indic Studies, Dartmought, USA, 2010, p. 246-7.
9. *Srimad-Bhagavatam* 1.3.5 purport & *Chaitanya-caritamrita*, *Madhya-lila* 20, 319-328.
10. *Bhagavad-gita* 8.17 & *Srimad-Bhagavatam* 3.11.20 & *Vishnu Purana*, Book One, Chapter Three, p. 35.
11. *Chaitanya-caritamrita*, *Adi-lila* 3, 7-10 & *Srimad-Bhagavatam* 4.30.49 purport.

CHAPTER FOUR

Developments in Writing and Language

WRITING

There has always been questions about where the original script came from, and how did it originate. However, in this regard, famous archeologist and specialist in scripts, A. B. Walawalkar and scribe L. S. Wakankar have, through their research proved that the Indian script originated in India itself and said that on the basis of phonetics, the tradition of writing was present even in the Vedic times. [1]

The name *Sanskrit* actually refers to a language brought to formal perfection, aside from the common languages at the time, like Prakrit. The form of Sanskrit that has been used for the last 2500 years or more is commonly known as Classical Sanskrit, which had been established by the ancient grammarians, and most scholars accept that it was finalized by Panini in the 5th century BCE. That is what became the standard for correct Sanskrit with such comprehensive authority that little has changed it down to the present day.

Kamlesh Kapur provides further insight into Sanskrit writing in her book *Portraits of a Nation: History of India*: "Sanskrit language is composed of 50 sounds and letters in its alphabet. It has 11,000 roots from which to make words. The English language has 500,000 words. Sanskrit language has 1700 *Dhatu* (root verbs), 80 *Upasargas* (suffixes, prefixes), and 20 *Pratyaya* (declensions). It is believed that Sanskrit has roughly 74,000,000 words. In fact, using these rules and by adding prefixes and suffixes, Sanskrit can provide an infinite number of words whose meaning is completely determined by the grammatical process.

"Several languages spoken and written today in India have been derivatives of Sanskrit. Bengali, Gurumukhi, Gujarati, Marathi, Oriya and

Hindi have been derived from Sanskrit. Languages of the South have been influenced by Sanskrit. Recently, Washoe County of Nevada (USA) proclaimed January 12, 2008 as Sanskrit Day. The proclamation says that, "As Hinduism expands in the West, it is important that to understand Hinduism, one should have a working knowledge of Sanskrit." [2]

However, India also has a strong tradition in its Vedic culture that describes the possible origin of its script. There are a few examples of this. One is that the text known as *Yaju Taittariya Samhita* tells the story of how the *devas* faced the problem that since sound vanishes once the words are spoken, what method could be applied to give it shape? So, they went to Indra and said, *"Vachanvya kurvit,"* which means "grant sound a shape." Then Indra said that he would have to take the help of Vayu, the wind god. The other gods agreed and Indra gave a shape to sound in the form of the knowledge of writing or script. This is famous as *Indra vayavya vyaakaran*, or the grammar pertaining to the aerial Indra. [3]

Another example gives credit to Lord Shiva. This one describes that with the death of various sages, particular branches of Vedic knowledge started disappearing. So, with a prayer to save them, great sages like Sanaka went to Shiva in the south Indian place of Chidambaram. Hearing their prayers, Lord Shiva strummed his damru instrument nine and then five more times during the interval of his cosmic dance. Thus, fourteen sources of sound were born. These came to be known as the *Maheshwar Sutra*. [4]

Another story from the Vedic tradition is that when the great Vedavyas was thinking of writing the *Mahabharata*, he faced the problem of who would write it. To solve this problem he thought of Ganesh. When Ganesh came, Vedavyas said, "You be the writer of the Bharat Granth." Ganesh agreed only if Vedavyas would not pause or stop, and Vedavyas agreed as long as Ganesh would not write anything unless he understood the meaning of everything that Vedavyas dictated. This was supposed to have happened shortly after the beginning of the age of Kali-yuga began, which is accepted to be in the year 3102 BCE. So there had to have been the knowledge of the Sanskrit script at that time.

Nonetheless, the archeologist Balawalkarji studied the scripts of the ancient coins and proved that it was mainly the Maheshwari script which was the Vedic script. According to him, it was only later that the Brahmi and the Nagari script developed from this.

original language of the earth. All Western scholars who readily apply their mind to the problem will find themselves concurring with Halhead that Sanskrit is the oldest language and that it was spoken all over the world. Other world languages are shattered and twisted bits of Sanskrit."

The Great Sanskrit scholar Bopp wrote in his *Edinborough Review* (Volume 33, page 43): "At one time Sanskrit was the one language spoken all over the world."

As the study and interest in Sanskrit grew, there were many scholars and researchers who gave praise to it. In 1777, the French astronomer Bailly figured that the earliest humans had to have been located on the banks of the Ganges. Bailly also once stated, "The Brahmans are the teachers of Pythagoras, the instructors of Greece, and through her the whole of Europe." [7]

Voltaire also opined, "In short, Sir, I am convinced that everything–astronomy, astrology, metempsychosis, etc.–comes to us from the banks of the Ganges." [8]

The French naturalist and traveler Pierre de Sonnerat (1782) also believed all knowledge came from India, which he considered the cradle of the human race. [9]

Then in 1807, Schelling, a metaphysician who was well-known in his day, wondered "what is Europe really but a sterile trunk which owes everything to Oriental grafts." [10]

In 1808, Friedrich von Schlegel argued that "the Northwest of India must be considered the central point from which all of these nations had their origin." [11] Schlegel, who also helped popularize German interest in Sanskrit, in his study of comparative grammar came to the conclusion that "the Indian language is older, the other younger and derived from it."

In 1845, Eichhoff boldly proclaimed that "all Europeans come from the Orient. This truth, which is confirmed by the evidence of physiology and linguistics, no longer needs special proof." [12] And this, I might add, is before genetics confirmed the same thing.

In 1828, Vans Kennedy related, "Sanscrit itself is the primitive language from which the Greek, Latin, and the mother of the Teutonic dialects were originally derived." [13]

Then in 1855, Lord A. Curzon, the British governor-general of India and later chancellor of Oxford, was fully convinced that "the race of India branched out and multiplied into that of the great Indo-European family.... The Aryans, at a period as yet undetermined, advanced toward and invaded the countries to the west and north-west of India, conquered the various tribes who occupied the land." [14]

Michelet was another that had the opinion that the *Vedas* "were undoubtedly the first monument of the world",[15] and that India emanated a torrent of light and the flow of reason and Right."[16]

Plus, Godfrey Higgins, in his book *The Celtic Druids* (page 61), writes: "There are many objections to the derivation of the Latin from the Greek. Latin exhibits many terms in a more rude form than Greek. Latin was derived from Sanskrit."

The roots of many languages are found in Sanskrit, which some called the mother of all languages, distinguished from the rest by its longevity, stability of form over the many millennia, and showed the status of a sacred language. The fact is that the farther back in time we trace the European languages, the more they begin to resemble Sanskrit. The farther we go back in time, the more we see that European and Vedic culture coalesce.

Sri Aurobindo observed that Sanskrit is "one of the most magnificent, the most perfect and wonderfully sufficient literary instruments developed by human mind... at once majestic and sweet and flexible, strong and clearly formed and full and vibrant and subtle..." [17]

We can see many Sanskrit words in other languages, or continuations of them in Lithuanian, Russian, or English. In fact, there are many words in Lithuanian that are related to or a part of Sanskrit. I have already spent a chapter or two of *Proof of Vedic Culture's Global Existence* comparing Sanskrit with numerous English words, so we will not go into it here.

One of the reasons why remnants of Sanskrit appear in places around the world, since Sanskrit was the language of early India, or Bharatvarsha, was that people of the region spread or migrated to other parts of the world. Then they named oceans, rivers, mountains, and regions with Sanskrit names. Anybody can see this if they are simply a little educated in it. For example, we can see it in names like Indonesia, Indochina, West Indies, etc., or in other places we have Afghanistan, Baluchastan, Turkasthan, Kurdisthan, Kazaksthan, and Uzbekisthan, all which show the Sanskrit based *sthan*, and which gives a hint of the past influence of the global Vedic tradition. Looking further, there are also many Sanskrit names in the countries of the Far East and South Pacific.

Unfortunately, the similarities in languages were used to help support the Aryan Invasion Theory, the idea that Sanskrit and the Vedic culture came into ancient India from outside. But more than anything, it was not that Sanskrit traveled into India, but that it traveled west and was then adopted to varying degrees by others, thus giving way to what had been called the Proto-Indo-European language that was supposed to have pre-dated Sanskrit. Of course, this has yet to be proved, and the idea came about mostly because of the Euro-centric way of looking at things. With new evidence that has come out, we can conclude that there was a westward movement or migration of people out of India that brought Sanskrit with them, which was absorbed into the existing languages of several central and west Asian regions.

With the advanced nature of the Sanskrit language and alphabet, some feel that, like the traditional source of the *Vedas*, Sanskrit was given by Divinity to humanity. It could not have been developed by the slow process of a human agency. After all, in the time period in which Sanskrit appeared, mankind was considered by some to be barbarians. But how could such a people, if that is what they were, develop such a refined language like Sanskrit? For such a language to appear, it would have to come from an equally refined and advanced civilization. Otherwise, why, after thousands of years of our advanced scientific civilization, have we not seen a better or more sophisticated language?

To help substantiate this, we can relate the following quote which appeared in the 1985 spring issue of *AI* (*Artificial Intelligence*) magazine, written by NASA researcher Rick Briggs: "In the past 20 years, much time, effort, and money have been expended on designing an unambiguous representation of natural languages to make them accessible to computer processing. These efforts have centered around creating schemata designed to parallel logical relations expressed by the syntax and semantics of natural languages, which are clearly cumbersome and ambiguous in their function as vehicles for the transmission of logical data. Understandably, there is a widespread belief that natural languages are unsuitable for the transmission of many ideas that artificial languages can render with great precision and mathematical rigor. But this dichotomy, which has served as a premise underlying much work in the areas of linguistics and artificial intelligence, is a false one.

"There is at least one language, Sanskrit, which for the duration of almost 1000 years was a loving spoken language with a considerable literature of its own. Besides works of literary value, there was a long philosophical and grammatical tradition that has continued to exist with undiminished vigor until the present century. Among the accomplishments of the grammarians can be reckoned a method for paraphrasing Sanskrit in a manner that is identical not only in essence but in form with current work in Artificial Intelligence."

On another level, the ancients and rishis called Sanskrit the language of the gods, or *devevani* or *devabhasha*. The script was called *devanagari*, the script of the gods. And the fact is, the most spiritual of Vedic literature is in Sanskrit. In the *Rig Veda*, Sanskrit has been called *vacho aggram*, or the earliest language. It is no doubt the main language used by the great rishis or sages to disseminate the knowledge of enlightenment that had been received by them ever since the time of the universal creation. Sanskrit was able to invoke the spiritual energy of which it speaks, and the vibration for propelling the consciousness to the higher realms it depicts. The great epics and codes of knowledge are all in Sanskrit. Even the great *acharyas*, like Shankar, Ramanuja, Madhva, Nimbarka, Vallabha, and other poets and philosophers wrote in Sanskrit. Sanskrit stood for at least three millennia, if not much longer, as the carrier of Vedic thought before its dominance gradually gave way to the vernacular dialects that eventually evolved from it as the modern languages of Hindi, Gujarati, Bengali, Tamil, Telugu, Kannada, and so on.

There are officially 25 languages in India, along with 33 different languages and 2000 some dialects that are known to be used. In this regard Will Durant relates in *Our Oriental Heritage* (p. 406): "The Sanskrit of the *Vedas* and the epics has already earmarks of a classical and literary tongue, used only by scholars and priests; the very word *Sanskrit* means 'prepared, pure, perfect, sacred.' The language of the people in the Vedic age was not one but many; each tribe had its own Aryan dialect. India has never had one language."

SANSKRIT GRAMMAR

The grammar of Sanskrit is also known to be without comparison. Sir William Wilson Hunter wrote in *The Indian Empire*: "The grammar of Panini stands supreme among the grammars of the world, alike for its precision of statement and for its thorough analysis of the roots of the language and of the formative principles of words. By applying an algebraical terminology, it attains a sharp succinctness unrivaled in brevity. It arranges in logical harmony the whole phenomenon which the Sanskrit language presents and stands forth as one of the most splendid achievements of human invention and industry. So elaborate is the structure that doubts have arisen whether its innumerable rules of formation and phonetic change, its polysyllabic derivatives, its ten conjugations with its multiform aorist and long array of tenses could even have been the spoken language of a people."

Though we give much credit to Panini for being one of the first if not the first grammarian of Sanskrit, we should still remember that in his writings, Panini himself mentions at least 10 grammarians who preceded him. [18]

Furthermore, it is known that Sanskrit was a vocal tradition long before it was put into written form. This tends to show that Sanskrit had been existing for many years before Panini, and that Panini may have also existed at a much earlier time period than many people think.

The fact that Panini listed previous philologists indicates that there had to have been a fully existing language of Sanskrit in ancient India long before he formed his book on Sanskrit grammar. Otherwise, the complex literature could not have been passed down to future generations to continue in such a flawless manner in an oral tradition. Panini did not develop Sanskrit but only compiled the rules of Sanskrit.

Dr. Cardona, a Professor of Linguistics at the University of Pennsylvania in Philadelphia, a known Panini grammarian, places Panini in the 6th century BCE, but believes that Panini could have been much earlier. In this regard, Count Bjornstjerna, even with what early evidence he could uncover, writes in his *Theogony of Hindoos* that Hindus possessed written texts of religion before 2800 BCE. So it is likely that it could have been long before then.

The earliest of glossaries on Vedic words goes back to the *Nighantu*, written by the ancient etymologist Yaska. Yaska explained that he compiled this based on previous glossaries, the most important of which was the *Nighantuka-Padakhyana*, which is attributed to Kashyapa Prajapati. Yaksa himself described at least twelve previous etymologists before him. As listed in his *Nirukta*, it includes Aupamanyava (*Nirukta* 1.1), Audambarayana (1.1), Varshayayani (1.2), Gargya (1.3), Shakatayana (1.3), Agrayana (1.9), Shakapuni (2.8), Aurnavabha (2.26), Taitiki (4.3),

Sthaulastivi (7.14), Kraustuki (8.2), and Kathakya (8.5). So his own commentary, the *Nirukta*, is based on a long tradition of Vedic Sanskrit, and was a compilation and codification of the etymological knowledge that went all the way back to the pre-historic time of Kashyapa Muni.

Obviously, Sanskrit was the earliest of developed languages, and no country but ancient India, and no language except Sanskrit can boast of a possession so ancient or venerable. No people but the Hindus, the Vedic Aryans, can show such a sacred heirloom in its history, so high in its grandeur and glory when compared with other languages. The *Vedas* and Vedic literature, such as the *Ramayana* and *Mahabharata*, serve as a beacon of divine light for the onward progress for humanity.

Sir W. Hunter said: "The grammar of Panini stands supreme among the grammars of the world, alike for its precision of statement and for its thorough analysis of the roots of the language and of the formative principles of words. By applying an algebraical terminology, it attains a sharp succinctness unrivaled in brevity, but at times enigmatical. It arranges in logical harmony the whole phenomena which the Sanskrit language presents, and stands forth as one of the most splendid achievements of human invention and industry. So elaborate is the structure that doubts have arisen whether its innumerable rules of formation and phonetic change, its polysyllabic derivatives, its ten conjunctions with its multiform aorists and long array of tenses could ever have been the spoken language of a people." [19]

Mrs. Manning also relates: "Sanskrit grammar is evidently far superior to the kind of grammar which for the most part has contented grammarians in Europe." [20]

Mr. Elphinstone agrees in the same way: "His (Panini's) works and those of his successors have established a system of grammar, the most complete that ever was employed in arranging elements of humans speech." [21]

Professor Sir Monier Williams says: "The grammar of Panini is one of the most remarkable literary works that the world has ever seen, and no other country can produce any grammatical system at all comparable to it, ether for originality or plan or analytical subtlety. . . His Sastras are a perfect miracle of condensation." [22]

Sages engaged in chanting the ancient Vedic texts in a temple in Jagannatha Puri.

THE VEDIC TEXTS

Sanskrit is the foundation of Vedic literature, which is the basis of the Vedic philosophy. The Vedic literature is a complete library for understanding life, the purpose of the creation, how the cosmos manifested, and what is the spiritual identity of the individual soul, Supersoul, and Supreme Being; plus, the relationship between them, and the pathways for directly realizing and perceiving these. This is what is called *Sanatana-dharma*, the eternal duty of life and the eternal state of being, meaning complete harmony and balance that we should all reach. This is the main purpose of the human form of life according to the Vedic system.

The original compositions of many of the Vedic hymns were given credit to the early sages or seers, such as Brigu, Angirasa, Marichi, Atri, Vashistha and his brother Agastya, and Vishvamitra. It was Brigu, Angirasa, Marichi, and Atri from whom came the seven rishis (Saptarishis) who became the main lineages or *gotras* that we refer to today. These consist of: Jamadagni from Bhrigu; Bharadvaja from Angirasa; Gautama from Angirasa; Kashyapa; Vashistha from Marichi; Agastya from Marichi; Atri; and Vishvamitra from Atri. It is said that Bhrigu and his descendants lived in the western part of the Asian subcontinent and Vashistha and Vishvamitra lived in the Sarasvati region. Later, the great sage Vedavyasa compiled it all into written form. (A detailed analysis of the Vedic literature and its numerous books has been provided in a previous book of mine called *The Heart of Hinduism*. So I will not included that elaboration here.)

The point to remember is that the Vedic literature held universal spiritual knowledge. Even the *Puranas*, which are considered to be the interplanetary histories and elaborations of the spiritual knowledge of the Vedic *samhitas*, such as the *Rig, Sama, Atharva*, and *Yajur Vedas*, are said to be universal in nature. In other words, they were not exclusive to the region of India.

One little story that can help point this out is how, with the use of the Vedic knowledge, the source of the Nile River was found. The British explorer John Hanning Speke, who in 1862 discovered the Nile in Lake Victoria, acknowledged that the Egyptians themselves did not have any idea of where the Nile's source was located. However, it was from British Lt. Colonel Wilford's description of the Hindus' intimate awareness with ancient Egypt that led Speke to Ripon Falls, at the edge of Lake Victoria. This was outlined in Wilford's essay on Egypt from the *Puranas*, called *Ancient Book of the Hindus' Asiatic Researches* (Vol. III, 1792). What was also most helpful was that Lieutenant Speke constructed a map based on the information from the *Puranas*, as described in his book, *Journal of the Discovery of the Source of the Nile* (1863). He explained, "All our previous information concerning the hydrography of these regions originated with the ancient Hindus who told it to the priests of the Nile; and all these busy Egyptian geographers who disseminated their knowledge with a view to be famous for their long-sightedness, in solving the mystery which enshrouded the source of their holy river, were so many hypothetical humbugs. The Hindu traders had a firm basis to stand upon through their intercourse with the Abyssinians."

Thus, the map coursed the river through Kushadvipa, from a great lake in Chandristhan, "Country of the Moon," while it gave the correct position in relation to the Zanzibar islands. Speke wrote that some Hindu Pundits knew the Nile as Nila and Kaali. The word *Nile* means blue and *Kali* means dark, which were appropriate descriptions of the Nile River.

There names are mentioned in some *Puranas*, including the *Bhavishya*. This went against the idea of that time because Lake Victoria was unknown then.

Sir Richard Burton, the leader of the Nile expedition had identified Lake Tangyanika as the source. Speke, however, following the advice of a Benares Pundit insisted that the real source was a much larger lake that lay to the north. By following this advice, Speke was able to discover Lake Victoria and the source of the Nile. The Pundit also told him that the real source were the twin peaks known as Somagiri. *Soma* in Sanskrit indicates the moon, and *giri* means hill or mountain. Thus, Somagiri indicated the fabled Mountains of the Moon in Central Africa.

The wonderful inventive genius and high level of consciousness of the Vedic Aryans enabled them to produce or utilize a language which contributed materially in the creation of a literature that remains unparalleled for richness, sublimity and range. The particular beauty inherent in the language of such intellectual powers were greatly enhanced by the scientific upbringing that had developed into what is now such a model of perfection that it was known as *devanagari*, or the language of the gods.

Professor Monier Williams was also highly impressed with the *Ramayana*. He had written: "*Ramayana* is undoubtedly one of the greatest treasures in Sanskrit literature." However, later he went into more detail on his appreciation for it: "There is not in the whole range of Sanskrit literature a more charming poem than the *Ramayana*. The classical purity, clearness and simplicity of its style, the exquisite touches of true poetic feeling with which it abounds, its graphic descriptions of heroic incidents, nature's grandest scenes, the deep acquaintance it displays with the conflicting workings and most refined emotions of the human heart, all entitle it to rank among the most beautiful compositions that have appeared at any period or in any country. It is like a spacious and delightful garden, here and there allowed to run wild, but teeming with fruits and flowers, watered by perennial streams, and even its most tangled jungle intersected with delightful pathways. The character of Rama is nobly portrayed... " [23]

The *Mahabharata* also was not in want of its western admirers, even from years ago, such as Dr. F. A. Hassler of America, in his letter to P. C. Roy, dated July 21, 1888, which was published in P. C. Roy's English translation of the *Mahabharata*: "In all my experience in life, I have not found a work that has interested me as much as that noble production of the wise, and I do not hesitate to say, inspired men of ancient India. In fact I have studied it more than any other work for a long time past, and have made at least 1,000 notes which I have arranged in alphabetical order for the purpose of study. The *Mahabharata* has opened to me, as it were, a new world, and I have been surprised beyond measure at the wisdom, truth, knowledge, and love of the right which I have found displayed in its pages. Not only so, but I have found many of the truths which my own heart has taught me in regard to the Supreme Being and His creations set forth in beautiful, clear language."

The early American ethnologist, Jeremiah Curtin, who also had written to Baba P. C. Roy about his edition of the *Mahabharata*, also had deep appreciation for what he found within it. He relates in his letter, which appeared in Part XXX of the book: "I have just finished reading carefully from beginning to end, 24 numbers of your translation of the *Mahabharata*, and can honestly say that I have never obtained more pleasure from reading any book in my life. The *Mahabharata* will open the eyes of the world to the true character and intellectual rank of the Aryans of India. You are certainly doing a great work... The *Mahabharata* is a real mine of wealth not entirely unknown, I suppose, at present to any man outside your country, but which will be known in time and valued in all civilized lands for the reason that it contains information of the highest import to all men who seek to know in singleness of heart, the history of our race upon the earth, and the relations of man with the Infinite Power above us, around us and in us."

This shows that it is not a matter of proselytizing, but only a matter of sharing the Vedic knowledge and wisdom with others that will attract numerous people to find that the deeper levels of spirituality that they are looking for is already existing and waiting for them within the open texts of the Vedic literature.

CHAPTER NOTES
1. Suresh Soni, *India's Glorious Scientific Tradition*, Ocean Books Pvt. Ltd., New Delhi, 2010, p. 199.
2. Kamlesh Kapur, *Portraits of a Nations: History of India*, Sterling Publishers, Private Limited, 2010, p. 401.
3. Suresh Soni, *India's Glorious Scientific Tradition*, Ocean Books Pvt.

Ltd., New Delhi, 2010, p. 199.

4. Ibid., p. 200.

5. Pococke, *India in Greece*, p. 18.

6. Pritchard, *Dr. Pritchard's Physical History of Man*, Vol. I, p. 502.

7. Jean-Sylvan Bailly, *Lettres sur l'origine des sciences et sur celle des peuples de l'Asie*, Paris, Freres Bebure, 1777, p. 51.

8. Ibid., 1777, p. 4.

9. Pierre Sonnerat, *Voyages aux Indes Orientales et la Chine*, Paris, 1782.

10. L. Poliakov, *The Aryan Myth*, Sussex University Press, London, 1971, p. 11.

11. Friedrich von Schlegel, *Uber die Sprache und die Weisheit der Indier*, Amsterdam Studies in the Theory and Hindistory of Linguistic Science, Amsterdam, Benjamins, 1977, p. 505

12. E. W. Eichhoff, *Vergleichung der Sprachen von Europa und Indien*, Schrey, Leipzig, 1845.

13. Vans Kennedy, *Researches into the Origin and Affinity of the Principal Languages of Asia and Europe*, Longman, London, 1828, p. 196.

14. *Journal of the Royal Asiatic Society*, 16, 172-173.

15. J. Michelet, *Bible de l'humanite*, Paris, Chamerot, 1864, p. 26.

16. Ibid., p. 485.

17. *Pride of India: A Glimpse into India's Scientific Heritage*, Samskriti Bharati, New Delhi, 2006, p. 130.

18. Nicholas Kazanas, *Indo-Aryan Origins and Other Vedic Issues*, by Aditya Prakashan, New Delhi, 2009, p. 199.

19. *Imperial Gazetteer of India*, Art, "India", p. 214.

20. *Ancient and Medieval India*, Vol. I, p. 381.

21. *Elphinstone's History of India*, p. 146.

22. Monier Williams, *Indian Wisdom*, p. 172.

23. *Indian Epic Poetry*, p. 12.

CHAPTER FIVE

Developments in Mathematics

THE NUMERICAL SYSTEM OF INDIA

The numeral script from India is one of the greatest contributions to the world. The Greek alphabet, for example, was a great hindrance to calculating. The Egyptians also did not have a numerical system suitable for large calculations, in fact it was a hindrance. For the number 986 they had to use 23 symbols. Even after the Greeks, the Romans also were in want of a system of numbers for mathematical calculations. China's pictorial script was also not ideal for such calculations. Actually, the mathematical systems of the Egyptians, Babylonians, Romans, and even the Chinese, all using independent symbols, had advanced as much as they could until they received help from the numeral system from India. Only after they adopted the Indian system that was called Arabic numerals did they find what they needed.

The work of the Greek mathematicians Euclid and Archimedes helped bring about many new perspectives and insights, but later Carl Friedrich Gauss, the "prince of mathematics," was said to have lamented how much more advanced science would have been if Archimedes in the third century BCE had not failed to foresee the advanced nature of the Indian system of numeration. Pierre Laplace, one of the world's greatest mathematicians from France, wrote: "It is India that gave us the ingenious method of expressing all numbers by ten symbols, each symbol receiving a value of position, as well as an absolute value. We shall appreciate the grandeur of this achievement when we remember that it escaped the genius of Archimedes and Appolonius." It was the Indian numerical system that finally set free the other forms of mathematics. By 500 CE, mathematicians of India had solved the problems that baffled the world's greatest scholars of all time.

In *History of Sanskrit Literature* (page 424), Professor MacDonnell writes, "There is in the first place, the great fact that the Indians invented the numerical figures used all over the world." Brian Clegg, in *The Quest to Think the Unthinkable* (pages 54-60), mentions, "the characters we use for the numbers arrived here from India via the Arabic world." Leonardo of Pisa, known by his nickname of Fibonacci, commented in his book *Liberabaci*, written in 1202, that he was "introduced to the art of India's nine symbols," and it was this book that really brought the Vedic system of numbers to the West.

The numerical system of India spread to Arabia through traders and merchants, and from there up into Europe and elsewhere. It became known as the Arabic numerals, yet the Arabians had called them "Indian figures" (Al-Arqan-Al-Hindu) and the system of math was known as *hindisat*, or the Indian art.

Al-Khwarizmi wrote numerous books that played important roles in arithmetic and algebra. His work, *De Numero Indorum* (*Concerning the Hindu Art of Reckoning*), was based presumably on an Arabic translation of Brahmagupta's work, where he gave a full account of the Vedic numerals which was the first to expound the system with its digits of 0,1,2,3,4,5,6,7,8,9, and the decimal place value which was a fairly recent arrival from India. It was because of this book and its Latin translations that a false presumption was made that our system of numerals is Arabic in origin. The new notation came to be known as that of al-Khwarizmi, or more carelessly, algorismi; ultimately the scheme of numeration making use of the Vedic numerals came to be called simply algorism or algorithm, a word that originally derived from the name al-Khwarizmi. This now generally means any peculiar rule of procedure or operation. [1]

This development obviously took much time and imagination, and a great ability for abstract thinking. The one thing that made this possible was that it came from an atmosphere within the Vedic civilization that provided for much mystical, philosophical, cosmological, and metaphysical appreciation. The point is that, as with Sanskrit, the study of numbers and mathematical research was developed with a combination or along side the metaphysical and spiritual insights and realizations of the time. This provided for the broad-mindedness that was necessary to evolve the developments for which India became known. They were not restricted by any narrow view of the world or particular cosmology or spiritual identity that limited much of the rest of the planet. They had been a culture that always looked at a wide variety of views, open to what possibilities humanity could arrive at, based primarily on the spiritual philosophy of its culture. In fact, so deeply has this been ingrained in the culture that you can see this aspect in all other areas of study within Vedic culture and the civilization that arose from it. This itself is probably the greatest contribution to humanity, of which the world has never seen since, or in any other part of it. We can safely say, after much study on this, that the area of India was indeed the center for most civilizational development of the time. One example is that recent evidence of geometrical drawing instruments from as early as 2500 BCE have been found in the Indus Valley. Weights and measures and scales with decimal divisions have been found from that early period, all of which are still quite accurate.

From the numerical system came the means to develop a highly sophisticated mathematical system. Time and time again we have seen that many of the inventions we enjoy today are because of the developments that took place in ancient India. But how many times is this overlooked or underestimated, negated, or even distorted to the point where credit is given to someone else from some other place? In fact, Dr. David Gray, in his book *Science and Mathematics in India*, writes: "The study of mathematics in the West has long been characterized by a certain ethnocentric bias, a bias which most often manifests not in explicit racism, but in a tendency toward undermining or eliding the real contributions made by non-Western civilizations. The debt owed by the West to other civilizations, and to India in particular, go back to the earliest epoch of the Western scientific tradition, the age of the classical Greeks, and continued up until the dawn of the modern era, the renaissance, when Europe was awakening from its dark ages. . . The role played by India in the development (of the scientific revolution in Europe) is no mere footnote, easily and inconsequentially swept under the rug of Eurocentric bias. To do so is to distort history, and to deny India one of its greatest contributions to world civilization." Therefore, it is time, as we proceed to view the historical and chronological order of developments from India, that we give credit where credit is due.

For example, Mrs. Manning writes in her *Ancient and Mediaeval India*, (Volume I, page 374-5): "Hindus were peculiarly strong in all the branches of Arithmetic. . . The Arabs were not in general inventors but recipients. Subsequent observation has confirmed this view; for not only did algebra in an advanced state exist in India prior to the earliest disclosure of it by the Arabians to modern Europe, but the names by which the numerals have become known to us are of Sanskrit origin."

Even Professor Monier Williams relates in his *Indian Wisdom* (page 185): "To the Hindus is due the invention of algebra and geometry and their application to astronomy."

When comparing the Hindus and Greeks as regards to their knowledge of mathematics, Sir Mountstuart Elphinstone explains in *History of India*: "There is no question of the superiority of the Hindus over their rivals in the perfection to which they brought the science. Not only is Aryabhatta superior to Diaphantus (as is shown by his knowledge of the resolution of equations involving several unknown quantities, and in general method of resolving all indeterminate problems of at least the first degree), but he and his successors press hard upon the discoveries of algebraists who lived almost in our own time."

A. L. Basham, who everyone knows as a writer on ancient India, writes in his *The Wonder That was India*: "Medieval Indian mathematicians, such as Brahmagupta (seventh century), Mahavira (ninth century), and Bhaskara (twelfth century), made several discoveries which in Europe were not known until the Renaissance or later. They understood the import of positive and negative quantities, evolved sound systems of extracting square and cube roots, and could solve quadratic and certain types of indeterminate equations."

Furthermore, B. B. Dutt explained in his article *The Modern Way to Express Numerals* (as appeared in *Indian Historical Quarterly*, Issue 3, pp. 530-540): "The Hindus had adopted the decimal system a long time back. The numerical language of no other country had been able to achieve or acquire the scientific caliber and the completeness that ancient India had. The ancient Indians had achieved success in expressing any number beautifully and easily with the help of only ten symbols. The beauty of Hindu numeral markings attracted the civilized world and they gladly adopted it. . . These numerals slowly reached the west via north Arabia and Egypt and by the 11th century reached Europe. The Europeans called them Arabic numerals because they got them from Arabia, but the Arabs themselves unanimously called them Hindu numerals (Al-Arkan, Al-Hindu)."

Professor Ginsberg further explains this in his article *New Light on Our Numerals* (as published in *The Bulletin of the American Mathematical Society*, pp. 366-69): "In around 770 AD, Abba Sayeed Khalifa Al-Munsur of Baghdad had invited the famous Hindu scholar Kank of Ujjain to the famous court of Baghdad. Kank taught Hindu astrology and mathematics to the Arab scholars. With Kank's help, they even translated Brahmagupta's *Brahma Sphut Siddhant* into Arabic. French scholar M. F. Nau's latest discovery proves that Indian numerals were known in Syria in the 7th century and were also praised."

As the decimal system traveled from India, the names of the numbers changed slightly according to language, such as *Ekam* in Sanskrit became known as *ek* in Hindi and *one* in Arabic and Greek, while the *shunya* became *sifar* in Arabic, *jeefar* in Greek and *zero* in English. [2]

VEDIC MATHEMATICS

What many people do not realize is that ancient India is the father of the great mathematical developments. What we enjoy today has come, primarily, from the early accomplishments that came out of the Vedic civilization. The difference in the systems of math in other parts of the world and what we find in the Vedic tradition is that Vedic mathematics had developed the system of tens, hundreds, thousands, etc., and the basis of carrying the remainder of one column of numbers over to the next. This made for easy calculations of large numbers that was nearly impossible in other systems, as found with the Greeks, Romans, Egyptians and even Chinese. The Vedic system had also invented the zero, which has been called one of the greatest developments in the history of mathematics.

Much of the world, when we look at its history, does indeed acknowledge the advancements of ancient India. For example, the oldest European book on mathematics is known as *Coda Vigilanus*, which can be found in the Museum in Madrid. Therein it says, "From the signs of counting (numerals), we experience that the ancient Hindus had very sharp brains and that the other countries were much behind them in counting and in geometry and other sciences. This is proved by their nine numerals with the help of which any number can be written."

This is very much like the quote from Albert Einstein who once mentioned that we should be thankful to India, who taught us how to count.

Bharti Krishna Teerthaji, the Sankaracharya of Puri, mentions in the foreword of his book *Vedic Mathematics* (p. xviii) other scholars who have recognized the value of India's contribution to the world of mathematics: "It gives me great pleasure to say that some well known modern mathematicians like Prof. G. P. Halstand, Prof. D. Morgan and Prof.

Hutton, who are researchers and lovers of truth have, in contrast to Indian scholars, adopted a scientific outlook and have wholeheartedly praised India's unique contribution to the progress of mathematical knowledge."

In this light, Prof. G. P. Halstand says, in his book *The Foundation and Process of Mathematics* (p. 20), "The significance or importance of the discovery of the zero can never be explained. Giving not just a name but authority, in fact, power to 'nothing,' is the characteristic of the Hindu community, whose invention it is. It is like giving the power of the dynamo to nirvana or salvation. No other single mathematical invention has been more effective than this in the general development or progress of intelligence and power."

The French-Moroccan scholar Georges Ifrah also commented about the advancements of Vedic culture and its mathematical systems in his three-volume work *The Universal History of Numbers*:

"Finally it all came to pass as though across the ages and the civilizations, the human mind had tried all the possible solutions to the problem of writing numbers, before universally adopting the one which seemed the most abstract, the most perfected and the most effective of all. ...The measure of genius of the Indian civilization, to which we owe our modern system, is all the greater in that it was the only one in all history to have achieved this triumph."

In this way, Vedic mathematics is another example of India's contribution to world progress. It is an ancient development that continues to play an important part in modern society. Without the advancements in math that had been established by Vedic culture as far back as 2500 BCE and passed along to others, we would not have many of the developments and inventions that we enjoy and take for granted today.

THE SHULBA SUTRAS

It was the *Shulba Sutras* that recorded the basis of these geometrical formulas used for the Vedic temples and altars. For example, it explains how to make a square of the same area as that of a triangle, a circle of the same area as that of a square, and make a circle double, triple or one third of the area of a square. Bhaskaracharya's *Lilavati* tells us that an arm of an equal tetragon, pentagon, hexagon, octagon in a circle, is in definite proportions to the diameter of the circle.

The *Shulba Sutras* are named after their propounders, such as Baudhayanam, Apastambha, Katyayana, etc. The *Shulba Sutras* form part of the *Vedangas*, which further belong to the *Kalpa Vedanga* or *Kalpa Sutras*. Among the nine *Shulba Sutra* texts the most important are of *Baudhayana*, *Apastamba* and *Katyayana*. Pandit Venkatachalam (1885-1959 CE) has shown that Baudhayana lived during 3200 BCE. [3]

The *Shulba Sutras* preserved the constructional measurements and different geometrical shapes for the altars and arenas used for the religious rituals. The Vedic system of math, as explained in the *sutras*, also reduced the number of steps in calculations to merely a few that otherwise required many steps by conventional methods. Thus, this ancient science is still worthy of study today.

Vedic culture already had an established mathematical system that had been recorded in the *Shulba Sutras*. These are known to date back to the 8th century BCE. However, new research by scholars now date them as far back as 3200 BCE. The name *Shulba Sutras* meant "codes of rope." This was because such calculations were used for measuring precise distances for altars and temple structures by using lengths of rope.

The *Shulba Sutras* were actually a portion of a larger text on mathematics known as the *Kalpa Sutras*. These and the Vedic mathematicians were recognized for their developments in arithmetic and algebra. Indians were the first to use letters of the alphabet to represent unknowns. But they were especially known for what they could do in geometry. Furthermore, what became known as the Pythagorean theorem was already existing in the *Baudhayana*, the earliest of the *Shulba Sutras*. This was presented by Pythagoras around 540 BCE after he discovered it in, what some say, his travels to India. So this shows the advanced nature of the Vedic civilization.

The *Shulba Sutras* actually explain that they represent the premises that were taught in the *Samhitas* and *Brahmanas*, such as the *Taittiriya Samhita* and the *Shatapatha Brahmana*. They were not presenting something new or original. They were but compilations of formulas for the construction of altars in various shapes, each shape depending on the need required by the ritual. Some of these shapes could be square, circular, trapezoid, or falcon shaped. These formulas could and were also used for secular purposes as well, such as in architectural projects, the likes of which spread throughout India and were greatly advanced to the level of knowledge of the later invaders into the region.

In 1978, Dr. Abraham Seidenberg, a professor of mathematics at the University of California in Berkeley, as noted in a paper called *The Origin of Mathematics* (p. 301, 1978) mentioned two different forms of mathematics, namely the algebraic and the geometric. Therein he explains, "If it could be shown that each of these has a single source – and there are many rather familiar facts that suggest this is so – and if, moreover, in both cases the sources turn out to be the same, it would be plausible to claim we have found the unique origin of mathematics."

He concluded, "Old Babylonia (1700 BC) got the theorem of Pythagoras from India, or both Old Babylonia and India got it from a third source. Now the Sanskrit scholars do not give me a date so far back as 1700 BC. Therefore, I postulate a pre-Old Babylonian (i.e. pre-1700 BC) source of the kind of geometric rituals we see preserved in the *Shulba Sutras*, or at least for the mathematics involved in these rituals." In this paper, Seidenberg established that the *Shulba Sutras* were the basis for the mathematics in Egypt, Babylon, and Greece.

In this way, Seidenberg also recognized the similarities of the *Shulba Sutras* with Pythagorean Greek mathematics. He went on to trace the unique origin of these forms of mathematics to the *Shulba Sutras*. His research led to the conclusion that the Sutra literature preceded the mathematics of both Old Babylonia (c. 1900–1750 BCE) and of the Egyptian Middle Kingdom (c. 2100–1800 BCE). However, even more than this, Seidenberg showed that the mathematics of both the Old Babylonia and Egypt must have derived from ancient India in the *Shulba Sutras*, as others have confirmed. As Seidenberg concludes: "The elements of ancient geometry found in Egypt and Babylonia stem from a ritual system of the kind observed in the *Shulba Sutras*." [4]

As N. S. Rajarama has also shown through analysis, Vedic mathematics already had to have been existing during the time of the Harappan cities. It was this development that contributed to the advanced nature of the construction of these places. [5]

THE GREAT MATHEMATICIANS

Many years after the *Shulba Sutras*, Vedic mathematics enjoyed further development in the field of Jyotish, Vedic astronomy, which used all forms of math. Indian mathematicians continued creating systems that were not known in Europe until much later in the Renaissance period. For example, Aryabhata was one such mathematician. He is said to have been born in 476 CE and lived to 550 CE in Kusumapura in the Magadha empire not far away from the Nalanda University. There is some thought that he was also a chancellor at the university. Aryabhatta introduced sines and versed sines, and is credited as the inventor of algebra. His best known works are the *Aryabhatiya*, a compendium of mathematics and astronomy that survives to the present day, and the *Arya-siddhanta*. These works had dominated the field of astronomy for many years, and also many commentaries had been written on them, starting with Bhaskara's commentary in 629 CE. His ideas had spread all over, even to include works in Tamil, Telugu and Malayalam. The calendar of India was based on the work of Aryabhata until the presence of the Gregorian calendar.

It is said that while he did not use the zero, the knowledge of it was there as a place holder for the values of ten. He is said to be the first to state that the Earth rotates about its axis daily, and that the Earth travels around the sun. However, the ancient Vedic texts have described this many years earlier, which shows the wisdom of the early Vedic seers.

This was not developed by the Greeks, but had been stated in the early *Puranas*. He also calculated the length of the year to be 365.258 days. He gave a close estimate of the size of the earth and stated that it also turns on its own axis, and that the planets were spherical.

Dick Teresi, a science historian, mentions Aryabhata in his book *Lost Discoveries* (page 133) in this way: "The *Aryabhatiya* is a summary of Hindu mathematics up to his time, including astronomy, spherical trigonometry, arithmetic, algebra, and plane trigonometry. In it one of Aryabhata's main goals was to simplify the even more complex computational mathematics of Indian astronomy. He had a practical purpose for this: to fix the Hindu calendar for easier forecasting of eclipses and movements of celestial bodies." [6]

Varahamihira was another Indian mathematician and astronomer of the times (505-587), who lived in Ujjain. Tradition says that the title of Varaha before his name of Mihira was given to him by Vikramaditya, the King of Ujjain. That was because Mihira correctly predicted that the King's son would die at the age of 18. His main work was *Panchasiddhantika* (*Treatise on the Five Astronomical Canons*), written around 575 CE. This provides information about older texts that are now lost, but also summarizes five earlier treatises, which include the *Surya Siddhanta, Romaka Siddhanta, Paulisa Siddhanta, Vasishtha Siddhanta*, and the *Paitamaha Siddhanta*. This covered Vedanga Jyotisha along with Hellenistic astronomy, which included Greek, Egyptian and Roman aspects. He also composed the *Brihat-Samhita*, which covered a wider range of topics, such as astrology, planetary movements, eclipses, architecture, agriculture, gems, domestic relations, clouds, rainfall, etc.

According to the *Surya Siddhanta*, in every *Mahayuga* or *Chaturyuga* (every 4,320,000 years) there are slight differences in our perception of the motions of the planets which make it necessary to correct the astronomical texts to suit the altered conditions. Varahamihira did not include the foregoing *Siddhantas* since they belonged to the earlier *Mahayugas*. He only codified those *Siddhantas* which belonged to the present *Mahayuga*. Few are those who understand the differences in the planetary motions or positions from one Mahayuga to the next.

Besides the *Surya Siddhanta* which is probably spoken about most often and is the oldest of the existing *Siddhantas*, there were a total of nine *Siddhantas*, the eight remaining of which include the *Brahma Siddhanta*, the *Soma Siddhanta, Vrihaspati Siddhanta, Gargya Siddhanta, Narada Siddhanta, Parashara Siddhanta, Pulastya Siddhanta*, and the *Vashishta Siddhanta*.

Varahamihira was followed by Brahmagupta (7th century, 598-668 CE) who was the great mathematician and astronomer that especially developed the use of zero, and was the first to use algebra to solve problems in astronomy. He was the head of the astronomical observatory in Ujjain, which you can still see today. It was the Hindu ruler Sawai Raja Jai Singh (1724-1730) who built the astronomical observatories that are still quite accurate, called Jantar Mantar in the places of Delhi, Jaipur, Varanasi, Ujjain, and Mathura. Interestingly enough, I have been to all of them but the latter and they are all very interesting to view.

Brahmagupta is said to be the founder of Numerical Analysis. He made several original contributions in algebra and trigonometry. His best known works include the *Cadamekela*, his most famous work the *Brahmasphuta Siddhanta*, the *Khandakhadyaka*, and the *Durkeamynarda*. The four fundamental mathematical operations (addition, subtraction, multiplication, and division) were known to many cultures long before

One of the astronomical instruments at the observatory in Ujjain, built by Sawai Raja Jai Singh, where some of the great mathematicians like Brahmagupta and Bhaskaracharya studied for some time.

Part of the large Jantar Mantar observatory in Jaipur

Brahmagupta, such as the Sumerians as far back as 2500 BCE. However, the way we use them today with the Arabic numerals are first known to appear in his *Brahmasphuta Siddhanta*.

The *Brahmagupta-siddhanta* was based mostly on the *Aryabhatiya*, and the *Khandakhadyaka* was like a simplified form of the *Aryabhatiya*. However, the latter book, in two parts, included a section on where Brahmagupta differed from Aryabhata. Nonetheless, both of his books were later translated into Arabic (*Zij-al-Arkand* and *AZ-Zij Kandakatik al-arabi*) by Persian scholar Al-Biruni. These were later translated into Latin in 1126 CE from the Arabic versions by Ya'qub ibn Tariq. From there they entered into Europe along with its theories. Kapler's theory of Parallax is a repeat of the *Khanda-khadyaka*.

Brahmagupta was the first to give the exact formula for the area of a cyclic quadrilateral in his famous book *Brahma Sphuta Siddhanta*. Equally important were the equations he developed for the diagonals of a cyclic quadrilateral, hailed as the most remarkable in Vedic geometry. The first equations for the diagonals of a cyclic quadrilateral were first given in the West by W. Snell in 1619. [7]

Brahmagupta also described the law of gravity more than 500 years before Newton. He related that "all things fall to the earth by a law of nature, for it is the nature of the earth to attract and keep things."

Then there was Bhaskara I (c. 600-c. 680) who was another mathematician who gave a unique commentary on Aryabhata's main work, called the *Aryabhatiyabhasya* (written in 629 CE) with a most noteworthy approximation of the sine function. This is the oldest known work in Sanskrit on Vedic mathematics and astronomy. His other works include *Mahabhaskariyam* and *Laghu Bhaskariyam*.

Next was Mahavira (9th century, 815 CE), an Indian Jain mathematician who made great strides in the use of fractions, permutations, and combinations, and figuring out how to divide one fraction by another. His best known written work was the *Ganit Saar Sangraha*. His writings were inspirational to other mathematicians since he expressed the subjects of Aryabhata and Brahmagupta in clearer terminology that became a standard after that.

It was also Vardhamana Mahavira who is considered to have established Jainism and was also a contemporary of Gautama Buddha (1894-1814 BCE). Thus, Jainism is as old as Buddhism. But Jain mathematicians also helped develop many aspects of Indian mathematics. To them it was more of an abstract discipline cultivated for its own sake, and not necessarily as part of a spiritual tradition. Some of the older texts in this line include the *Sthananga Sutra* (50 CE), which outlined the science of numbers, geometry, fractions, equations, square roots, cubes and cube roots. The *Anuyogadwara Sutra* gave lists of successive squares and square roots. The *Bhagavati Sutra* (300 BCE) elaborated on number problems involving permutations and combinations. Other Jain texts included the *Surya Pragnapti, Jambudvipa Pragnapti*, and *Triloka Pragnapti* (all from around 300 BCE), and others which include, *Sthananga Sutra, Uttaradyyana Sutra, Bhagvati Sutra*, and *Anuyoga Dvara Sutra*. The *Sthananga Sutra* provided such things as the theory of numbers, arithmetical operations, geometry, fractions, simple equations, cubic equations, and so on. [8]

There was also the mathematician Sridharacharya in the latter half of the 10th century. He worked in the area of arithmetic, mensuration, and geometry, extraction of roots, cube roots, etc. He was the first to solve the quadratic equation in one variable. His work on arithmetic and geometric series became a standard reference work.

Then there was Bhaskara II (12th century, 1114-1185), also called Bhaskaracharya, who made progress in spherical trigonometry and principles of calculus before Newton by 500 years. He used it to determine the daily motion of planets. He was called the greatest of the medieval mathematicians of India. His greatest work was the *Siddhanta Shiromani* (Sanskrit meaning "Crown of Treatises," written in 1150 when he was 36 years old) which is divided into four parts called Lilavati, Bijaganita, Grahaganita on mathematics of the planets, and Goladhyaya on astronomy. This covered arithmetic, algebra, trigonometry, and astronomy, and mathematics regarding planetary and spherical problems. Another important work by him was his *Karnakutuhala*.

Bhaskaracharya also produced extensive treatises on plane and spherical trigonometry and algebra, which contained remarkable solutions of problems which were not discovered in Europe until the 17th and 18th centuries. Bhaskara is also associated with the Ujjain school of astronomy and is also a commentator of Aryabhata. [9]

It was Bhaskaracharya II who had developed his science as the father of modern calculus many centuries before Leibnitz and Newton. It is regrettable that much of the world never knew of Bhaskaracharya's contributions. Bhaskaracharya made significant progress in the field of trigonometry, though it had originated centuries before him. Aryabhatta I, Aryabhatta II, Lalla, and Brahmagupta all contributed to its development, though none were the originator of it since it had been in existence long before this, probably connected with the science of ancient Indian astronomy. [10]

Madhava of Sangamagrama (1340-1425 CE) was perhaps the greatest of the Indian medieval astronomer-mathematicians. Madhava was the famous Kerala mathematician and the originator and leader of the Kerala school of mathematics. This school flourished during 1300-1750. He took the finite procedures of ancient mathematics toward their limit to infinity. His work on the power series for pi and for the discovery of the sine and cosine functions as an infinite series was about 300 years before Newton. His work is referred to with reverence by several later writers. This work made its first appearance in Europe in 1676 in a letter by Newton to the Secretary of the Royal Society, Henry Oldenburg. Madhava also made amazing contributions in the area of infinite-series expansions of circular and trigonometric functions, and finite-series approximations to them. He was considered, basically, as one of the founders of Mathematical Analysis. [11]

Madhava in Kerala developed a power series for arc tangents, apparently without calculus, which allowed the calculation of pi to any number of decimal places. It is not known whether he invented a system as good as calculus, or did it without calculus, but it is remarkable either way.

Madhava's famous works include *Venvaroha, Laghu Prakarana, Sphuta Chandrapti* (1400), *Aganita* (1418), *Golavada*, and *Mahajyanayana Prakarana*. The first two works gave solutions for the notoriously difficult problem of lunar motion. Later, astronomers gave him the title of "master of the sphere." Madhava also gave a more accurate value for the pi in the Bhuta Sankya notation at 3.14159265359. Jyesthadeva and others in their works (1530) gave credit to Madhava with the mathematical notation that only later became known as the Gregory series (1671) in England and as the Leibniz series in Germany.

We have the formulas for Madhava's sines and cosine series as outlined in the *Yuktibhashah* (Chapter 6, verse 12-13) said to be compiled by Jyeshthadevah (1500-1610 CE), but only later became known through

Newton (1642-1727 CE) and Brook Taylor (1685-1731 CE) who had formulated similar sine and cosine series through a different approach. We also see the first tangent series of Madhava's as described in the *Kriyakramakari* (Chapter 2, verse 40) by Putumana Somayaji (1350-1410 CE). It was later that James Gregory (1638 CE) and G. W. Leibnitz (1644 CE) developed their tangent series through a calculus approach. In the *Tantra-sangraha* by Nilakanthah (1445-1545 CE) we also find Madhava's infinite series for pi, which was later discussed in the West by John Wallis (1655 CE) and Abraham Sharp (1717 CE). This was later taken to many new developments by Ramanuja (1887-1920). Madhava also developed what later became known as the Taylor Power Series (1685-1731), thus predating Taylor by more than 300 years. [12]

Neelakantha Somayaji was another important figure in the Kerala school. In his work *Aryabhatiya Bhashya*, he tried to grasp the hidden meanings of Aryabhata, expound the principles, reconcile contradictions, and point out wrong interpretations. His main work was the *Tantra Sangraha*, composed in 1500 CE. [13]

Other prominent mathematicians of this Kerala school include Jyeshthadevah who authored *Yuktibhashah* (1520); Putumana Somayaji, author of *Karana Paddhati* (1730); and Raja Sankara Varma, author of *Sadratnamala*.

ALGEBRA AND GEOMETRY

Such systems of mathematics as Algebra also had its beginning in India. With the time of the *Shatapatha Brahmana* known to be prior to the 6th century BCE, the time of geometric algebra in ancient India dates back well before 800 or 1000 BCE if not much before then. B. B. Dutta, in the Preface of his *History of Hindu Mathematics*, says: "The use of symbols-letters of the alphabet to denote unknowns and equations are the foundations of the science of algebra. The Hindus were the first to make systematic use of the letters of the alphabet to denote unknowns. They were also the first to classify and make a detailed study of equations. Thus, they may be said to have given birth to the modern science of Algebra."

The Arab scholar Moosa-al-Khawarizmi came to India in the 9th century to learn this system and wrote a book called *Alijeb Oyal Muquabila*. From this the knowledge of it traveled to Europe.

We also know that in the Vedic culture, altars and temples were made based on mathematical formulas, which was the basis for the system of geometry. It is said that in at least 800 BCE Baudhayana and Apastambha gave the necessary architectural specifications for the construction of these altars and platforms.

In this regard, there is probably no one who has written as clearly as A. L. Basham about the lofty and advanced nature of Vedic mathematics.

"Through the necessity of accurately laying out the open-air site of a sacrifice, Indians very early evolved a simple system of geometry, but in the sphere of practical knowledge the world owes most to India in the realm of mathematics, which were developed in Gupta times to a stage more advanced than that reached by any other nation of antiquity... While Greek mathematical science was largely based on mensuration and geometry, India transcended these conceptions quite early, and, with the aid of a simple numeral notation, devised a rudimentary algebra which allowed more complicated calculations than were possible to the Greeks, and led to the study of number for its own sake.

"...For long it was thought that the decimal system of numerals was invented by the Arabs, but this is certainly not the case. The Arabs themselves called mathematics 'the Indian (art)' (*hindisat*), and there is now no doubt that the decimal notation, with other mathematical lore, was learnt by the Muslim world either through merchants trading with the west coast of India, or through the Arabs who conquered Sind in A. D. 712.

"The debt of the Western world to India in this respect cannot be over-estimated. Most of the great discoveries and inventions of which Europe is so proud would have been impossible without a developed system of mathematics, and this in turn would have been impossible if Europe had been shackled by the unwieldy system of Roman numerals..." [14]

Geometry was a highly developed science in ancient India. The *Vedas* contain an important and necessary act of *yajna* [Vedic ritual]. The altars, their construction, and measurement involved deep and accurate knowledge of mathematics, particularly geometry.

The *Shulba Sutras*, contained all these rules... In more modern times, we find that several mathematicians, such as Bhaskara I, Brahmagupta, and Mahavira showed deep knowledge of these techniques. [15]

For example, therein the *Shulba Sutra* (Chapter 1, verse 12) we find the formula, "The areas (of the squares) produced separately by the length and breadth of a rectangle together equal the area (of the square) produced by the diagonal." This was only later known as the theorem of Pythagoras. But Indian scholars had been using this since the Vedic period. [16]

Another theorem described in the *Brahma-sphuta-siddhanta* (Chapter 12, verse 28) by Brahmagupta around 628 CE, is "The sums of the products [distances] of the sides about the diagonal should be divided by each other and multiplied by the sum of the products of the opposite sides. The square roots of the quotients are the diagonals in a Vishama quadrilateral." This only later became recognized as Snell's theorem about one thousand years later in 1619 CE. [17]

Trigonometry concepts, formulas, tables, etc., were also found in the old texts of the *Surya Siddhanta*, and Varahamihira's *Pancha Siddhanta*, and Brahmagupta's *Brahma Sphuta Siddhanta*.

The antiquity of mathematics of ancient India is further expressed by Professor Wallace in *Mill's India* (Vol. II, p. 150) wherein he says: "However ancient a book may be in which a system of trigonometry occurs, we may be assured it was not written in the infancy of the science. Geometry must have been known in India long before the writing of the *Surya Siddhanta*."

This is corroborated in the early edition of the *Edinburgh Encyclopedia* on the section under Geometry (p. 191) where Professor Wallace is quoted: "The researches of the learned have brought to light astronomical tables in India which must have been constructed by the principles of geometry, but the period at which they have been framed has by no means been completely ascertained. Some are of the opinion that they have been framed from observation made at a very remote period, not less than 3,000 years before the Christian era; and if this opinion be well founded, the science of geometry must have been cultivated in India to a considerable extent long before the period assigned to its origin in the West; so that many elementary propositions may have been brought from India to Greece."

In *Ancient and Medieval India* (Vol. II, p. 375), Professor Monier Williams outrightly says: "To the Hindus is due the invention of algebra and geometry and their application to astronomy."

ADVANCED MATHEMATICS FIRST CAME FROM INDIA

It should be obvious now that for years much of the world has thought that the advancements in mathematics came from the Arab countries, but nothing can be farther from the truth. They only inherited the advanced formulas from the Hindus, wrote about them, and then helped transfer them to Europe through Spain.

To quote from Carl B. Boyer in his *History of Mathematics* (pages 227-228): "Mohammed ibn-Musa al-Khwarismi... who died sometime before 850, wrote more than a dozen astronomical and mathematical works, of which the earliest were probably based on the *Sindhind* derived from India. Besides... [he] wrote two books on arithmetic and algebra which played very important roles in the history of mathematics... In this work, based presumably on an Arabic translation of Brahmagupta, al-Khwarizmi gave so full an account of Hindu numerals that he probably is responsible for the widespread but false impression that our system of numeration is Arabic in origin..."

This same premise is repeated in another research article on Al-Khwarizmi by Shawn Overbay, Jimmy Schorer, and Heather Conger which explains, "Al-Khwarizmi wrote numerous books that played important roles in arithmetic and algebra. In his work, *De numero indorum* (*Concerning the Hindu Art of Reckoning*), it was based presumably on an Arabic translation of Brahmagupta where he gave a full account of the Hindu numerals which was the first to expound the system with its digits 0,1,2,3,... 9 and decimal place value which was a fairly recent arrival from India. Because of this book, with the Latin translation, [it] made a false inquiry that the system of numeration is Arabic in origin." [18]

Another very well researched online article, "Numbers: Their History and Meaning," concludes that the Indian system is the earliest form of mathematics that we use today. It explains: "It is now universally accepted that our decimal numbers derive from forms, which were invented in India and transmitted via Arab culture to Europe, undergoing a number of changes on the way. We also know that several different ways of writing numbers evolved in India before it became possible for existing decimal numerals to be marred with the place-value principle of the Babylonians to give birth to the system which eventually became the one which we use today.

"Because of lack of authentic records, very little is known of the development of ancient Hindu mathematics. The earliest history is preserved in the 5000-year-old ruin of a city at Mohenjo Daro, located northeast of present-day Karachi in Pakistan. Evidence of wide streets, brick dwellings and apartment houses with tiled bathrooms, covered city drains, and community swimming pools, indicates a civilization as advanced as that found anywhere else in the ancient Orient.

"These early peoples had systems of writing, counting, weighing, and measuring, and they dug canals for irrigation. All this required basic mathematics and engineering." [19]

The reality and conclusion of this study is that the so-called "Arab" contribution to mathematics was substantially built on prior knowledge of the Hindus and the Greeks, and while the Greek influence and origins are frequently recognized, the Hindu contribution is very rarely acknowledged or mentioned.

HOW INDIAN MATH SYSTEMS WENT WEST

As explained in the book *Science and Technology in Ancient India*, "Said-al-Andalusi, probably the first historian of science, who belonged to the eleventh century A.D., in his book, *Tabakat-al-Umam* (*The Book of the Categories of Nations*), accorded the first place to Hindus among the right culture groups that had developed sciences by that time. The reason was not far to seek. India had registered remarkable progress in mathematics, astronomy, medicine and metallurgy. Indian astronomical-mathematical texts, especially of Brahmagupta, were rendered into Arabic in the Caliphate at Baghdad during the 8th - 9th century A.D. Likewise, the Ayurvedic classics, the *Charaka* and *Sushruta Samhitas* as well as Vagbhata's *Ashtanga-hridaya* and *Madhava Nidana*, were also translated into Arabic. Indian scholars in astronomy, mathematics and medicine were held in high esteem, not only at home but even in Islamic countries. Islamic savants like Al-Khwarizmi [in the 9th century] and Al-Biruni played an important role in the transmission of Hindu mathematics and astronomy into the West. Along with Al-Kindi, they spread the decimal place-value system and the Hindu (Brahmi) numerals far and wide. The Ayurvedic knowledge and practices too were passed on to the west, specially by Al-Razi through his medical compendium." [20]

HOW INDIAN MATHEMATICS ENTERED ARABIA

Further information is supplied by an Arab historian, Al-Qifti (1270 CE) who reported that in the year AH 146 (or 773 CE), a man well versed in astronomy by the name of Kanaka came to Baghdad on a diplomatic mission from Sindh in northern India, with 20 other scientists. He brought with him books like *Surya Siddhanta* and the works of Brahmagupta and Bhaskaracharya. Calif al-Munsur ordered that these books be translated into Arabic, after which a handbook should be produced for Arab astronomers outlining the principles in the books. The job was given to Al-Fazari, who made a text which was later known as the *Great Sindhind*. The word *sindhind* is said to come from the word *Siddhanta*, which meant an astronomical text. It was because of this text that al-Khwarizmi constructed his Zij.

Thereafter, a Latin translation made in 1126 CE from an edited version provided by Maslama al-Majriti, a Spanish astronomer from Cordoba, became one of the most influential astronomical texts in medieval Europe. [21]

HOW INDIAN MATHEMATICS REACHED EUROPE

It was Al-Fazari's translation of the *Siddhantas* that reached its height of popularity with a native from Khiva, Muhammad ibn Musa Al-Khwarizmi, who lived around 825 CE. It was the Arab mathematician Al-Khwarizmi who learnt Sanskrit and wrote several books on mathematics and astronomy of the Hindus. His arithmetic explained the Hindu system of numeration. This book was later translated into Latin in the 12th century under the title of *Algorithimic de numero Indorum*. This is what especially helped rapidly spread the use of the Hindu numbers and math systems throughout Europe, and how they became acquainted with the decimal position. Al-Khwarizmi's algebra had the title *Hisal al-jabar wal-muqabala* (science of reduction and confrontation). This became known through the Latin translations and they made the word *al-jabr* synonymous with the whole science of algebra. [22]

ALTERNATIVE DATES FOR INDIA'S MAJOR
MATHEMATICIANS

In spite of the conventional dates for the major mathematicians of India, as we have been using, the authors of *The Origin and History of Mathematics* present a new time line based on calculations of the Vedic calendar. I will let them explain it and you can decide to agree or not:

"The modern period starts in India from the time of the *Mahabharata* war in 3138 B. C., thirty-six years before Kali Yuga that commenced in 3102 B. C. We find detailed information of the dynasties, including the names of the kings in each dynasty and the corresponding duration of their reign. At the end of the *Mahabharata* war, the victorious Yudhisthira of the Pandavas was crowned as the emperor of Bharat Varsha (Greater India) at Hastinapur. Thus, Yudhisthira Era began in 3138 B.C. The Sapta Rsi Era began in 3076 B.C. (26 Kali Era), which was the year of the demise of Yudhisthira, when Sapta Rsi Mandala (the Big Bear) left the star Magha. This era is also known as Laukikabda Era as well as Swargarohana (journey for emancipation) time of Yudhisthira.

"In the modern period of Bharat (India), Aryabhatta is the first famous mathematician and astronomer. In his book *Aryabhattiyam*, Aryabhatta clearly provides his birth date. In 10th stanza, he says that when $60 \times 6 = 360$ years elapsed in this Kali-Yuga, he was 23 years old. The stanza of the *shloka* starts with *sastyabdanam sadbhiryada vyatitastra yashcha yuga padah*. *Sastyabdanam sadbhi* means $60 \times 6 = 360$. While printing the manuscript, the word *sadbhi* was altered to *shashti* to imply $60 \times 60 = 3600$ years after Kali Era. As a result of this intentional arbitrary change, Aryabhatta's birth time was fixed as 476 A.D. Since in every genuine manuscript, we find the word *sadbhi* and not the altered *shashti*, it is clear that Aryabhatta was 23 years old in 360 Kali Era or 2742 B.C. This implies that Aryabhatta was born in 337 Kali Era or 2765 B.C., and therefore could not have lived around 500 A.D., as manufactured by the Indologists to fit their invented framework.

"Bhaskara I is the earliest known commentator of Aryabhatta's works. His exact time is not known except that he was in between Aryabhatta (2675 B.C.) and Varahamihira (123 B.C.). Bhaskara mentions the names of Latadeva, Nishanku and Panduranga Svami as disciples of Aryabhatta. Moreover, he says that Aryabhatta's fame has crossed the bounds of the oceans and whose works lead to accurate results even after lapse of so much time. This shows that Bhaskara I was living quite a lot of time later than Aryabhatta. His works are *Mahabhaskariyam, Aryabhatiya Bhashyam* and *Laghu Bhaskariyam.*

"Next is Varahamihira who says that he was writing his *Pancha Siddhanta* in the year 427 Shaka Kala. Since Shaka Kala or Shaka Era started in 550 B.C., it means that 550 - 427 = 123 B.C. Varahamihira also indicates how to find Shaka Kala in *Brihat Samhita,* which is equal to the Svargarohana time of Yudhisthira coupled with 2526 years, that is 3076 - 2526 = 550 B.C. Svargarohana time of Yudhisthira is 26 years after Kali Era and therefore 26 + 2526 = 2552 Kali Era as the starting point of Shaka Kala or Shaka Nripa Kala. Thus the Cyrus Era which was in vogue in Varahamihira's time began in 550 B.C.; and Cyrus Era was the Persian Shaka King. The special contribution of Varahamihira was *Pancha Siddhanta* in which he codified the then existing five *Siddhantas,* namely, *Paulisha, Romasha, Vasishtha, Surya (Saura)* and *Pitamaha.* In addition, he wrote the famous *Brihat Samhita,* the theoretical and predictive astrology. Only *Surya Siddhanta* has been preserved. Varahamihira quotes a tribute paid to a Yavana (not Greek) astronomer, by an early astronomer Garga, namely 'the Yavanas are Mlechchas (people deviated from *Sanatana Dharma*) but amongst them this science of astronomy is duly established and therefore they are honored as Rsis.' Recall that there were Yavana kingdoms in South and Northwest of India even before Maurya Asoka's time (1472 -1436 B.C.). At that time, there were no Greeks. This tribute to Yavanas has been misinterpreted by the orientalists to imply the influence of Greek astronomy on Indian astronomy in Garga's time. Since Garga's time was long before Varahamihira's time and since Yavanas were not Greeks at that time, the conclusion of the influence of Greek astronomy on the astronomy of ancient India has no validity and is a clear fabrication.

"After Bhaskara I, we have Brahmagupta, who is a great mathematician and astronomer. According to Brahmagupta, he completed his work *Brahma Siddhanta* when he was 30 years of age in 550 Shaka Kala. This means Brahmagupta was born in 30 B.C.

"Next in line of astronomers and mathematical thinkers was Bhaskaracharya, known as Bhaskara II, who is the author of a popular work called *Siddhanta Shiromani.* He states that he compiled his work in 1036 Shaka Nripa Kala (the same time of Shaka king). Hence subtracting 550 from 1036 we get 486 A. D. as the time of compilation of *Siddhanta Shiromani.*" [23]

CHAPTER NOTES

1. Niranjan Shah, *Numerals is India's Next Great Contribution*, India Tribune, January 19, 2008.
2. Suresh Soni, *India's Glorious Scientific Tradition*, Ocean Books Pvt. Ltd., New Delhi, 2010, pp. 81-82.
3. V. Lakshmikantham and J. Vasundhara Devi, *The Origin and History of Mathematics*, Indian Foundation for Vedic Science, Rohtak, Haryana, India, 2004, p. 59.
4. Seidenberg, *The Ritual Origin of Geometry*, 1962, p. 515.
5. N. Jha and N. S. Rajaram, *The Deciphered Indus Script*, Aditya Prakashan, New Delhi, 2000, pp. 43-45.
6. *Pride of India: A Glimpse into India's Scientific Heritage*, Samskriti Bharati, New Delhi, 2006, pp. 60-61.
7. *Science and Technology in Ancient India*, by Editorial Board of Vijnan Bharati, Mumbai, August, 2002, p. 54.
8. V. Lakshmikantham and J. Vasundhara Devi, *The Origin and History of Mathematics*, Indian Foundation for Vedic Science, Rohtak, Haryana, India, 2004, p. 109.
9. *Pride of India: A Glimpse into India's Scientific Heritage*, Samskriti Bharati, New Delhi, 2006, pp. 61-62.
10. Ibid., p. 48.
11. V. Lakshmikantham and J. Vasundhara Devi, *The Origin and History of Mathematics*, Indian Foundation for Vedic Science, Rohtak, Haryana, India, 2004, pp. 92, 96, 98.
12. *Science and Technology in Ancient India*, by Editorial Board of Vijnan Bharati, Mumbai, August, 2002, p. 59.
13. Ibid., p. 61.
14. L. A. Basham, *The Wonder That was India*, Grove Press, Inc., New York, 1954, pp. 494-5.
15. *Pride of India: A Glimpse into India's Scientific Heritage*, Samskriti Bharati, New Delhi, 2006, p. 36.
16. Ibid., p. 37.
17. Ibid., p. 38.
18. http://www.ms.uky.edu/~carl/ma330/project2/al-khwa21.html
19. http://home.c2i.net/greaker/comenius/9899/indiannumerals/india.html
20. B. V. Subbarayappa, Foreword, *Science and Technology in Ancient India*, by Editorial Board of Vijnan Bharati, Mumbai, August, 2002.

21. V. Lakshmikantham and J. Vasundhara Devi, *The Origin and History of Mathematics*, Indian Foundation for Vedic Science, Rohtak, Haryana, India, 2004, p. 58.
22. Ibid., p. 25.
23. V. Lakshmikantham and J. Vasundhara Devi, *The Origin and History of Mathematics*, Indian Foundation for Vedic Science, Rohtak, Haryana, India, 2004, pp. 50-52.

The Jantar Mantar, astronomical instruments, in New Delhi, India

CHAPTER SIX

Vedic Astronomy

As previously mentioned, Vedic mathematics made great strides in its connection with Vedic astronomy, which also developed to a large extent with the advancements of mathematics. Such advancements can only flourish amongst a people who are already greatly civilized and progressive. This also proves the great character of the Vedic literature, in which was recorded numerous descriptions of the astronomical positions of the stars and planets, which give indications of the time periods in which they were recorded.

Some of the early comments about this include those of Count Bjornstjerna who writes in *Theogony of the Hindoos* (page 32): "Cassini, Bailly [Jean-Claude Bailly, 1736-93, who was later guillotined in the French Revolution], Gentil, and Playfair maintain that there are Hindoo observations extant which must have been made more than three thousand years before Christ, and which evince even then a very high degree of astronomical science." He goes on to say that: "According to true astronomical calculations of the Hindoos, the present period of the world, Kali-yuga commenced in 3102, years before the birth of Christ, on the 20th of February, at 2 hours, 27 minutes, the time being thus calculated to minutes and seconds. They say that a conjunction of the planets then took place, and their tables show this conjunction. Bailly states that Jupiter and Mercury were then in the same degree of the ecliptic, Mars at a distance of only eight, and Saturn of seven degrees; whence it follows, that at the point of time given by the Brahmanas as the commencement of Kali-yuga, the four planets above mentioned must have been successively concealed by the rays of the sun (first Saturn, then Mars, afterwards Jupiter, and lastly Mercury). They, thus showed themselves in conjunction; and although Venus could not then be seen, it was natural to say that a conjunction of the planets then took place. The calculations of the Brahmans are so exactly confirmed by our own astronomical tables, that nothing but an actual observation could have given so correspondent a result."

Count Bjornstjerna, an early reviewer of Vedic culture, also said: "But if it be true that Hindus more than 3,000 years before Christ, according to Bailly's calculation, had attained so high a degree of astronomical and geometrical learning, how many centuries earlier must the commencement of their culture have been, since the human mind advances only step by step in the path of science!" [1]

Research scholars like Bailly and Charles Francois Dupuis (1742-1809) also claimed that the Hindu Zodiac is the earliest known to man, and that the first calendar was made in India around 12,000 BCE. This was stated in *Bailly's Histoire de Astonomie Ancienne* and the proceedings of the Society of Biblical Archeology, December, 1901, part 1.

The historian James Mill, in the *History of British India* (Volume II, p. 106-7), mentions how Professor H. H. Wilson relates that, "The science of astronomy at present exhibits many proofs of accurate observation and deduction, highly creditable to the science of the Hindu astronomers. The division of the ecliptic into lunar mansions, the solar zodiac, the mean motions of the planets, the procession of the equinox, the earth's self-support in space, the diurnal revolution of the earth on its axis, the revolution of the moon on her axis, the dimensions of the orbits of the planet, the calculations of the eclipses are parts of the system which could not have been found amongst an unenlightened people. . . The originality of the Hindu astronomers is at once established, but it is also proved by intrinsic evidence, and although there are some remarkable coincidences between the Hindu and other systems, their methods are their own."

There are nine basic astronomical texts called *Siddhantas*, and these are: 1. Brahma, 2. Surya, 3. Soma, 4. Brihaspati, 5. Gargya, 6. Narada, 7. Parashara, 8. Pulastya (or Paulisa), and 9. Vashistha. Of these, most people are aware of the *Surya Siddhanta*, which is known as the oldest of all of them. Different scholars give varying dates for the *Surya Siddhanta*, but the author provides two verses in which he states about when the book was composed: "Six *manvantaras* have passed since the beginning of this *kalpa*, and of the seventh *manvantara*, 27 *chaturyugas* have passed. The Satya-yuga of the 28th *chaturyuga* has also passed." From this description the time of the compilation of this book may be inferred to mean that the book is many thousands of years old. Those who understand the lengths of time in *manvantaras* and *chaturyugas*, as explained in a previous chapter, can calculate the age of the *Surya Siddhanta*.

Some of the earliest references to the Vedic astronomical understanding can be found in such texts as the *Yajur Veda*, which states that the earth is kept in space owing to its attraction (or gravitational pull) of the sun. The *Atharva Veda* also states that the moon is dependent on the sun for its light.

There were other noteworthy books on astronomy, such as *Vedanga Jyotisha*, *Bhrigu Samhita*, and *Jyotish Sashtra*. Indian astronomers were quite knowledgeable for their position. They knew the shape of the earth and orbits of other planets, and the position of the moon in relation to the stars, and the moon's cycle. Through this insight, they could tell the most auspicious days for performing religious rites.

The advancements of Vedic culture is also reflected in its astronomical records. For example, the passage of Saturn and Mars through the head of the constellation of Taurus is call Rohini Shakat Bhed. This event was supposed to be quite malevolent to happenings on earth. That is why this event is recorded in various Sanskrit texts. The head of the Taurus constellation is like a reverse triangle with what is called Aldebaran at one of the corners. Orbits of Saturn and Mars intersect the ecliptic at two different points called nodes. The nodes have retrograde motion. The nodes of Saturn are said to complete one circle in 40,000 years, while those of Mars in 50,000 years. The mention of the Rohini Shakat Bhed in the ancient Sanskrit literature indicates that Hindus were familiar with the motion of planets at least 5,000 years ago. Saturn passed through Rohini Shakat in 3200 BCE and Mars much earlier than that. [2]

The advanced knowledge that was known in the field of Vedic astronomy, such as outlined in the *Siddhanta Shiromani* by Bhaskaracharya, includes the fact that earth's revolutions are 365.257 days, while Aryabhata determined it to be 365.259 days, with the modern calculation being 365.256 days. Aryabhata, in his *Aryabhatiya*, also gives revolutions for the moon as 27.322 days, while the modern calculation is also 27.322 days. For Mars he determined 1.881 years, which the modern calculation agrees. For Jupiter it is 11.861 years by Aryabhata with a modern calculation of 11.862 years. For the sun Aryabhata determined 29.477 years, with a modern calculation of 29.458 years.

Jean-Sylvan Bailey, a nineteenth century French astronomer, was also impressed with the accuracy of the astronomical tables compiled by the ancient Hindus. He had observed, "...the motions of the stars calculated by the Hindus before some 4500 years vary not even a single minute from the tables of Cassine and Meyer [used in Europe in the nineteenth century]. The Indian tables give the same annual variation of the moon as that discovered by Tycho Brahe–a variation unknown to the school of Alexandria and also to the Arabs who followed the calculations of the school. ...The Hindu systems of astronomy are by far the oldest and that from which the Egyptians, Greeks, Romans, and even the Jews derive their knowledge."

British astronomer John Playfair also estimated that Hindu astronomy must go back at least to 5000 BCE. In fact, both David Frawley and Lokamanya Tilak found references in the *Rig Veda* that provide dates before 6000 BCE. [3]

The Calcutta Newspaper, *The Telegraph* (December 12, 1992) writes that there is evidence of astronomical observations as early as 4000 BCE in the *Rig Veda*, which is assigned by different scholars to different periods from 12,5000–1500 BCE. [4]

THE HELIOCENTRIC THEORY

Things like the Heliocentric Theory were known for many years in ancient India before Europe ever came to accept it. Even from the time of the *Yajur Veda* we find (*Taittiriya-samhita*, Kandah 3, Prapatakah 4, Anuvakah 10, mantra 34) it stated, "The sun holds the earth and the celestial region. The sun is the attracting power [by its gravitational pull]." And this is further elaborated in books such as the *Vishnu Purana* (Book 2, chapter 8, verse 15), "There is, in truth, neither rising nor setting of the sun, for it is always there, and these terms (of rising and setting) merely imply his presence and disappearance."

Also in the *Rig Veda* (Mandalam 1, Suktam 50, verse 4), "Oh Sun! (You) overwhelm all in speed, visible to all, source of light. (You) shine pervading the universe." This indicates that the sun has its own orbit through the universe as it shines forth, lighting whatever it goes. And later in *Sayanacharya's Commentary* (14th century CE), we find where he explains, "It is remembered (that) Salutations to Thee (sun), the traveler of 2,202 *yojanas* in half a *nimisha*." Herein one *yojana* is about 9 miles, and half a *nimisha* is the time of about .114286 of a second. Therefore, 2,202 *yojanas* in half a *nimisha* equals to about 186,282.397 miles per second. The speed of light was calculated in the West only about 1676 CE by Olaus Roemer, a Danish astronomer, and then in 1887 Michealson and Morley established the velocity of light as 186,300 miles per second. [5]

The fact that the planets also had their own elliptical orbits was also understood in ancient days of India as we read in the *Rig Veda* (Mandalam 1, Suktam 164, mantra 2), "The elliptical path through which all the celestial bodies move is imperishable and unslackened." It was only later when Johannes Kepler (1571-1630) proposed that the path of all the planets and other celestial bodies is elliptical. [6]

JYOTISH

Tied with Vedic astronomy comes the Vedic system of astrology, known as Jyotish. Hasmukh Patel, a Vedic astrologer and editor of *Star N Life* from India, explains that "Astrology in India begins with the *Bhrigu Samhita*. The *Bhrigu Samhita* is an astrological classic attributed to Maharishi Bhrigu during the Vedic period Treta-yuga, although the available evidence suggests that is was compiled over a period of time by the various students in the lineage of Maharishi Bhrigu."

This compilation is now called the *Brihat Parasara Hora Shastra*. Bhrigu had deep insight into the past, present and future with the help of divine powers, and compiled about 500,000 horoscopes, which formed a database for further research and study, the total permutations of which can go up to 45 million. Bhrigu taught this art to his son or grandson, Shukra and other pupils, which has extended down through time.

As explained by journalist Niranjan Shah: "Everything in the *Bhrigu-Samhita* is written in a dialogue form. The dialogue is between the sage Bhrigu and his disciple, sage Acharya Shukra. Both of them are engaged in discussion about the welfare of those who would seek their audience. The sage also refers to specific problems and prescribes prayers and other remedies to surmount those problems. If these prayers and remedies are performed carefully and with devotion, the individual concerned is freed from the sins of the past lives. The sage then assures the fulfillment of the prediction of the prophecies made by him.

"*Bhrigu Samhita* covers all important aspects of one's like. The predictions and prophecies in the *Bhrigu Samhita* are a synthesis of astrology and ancient Indian system of mantra, tantra, prayers, penance, meditation, and yoga. In certain cases, the *Samhita* also provides diagnosis of diseases along with their remedies. It is a miracle that exceeds all powers of imagination. The best way is only to experience one-self. It is for this reason that Lord Krishna proclaimed in the *Gita*, the Song Divine, of Maharishis, I am Bhrigu, and among the wise, I am Shukracharya."[7]

Jyotish, the ancient science of Vedic astrology, is also being accepted and gaining popularity in the West. Vedic Astrology is meant to help the individual better find his or her way through life. It is to assist in discovering one's highest proclivities, personality, character, qualities, and traits and what may be one's best direction for a career, and other things. Thus, a person will least likely waste one's time in unfulfilling or even dissatisfying activities, professions or pursuits.

To further our understanding of Jyotish, I let Chakrapani Ullal, one of the most well-known Vedic Astrologers in the West, describe it as taken from the book, *Vedic Culture: The Difference It Can Make in Your Life*:

"We turn our attention now to the subject of a branch of the *Vedas* called Vedic astrology or Jyotish, which is called the 'eye of the *Vedas*'. It has a cognizing influence of the truth of life and self-knowledge. It acts as a mirror to an individual without which one may not know how to approach life most effectively. It is also called the 'Science of Time'. Time is the source power that rules the universe. All things originate through the procession of time. Hence, Vedic Astrology constitutes the science that maps the structure of time. Astrology is considered divine knowledge that is pure, supreme, secret, and exalted.

"Astrology can be defined as the science of correlations of astronomical facts with terrestrial events, and demonstrates the Vedic understanding of the universal interconnectedness and interdependence of all phenomenon, that microcosm and macrocosm are but reflections of one another. Just as mathematics is the organizing principle of science when dealing with inanimate matter, so also astrology is the organizing principle which deals with life and its significance in relation to all living bodies. The planets are seen as reflectors or transmitters of light and solar energy. The solar and planetary rays, like radio waves, affect biological and psychological processes. The rays of influence are unseen vibrations that are not perceptible to the physical eye.

"Astrology gives insight and guidance to the fortunes and misfortunes of men, issues of empires and republics, floods and earthquakes, volcanic eruptions, plagues, pestilence and other incidents concerning terrestrial phenomena in relation to the regular movements of the planets.

"Over 10,000 years ago the ancient sages, in their super-conscious state, cognized that there is energy in planets, and that they send out different rays at different angles which bear influence on everything animate and inanimate on other planets. Through their sensitized intuition and repeated observations these highly evolved souls were able to find out the different characteristics inborn in the planets and also discovered that each rules a distinctive part of the human mind/body. It was also found that particular groups of stars known as constellations have different characteristics, and that they modulate the influence of the planets.

"Astrologers say that there are two forces, Daiva and Purushakara, fate and individual energy. The individual energy can modify and even frustrate fate. Moreover, the stars often indicate several fate possibilities; for example, that one may die in mid-age, but that if, through determination, one gives attention in that area it can be overcome, one can live to a predictable old age. Thus, astrology does not say that events must and should happen, but gives the benefic and malefic tendencies which can be directed or modified through conscious effort. The horoscope shows a man's character and temperament. Though it may show that he could become a criminal, it does not mean he is fated to become so. What it means is that he is just the sort of person who will have criminal tendencies, but they can be checked by proper care and training. Additionally, if emotional and financial challenges are indicated in any particular year, one can certainly meet the crisis better if one knows that it might occur.

"Then, how would one define astrology? It is the philosophy of discovering and analyzing past impulses and future actions of both individuals and nations in the light of planetary configurations. Astrology explains life's reactions to planetary vibrations." [8]

CHAPTER NOTES
1. *Ward's Mythology*, Vol. I, p. 114.
2. *Science and Technology in Ancient India*, by Editorial Board of Vijnan Bharati, Mumbai, August, 2002, p. 22.
3. N. S. Rajaram, *Sarasvati River and the Vedic Civilization*, Aditya Prakashan, New Delhi, 2006, p.134.
4. *Science and Technology in Ancient India*, edited by Dr. Manabendu Banerjee, Dr. Bijoya Goswami, Sanskrit Pustak Bhandar, Calcutta, 1994, p. 35.

5. *Pride of India: A Glimpse into India's Scientific Heritage*, Samskriti Bharati, New Delhi, 2006, p. 67.

6. Ibid., p. 72.

7. Niranjan Shah, *Bhriga Samhita is Ancient Hindu Astrological Treatise*, India Tribune, June 21, 2008.

8. Chakrapani Ullal, in *Vedic Culture: The Difference It Can Make in Your Life*, edited by Stephen Knapp, 2005, (pp. 197-198, 202-203.

CHAPTER SEVEN

Vedic Architecture and Temples

Architecture in India was an extremely rich form of expression and highly developed science, with a deep heritage of spirituality in it. It is evident that one of the primary purposes of much of the significant architecture was to display the prevailing spiritual consciousness of the people.

The center of all architectural development was the temple. The temple or *Mandir* was the earthly home of God, and like the launching pad for the devotee's consciousness to soar toward the Divine and the spiritual world. The *murti* or deity of the Divine would be placed in the temple sanctum, around which all temple activity would revolve. Such buildings were often elaborately decorated with stone, wood, plaster, etc. and carved or cut to depict the stories from the *Puranas* or other sacred texts. Temples were always the center of religious, social and educational activities, practically more so in ancient times than today.

During a span of more than two thousand years various dynasties were known for constructing glorious temples, some of which include the Mauryan, Ashoka, Gupta, Satavahana, Chedi, Chandella, Chalukya, Solanki, Pallava, Shola, Hoysala, Vijayanagar, and others. Many of these temples remain beautiful architectural wonders today.

The *Mandirs* were composed of various parts, which included the *Garbhagriha* or sanctum; the *Sukanasi* or nose of the structure; the *Antarala* or adjoining passages; the *Mandapa* or main hall; the *Dhwaja sthambha* or flag post; and the *Bali peeth*, or the pedestal for the offerings. The temple was the microcosm that reflected the macrocosm, or the symbol of the cosmic being.

The temples played a most prominent center of village and community life. Of course, they were places of worship, but they were also places of preserving and teaching basic education along with the culture by which the community thrived. They also utilized and employed many artists, musicians, dancers, cooks, architects, priests, carpenters, weavers, florists, etc., for maintaining the temple and participating in festivities on the holy days. Farmers and landowners would also donate food and produce to the temple, which would be used for offering to the deities and then distributed to the devotees and pilgrims. Thus, everyone participated and benefitted at the same time.

Temple construction was more specific because of the higher purpose involved. The science of construction goes all the way back to the time of the *Atharva Veda*, which contains several hymns on the topic in its *Shala-nirmana-sukta*. Other hymns that discuss the ways of testing soil for construction, what should be avoided, or what materials to use are also found in the *Matsya Purana* (Adhyayah 253, verse 11), *Vastu Shastra* (verse 5), *Bhrigu-samhita* (Adhyayah 4), and *Kashyapa-shilpah* (Adhyayah 4).

Additional Sanskrit literature that contained references to architecture included *Agni Purana*, the *Brihat Samhita* and *Arthashastra*, and the *Vastu Sashtra* texts like the *Maya-mata*, *Manasara*, and *Samarangana-sutradhara*. These all included such points as the selection of stone, soil testing, making of bricks, mortar, the carving of the deities, and even the use of chisels and carving tools.

The references in both the *Ramayana* and *Mahabharata* mention the two great architects, namely Visvakarma of the gods and Maya Danava. The existence of Maya in the Khandara forest and his building the Sabha of the Pandavas, and his knowing of the city near Kailasha is because of his expertise in this subject. The *Ramayana* also explains different kinds of architects used in house construction, according to the *Silpa Shastra*. These include the Sthapati, Vardhaki, Takshaka, and Sutradhara. The different houses were called Prasada, Saudha, Vimana, Harmmya, Sabha, and so on. The *Mahabharata* describes six kinds of forts, as also found in the *Silpa Shastra*. From the information of Vastu as also found in Kautilya's *Arthashastra*, which is known to have been in existence no later than the 1st century CE or even by the 4th century BCE, we can understand that all of such knowledge would have been developed before then. [1]

Other information from ancient times included the use of timber, bricks and stones, the foundation and picking the proper sites, shape of the land, soil condition, and then the construction of the building.

The huge gopuram or tower to the largest Vishnu temple in India, Sri Rangam, an architectural wonder.

ARCHITECTURE IN HARAPPA

By the time we see the Harappan civilization, architecture is already well developed. This is explained as follows:

"The Harappa civilization was in a fairly matured state as early as 3000 B.C. Investigations have revealed a culture in which the finished quality of materials employed the high standard of their manipulation, and the stability of the construction as a whole is astonishing.

"In the first place, the builders of these cities had acquired experience of town planning, as proved by the methodical manner in which they were laid out with straight streets at right angles, the main thoroughfares running almost due north and south, east and west.

"The principal buildings were fairly regularly oriented having their sides towards the cardinal points. They were laid in mud-mortar, care being taken to stagger the joint where necessary, the entire process indicating that the Indus builders were thoroughly experienced in the technique of the bricklayer's craft." [2]

VASTU ARCHITECTURE

Vastu Shastra is the Indian science of arranging the interior of architecture so that the energies flow through the buildings for the occupant's best health, peace, harmony, wealth, etc. Vastu is especially used for Hindu temples and architecture, or Hindu homes. However, it has been shown well worth applying it for secular buildings, too, and has also traditionally been applied to forts, apartments, houses, and nowadays offices as well.

Vastu can be divided into two parts, first for determining the potential of the plot, depending on the purpose of its use. This can be for residential or commercial. Plots facing east and north are always better than ones facing south or west. This can be corrected with special care during the building of the structure on the plot. Roads around the plot and levels of the ground are also significant.

Vastu applied to buildings use principles that govern the construction. This is used for determining where to put the rooms and what the purposes of each room will be. The science of it can go into much depth on how to construct the buildings, or how to arrange things in the house even after it has been built. But it is always better to design the house according to the principles of Vastu before it is built.

Our purpose is not to explain the whole science of Vastu here, which can be learned in various books which specialize on it. But we want to explain a little about the origins of Vastu and how old it is. Traditionally it is linked back to the time of Mahamuni Maya, the Danava demon architect in the southern part of India, as well as to Visvakarma in the north. Both of these personalities are mentioned in such texts as the *Ramayana* and *Mahabharata*. So this gives us some idea that it goes back more than 5000 thousand years ago.

Furthermore, *Vastu Shastra* is a part of the *Stapatya Veda*, which is an *upaveda* of the *Atharva Veda*. Mention of the science of arranging buildings properly, as according to Vastu, can be found in the *Matsya Purana, Skanda Purana, Agni Purana, Garuda Purana, Vishnu Purana, Bhagavata Purana*, and texts that are more specific to Vastu including the *Vishvakarma Prakash, Samraangan Sutradhar, Kashyapa Shilpashastra, Brihad Samhita*, and *Praman Manjaree*. The point here is that the principles of Vastu started from thousands of years ago and has become a time-tested system that has held firm up to modern times, as long as it is understood and applied properly. Thus, a good teacher is also required to go into the depths of it by any sincere student.

CHAPTER NOTES
1. Dr. Manabendu Banerjee, Dr. Bijoya Goswami, *Science and Technology in Ancient India*, edited by Sanskrit Pustak Bhandar, Calcutta, 1994, pp. 66-67.
2. *Science and Technology in Ancient India*, by Editorial Board of Vijnan Bharati, Mumbai, August, 2002, p. 14.

CHAPTER EIGHT

The Vedic System of Medicine

Medicine and treatment of disease is a science in India which has an origin that is lost in antiquity. However, according to the *Charaka Samhita*, one of the earliest texts on ancient Indian medicine, it was Brahma, the secondary creator of the universe, who propounded the knowledge of Ayurveda, an *upaveda* of the *Atharva Veda.* Daksha Prajapati learnt Ayurveda from Brahma and passed it along to the celestial twins and physicians of the gods, the Ashwins. Lord Indra got this knowledge from the Ashwini twins, then from him it went to Sage Bharadwaj, then Atreya Punarnava, then his disciples Agnivesh, Bhel, Hareet, etc. After being handled by a few more sages, the science of Indian medicine, Ayurveda, was developed into three schools by the sages Charaka, Sushruta and Kashyapa, all of whom have compendiums named after them.

When it comes to the development of medicine from the times of ancient India, there are two major areas, which are *Kaya Chikitsa,* or the science of general medical treatment specially of the body, and *Shalya Chikitsa,* or surgery. Soon after this had been established, the branches were standardized into eight, resulting into *Astanga Ayurveda.* These include *Shalya* (surgery in general), *Shalakya* (supraclavicular surgery, mainly head and neck), *Kaya Chikitsa* (medical treatment of the body), *Bhuta Vidya* (management of mental diseases or psychiatry), *Kaumarya Bhritya* (pediatrics), *Agada Tantra* (toxicology), *Rasayana* (elixirization), and *Vaji Karana* (counseling on sex and geriatrics).

Many of the old treatments have been mentioned in regard to the ancient Vedic traditions, such as how to rejoin the head of a horse after it had been severed in a *yajna* [Vedic ritual], or the restoration of sight to the sage Chyawan, or restoring his senility, etc. But many more developments were made from the medical foundation.

To explain further, the teacher/disciple lineages are traced to three original teachers: Atreya for internal medicine; Dhanvantari for surgery;

and Kashyapa for gynecology and pediatrics. The teachers who provided the means to extend the teachings of these systems are Sushruta (generally accepted to be around the 6th century BCE) of the Dhanvantari tradition who codified surgical practices; Charaka (1st century BCE) of the Atreya school, who codified the precepts and practices in internal medicine; and Vagbhata II (6th century CE) of the Kashyapa school, dealing with gynecology and pediatrics. Bhela (7th century CE) was another scholar of the Atreya school whose compilation of the *Bhela-samhita* has survived the years. However, one point to consider is that the knowledge for these traditions existed for at least several centuries if not thousands of years before they were codified, such as found in the *Atharva Veda* and the associated *Garbhopanishad* which are repositories of knowledge in this field.

Medicine is primarily in the Atreya tradition, and the sage Charaka is famous for propagating this tradition with his *Charaka Samhita*, said to be the first and main book of *Ayurveda*.

Treatments like surgery are in the Dhanvantari tradition, from which the famous surgeon Sushruta propagated this tradition with his *Sushruta Samhita*. It is considered that in 600 BCE, Sushruta recorded complicated surgeries like cesareans, cataract, artificial limbs, fractures, hernia, intestinal surgery, bladder stone removal, rhinoplasty or plastic surgery of the nose, and brain surgery, plus suturing, the knowledge of the instruments needed for particular operations, types of forceps, surgical probes, needles, and cutting instruments.

Over 125 surgical instruments were described and used, including lancets, forceps, catheters, etc., many of which are the same or similar as those we still have today. Deep knowledge of anatomy, physiology, etiology, embryology, digestion, metabolism, genetics, and immunity is also found in these texts. The *Sushruta Samhita* is over a thousand pages of descriptions of various diseases, their causes, likelihood of getting them, and treatments. Therein many topics are clarified further with dialogues between Dhanvantari and his disciples. The *Sushruta Samhita* has 192 chapters, the first nine of which are about 125 different surgical instruments, what they are, what material they are made of, and which type of surgical procedure for which they are used. This also describes ways of stitching wounds and different dressings for various wounds.

Though he mentions many different kinds of surgical instruments, he emphasized so much on the cleanliness of the atmosphere and sterilization of the instruments before or after the surgery, and the ways to do it, that even modern surgeons are amazed. He also wrote about how to make the patients senseless, or the first mention of the use of anaesthetics to help in operations or surgery.

In addition to general surgery, he also discusses trauma and describes six varieties of injuries involving almost all parts of the body. He also gives treatments for 12 varieties of fractures and six types of dislocations, as well as amputations and principles of traction, manipulation, and post operative physio-therapy. Sushruta also made contributions in the development of rhinoplasty in nose and ear replacement, which was a branch of surgery that Europe ignored for another 2000 years. No single surgeon in history has the credit of such contributions, making him the most versatile genius in medical history. [1]

The *Sushruta Samhita* also mentions the surgical removal of harmful tissues or elements born out of what would be cancer in such organs as the intestines.

Even as far back as the times of the *Shatapatha Brahmana*, which goes back several thousand years, we find a complete description of the function of the heart. It explains that the heart functions through three actions of taking, giving or propelling, and circulating. The *Naadi Gyanam Granth* also explains that the heart acts in contraction and expansion over and over again. The *Bhel Samhita* also describes that it is the heart from which the blood flows out and goes to various parts of the body. [2]

The ancient advancements in understanding the various functions of the body can be illustrated by the fact that Harvey, of the 17th century, is usually credited to be the discoverer of blood circulation. However, both Sushruta and Bhela as well as Charaka clearly indicate not merely the existence of blood circulation, but also the purpose of blood supply to the whole body, viz. to supply nutrition. It is most noteworthy that Bhela goes to the extent of describing blood circulation even in the foetus. It is understood that blood is a transitory but vital constituent of the body, transitory in the sense that it is always replenished and is ever on the move. Its flow never ceases as long as life exists and why should it flow like this incessantly is an inexplicable mystery (*adrustha hetunal*). It is nothing but the essence of the food that we take which is transmuted by the *rasa kriya* or the chemical action of the body to an assimilable form, as the *Sushruta Samhita* explains (14.3).

Therein it describes that which is the lustrous essence of the well processed food, which is also greatly subtle, that is called *rasa*. Its place (when it forms a constituent of blood) is the heart. Entering into the 34 arteries from the heart... it satisfies, nourishes and develops, bears and supports, and also continues to maintain for so long the entire body.

We can find additional knowledge of veins and arteries in the *Atharva Veda* (1.17.1) and the earliest mention of surgery is found in the *Rig Veda* (1.116.15) where the Ashvins fitted an iron leg to Vishpala who lost her leg in a war. Then in the *Atharva Veda* (4.12.3-5) we also find a prayer for joining the disjointed parts of the body. [3]

The *Bhela Samhita* (20.3) further points out that it is from the heart that *rasa* issues forth and from this, the latter goes on to all places (as arteries or *dhamanies*). The heart is reached by the veins and therefore the veins are said to be born of the heart. (This is a clear conception of the heart-artery-body-vein-heart cycle or circulation of blood with heart as the center.) [4]

The *Charaka Samhita* was the book by the sage Charaka some 2500 years ago. This is the main treatise of the system of Ayurvedic medicine. It consists of 120 chapters in eight sections on surgery, eye and head treatment, therapeutics, toxicology, pediatrics, pharmacology, and medicine preparation, mental diseases, and treatment of reproductive systems. Charaka is the first to point out the effects of diet and activity on the mind and body. He also understood the fundamentals of genetics, and how to determine the sex of a child being carried in the mother. He also established how birth defects was not necessarily due to any defect in the mother or father, but to the ovum or sperm of the parents. He also counted 360 bones in the body, including teeth.

The sage Charaka also explained that nature provides all the natural medicines in the area a person lives. The *Rig Veda* also names over 1000 herbs and plants used for medical purposes. Thus, a person must investigate the plants and vegetables around oneself and use them. The *Charaka Samhita* talks about 341 plant-generated medicines, another 177 from animals, and 64 from minerals. The *Sushruta Samhita* also discusses 385 plant-generated, 57 animal-generated and 64 mineral-generated medicines and how to use them. All kinds of powders, distillates, decoctions, mixtures, gels, and various other kinds of medicines were produced from these. [5]

According to a World Health Organization report, there are about 400 families of flowering medicinal plants of which 315 families of plants can be found in India. In the old days, the Ayurvedic practitioners prepared medicines from the flowering plants individually for each of his patients, which, unfortunately, is not the way it has been done for many years.

Historically, though surgery in Bharatvarsha had developed to a great extent in ancient Ayurveda, it declined from the period of Buddha onwards because of emphasis on non-violence to the extent of banning dissection. Hence the contents of present day Ayurveda are essentially of *Kaya Chikitsa* and its medical material. The developments of knowledge and its practice as medicine had reached a zenith much before the times of Buddha, while the Greek civilization and its achievements in medicine are principally post Buddhistic, such as after 620 BCE. The historians of western (modern) medicine trace its origin to this Greek civilization. [6]

Nevertheless, we can understand that surgery and medicine was already highly developed in India while the rest of the world remained completely unaware of these possibilities. Nevertheless, a well-developed medical system was fully in existence by the 1st century CE. Progress in medicine led to developments in chemistry and the production of medicine, alkaline substances and glass. This also brought about colorfast dies and paints that were developed to remain in good condition over the centuries. The paintings in the caves of Ajanta are a testimony to this.

PRINCIPLES OF AYURVEDA

The *Charaka Samhita* explains, "The basic aim of the concepts and fundamental principles of all sciences is to establish happiness in all living beings. But a correct and thorough knowledge of the basic principles of the universe and the body leads to the correct path to happiness, while deceptive knowledge leads to the wrong path."

The whole point of Ayurveda is found in the meaning of the word, which is *Ayur* (span of life) and *veda* (the knowing thereof). This means it is a knowledge of the span of living given to an individual, to extend it, to render it healthy, happy, salutary, and exuberatingly excellent. In this light, diseases are accidents brought about by *pragna aparadha*, meaning the willful transgression of the laws of living, which confer *svasthya* or health. Its specialty is that it recognizes self or soul as integral to living, and mind is but an organ of it, best employed so the mind does not lead it astray. This is *jitendriyatva*, control of the senses–the surest way to never get a disease. [7]

To explain more clearly, Ayurveda is the Vedic system of holistic medicine. It has become quite popular in the West and is continuing to gain ground and acceptance. Acharya Charaka has been called the father of medicine, known most for his work, the *Charaka Samhita*, which is like the encyclopedia of Ayurveda. What he covers still hold its value even after three millennium. These include human anatomy, embryology, pharmacology, circulation, and diseases, such as diabetes, tuberculosis, heart problems, etc.

Ayurveda is traditionally divided into eight branches, according to Charaka, which are: 1. *Sutra-sthana*, general principles, 2. *Nidama-sthana*, pathology, 3. *Vimana-sthana*, diagnostics, 4. *Sharana-sthana*, physiology and anatomy, 5. *Indriya-sthana*, prognosis, 6. *Chikitsa-sthana*, therapeutics, 7. *Kalpa-sthana*, pharmacy, and 8. *Siddhi-sthana*, successful treatment.

Sushruta was another noted physician who greatly developed the Vedic system of medicine. He had been a professor of medicine in the University of Benares nearly 3000 years ago, and wrote his *Sushruta Samhita* in Sanskrit, a process of diagnosis and therapy, which had been given to him by his teacher, known as Divodas Dhanvantari. Two other authorities appeared later, which were Vagbhata, who was present in Sindha about two centuries before Christ, and Madhava, who appeared in Kishkindha in Andhra in the 12th century. There is a Sanskrit verse which explains, "Madhava is unrivaled in diagnosis, Vagbhata in principles and practice of medicine, Sushruta in surgery, and Charaka in therapeutics." It is known that the Arabs and Persians translated the knowledge of Sushruta and Charaka into their own language in the eighth century CE.

It should be understood, however, that many surgeons were known in India before Shusruta, but he was the one who compiled the knowledge which came from the teachings of Divodas Dhanvantari, who had been king of Kashi according to the *Sushruta Samhita*. Panini, said to have appeared around 800 BCE according to historians, mentions both Charaka and Sushruta, so they had to have appeared sometime before that. This means the dates that are generally accepted for their appearances, as previously listed, are too late and not accurate.

In any case, the impressiveness of the medical system of India was noted by many people. For example, Arthur Selwyn-Brown, who came to

India during the British rule as an English dental surgeon and studied Indian medicine, wrote in his two-volume publication *Physicians Through the Ages*, "Indian medicine is an extremely old science. Ayurveda, the most ancient medical science of India, is the oldest medical science of the world, and history has distinctly shown that Western medicine is the offspring of Ayurveda."

Sir W. W. Hunter explains in *History of Hindu Chemistry*: "The surgery of the ancient Indian physicians was bold and skillful. They conducted amputations, arresting bleeding by pressure, a cap-shaped bandage and boiling oil; practiced lithotomy; performed operations in the abdomen and uterus; cured hernia, fistula, piles; set broken bones and dislocations; and were dexterous in the extraction of foreign substances from the body. A special branch of surgery was devoted to rhinoplasty, or an operation for improving deformed ears and noses and forming new ones, a useful operation which European surgeons have now borrowed. The ancient Indian surgeons also mention a cure for neuralgia, analogous to the modern cutting of the fifth nerve above the eyebrow. They devoted great care to the making of surgical instruments and to the training of the students by means of operations performed on dead bodies spread over a board or on the tissues and cells of the vegetable kingdom, and upon dead animals. They were expert in midwifery, not shrinking from the most critical operations, and in the diseases of women and children."

To understand more about what Ayurveda is, I let Pratichi Mathur, an Ayurvedic practitioner herself, tell us about it from the book, *Vedic Culture: The Difference It Can Make in Your Life*:

"So what is Ayurveda exactly? Literally translated from Sanskrit it is composed of two words '*Ayus*' which means life and '*Veda*' which denotes knowledge. So Ayurveda is the knowledge of healthy living and is confined not only to the treatment of diseases. Life is a vast, and an all-encompassing phenomena, which includes death. On one end, life is a celebration of birth, growth, child bearing, youth and sexuality; on the other end, life also brings forth disease, decay, aging, and loss of vigor. Ayurveda is that ancient art and science that helps us understand this very 'life' with all its different shades and colors; understand how best we can undertake this journey; and how we transition through its different phases, example from teenage, to adulthood, to maturity, etc. Following the principles of Ayurveda brings about a profound understanding of the inner ability to have sound body, mind and spirit. From this point of view, Ayurveda is a compendium of life and not disease. This is a major agenda indeed for any system of medicine, but can it be any less--especially if true healing has to take place. Perhaps, this is exactly why Ayurveda manages to get to the root of the disease that distresses the mind or the emotion that ails the body.

"Ayurveda has twin objectives--maintaining the health of the healthy, and cure illnesses of the diseased. Ayurveda, which is not just a system of disease and its management, but literally a living dynamic philosophy and manual on the art of living, is well fitted to meet its objectives. On one hand Ayurveda offers treatments like *Panchakarma* or even surgery for the diseased; and on the other hand Ayurveda offers preventative medicine for the healthy. These include elaborate details for following ideal daily and seasonal routines, specialized diets for optimizing health and immunity (Ojas), *Rasayana Chikitsa* (promotive therapy), *Vajikarna Chikitsa* (aphrodisiac therapy), *Swasthavritta* (regimen to stay healthy furnishing details on topics such as exercise, smoking for health), *Sadachar* (social hygiene), etc.

"Ayurveda advocates a complete promotive, preventive and curative system of medicine and includes eight major clinical specialties of medicine namely, (1) Medicine (*Kayachikitsa*), (2) Surgery (*Salya Tantra),* (3) ENT (*Salakya Tantra),* (4) Pediatrics (*Kaumatabhritya),* (5) Psychiatry (*Bhutvidya*), (6) Toxicology (*Agad Tantra*), (7) Nutrition, rejuvenation and geriatrics (*Rasayan tantra*), and (8) Sexology and virilization (*Vajikarana).* This shows what a developed science Ayurveda was in ancient times.

"The exact origin of Ayurveda is lost in the mists of antiquity. Since Panini is placed at 7th century BC and Ayurveda depicts non-Paninian Sanskrit grammar, it is logical to place Ayurveda between 6th–10th Century BC. Tracing the continuity of Ayurveda, it is natural to look for the continuing thread in India's ancient Vedic tradition. Although the term Ayurveda does not seem to appear in the *Vedas,* and it appears first in Panini's *Ashtadhayayi,* however, there are positive evidences to show that in the Vedic period, medicine as a profession was prevalent. The *Rig Veda* and the *Atharva Veda* both mention that there were thousands of medical practitioners and thousands of medicines. References to Ayurveda are found as early as the *Rig Veda.* The three Rig Vedic gods Indra, Agni and Soma relate to the three biological humors: Vata, Pitta and Kapha. References are made of organ transplants as in the case of the artificial limb of queen Vishpala, daughter of King Khela. The functions of physicians are also described in the *Rig Veda.*

"Rishi Sushruta, famous Ayurvedic surgeon, also holds that Ayurveda is a supplement (*upanga*) of the *Atharva Veda*. While several other sources including the famous Hindu epic *Mahabharata* speak of Ayurveda as an *upanga* of *Atharva Veda*; several other schools of thought hold Ayurveda as a fifth *Veda* (*Panchamveda*). Perhaps Ayurveda grew from *Atharva Veda* first as a branch and then as a comprehensive vast system deserving it's own status, or it developed parallel to the four *Vedas* as an independent knowledge (with close resemblance to the *Atharva Veda*)." [8]

THE HIPPOCRATIC OATH

Long before there was the Hippocratic oath, the basis of the attitude the medical practitioners should have, there was the oath described in the *Charaka Samhita* (*Vimana Sthana Adhyaya* 6.8-14), which says, "If you desire success in profession, success in wealth, attainment of fame and heaven after death, you shall pray everyday while you get up or while you sit, for the welfare of all creatures beginning with the cows and the brahmanas. With all your attention, endeavor to secure the health of your patients. You shall not desert or injure your patients even for the sake of your living. You shall not commit adultery with others' women even in mind. Similarly, you shall not covet others' possessions even in mind. You shall not be a drunkard or a sinful man, nor should you associate (yourself) with the abettors of crime. You should speak words that are gentle, pure and righteous, pleasing, worthy, true, wholesome, and moderate. Your behavior must be in consideration of time and place, and heedful of the past experience (you have gained in all these matters). You shall act always with a view to the acquisition of (new) knowledge and the excellence of the equipment (as are needed for your exciting profession)."

In this way, the *atreya anushasana*, or oath taking ceremony prescribed for both students and teacher by Charaka is much more comprehensive and elegant compared to the Hippocratic oath taken by the modern medical students. This *samhita* tradition dates to 7,000 years back, whereas the Hippocratic oath dates back to only the 4th century BCE.

PLASTIC SURGERY

In regard to surgery, what became known as plastic surgery had already been known in India for many years. However, as described in *India's Glorious Scientific Tradition*, by Suresh Soni (pp.183-84) one example of its affects were witnessed by two British doctors named Dr. Thomas Crasso and Dr. James Findlay. This was in 1793 when a person, a Marathi coachman named Kavaasji, had to have a new nose. The doctors watched and submitted a report with pictures in the *Madras Gazette*, which was republished in the October, 1794 edition of *Gentleman Magazine*, London. It is described therein:

"An artificial nose made of fine wax is placed instead of the nose that has been cut off. This wax is spread on the forehead of the person (who has to undergo the plastic surgery). An outline is marked out and the layer of wax is removed. Then, the surgeon takes out the skin of the similar shape from the patient's forehead while it remains stuck to a small portion below the eyes. Because of this joint, the portion of the old nose that is left is divided into two. An incision is made behind it. Now, the skin from the forehead is brought down and stuck to the incision.

"Terra Japonica (yellow *kattha*) is made into a dough after mixing it with water and spread over a piece of cloth. Five or six such pieces are placed one on top of the other and kept in the place of the surgery. After keeping this kind of a bandage for four days, a piece of cloth soaked in ghee is placed on it. After twenty days, the joined skin (from the center of the eye) is removed and the new nose is given the proper shape. The patient has to keep lying down for the first five days after the surgery. On the tenth day, cylindrical pieces of cotton wool or soft cloth are placed inside the new nostrils to keep them open.

It was further explained, "This operation was always successful. The new nose used to stick permanently and would start looking like the old nose. Even the mark on the forehead, made by removing the skin, would vanish after sometime."

Obviously, this report created reactions at the time in the European medical world. The entire process for nose replacement, along with over 300 other surgical operations, had been given in the *Sushruta Samhita*. Nonetheless, the surgeons from all over Europe studied the above process, and after understanding the method, a 30-year-old surgeon named Dr. J. C. Carpew transplanted the nose of a man in 1814. This operation was also successful. This brought about a revolution in surgical treatment and it was given the name "Plastic Surgery." All surgeons, including Dr. Carpew, unanimously agreed that plastic surgery was a gift from ancient India.

INOCULATIONS

We also find a description of the process of vaccinations that was used for the small pox disease in Bengal in an article called *An Account of the Disease of Bengal; Calcutta*, of February 10, 1731. It explains that there are many cases of small pox in Bengal. For this, vaccination is given in the same way that Dr. Jenner [who is said to have discovered vaccination in 1798] had later done by making a vaccine out of the pus. In Bengal too, pus was collected from the blisters of small pox patients and stored for use the following year. The entire process had been given in detail in this journal. In this way, the process had been performed in India years before it had been done in Europe.

Another example is from the book, *Operation of Inoculation of the Small Pox as Performed in Bengal: 1731*. This describes the process that was done. But it is interesting that in reply to the question to the villagers regarding how long this process had been going on, the author says that it was evident from at least 150-200 years earlier, but in answer to who discovered it, the villagers of Bengal replied that Dhanvantari had showed them the path. This makes the method so old that it is lost in antiquity.

EMBRYOLOGY IN VEDIC TIMES

As it is explained by B. B. Chaubey in *Science and Technology in Ancient India*, "It would be a great surprise for the modern scientists to know that India has to its credit besides many sciences, the development of embryology in the Vedic period. Though we do not find a systematic treatment of the subject, some hymns of the *Rig Veda* and the *Atharva Veda* and frequent references scattered in the Vedic texts give a clear picture of the knowledge of the Vedic seers about this branch of science. Hundreds of technical terms concerning the development of the infant from conception to birth occurring in Vedic texts are testimony to the fact that the Vedic scientists had a very sound knowledge of embryology in that hoary past when people of most of the countries were living a savage life. How the semen (*ritas*) is formed and how does it develop together with Rajas after being placed in the womb, all these things have been described in Vedic texts. The Brahmanas have many references to the process how the male and female child is born, giving *arthavada* [or authority] to the ritualistic injunctions [that describe how to conceive a male or female]. The *Vedanga* literature too supplies ample material in this regard. The *Puranas*, especially the *Garuda Purana* [along with the *Bhagavata* and others] gives the details how a man appears in the womb." [9]

Furthermore, the knowledge of the body was quite precise. The *Sushruta-samhita* (Sharirasthanam, Adhyayah 5, paragraph 6) gives a description of the body as "a collection of 7 layers of skin, 7 tissues, 7 receptacles, 7 elements, 700 tubular vessels, 500 muscles, 900 sinews, 300 bones, 210 joints, 107 vital parts, 24 (blood) vessels, 3 humors, 3 impurities, 9 sense organs, 16 tendons, 16 plexuses, 6 bunches of muscles, 4 muscular chords, 7 (fibrous) sutures, 14 bony complexes, 14 terminal formation, 22 capillaries, and 2 intestines." Hardly any book of that era gave such details.

How these develop in the body is also explained in the *Sushruta-samhita*, which offers a rare explanation, especially considering the time in which this was written: "In the fourth month, the division of all the major and minor organs manifests. Because of the manifestation of the heart, the gaining of consciousness becomes evident. How? Because of its position. Therefore, in the fourth month of pregnancy (the foetus) seeks sense objects. (The foetus) communicates its desire to the pregnant woman. By the dishonoring of such desires, the woman generates a hunchbacked, crippled, lame, paralytic, dwarfed, cross-eyed or blind child. Therefore, whatever she desires, have them given to her. The pregnant woman who gets what she desires generates energetic and long-living child."

DENTISTRY

As we would expect, if the ancient area of India was known for its advancements in medicine and surgery, it would also have developed the means for progress in dentistry. There is evidence from the Neolithic site of Mehrigarh in Pakistan on 11 individuals from 7500 to 9000 years ago. This is long the main route between Afghanistan and the Indus Valley. This is mentioned in a report in the April 6, 2006 issue of *Nature*. They discovered drill holes on a least 11 molars from people buried in the MR3 cemetery. Light microscopy showed the holes were conical, cylindrical or trapezoidal in shape. A few had concentric rings showing drill bit marks; and a few had evidence of decay. There were no fillings, but tooth wear on the drill marks indicate that each of these individuals continued to live on after drilling was completed. It is noted that the instruments were small flint tipped wooden drills to fix the teeth.

Dr. Arthor Selwyn-Brown writes in *The Physicians Through the Ages* (page 274): "You will be agreeably surprised to know that dentistry in all its branches was well known and practiced by the old Hindu doctors. Searching into Ayurveda, one finds that there is a whole chapter devoted to the mouth cavity, wherein are described all the operations that are known to the present-day Western dentistry, such as: 1. Extractions by forceps; 2. Extractions by elevators; 3. Lancing of the gums; 4. Removal of the Tartar; 5. Fitting of artificial dentures. That dentistry must have existed then is certain, for even today, we come across cases in which front teeth are decorated with gold or jewel studs by Indian jewelers. As a dental surgeon, I appreciate that difficulty of drilling a through and through hole which is required for such decorations, without killing the nerve of these teeth; and yet thousands of teeth are with impunity perforated for this decoration. The work is so well done that any modern dentist might be proud of it."

THE SOMA PLANT

In discussing the age-old medicine systems of ancient Bharatvarsha, we should also include a look at the special Soma plant, which was also known for its potency as a curative and energy giving ingredient of the ritualistic elixir of ancient Vedic ceremonies. It was a respected brew and medicine in its own right, used for heightening one's strength, vitality and consciousness.

As described in *The Rig Veda and the History of India*, by David Frawley, he explains what and where the Soma plant could be found. "...I identified Sharyanavat with Lake Manasarovar in Tibet, which is the source of the Sindhu, Sarasvati and Sarayu rivers of Vedic fame. Yet, while Lake Manasarovar was perhaps the ultimate Soma lake and source of the Sarasvati, the lakes in Kurukshetra and those in Kashmir were important

Soma areas as well. Soma referred to plants growing in the lakes of north and perhaps central India. However, it appears that the main Soma lakes were those in the Sarasvati region, which probably existed even before the river began to dry up.

"This may also explain why Soma disappeared. Soma was mainly a plant cult of the Sarasvati area and the Sarasvati-based Vedic religion. When the glaciers had largely melted and the Sarasvati stopped flowing, most of the Soma lakes and the areas of Soma worship also disappeared or shifted.

"*It cannot be a coincidence that the loss of Soma in the Vedic religion and the demise of the Sarasvati River went together and occurred about the same time! The [simultaneous] loss of the Soma plant and the loss of the Sarasvati River reflect the same geological, climatic and cultural changes at the end of the Vedic age! Vinashana Soma and Vinashana Sarasvati represent the same phenomenon!* That Sarasvati and Soma lost their earthly counterparts and became mythological in later texts shows their close connection." [10]

"According to Sushruta, the great Ayurvedic teacher, Soma grows in all the mountain regions of India. However, the main Soma lands are Kashmir, particularly its lakes, and beyond it across on the Indus in the mountains, the regions of Gilgit and Ladakh. These Somas are named after the meters of the Vedic hymns, showing their special importance in the Vedic ritual." [11]

EXPANSION OF INDIAN MEDICINE

After the early development of medicine in early India, it started to spread elsewhere, and it was in Tibet where it got its greatest popularity. It was there in the 8th century where a big work in four parts, *Chatustantra* in Tibetan, entitled *Amritahridaya*, was translated from Sanskrit to Tibetan. The teaching within it was ascribed to Buddha Bhaishajyaguru. But some of the passages are clearly quotations from the *Charaka* or *Sushruta Samhitas*. The work then went into Mongolia, and then into Russia in the following centuries where it again became quite popular. Several other texts were translated into Tibetan and were included in the Tibetan *Tanjur*. The first one was *Yogashataka*, and then the extensive *Ashtangahridaya* of Vagbhata, together with two extensive commentaries. Indian veterinary medicine is also included in the Tibetan *Tanjur*, with a translation of the *Ashvayurveda* by Shalihotra. [12]

From there, and from India itself, it spread into Europe and throughout the world. Today it has strong advocates in the West. More doctors are trained in it, more students study it, and an increasing number of people see and experience the advantages of following this holistic system of medicine, especially as a means of preventative medicine to keep the body healthy. In this way, here is another example of the old Vedic culture that remains as relevant today as ever.

When studying Ayurveda, the literature that was produced are of three basic categories:

1. The classical works, which include the *Samhitas* of Charaka, Sushruta, Kashyapa, Bhela, and so on. *Vagbhata* was another noteworthy text, along with later ones such as *Bhava, Prakash, Madhava Nidana*, and *Rasaratna Samucchaya*.

2. The second category includes the lexicons or famous *Nighantus*. These start with the *Dhanvantari Nighantu* of classical times up to the most recent *Shodala Nighantu*. These presented the medical material of the contemporary times.

3. The third category are those texts of modern times and authors that blended the Ayurvedic with contemporary medicine and more current techniques. These days, this third category can be found in numerous places around the world. [13]

CHAPTER NOTES

1. Niranjan Shah, *India's Sushrut Was First Surgeon of World*, India Tribune, July 5, 2008.

2. Suresh Soni, *India's Glorious Scientific Tradition*, Ocean Books Pvt. Ltd., New Delhi, 2010, pp. 172-174.

3. Dr. Manabendu Banerjee, Dr. Bijoya Goswami, *Science and Technology in Ancient India*, Sanskrit Pustak Bhandar, Calcutta, 1994, p. 5.

4. K. H. Krishnamurthy, *Medicine and Surgery in Ancient India*, a Yugayatri Publication, Bangalore, pp. 39-40.

5. Suresh Soni, *India's Glorious Scientific Tradition*, Ocean Books Pvt. Ltd., New Delhi, 2010, p. 177.

6. K. H. Krishnamurthy, *Medicine and Surgery in Ancient India*, a Yugayatri Publication, Bangalore, p. 3.

7. Ibid., p. 4.

8. Prathichi Mathur, in *Vedic Culture: The Difference It Can Make in Your Life,* edited by Stephen Knapp, 2005, pp. 165-166.

9. Dr. Manabendu Banerjee, Dr. Bijoya Goswami, *Science and Technology in Ancient India*, edited by Sanskrit Pustak Bhandar, Calcutta, 1994, pp. 72-3.

10. David Frawley, *The Rig Veda and the History of India*, Aditya Prakashan, New Delhi, 2001, pp. 146-7.

11. Ibid., p. 147.

12. Jean Filliozat, *The Expansion of Indian Medicine Abroad*, published in *India's Contribution to World Thought and Culture*, Published by Vivekananda Kendra Prakashan, Chennai, 1970, p. 69.

13. K. H. Krishnamurthy, *Medicine and Surgery in Ancient India*, a Yugayatri Publication, Bangalore, pp. 1-2.

CHAPTER NINE

Developments in Textiles in Ancient India

We also find that textiles played an important part of the contributions and developments for which ancient India became known. In *Our Oriental Heritage*, Will Durant explains, "the growing of cotton appears earlier in India than elsewhere; apparently it was used for cloth in Mohenjodaro. During the excavations at Mohenjodaro a small fragment of cotton fabric and a small piece of cotton string in the neck of a vessel were recovered. The quality of both fabric and the string leaves no doubt that a mature textile craft had existed in the Indus Valley civilization."

Dr. Stanley Wolpert, professor of history at UCLA wrote in the publication *India*: "Ancient Indians were the first humans to spin and weave cotton into cloth that continues to provide our most comfortable summer attire."

Furthermore, in *Cotton as World Power*, Dr. James A. B. Scherer explains, "India is the original home of cotton. Centuries passed before the new goods made any impression on England, whose people wore wool exclusively. When cotton goods did begin to come in, a fierce conflict ensued with wool, which was then styled, the revenue and blood of England—so important was it in the economic life of the people." [1]

How cotton finally spread to England can be described like this: It was in the 1st century when the Arab traders brought the fine muslin and calico from India and sold it to Italy and Spain. The Moors then introduced the cultivation of cotton into Spain in the 9th century. Fustians and Dimities were woven there in the 14th century, in Venice and Milan, at first with a linen warp. Little cotton cloth was imported to England before the 15th century, although small amounts were obtained chiefly for candlewicks. By the 17th century, the East India Company was bringing rare fabrics from India.

The medieval Arabs took up the art of textiles from India, and their word *quattan* gave the English word *cotton*. The word *quattan* is derived from the original Sanskrit word *kantan*, which means making a thread out of a cotton ball. The name *muslin* was originally applied to fine cotton weaves made in Mosul from Indian models; and calico was so called because it came from Calicut on the southwestern shores of India, first in 1631. [2]

Of course, cotton cannot become cloth unless there is a way to make the thread. And through a simple investigation we can find that the spinning wheel was one of India's earliest contributions to the famous cloth that they were able to produce. *Britannica's Concise Encyclopedia* relates: "The spinning wheel is an early machine for turning textile fiber into thread or yarn, which was then woven into cloth on a loom. The spinning wheel was probably invented in India, though its origins are unclear. It reached Europe via the Middle East in the Middle Ages."

Professor D. P. Singhal of the University of Queensland, Australia provides more clarity on this by writing in *India and the World Civilization* (page 176): "The spinning wheel is an Indian invention."

To give more credence to this line of thought, in her book *Spinning Wheels, Spinners and Spinning*, Patricia Baines reports of written evidence to the presence of spinning wheels in Persia in 1257, and linguistic evidence that suggests they came to Persia from India. Therefore it is most likely that they were in operation much earlier than this. The significance of the spinning wheel is that it is one of the first examples of a belt-transmission of power.

From the cultivation of cotton and the invention of the spinning wheel and the loom came some of the finest textiles the world has seen. India has been known for its brilliant and high quality cloth for hundreds of years. In *History of India*, Elphinstone writes: "The beauty and delicacy of (Indian cotton cloth) was so long admired, and which, in fineness of texture, has never yet been approached in any country." Murray also writes therein: "Its fabrics, the most beautiful that human art has anywhere produced, were sought by merchants at the expense of the greatest toils and dangers."

James Mill also writes in *History of India*: "Of the exquisite degree of perfection to which the Hindus have carried the production of the loom, it would be idle to offer any description; as there are few objects with which the inhabitants of Europe are better acquainted. Whatever may have been that attainment in this art of other nations of antiquity, the manufacturer of no modern nation can, in delicacy and fineness, vie with the textiles of Hindustan."

THE ANTIQUITY OF CLOTH MAKING

The making of cloth goes back to ancient times in Bharatvarsha (India). It is even described in the *Vedas* how Sage Gritsmad made the first cloth from sowing cotton, then making thread with a wooden bobbin, and then cloth. Of course, India has been known for its beautiful textiles for many years. Making saris from silk, or with colored dyes, or embroidered with gold or silver thread, have made them into a desirable item in all parts of the world.

Cotton was cultivated, then spun into threads and woven into cloth since ancient times in India, dating back at least 4000 to 5000 years ago. The Greeks did not know of cotton until Alexander invaded India where they found cotton for the first time. They had not found it in the previous countries through which they traveled, including Egypt, Mesopotamia or Persia. Previous to this, the Greeks had used only wool in their woven fabrics.

From the findings at Mohendjodaro, a piece of cotton has been discovered that shows people at that time, 5000 years ago, were aware of the means to make and use it for clothing. Cotton was greatly cultivated in fields near Kashi (Varanasi) as well, which was an important center for textiles since the times of Lord Buddha. The skills of the spinners and weavers enabled them to make them extremely fine. In fact, Buddhist literature includes many references to the magnificent cotton spinners and weavers, relating that the fabrics were so fine that even oil could not penetrate the cloth.

Later, Kashi also became a major center for its silk manufacturing and products. The area of Gandhara (modern northwest India and Pakistan) and Vahika, near the Sindhu, Sutlej and Beas Rivers, were also known for its fine woollen chadars and shawls. [3]

Many centers for the production of textiles existed. Kashmir was known for its woolen weaves and embroidery, places like Benares, Ujjain, Indore, and Paithan near Aurangabad, were known for their fine silks, as

The wonders of the loom, weaving new cloth in Kanchipuram

The unique fabrics and designs of Indian textiles have always been in demand

were places in the south like Kanchipuram. Rajasthan also specialized in all manner of patterned prints and dyed cloths, and also in carpet-making.

Traders from ancient Greece, Egypt and Arabia ordered cotton cloth from India. They were especially known for the sheer quality of the cloth. When the French traveler and trader Tavernier visited India in the 17th century, he described the cotton clothes, by saying, "They are so light and beautiful that you cannot even feel them with your hands, and the delicate embroidery is hardly visible." In another place he writes, "A Persian Ambassador went back from India and gifted a coconut to his Sultan. The courtiers were amazed at this petty gift. But more amazing was the fact that when the coconut was opened, a roll of 30 yards of [Dacca] *mulmul* [fabric] came out of it."

In 1835 Edward Benz wrote, "The Indians in every age have, in the textile industry, maintained an incomparable and matchless standard. Some of their *mulmul* clothes seem to have been made, not by humans but by fairies and butterflies."

DYES AND COLORING AGENTS

Further archeological evidence from Mohenjodaro shows that the knowledge of mordant dying was in existence from the second millennium BCE. And the use of block printing on textiles in India was known since 3000 BCE. Some historians view India as the original home of block printing. Stuart Robinson in his *A History of Printed Textiles* reports that the export of printed fabrics to China can be dated back to the fourth century BCE. They had been very much appreciated by the Chinese and even imitated by the Chinese craftsmen. Also at the Khmer capital of Angkor, Chou Ta-kuan, the Chinese observer, wrote at the end of the thirteenth century that the preference was given to Indian weaving for its skill and delicacy.

Prof. A. R. Vasudeva Murthy and Prasun Kumar Mishra explains the attraction for India's colored fabrics: "As already mentioned, India was in the forefront of the textile industry till the end of the 18th century. This was one of the most competitive industries of the country and probably the most successful textile industry of the world. Its beautiful and colored textile products of cotton, silk, wool, and jute attracted the whole world from time immemorial. The Indus Valley people were acquainted with the red color of the madder root. There were more than 100 coloring agents of both mineral and vegetable origin and possibly a few of animal origin for dyeing the fabrics and other articles of every day use. Indigo was the other most famous dye extracted from the plant *indigofera tinctoria* for dyeing various shades of blue. It may not be out of place to mention that indigo plantation was prevalent in India on 1.6 million acres of land till the beginning of the 20th century. Germany began to manufacture this coveted dye with cheap industrial raw materials on a commercial scale from 1897 onwards and gained the world monopoly. This practically killed the Indian indigo industry by 1914." [4]

TEXTILES WERE A MAJOR FACTOR IN INDIA'S TRADE WITH OTHER COUNTRIES

Ancient Rome was known for having good trade relations with Bharatvarsha, ancient India. The chronicles of the Greek *Periplus* show that a variety of spices, good textiles (muslins and cottons), along with iron, gems and ivory were traded. Rome also supplied in return such things as cut gems, coral, perfumes, papyrus, copper, tin, and lead. Payments were generally in gold or silver coins at that time. The Roman writer Pliny (23-79 CE) mentioned that the costs of such things were quite high. He also wrote that, "Not a year passed in which India did not take fifty million sesterces away from Rome."

It is interesting to note that Romans were great fans of Indian textiles, to the point that much of the gold of Rome was drained from its coffers to buy Indian textiles. Some of these gold coins of early Rome have been found in several parts of southern India. Roman records indicate that at one point the Roman senate banned the import of Indian muslin to stop the drain of their gold. [5]

The Greek geographer Strabo (63 BCE–20 CE) and the *Periplus* records also mention the Gujarat port of Barygaza (Broach) as a place that exported fine Indian textiles. The thirteenth century Chinese traveler Chau Ju-kua refers to Gujarat as a source of cotton fabrics of every color. Also Marco Polo recorded the exports of Indian textiles to China and South East Asia from the Masulipattinam (Andhra) and the Coromandel (Tamil) coasts in the largest ships in the thirteenth century.

The old Tamil text *Silappathikaarum* (*The Ankle Bracelet*) from the late 2nd century CE, describes the wealth of some of the cities and maritime trading ports in southern India at that time. It relates that the markets offered a great variety of precious and prized commodities. The city of Puhar was populated with merchants and traders where there was a spacious forum for stored bales of merchandise, marked to show the quantity, weight and owner's name. Even whole streets were specialized in particular commodities, such as coral, jewelry, pearls, sandalwood, gold, and other precious gems. Skilled craftsmen also brought finished items such as woven fabrics, silks, ivory carvings, jewelry and so on to be sold and later traded in far corners of the world. North India also had its centers for such trading as well, such as Taxila, Patilputra, and others.

John Guy in his *Arts of India, 1550-1900*, mentions that in Broach had also been the discovery of a hoard of gold and silver coins mostly from the fourteenth century, belonging to the Mamluk kingdom of Egypt and Syria, which suggests the serious trading in exchange for precious metals.

Even the rough fabrics were useful and became popular outside India. The early Indian sacks made of jute and hemp, used for packaging goods, were named after the Sanskrit word of *Goni* or *Gonika*, which became known as the "gunny sack" in English.

It is also reported that the attractiveness of fast-dyed, multi-colored Indian prints on cotton in Europe as one of the factors that lead to the formation of the London East India Company in 1600, followed by the Dutch and French counterparts thereafter. However, by the late 1600s, there was such overwhelming demand for Indian textiles, no matter whether from Bengal, Patna, or Surat, that ultimately the French and English wool and silk merchants prevailed on their governments to ban the importation of these imported cottons from India. The French ban came in 1686, while the English followed in 1701. Nonetheless, textile producing centers that catered to the internal or overland trade continued to prosper. Even today the uniqueness of India's textiles, whether in shoulder bags, purses, saris, shawls, clothes, sheets, carpets, etc., remains high in global interest and of prized possession.

CHAPTER NOTES
1. Niranjan Shah, *India is the Original Home of Cotton*, India Tribune, February 27, 2010.

2. Ibid.

3. *Science and Technology in Ancient India*, by Editorial Board of Vijnan Bharati, Mumbai, August, 2002, p.112, 4.

4. Prof. A. R. Vasudeva Murthy and Prasun Kumar Mishra, *Indian Tradition of Chemistry and Chemical Technology*, Samskrita Bharati, Bangalore, India, August, 1999, p. 48.

5. Kamlesh Kapur, *Portraits of a Nation: History of India*, Sterling Publishers, Private Limited, 2010, p. 416.

CHAPTER TEN

India's Developments in Metallurgy

India has a great history of metal work, and smelting of metals and deriving alloys, which was done as far back as 3000 BCE. The trade of metal products was extensive between India, Egypt and Rome. Tools of iron and steel from ancient India were of great demand for many purposes. It is indicated that the first weapons of steel for the people of the Mediterranean came from India.

Many of the ancient Sanskrit texts contain instructions on metal work, such as the building of furnaces as found in the *Brihad-vimana-shastram*, or bellows, or the making of metal powders or binders or glue, as in the *Rasendra-sara-sangrahah*, *Shilpa-ratnam*, and *Rasa-ratna-samucchaya*, all from the 9th, 11th and 12th centuries CE. [1]

"The *Atharva Veda* (Shukranti 4.7.194-196) mentions the procedure of production of lead shots or granules–the crude way of atomisation of liquid metals. These lead shots were used like bullets for punishing thieves." [2]

It is known that there are some 44 old texts that describe the process of Indian metallurgy. One of the most well-known of these texts is called the *Rasaratna Samucchaya*. In it we find descriptions of many aspects of this technology, including the structural arrangement and function of the chemical laboratory, the *kosthi yantra* (the furnace), the *tiryak patana yantra* (vessels for containing chemicals), the *dheki yantram* (the distillation pot), and other things, like the chemical work to be done in the laboratory.

The *Aswalanan Grihya Sutra* mentions that when a child is born, the father should feed him from a golden vessel with clarified butter and honey with which he has ground the gold dust. This rite was performed for the sake of longevity and the general health of the child.

Manusmriti (2.29) also mentions that before the navel string is cut, the *jatkarma* ceremony must be performed for a male child, feeding him gold dust, honey and clarified butter. This is also described in the *Sushruta Samhita* (Sarir 10.12)

According to the research done by the archeologist Jim G. Shaffer, he determined that iron ore was recognized and used by the late third millennium BCE in southern Afghanistan, and then used to make iron items. Iron ore and items made from it have also been found in eight bronze age Harappan sites, some as far back as 2600 BCE or earlier. This makes Shaffer's views quite convincing. This may have been a natural development from smelting copper, and then using it for the making of iron utensils. [3]

Kamlesh Kapur describes in her book *Portraits of a Nations: History of India* in regard to the metal objects found at various sites, such as Mehrgarh and Naushaqro: "The first metallic objects were found near the excavated burial grounds. These were mostly ornaments. Hammering of unalloyed copper seems to be the only technique used to manufacture these small ornaments. These are dated around 7th millennium B.C. Weapons, chisels, axes and blades were found near habitational sites. The date of these objects is around 4th millennia B.C., thus, it is clear that molding, casting and the use of copper-lead alloy indicate an advanced knowledge and skill of these ancient people."

"In Naikund, India, archeologists have found a smelting furnace dated to 800 B.C. The Deogarh temple in India (600 A.D.) has hundreds of iron objects."

"According to Will Durant, Hindus seem to have been the first people to mine gold. Greek visitors like Megasthenese have mentioned this in their records. Much of the gold used in the Persian Empire in the 5th century B.C. came from India. India also mined silver, copper, zinc, led, tin and iron. Indians also knew the techniques for isolation, distillation and use of zinc." [4]

"Iron is no doubt a metal of great antiquity. A great deal had been written about Indian iron. Robert Hadfield (1912), the British metallurgist, quotes 'Without doubt, the process of making iron and steel have been used in India for thousands of years.' Heath J. M. (1839) therefore rightly claims that the Hindus had been familiar with the manufacture of steel from time immemorial and confirmed the opinion of Hadfield that the stone works of

Egypt could only have been carried out by tools of iron, probably cemented or hardened steel from India.

"In the earlier part of the 19ᵗʰ century, iron-making was practiced in many areas of India. They were located at places where iron ore and charcoal were easily available. The descriptions of the iron making process have been given by many observers throughout the years, from Captain Hamilton (1708) all the way to Holland (1893). It is gathered that large furnaces with a charge of as much a one ton of ore at a time were operated in Malbar (South India)." [5]

STEEL MAKING

Another rather unknown early development of ancient India is the ability of its craftsmen to make high grade steel. S. Ramachandran relates in *Iron and Steel Technology: Opinions for India*: "Steel has been known in India since hoary antiquity and is referred in the *Vedas* as *Ayas*. It has been deduced from archeological evidence that ancient Indians knew the art of making steel."

The name of Wootz is figured to have is origin in the Kannada-Telugu word for steel, which is *wukku*. This steel was made through a process by mixing low carbon soft iron and high carbon brittle steel at high temperature. India used to export this kind of steel from the 2ⁿᵈ century onwards to places like Iran, Arabia, Damascus, etc., where they wanted strong armament. Most places, like Arabia, they only knew how to make the brittle steel, but when that was combined with the Indian steel, they could get stronger material. This is how Indian steel became identified with Damascus swords and became widely exported to the West and East. By 1500, it became a coveted commodity in international trade.

Also, in *Ancient and Medieval India*, Mrs. Manning writes: "The superior quality of Hindu steel has long been known, and it is worthy of record that the celebrated Damascus blades have been traced to the workshops of Western India. Steel manufacturing in Kutch enjoys at the present-day a reputation not inferior to that of the steel made at Glasgow and Sheffield."

In this way, we can see that ancient India knew the technology of making steel from iron, as well as welding and smelting it from times immemorial, a technology that became known only later in places like England.

Further evidence of this is confirmed by Mr. L. White Jr., as found in the April, 1960 issue of *American Historical Review*: "Eduardo Saline, an authority on the metallurgy of early medieval long swords, suggests that the marvelously skillful twisting and fagoting of thin rods of steel and iron of different qualities that produced the laminated Merovingian blades was inspired by Indian Wootz steel, which achieved similar results by crystallization."

Mr. J. Needham writes in *Science and Civilization in China*: "Steel was manufactured in ancient India, and it was being exported to China at least by the fifth century A.D."

More insight into the expertise of the early Indian metal workers is further explained as follows: "In metallurgy, Indian metalsmiths had unparalleled achievements to their credit. They were the first in the then known world, to have successfully developed the extraction of zinc from its ores. They had understood, even if empirically, the complicated nuances of zinc metallurgy, its endothermic reduction reaction and the reducing atmosphere needed for the downward distillation of zinc, even as early as 400 B.C. It was only two thousand years later that a similar process was adopted in the west. Indian ironsmiths had perfected the process of extracting iron from its ores in such a way that iron of as high a quality as 99.7% could be obtained. Their forge welding technique was equally remarkable, as evidenced by the massive Iron Pillar (late 4th century A.D.) Now standing majestic and serene near Qutab Minar in Delhi, unrusted for over 1600 years. This technique was not short-lived either. There were larger iron pillars and beams of high purity that speak volumes about the metallurgical skills of ancient Indian ironsmiths. Even in the production of steel, an iron-carbon alloy, they had won approbation and Indian steel, known as Wootz steel (with 1.3-1.6% carbon content) was sought after in West Asia for fabricating the famous Damascus swords. Metallic iron-casting with exquisite iconography and iconometry from about the 7th century A.D. was an accomplished metal craft in India." [6]

Regarding the iron pillar at the Qutab Minar, evidence shows that it was made in the 4th century. According to the Sanskrit inscription on it, it was set up by Chandra Raj as the flag post in front of the Vishnu temple in Mathura. It was likely the Garuda *stambha* with an image of Garuda,

Lord Vishnu's bird carrier on top. It was brought to Delhi in 1050 by Anang Pal, founder of Delhi. [7]

A chemical examination of the pillar in 1961 showed that it is made of surprisingly good steel and contains much less carbon in comparison to the steel of today. Dr. B. B. Lal, the chief chemist of the Indian Archeological Survey has concluded that the pillar is made by joining 20-30 kgs of hot iron pieces. It is believed to have been manufactured in 15 days by 120 workers. The fact that 1600 years ago the technique of joining pieces of hot iron was known is a matter of amazement because not a single joint can be seen in the whole pillar. The fact that it has not rusted after being in the open for 16 centuries amazes many expert scientists. [8]

As further related by James Ferguson in his book, *A History of Indian and Eastern Architecture* (p. 208, from 1910), "The Iron Pillar of Delhi opens our eyes to an unsuspected state of affairs, to find Hindus at that age capable of forge-welding a pillar of iron, larger than any that have been forged even in Europe up to a very late age, and not frequently even now. It is almost equally startling to find that after exposure to wind and rain for centuries, it has remained unrusted and the capital inscriptions are as clear and as sharp now as when put up fifteen centuries ago..."

Conclusions of elaborate scientific studies were that the iron pillar was made of wrought iron and has 99.7% iron content. The pillar is a low carbon steel heterogeneous structure with rather high phosphorous content. The pillar was not cast in one piece but fabricated ingeniously by forging and hammer-welding lumps of balls of hot pasty iron in step by step process. The presence of lead solder in the joint between the decorative bell capital and the main body of the Delhi pillar, confirmed by X-ray analysis, establishes the use of lead based solder. [9]

COPPER

Copper was another metal that the people of ancient India learned how to use expertly. From as far back as 2000 BCE, people had made fine copper axes with sharp cutting edges by casting the copper in molds. The capital of this technology was around Ujjain, as well as the Nasik-Ahmednagar-Pune and other districts. Also, bronze was known in the Indus Valley region before 3000 BCE. Items in bronze were made through the lost wax system, which is still used today. This was very well established

The famous non-rusting iron pillar at the Qutab Minar, Delhi

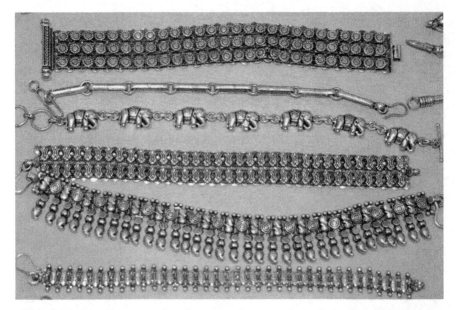

Hand made silver jewelry from a silversmith in Jaisalmer, Rajasthan

in Mohenjodaro, especially for art and decorative items. The copper alloy of brass was also used, which in its earliest form contained more than 28% zinc. References in Greek texts to zinc technology indicates that zinc objects were traded from India as far back as the 6th or 5th century BCE. [10]

   As explained further: "Pure copper was also used as a material for making instruments and vessels for medicinal purposes. A copper probe for applying Antimony to the eye has been found in the excavations of Bijnor and another in Bihar excavations. The sage Sushruta mentions a copper needle in the operation of cataract. Tin was also used as a material for blunt instruments. Sushruta mentions plates of tin to surround a tumor end to protect the healthy parts before the actual surgery. Such plates are recommended to be made of tin / lead / copper. Sushruta also mentions that use of lead probes, iron and silver cups. Among many other things, gold and silver needles are mentioned as necessary things for a lying-in-room, by Charaka. To cut the navel chord of the new-born child, he recommended a knife of either gold or silver or iron. In the *Manu-Smriti*, one meets before the section of the navel string, a ceremony is advised on the birth of a male-child, wherein little honey and ghee mixture is given to taste for the newborn with a golden spoon. A golden needle is mentioned by Sushruta for pricking the bulbs of some plants to extract its juice." [11]

SILVER AND GOLD

Iron, steel, zinc, and other metals were only a part of what came out of early India, along with the chemical processes that they had learned so many years ago. Silver and gold were also of importance. The archeological finds of silver artifacts have helped clarify the antiquity of the Vedic culture. Silver ornaments that had been found at Kunal, another Sarasvati site, prove that copper purification (which releases silver as a by-product) was known in India before 3000 BCE.

"Gold: a typical naturally occurring gold powder, is mentioned in the *Mahabharata* (2.52.2-4) was known as Pipilika Gold.

"Such gold powder was presented to the King Yudhisthira at the time of the Rajasuya Yagna ceremony by various kings like Khasa, Pulinda, Ekasana, Arha, Pradara, Dirghavenu, Parada, etc. These kings were residing beneath the shades of the bamboo trees on the banks of the Sailoda river flowing in between Meru and Mandarachala (Himalayas). Due to the high purity of the Pipilika Gold, it was a novelty and suitable item for the presentation to the royal families." [12]

CHEMICAL SCIENCE AND ADDITIONAL DEVELOPMENTS

Archeological excavations at Mohenjodaro in Sindh (now in Pakistan) and Harappa in Punjab (also now in Pakistan) have shown that the people of the Indus Valley civilization (2500-1800 BCE) were skilled in employing a wide variety of chemical processes. Bricks, water-pots, vessels, jars, earthenwares, terracotta, jewelry, metal vessels and implements, seals, painted pots, chrome glazed pottery, and glass vessels, and many other items have been found. The Indus Valley people used mortar consisting of lime, gypsum, sand plaster as construction materials for building houses and mansions. In metal working also the Indus people were experts in casting and forging. Copper and bronze (an alloy of copper and tin) were utilized for making tools and weapons, domestic utensils, statuettes, bangles, finger-rings, ear-rings, amulets, wires and rods. Gold and silver were used for jewelry and ornamental vessels. Later excavations have unearthed specimens of iron implements. Recent excavations in several other parts of India have revealed similar objects hidden under the ground. [13]

"Everyone is familiar with the chemical excellence of cast iron produced in ancient and medieval India. The tempering steel was brought to perfection in India unknown to Europe. Alexander received a precious gift of 30 pounds of not gold but steel from the Indian king. India was the leader of several chemical and pharmaceutical industries including dyeing, tanning, soap making, glass, and ceramics, cement and metallurgy. Indians were far ahead of European experts in several technologies involving melting, smelting, casting, calcination, sublimation, steaming, fixation, and fermentation. There were experts in the preparation of a variety of metallic salts, compounds and alloys, pharmaceutical preparations, perfumery as well as cosmetics. It is appropriate to mention that it is the Muslims who took much of the Hindu chemistry, medicine, astronomy, and mathematics, and other branches of science and technology to the Near East and then to Europe. It is well established that the secret of manufacturing of Damascus-steel was taken by the Arabs from Persians and the Persians from India." [14]

"Evidence suggests that nearly three thousand years back, Indians knew the art of making glass and coloring it by metal salts. In ancient India, glass was used to make beads, bangles and laboratory ware. There is also mention of India exporting a huge lens to China. Evidence of an ancient (5th century B.C.) glass factory at Kepica in Uttar Pradesh has been found. Lumps of glass of different sizes and colors, including one 40 cm x 42 cm x 26 cm and weighing over 10 kg, were found. Central Glass and Ceramics Research Institute in Calcutta tested the glass and found it to be of soda lime, with a high percentage of alumina. Today aluminum silicate glasses are used for making kitchen ware, which can be heated on a stove." [15]

According to the writings of Periplus, glass had been manufactured in India since the 3rd century BCE. In the writing of Pliny, he referred to the glass of India as being superior to all others.

Another aspect of this was the distillation of scents for making perfumes and fragrances in liquids or ointments. One speciality was sandalwood and its oil, used from ancient times. The sandalwood tree was native to India, such as Karnataka, where it was grown and used for its fragrant qualities. It became a great product for exporting to Greece,

Arabia, and other places. Musk was another fragrant item that became in demand, gathered from the secretions of the gland of the male musk-deer. Camphor was another fragrant item exported from India since ancient times, often used in rituals and prayer.

Lac was used as a varnish or protective covering on wooden furniture, or as a dye, such as for finger nails and cloth. Lac is the resin-like substance secreted on trees by the Lac insect.

POTTERY

Different areas were known to make pottery as far back as 4000 BCE. Most were naturally made for utilitarian purposes with the use of a potter's spinning wheel. There were also jars and even huge wares (3 meters in height) for storing grains, made of alluvial clay from the banks of the Sindhu River, tempered with sand containing fine mica particles.

From 2000 BCE in Mohenjodaro and Harappa, kilns were found which were used for making glazed pottery. There were eighteen sites from the 5th to the 1st century BCE in Northern and Central India that were known for producing pottery. These include Sarnath, Mathura, Patna, Sanchi, and other towns in this area. [16]

LAPIDARY SCIENCE

Diamonds and many other precious and semi-precious jewels were used in the art of Vedic culture. But this science was not only about how to recognize the value of the gems and how to use them for decoration, but also for their use in Jyotish and counteracting the evil or negative influence of planets, or even in heightening their positive forces. The *Garuda* and *Agni Puranas* contain a lot of this kind of information.

The *Garuda Purana* was also known for containing information on the locations of diamond minds. Such places included the Himalayas, and the mountainous or hilly regions of Saurastra, Kalinga (between the Mahanadi and Godavari), Venvatata (near Nagpur), etc.

CHAPTER NOTES
1. *Pride of India: A Glimpse into India's Scientific Heritage*, Samskriti Bharati, New Delhi, 2006, pp. 113-114.
2. Dr. V. K. Didolkar, *Metallurgy in Samskrita Literature*, Samskrita Bharati, New Delhi, Oct. 2000, p. 16.
3. Vans Kennedy, *Researches into the Origin and Affinity of the Principal Languages of Asia and Europe*, Longman, London, 1828, p. 185.
4. Kamlesh Kapur, *Portraits of a Nations: History of India*, Sterling Publishers, Private Limited, 2010, p. 408-9.
5. Dr. V. K. Didolkar, *Metallurgy in Samskrita Literature*, Samskrita Bharati, New Delhi, Oct. 2000, pp. 18-19.
6. B. V. Subbarayappa, *Foreword*, from *Science and Technology in Ancient India*, by Editorial Board of Vijnan Bharati, Mumbai, August, 2002.
7. *Science and Technology in Ancient India*, Vigyan Bharati, pp. 76-77.
8. Suresh Soni, *India's Glorious Scientific Tradition*, Ocean Books Pvt. Ltd., New Delhi, 2010, p. 53.
9. *Science and Technology in Ancient India*, by Editorial Board of Vijnan Bharati, Mumbai, August, 2002, p. 83.
10. Ibid., pp. 86-90.
11. Dr. V. K. Didolkar, *Metallurgy in Samskrita Literature*, Samskrita Bharati, New Delhi, Oct. 2000, pp. 7-8.
12. Ibid., p. 13.
13. Prof. A. R. Vasudeva Murthy and Prasun Kumar Mishra, *Indian Tradition of chemistry and Chemical Technology*, Samskrita Bharati, Bangalore, India, August, 1999, p. 3.
14. Ibid., pp. 1-2.
15. *Science and Technology in Ancient India*, by Editorial Board of Vijnan Bharati, Mumbai, August, 2002, p. 43.
16. Ibid., p. 44.

CHAPTER ELEVEN

India's Agricultural Developments

BOTANY

Plants and their many uses played an important part of the Vedic culture of India. India was one of the oldest regions for cultivated plants, which included rice, jute, cotton, pulses, black pepper, wheat, rye, linseed, walnuts, and fruits such as apple, pear, and mango. Earliest forms of vegetive propagation were of bananas, sugarcane, yam, palm, etc. Animals were also domesticated for agricultural purposes, such as cows, buffaloes, goats, sheep, fowl, and possibly elephants back then as well. It has been found that river boats were used in ancient times for agricultural trade. Devices such as seed grills, carts, and granaries were found in Harappan sites, and other places yielded implements for ginning, spinning, and weaving cotton.

Archaeological findings have revealed that several species of winter cereals, such as barley, oats and wheat, along with legumes like lentil and chickpeas, were domesticated and grown in Northwest India before the sixth millennium BCE. Such research has also shown that several other crops were cultivated 3000 to 6000 years ago. These included oilseeds such as sesame, linseed, safflower, mustards, and castor; legumes such as mung bean, black gram, horse gram, field pea, grass pea, and fenugreek were all grown in the region. There were other crops as well, such as sugarcane, barley, jute, ginger, turmeric, pumpkin, gourd, cucumber, pepper, sesamum, radish, peas, and other pulses. Of course, there were also crops like cotton along with fruits like jujube, grapes, dates, jackfruit, mulberry, and black plum.

In the *Rig* and *Atharva Vedas* agriculture was considered a noble occupation. In fact, the *Atharva Veda* regarded it almost as important as human procreation. Dried cow dung was prescribed and used as manure, which has also been found that when combined with cow urine and made into a dried paste, is one of the best fertilizers today for putting nutrients back into the soil, even more effectively and naturally than chemical fertilizers. From the Vedic literature it seems that Vedic-age farmers also knew how to maintain soil fertility by crop rotation and changing crops from season to season. [1]

People investigated, tested and examined nature and the world of plants and vegetables to a fine degree. In fact, the *Atharva Veda* divided plants into seven sub-parts, such as trees, grass, herbs for medicine, shrubs, creepers, etc. Then we find in such texts as the *Mahabharata, Vishnu Purana, Matsya Purana*, etc., along with books by Parashar, Charaka, Sushruta, Udayan, and so on, greater descriptions and analysis of the various plants. They even recognized the presence of the life-force within them. For example, the sage Charaka explains that trees also have life similar to other living beings, and also have feelings. [2]

In the ancient *Krishi-Parashara* from about 400 BCE, we find the details for designing the plow with the names for its different parts in Sanskrit, with little differences in the basic plow that we see today. This text has been translated by the Asian Agri-History Foundation in Secunderabad, India. It gives lists of tools to be used, methods of good farming management for the high yield of crops, implements to be used, operations, harvesting, dealing with rainfall, management of cattle, along with advice on seed collection and storage, etc. The *Krishi-Parashara* and the *Brihat Samhita* also were known to give simple astrological models for predicting rain by using basic astrology with climate conditions, depending on the season. For example, Parashar's method utilized the positions of the Moon and Sun, while the *Brihat Samhita*, by Varahamihira (505-587 CE) considered lunar mansions. These methods are still used today by many farmers in India.

The *Krishi-Parashara* also provided descriptions of what the cow shed should be, and discussed the importance of cleanliness to keep the cows protected from diseases. The *Rig Veda* also includes references on how best to maintain cows and manage them properly with the right foods or fodder to eat and water to drink. Cow killing for food was never encouraged in the Vedic period.

The *Vrikshayurved Parashar* (1st century BCE or CE), also said to be by the sage Parashar, gives knowledge of advanced botany in six parts: 1. Plant morphology, 2. Nature, properties and classification of soils, 3. Description and distribution of forests, 4. Flowers–parts, functions, and classification, 5. Definition, function and classification of fruits, 6. Plant limbs–root, stem, bark, heart wood, sap, excretions, oleoginous products, spines and prickles, seeds, and embryonic plants. [3]

In a closer analysis of the *Vrikshayurveda Parashar*, we find a detailed description of the process of the growth of a tree from the seed. He explains that at first the water is absorbed in the jelly-like structure and a nucleus is formed and then slowly it takes up the energy and nutrition from the earth. Then the structure develops into an incipient seed and later takes the form of a solid tree. This is the process of formation and protoplasm which has been described in the chapter Beejatva Adhikaran.

The second chapter deals with the soil and the kinds and qualities of the soil. The third chapter describes fourteen different kinds of forests. The fourth chapter, Vrikshang Sutradhyay, deals with the physiology of plants and trees, including photo-synthesis. Pushpaang Sutradhyay in the fifth chapter outlines flowers, including the many kinds of flowers, the parts of them, and what are these parts. The sixth chapter, Falaang Sutradhyay, deals with the many kinds of fruits, their qualities, diseases, and classifications. The seventh chapter deals with parts of the tree, and the eighth chapter describes the process of the growth of the tree. Thus, Parashar went very deeply into the whole process of growth, development and care for the plants. [4]

Sage Parashar also describes various aspects of the microscopic nature of the cell. He says that it has protoplasm and cell membranes, and is created in the phase of the seed in which it absorbs terrestrial juices and energy. The cell has an outer wall and gap with colored matter, and inner wall, and then that which is not visible to the naked eye. Thus, we find here that he is practically describing the parts that could hardly be seen without a microscope.[5]

All branches of botany were known in ancient India, in whatever rudimentary a form, whether it was morphology, plant physiology, etc. Other important works that deal with botany include the *Brihatsamhita* by Varahamihira (500 CE), *Krishi-sukta* of Kashyapa (800 CE), and *Upavanavinoda* (from the *Sarngadhara-paddhati*) on horticulture of the 13th century. Many of the *Puranas* also dealt with various degrees of botany, such as the *Agni, Padma, Matsya, Varaha, Bhagavata*, or the *Arthashastra*, all contained sections on agricultural practices, such as seasonal crops, crop rotation, classification of plants, their health, land-use, seed management, their treatment for diseases, etc.

Furthermore, the means of plant nourishment, use of water and wind, fertilizers, grafting, cures for plant diseases, etc., were also known. Even the sleep and reaction to touch, or even heat, cold, thunder, and smell among trees were understood. This means that the discovery of life in plants by Sir J. C. Bose was not a discovery, but only a reconfirmation of what the *Vedas* and ancient India already knew. In fact, this is confirmed in the *Rig Veda* (10.97.21), and in the *Mahabharata* (Shanti Parva, Chapter 184). Even the idea of rotation of crops can be found in the *Taittiriya samhita* (5.1.7.37). [6]

AGRICULTURE

Botany was used first to develop a good system of agriculture. India also had a long agricultural heritage that went back before 3700 BCE, and had the first written texts on the topic. One of the oldest books, as previously mentioned, is the *Krishi-Parashar*, which means "Agriculture by Parashara."

Another text on agriculture was the *Kashyapiyakrishisukti*, traditionally said to be originally provided by Kashyapa (but said to be in circulation around 700-800 CE). This describes the means of producing certain crops, cattle management, soil properties, laying out gardens, means of irrigation, marketing, ways of support from the government, as well as mining, and even a personal code of conduct for farmers.

The *Vrikshayurveda* (*The Science of Plant Life*), information compiled by Surapala, was another book that appeared later (c. 1000 CE). This dealt with the application of Ayurveda to various kinds of trees. However, it also contained knowledge of raising orchards, seed management, selection of soil, ways of irrigation, finding groundwater, using fertilizers, dealing with plant diseases, and so on. These books recommend practical ways of efficient farming while preserving the world's resources and environment, along with the means by which humanity can achieve the essential aims of life, such as *dharma, artha, kama* and *moksha* (which means spiritual purpose or duty, economic development, sensual fulfillment, and liberation through spiritual advancement), all things that we should still consider today.

In Kautilya's *Arthashastra*, written during the reign of the Mauryan kings, we also find descriptions of agriculture and the appointment of officials to encourage it. The Greek traveler Megasthenes writes that the king used to appoint officials to examine the river and the wells to ensure equal distribution of water to the main drains and branches.

The Vedic age saw the use of instruments like the plough and sickle, along with the cultivation of wheat, rice, and barley. Knowledge of what kind of ploughs to be used on what kind of soil had been implemented at that time, along with the best kind of oxen for ploughing and how to care for them in a humanitarian way.

The farmers of that time were already using crop rotation to increase the fertility of the soil, and sowing in rows had been known since ancient times, though it was first used in Austria only in 1662, and in England in 1730. Irrigation and water collection was also used to help with agriculture. Thus, the science of agriculture was far more advanced in India than in Europe.

The Vedic texts also had outlined the treatment of animals. The *Agni Purana* also has detailed descriptions on the care and treatment of horses and cows, along with the treatment and methods to control elephants. We also find that the *Garuda Purana* and the *Agni Purana* offers instruction on dealing with animal disorders and livestock. There is a separate portion of *Ayurveda*, called *Shalihotra Samhita*, which is most significant for the treatment of horses.

It is said to be from around 800 BCE, and is also called the *Haya Ayurveda* and *Turagshastra*. It is comprised of some 12,000 slokas and is divided into eight parts, only a few of which are now available. This was translated into Arabic, Persian, Tibetan, and English. It offers the symptoms of diseases, treatments, medicines, and how to safeguard the health of the horses. According to some veterinary specialists, this book is better than the modern books on the treatment of horses. (*Pracheen Bharat Mein Vigyan Shilip*, pp.125-126)

WATER CONSERVATION

Regarding the arid landscape of the area, collecting and conserving water was extremely important, and they devised ways to do that. Water preservation was especially important in the southern part of India. Rulers felt it was an obligation as part of their duty to the people and kingdom. It was the only way to make sure their kingdoms would remain fertile. In

The Royal Palace in the hilltop fort in Jaisalmer, Rajasthan, designed to utilize every breeze that blows and every drop of rain that falls

The Pushkarini water tank, Hampi, designed to collect and store water

preparation for durations without enough rain, storage of large amounts of water, and to collect as much as possible during times of rain and monsoons, they built wells, tanks, large reservoirs, lakes, canals between rivers, and small dams to preserve and provide for irrigation water for farmers and for drinking until the next season. You can still see many of these as you travel through India. Satellite pictures have shown as many as 1.2 million of such ponds in India. These were much more effective than the environmentally damaging dams they are building along the rivers today. And if China begins to monopolize or divert the water and rivers that come out of Tibet, this may again become an important system to use. In some areas these have been put back in use.

In Jaisalmer, for example, in the western desert of Rajasthan, the king's palace in the central fort was constructed in such a way that it would collect every drop of water that fell to be used and stored for later. And the passageways were made to collect the slightest breeze made by the wind so that every part of the palace would have whatever cooling effect that could be felt.

IRRIGATION IN ANCIENT INDIA

In order to make the cultivation of certain crops in particular areas, irrigation was an important development. Even today many different plans for the distribution of water in India is on the drawing boards. And there are many places where you can see how water was collected through pipes or small channels, and in step wells that sometimes became works of art.

The history of irrigation in India can be traced back to prehistoric times. The *Vedas* and ancient India scriptures have references to wells, canals, tanks, and small dams, which were beneficial to the community. In fact, building such things were considered part of the acts of piety and public benevolence that earns a person good merit. In the *Rig Veda* are many references to irrigation. The word for well frequently occurs and is described as "unfailing and full of water." (10.101.6) The *Vishnu* and *Bhagavata Puranas* also have references to the importance of establishing wells and water tanks. But these wells and tanks, once built, were then to be maintained by the state or the rulers of the area. It was the spread of agricultural communities to less fertile areas that lead to co-operation and the development of irrigation and reservoirs.

EARLY DEVELOPMENT OF RICE IN INDIA

No one can deny the importance of rice in the diet of millions of people around the world. But rice cannot be cultivated without plenty of water, for which irrigation is one of the main needs. So with the development of irrigation in ancient India, it became a place where rice could easily be grown.

The *Krishi-Sukti* by Kashyapa is the main treatise on rice cultivation, which describes a method 2000 years ago or more that, for the most part, is still followed today. [7]

Rice seems to be first mentioned in the *Yajur Veda*, and then found elsewhere in other Sanskrit texts. Both Hindu and Buddhist scriptures make frequent reference to rice, and in both religions the grain is used as a major offering to the gods. Rice is often directly associated with prosperity and fertility. It is also considered a representation of Lakshmi, the goddess of fortune. It is also one of the first foods offered to babies when they start eating solid food.

It is known that rice has been cultivated in Asia for over 10,000 years. Historians believe that the "indica" variety of rice was first domesticated in the area covering the foothills of the Himalayas, such as in northeastern India, and the lower plains, which then stretched through Orissa, Bengal, Burma, Thailand, Laos, Vietnam, and Southern China. The "japonica" variety was domesticated from wild rice in southern China. Chinese records of rice cultivation go back 4000 years. However, perennial rice still grows in Assam and Nepal. This seems to have appeared around 1400 BCE in southern India after its domestication in the northern plains and watered by rivers. Cultivation and cooking methods are thought to have spread west rapidly by medieval times, and southern Europe saw the introduction of rice as a hearty grain. Today the majority of rice comes from India, China, Japan, Indonesia, Thailand, Burma, and Bangladesh. Asian farmers still account for 92 percent of the world's total rice production.

Evidence shows that rice was cultivated in the Mohenjodaro area from before 3000 BCE. It became a major crop in Sri Lanka by 1000 BCE. From Greece and Sicily rice spread gradually throughout the southern portions of Europe and to a few locations in North Africa. [8]

CHAPTER NOTES

1. Dr. W. B. Rahudkar, *Ancient Indian Science & Technology of Agriculture*, in *Bharatiya Bouddhik Sampada*, August, 2000, pp. 6-7.
2. Dr. Vidyadhar Sharma, *Sanskrit Mein Vigyan*, p. 143.
3. P. M. Tamboli and Y. L. Nene, article in *Science in India with Special Reference to Agriculture*.
4. Suresh Soni, *India's Glorious Scientific Tradition*, Ocean Books Pvt. Ltd., New Delhi, 2010, p. 149.
5. Ibid., p. 151-52.
6. Dr. Manabendu Banerjee, Dr. Bijoya Goswami, *Science and Technology in Ancient India*, Sanskrit Pustak Bhandar, Calcutta, 1994, pp. 37-38.
7. P. M. Tamboli and Y. L. Nene, from the article *Science in India with Special Reference to Agriculture*.
8. Niranjan Shah, *Rice, A Practical Blessing Conferred by India*, from India Tribune, July 3, 2010.

CHAPTER TWELVE

The Vedic Arts

THE VEDIC SYSTEM OF MUSIC

Along with the other developments came the Vedic arts, and music has been a great favorite of the people of Bharatvarsha (ancient India) for many centuries. Much of this knowledge is said to have been originally given to humanity through the *Gandharva Veda*. And the many different forms of music and the serious nature of learning the numerous kinds of instruments confirms their advancements in it.

Music was known and understood in Baratvarsha from the earliest of times, and was a primary basis of the *Sama Veda* for the chanting of the mantras within it. The *Gandharva Veda* specialized in music, but this has been lost. Nonetheless, the knowledge of music remains and the number of the Ragas and Ragnis are innumerable. However, the subtle differences between these are often so subtle that an untrained ear will not tell the difference.

The main Indian musical instruments that accompanied the songs were the sarod, veena, sarangi, tambora, ghata, tabla, sitar, etc. These instruments were not simple, but required special material, craftsmanship and processes to construct them, along with years of arduous practice to master them.

Alain Danielou, a French historian and head of the UNESCO Institute for Comparative Musicology explained his theory of how the Indian form of music was developed in the publication *Northern Indian Music*: "The ancient Hindus (Vedic Indians) were familiar with the theory of sound, and its metaphysics and physics. The hymns of the *Rig Veda* contain the earliest examples of words set to music, and by the time of the *Sama Veda*, a complicated system of chanting had been developed. By the time of the *Yajur Veda*, a variety of professional musicians had appeared, such as lute players, drummers, flute players, and conch blowers. Thus, music has been cultivated in very early ages by the Indians, as the abridged names of the seven notes, sa (shadja), ri (rishabha), ga (gandhara), ma (madhyama) pa (pancha-ama), dha (dhaivata), ni (nishada), occur in the *Sama Veda*, and in their present order."

In this regard, another person who explained the advanced nature of the Vedic system of music is Sir William Hunter, who stated in *The Indian Empire*: "A regular system of notation had been worked out before the age of Panini and the seven notes were designated by their initial letters. This notation passed from [Vedic] Brahmins through the Persians to Arabia, and was then introduced into European music by Guido d'Arezzo at the beginning of the 11th century. . . Hindu music after a period of excessive elaboration, sank under the Muhammadans into a state of arrested developments."

This refers to how the Islamic invasions forced musicians and dancers, and almost everyone else who practiced anything but Islam, to take cover and remain unable to practice their crafts. Thus, dancing and music came to a standstill, since it was banned by Muslims. However, to save themselves, numerous Hindu musicians converted to Islam, such as during Akbar's rule, and then continued as Muslim Gharanas. Thus, the Vedic system of music continued, but under the guise of being an Islamic contribution to the area. Therefore, again we find the common sense point of view that most Muslims in Indian come from a Hindu or Vedic heritage or family lineage. As such, many of the Islamic musicians are but carry-overs from the Vedic system of music.

To summarize, Anne C. Wilson relates in *A Short History of the Hindu System of Music*: "It must, therefore, be a secret source of pride to them (Vedic Indians) to know that their system of music, as a written science, is the oldest in the world. Its principal features were given long ago in Vedic writings."

One of the early purposes of the Vedic system of music was to help hold intact the means of chanting the Vedic texts with the proper pronunciation through the oral tradition. This was done through the use of musical notes with varying meters. Of course, we know the *Sama Veda* was especially focused on music, and it gave or at least utilized the system of seven notes, called *saptak*. This also became the backbone of the Western system of music. Sarjerao Ramrao Gharge-Deshmukh goes on to explain this in his book, *Ramayana: A Fact or Fiction?*:

"In both the Indian and Western systems, the first note of the *saptak* gets repeated at the end and the repeat note belongs to the next higher scale. The difference is that in the Indian tradition the repeat note is not counted in the *saptak* while in the West the ascending notes including the repeated one at the end are grouped in eight, making it an octave. In an octave, the eighth note is the same as the first one in a *saptak*, but belongs to the next higher scale. The Indian *sapta-svaras* (seven notes) and Western octave are as follows:

Indian *Sapta-svaras*: Sa Ri Ga Ma Pa Dha Ni Sa
Western Octave: Do Re Me Fa So La Ti Do

"In the Indian system, since the *Sa* is repeated it is not recounted in the *sapta-svaras*, as such making it a group of seven notes verses eight in the Western music. While defining *thhats* or scales, although the Indian system is based on a *saptak*, it makes use of an octave by dividing a *saptak* (eight notes) into two groups of four each...

"Ragas were based on *saptakas*. The Indian melody or raga system comes from 72 parent *thhats* or scales. *Thhats* include all seven notes while a raga need not include them all. In a *thhat*, the *sapta-svara* or seven notes are divided into two groups starting with *achal svara*, i.e., a constant note that cannot be interchangeably used as a soft (*komal*) or sharp (*teevra*) note...

"Thus, the Indian *thhats* are made of two groups of four notes and are equivalent to the Western octave. The 72 *thhats* are made using the combinations of the above notes with the *achal svara* rule by changing the order of the notes that are not *achal*. The intricacies of *ragas* involve rendering style, its constitution, and its body [through systematized methods]...

In conclusion, " All Vedic literature is nothing but poetry supported by elaborate system of music with rules and conformity to multiple meters suitable for differing emotions. As such, in Indian tradition, literature and music are inseparable. Thus... it is accepted that every nation and every region has its own poetic legacy, however, most of them lack the antiquity of the Indian literature and the orders of music." [1]

Western music is divided up to half tones, while the Indian music has up to quarter tones. Furthermore, there are six basic male ragas associated with 36 female ragnis which differ in a softer and more feminine

The beautiful and heart-melting Manipuri style rasalila dance, Manipur

*Musicians playing and singing bhajans to glorify Lord Krishna,
Vrindavana*

degree. From these 36 ragnis there are additional ragnis which bear
particular differences from the main ragas. Many are assigned to various
times of the day or night, or seasons of the year to invoke particular moods
and feelings. Thus, if they are sung at inappropriate times, it would indicate
the ignorance of the performer.

Six of the principal ragas include: 1. Hindaul, played to produce in
the mind of the hearers the sweetness and freshness of spring; 2. Sri Raga,
which invokes the calmness and silence of the evening; 3. Meg Mallar,
which brings the mood of an approaching thunder storm and rain; 4.
Deepuck, now extinct, called to light the lamps of approaching death, or
even to cause the body of the singer to burst into flames by which he dies
(No wonder it is now extinct or hardly known); 5. Bhairava, very popular
and brings to mind the effect of the approaching dawn and the freshness of
the new day and caroling of birds; 6. Malkos, which produces a feeling of
gentle stimulation.

VEDIC DANCE

As with art, dance in India was not merely an expression of an artist's emotional mindset or imagination, but was meant to be an interpretation or conveyance of higher spiritual principles or pastimes of the Divine. In fact, in the Vedic pantheon Shiva is known as Nataraja, the king of dancers. Shiva's dance was also not without a more significant purpose. His dance was based on the rhythm of cosmic energy that pervades the universe, and the destruction of the illusory energy by which all souls are given the opportunity for release from the illusion to attain liberation, *moksha*.

In this way, traditional Indian dance is highly spiritual and often accompanies important religious rituals and holy days and festivals. Vedic dance goes back to prehistoric times. Bharata Muni wrote his *Natya Shastra*, science of drama and dance, over 2000 years ago. Some scholars feel he belongs to the 5th century BCE. In his text he explains that it was Lord Brahma, the secondary engineer of the universal creation, who brought dance (*natya*) and drama to the people of planet Earth millions of years ago, shortly after the Earth was created.

Ranjani Saigal elaborates on how this was supposed to have happened: "Once gods and goddesses pleaded with Lord Brahma for another *Veda* to be created that would be simple for the common man to understand, which is particularly important in Kali-yuga. Granting their wish, Lord Brahma created the *Panchama-Veda*, the *Fifth Veda*, or *Natya Veda*, a quintessence of the main four *Vedas*. Brahma took *pathya* (words) from the *Rig Veda*, *abhinaya* (communicative elements of body movements, or mime) from the *Yajur Veda*, *geeth* (music and chant) from the *Sama Veda*, and *rasa* (vital sentiment and emotional feeling and expression) from the *Atharva Veda* to form the *Fifth Veda*, *Natya Veda*. After creating this *Veda*, Lord Brahma handed it to the sage Bharata and asked him to propagate it on Earth. Obeying the fiat of Lord Brahma, sage Bharata wrote the *Natyashastra*. Bharata together with groups of the Gandharvas [angelic beings] and Apsaras [heavenly dancing girls] performed *natya*, *nritta* and *nritya* before Lord Shiva. It became the most authoritative text on the artistic technique of classical Indian dancers, especially Bharatnatyam and Odissi. It is also possible that the term *Bharatnatyam* partly owes its name to sage Bharata."

Now Vedic or Indian dance has evolved into a tradition involving various schools and styles but with strict discipline. It is not uncommon that Indian families will have their daughters spend at least several years or more in such study and practice. There is a precise method of postures, facial and hand gestures (*mudras*), and movements, along with footwork that must be learned and synchronized to the beat and music in order to convey specific meanings, moods and stories to the audience. Many temples, especially in South India, were known for maintaining large groups of dancers that performed at festivals and religious functions. The Chidambaram temples in south India show 108 sculpted poses on the walls of the temples.

Many of the dance techniques are derived from the Natyashastra, such as Bharatnatyam, Kuchipudi, Kathak, Kathakali, Odissi, Mohiniattam, Krishna Atam, Bhagavata Mela, Manipuri, etc. These also have developed from various ways of telling the stories based on the epics, like the *Mahabharata, Ramayana,* or the *Panchatantra, Hitopadesha,* or Krishna-lila from the *Bhagavata Purana,* or stories from other *Puranas.* Other traditions of dance dramas also can be seen, such as Dashavatara in Maharashtra, or Yakshagana in Karnataka.

In these styles of dances, movements with the music and facial and hand expressions (*hastas* and *mudras*), which convey varying moods, such as anger (*krodha*), envy (*matsara*), greed (*lobha*), lust (*kama*), ego (*mada*), and so on, have become a part of the dance routines in order to help convey whatever pastime that it depicts.

When the dance is performed according to the spiritual standards, which some view as similar to the practice of yoga, even the dancers can invoke a high degree of spirituality in their own consciousness and bring unity between their inner selves and God. Then the transcendental atmosphere can manifest and draw the Divine to appear in the performers on stage. Thus, the environment becomes transformed and the audience may also experience *darshan* of the Divine and experience an inspiring upliftment in their own consciousness. In this way, the dance is divine beauty in motion. Or it is a way of invoking the spiritual dimension into our midst. Few other forms of dance attempt to do this.

Considering the spiritual nature and purpose of the dances, they would often be performed on special holy days during festivals, and performed at temples for the pleasure of the Deity and the audience who would attend such festive occasions. Thus, the dance was both art and worship together.

Ancient Indian classical dance was so influential that it is not difficult to see the affects of it in nearby areas, such as in Burma, Thailand, Indonesia, etc. Nowadays this ancient art of Indian dance is enjoying a wide audience and a prominent place on the international stage.

THEATER

Dance gave way to theater and drama as far back as at least the times of the *Rig Veda*. It is Bharatamuni who is said to have preserved and presented the text for dance and drama, but even he admitted of not knowing how long ago it began. Tradition further relates that the origins of drama is Lord Brahma. But the work of Lord Brahma was said to be quite complex, and Bharatamuni simplified it and made it more accessible to the masses in a systematic manner. *Natyashastra* encompasses all modes of emotional expression in speech, gestures, movements, and intonations in actions. Some of the great dramatists includes Kalidasa, the playwright of the Gupta court in Ujjain, and Bhavabhuti. In this way, the art of dance and drama have always been a part of the spiritual path of Vedic culture.

VEDIC ART

Vedic art is another ancient development that still holds much appreciation in modern times. Art in the Vedic tradition was never a mere representation of an artist's imagination. It was always a vehicle to convey higher truths and principles, levels of reality that may exist beyond our sense perception. It was always used to bring us to a higher purpose of existence and awareness. In this way, it was always sacred and beheld the sacred. Still today it is used to allow others to enter into a transcendental experience. It may also present the devotional objects of our meditation.

Vedic paintings or symbols are unique in that they can deliver the same spiritual energy, vibration and insight that it represents. In other words, through the meditation and devotional mood of the artist, the art becomes a manifestation of the higher reality. In this way, the painting or symbol becomes the doorway to the spiritual essence contained within.

They are like windows into the spiritual world. Through that window we can have the experience of what is called *darshan* of the Divine or divinities, God or His associates. *Darshan* is not merely seeing the Divine but it is also entering into the exchange of seeing and being seen by the Divine.

Thus the art, or the deity, is beyond mundane principles or ingredients, such as paint, paper, stone or metal with which it may be made, but it becomes completely spiritual through which the deity can reveal Himself or Herself. Thus, the truth of spiritual reality can pierce through the darkness of the material energy and enter our mind and illuminate our consciousness.

To convey higher realities in paintings and sculpture, everything has a meaning. The postures, gestures, colors, instruments or weapons, everything conveys a principle or purpose, which often must be explained to those who lack understanding. Thus, knowing the inner meaning of the painting increases its depth for those who can perceive it, which makes it worthy of further meditation and contemplation.

In describing his appreciation of the artists of the paintings in the caves of Ajanta, the British researcher Mr. Griffith says, "The artists who did the paintings in Ajanta were the topmost people in the world of creations. Even the straight vertical lines drawn with easy brush-strokes on the walls of Ajanta are amazing. But when one looks at the lines drawn parallel to the horizon and the curves sees the similarity and wonders at the thousand complexities of creation, it is felt that this is nothing short of a miracle." [2]

The caves at Ajanta, for example, used a combination of indigo and varnish, the painters of which might combine 14 colors of natural plant products until they got the right shade they needed. The use of such paints predates the use of paints in Europe.

Until today, the unique art and paintings of Indian culture has continued to captivate the world with its colors, details, the moods they invoke, and the pastimes they illustrate.

CHAPTER NOTES
1. Sarjerao Ramrao Gharge-Deshmukh, Pratibha Deshmukh, *Ramayana: A Fact or Fiction?,* Pune, October, 2003, pp. 220-3.
2. *Shilp Sanshodhan Pratishthan*, Nagpur, p. 12.

CHAPTER THIRTEEN

Ancient India's Maritime Developments

Now let us take a look at India's ancient maritime history, which is referenced as far back as the early Vedic texts. The fact is that the ancient Vedic texts, such as the *Rig Veda*, *Shatapatha Brahmana*, and others refer to the undertaking of naval expeditions and travel to distant places by sea-routes that were well-known at the time. For example, the *Rig Veda* (1.25.7) talks of how Varuna has full knowledge of all the sea routes that were followed by ships. Then (2.48.3) we find wherein merchants would also send out ships for foreign trade. [1]   Another verse (1.56.2) speaks of merchants going everywhere and frequently to every part of the sea. Another verse (7.88.3-4) relates that there was a voyage by Vasistha and Varuna in a ship skillfully fitted for the trip. Then there is a verse (1.116.3) that tells of an expedition on which Tugra, the Rishi king, sent his son Bhujya against some of his enemies in the distant islands. However, Bhujya becomes ship wrecked by a storm, with all of his followers on the ocean, "Where there is no support, or rest for the foot or hand." From this he is rescued by the twin Ashvins in their hundred oared galley. Similarly, the *Atharva Veda* mentions boats which are spacious, well constructed and comfortable.

An assortment of other books also referred to sea voyages of the ancient mariners. Of course, we know that the epics, such as the *Ramayana* and *Mahabharata* referred to ships and sea travel, but the *Puranas* also had stories of sea voyages, such as the *Matsya*, *Varaha*, and *Markandeya Puranas*. Other works of Classical Sanskrit included them as well, such as *Raghuvamsha*, *Ratnavali*, *Dashakumaracharita*, *Kathasaritsagara*, *Panchatantra*, *Rajatarangini*, etc.

The *Shangam* works of the South Indian Tamils have numerous references to the shipping activities that went on in that region, along with the ports, articles of trade, etc. Such texts included *Shilappadikaram Manimekalai, Pattinappalai, Maduraikhanji, Ahananuru, Purananuru,* etc. [2]

In the *Ramayana*, in the Kishkindha Kand, Sugriva gives directions to the Vanar leaders for going to the cities and mountains in the islands of the sea, mainly Yavadvipa (Java) and Suvarna Dvipa (Sumatra) in the quest to find Sita. The *Ramayana* also talks of how merchants traveled beyond the sea and would bring presents to the kings.

In the *Mahabharata* (Sabha Parva), Sahadeva is mentioned as going to several islands in the sea to defeat the kings. In the Karna Parva, the soldiers of the Kauravas are described as merchants, "whose ships have come to grief in the midst of the unfathomable deep." And in the same Parva, a verse describes how the sons of Draupadi rescued their maternal uncles by supplying them with chariots, "As ship wrecked merchants are rescued by means of boats." However, another verse therein relates how the Pandavas escaped from the destruction planned for them with the help of a ship that was secretly and especially constructed for the purpose under the orders of the kind hearted Vidura. The ship was large, and provided machinery and all kinds of weapons of war, and able to defy storms and waves.

Actually, ships have been mentioned in numerous verses through the Vedic literature, such as in the *Vedas, Brahmanas, Ramayana, Mahabharata, Puranas,* and so on. For example, in the Ayodhya Kaand of Valmiki's *Ramayana*, you can find the description of such big ships that could hold hundreds of warriors: "Hundreds of oarsmen inspire five hundred ships carrying hundreds of ready warriors." The conclusion is that ships have been in use since the Vedic age.

Also, in Kautilya's *Arthashastra* we find information of the complete arrangements of boats maintained by the navy and the state. It also contains information on the duties of the various personnel on a ship. For example, the Navadhyaksha is the superintendent of the ship, Niyamaka is the steerman, and Datragrahaka is the holder of the needle, or the compass. Differences in ships are also described regarding the location of the cabins and the purpose of the ship itself. [3]

In the *Brihat Samhita* by Varahamihir of the 5th century, and in the Sanskrit text *Yukti Kalpataru* by Narapati Raja Bhoj of the 11th century, you can find information about an assortment of ships, sizes, and materials with which they were built, and the process of manufacturing them. For example, one quote explains, "Ships made of timbers of different classes possess different properties. Ships built of inferior wood do not last long and rot quickly. Such ships are liable to split with a slight shock." [4] It also gives further details on how to furnish a ship for accommodating the comfort of passengers, or for transporting goods, animals, or royal artifacts. The ships of three different sizes were the Sarvamandira, Madhyamarmandira, and the Agramandira.

Ancient Indians traveled to various parts of the world not only for purposes of trade, but to also propagate their culture. This is how the Vedic influence spread around the world. For example, Kaundinya crossed the ocean and reached south-east Asia. From there, evidence shows that rock inscriptions in the Sun Temple at Jawayuko in the Yukatan province of Mexico mentions the arrival of the great sailor Vusulin in Shaka Samvat 854, or the year 932. In the excavations in Lothal in Gujarat, it seems that trade with countries like Egypt was carried out from that port around 2540 BCE. Then from 2350 BCE, small boats docked here, which necessitated the construction of the harbor for big ships, which was followed by the city that was built around it. [5]

In the period of 984-1042 CE, the Chola kings dispatched great naval expeditions which occupied parts of Burma, Malaya and Sumatra, while suppressing the piratical activities of the Sumatra warlords.

In 1292 CE, when Marco Polo came to India, he described Indian ships as "built of fir timber, having a sheath of boards laid over the planking in every part, caulked with iron nails. The bottoms were smeared with a preparation of quicklime and hemp, pounded together and mixed with oil from a certain tree which is a better material than pitch." He further writes: "Ships had double boards which were joined together. They were made strong with iron nails and the crevices were filled with a special kind of gum. These ships were so huge that about 300 boatmen were needed to row them. About 3000-4000 gunny bags could be loaded in each ship. They had many small rooms for people to live in. These rooms had arrangements for all kinds of comfort. Then when the bottom or the base started to get spoiled, a new layer would be added on. Sometimes, a boat would have even six layers, one on top of another."

A fourteenth century description of an Indian ship credits it with a carrying capacity of over 700 people giving a fair idea of both ship building skills and maritime ability of seamen who could successfully man such large vessels.

Another account of the early fifteenth century describes Indian ships as being built in compartments so that even if one part was shattered, the next remained intact, thus enabling the ship to complete her voyage. This was perhaps a forerunner of the modern day subdivision of ships into watertight compartments, a concept then totally alien to the Europeans.

Another traveler named Nicolo Conti came to India in the 15th century. He wrote: "The Indian ships are much bigger than our ships. Their bases are made of three boards in such a way that they can face formidable storms. Some ships are made in such a way that if one part becomes useless, the rest of the parts can do the work."

Another visitor to India named Bertham writes: "The wooden boards are joined in such a way that not even a drop of water can go through it. Sometimes, the masts of cotton are placed in such a way that a lot of air can be filled in. The anchors were sometimes made of heavy stones. It would take a ship eight days to come from Iran to Cape Comorin (Kanyakumari)." [6]

The famous archeologist Padmashri Dr. Vishnu Shridhar Wakankar says, "I had gone to England for studies, I was told about Vasco da Gama's diary available in a museum in which he has described how he came to India." He writes that when his ship came near Zanzibar in Africa, he saw a ship three times bigger than the size of his ship. He took an African interpreter to meet the owner of that ship who was a Gujarati trader named Chandan who used to bring pine wood and teak from India along with spices and take back diamonds to the port of Cochin. When Vasco da Gama went to meet him, Chandan was sitting in ordinary attire, on a cot. When the trader asked Vasco where he was going, the latter said that he was going to visit India. At this, the trader said that he was going back to India the very next day and if he wanted, he could follow him. So, Vasco da Gama came to India following him. [7]

Sir William Jones, in *The Journal of the Royal Asiatic Society–1901*, relates how the Hindus, "must have been navigators in the age of Manu, because bottomry is mentioned in it. In the *Ramayana*, practice of bottomry is distinctly noticed." Bottomry is the lending of insurance money for marine activities. [8]

MARITIME TRADE

Further evidence shows that shipping from Bharatvarsha was a national enterprise and the country was a leader in world trade relations amongst such people as the Phoenicians, Jews, Assyrians, Greeks, and Romans in ancient times, and more recently with Egyptians, Romans, Turks, Portuguese, Dutch, and English.

The simple fact is that India's maritime history predates the birth of Western civilization. The world's first tidal dock is believed to have been built at Lothal around 2300 BCE during the Harappan civilization, near the present day Mangrol harbor on the Gujarat coast.

The earliest portrayal of an Indian ship is found on an Indus Valley seal from about 3000 BCE. The ship is shown being elevated at both bow and stern, with a cabin in the center. It is likely to have been a simple river boat since it is lacking a mast. Another drawing found at Mohendjodaro on a potsherd shows a boat with a single mast and two men sitting at the far end away from the mast. Another painting of the landing of Vijaya Simha in Ceylon (543 BCE) with many ships is found amongst the Ajanta caves.

That India had a vast maritime trade, even with Greece, is shown by the coins of the Trojans (98-117 CE) and Hadrians (117-138 CE) found on the eastern coast of India, near Pondicherry. This is evidence that Greek traders had to have visited and traded in the port cities of that area.

Kamlesh Kapur explains more about this in *Portraits of a Nation: History of India*: "Recent archeological excavations at Pattanam in Ernakulum district of Kerala by the Kerala council for Historical Research (KCHR) indicate that there was thriving naval trade around 500 B.C. According to the Director of KCHR, 'The artifacts recovered from the excavation site suggest that Pattanam, with a hinterland port and a multicultural settlement, may have had links with the Mediterranean, the Red Sea, the Arabian Sea, and the South China Sea rims since the Early Historic Period of South India.' KCHR has been getting charcoal samples examined through C-14 and other modern methods to determine the age of these relics. These artifacts were from the Iron Age layer. The archeologists also recovered some parts of a wooden canoe and bollards (stakes used to secure canoes and boats) from a waterlogged area at the site.

"The radiocarbon dating from Pattanam will aid in understanding the Iron Age chronology of Kerala. So far, testing done by C-14 method to determine the ages of the charcoal samples from the lowermost sand deposits in the trenches at Pattanam suggests that their calibrated dates range from 1300 B.C. to 200 B.C. and 2500 B.C. to 100 A.D. Thus there is strong evidence that Kerala had sea trade with several countries in Western Asia and Eastern Europe from the second millennia B.C. onwards." [9]

The influence of the sea on Indian Kingdoms continued to grow with the passage of time. North-west India came under the influence of Alexander the great, who built a harbor at Patala where the Indus branches into two, just before entering the Arabian sea. His army returned to Mesopotamia in ships built in Sindh. Records show that in the period after his conquest, Chandragupta Maurya established an admiralty division under a Superintendent of ships as part of his war office, with a charter including responsibility for navigation on the seas, oceans, lakes and rivers. History records that Indian ships traded with countries as far as Java and Sumatra, and available evidence indicates that they were also trading with other countries in the Pacific, and Indian Ocean. Even before Alexander, there were references to India in Greek works and India had a flourishing trade with Rome. Roman writer Pliny speaks of Indian traders carrying away large quantity of gold from Rome, in payment for much sought exports such as precious stones, skins, clothes, spices, sandalwood, perfumes, herbs, and indigo.

The port cities included such places as Nagapattinam, Arikamedu (near Pondicherry), Udipi, Kollam, Tuticorin, Mamallapuram, Mangalore, Kannur, Thane, and others, which facilitated trade with many foreign areas, such as Indonesia, China, Arabia, Rome, and countries in Africa. Many other inland towns and cities contributed to this trade, such as Madurai, Thanjavur, Tiruchirapalli, Ellora, Melkote, Nasik, and so on, which became large centers of trade. Silk, cotton, sandalwood, woodwork, and various types of produce were the main items of trade.

Trades of this volume could not have been conducted over the countries without appropriate navigational skills. Two Indian astronomers of repute, Aryabhatta and Varahamihira, having accurately mapped the positions of celestial bodies, developed a method of computing a ship's position from the stars. A crude forerunner of the modern magnetic compass called Matsyayantra was being used around the fourth or fifth century CE. Between the fifth and tenth centuries CE, the Vijayanagara and Kalinga kingdoms of southern and eastern India had established their rules over Malaya, Sumatra and Western Java. The Andaman and Nicobar Islands then served as an important midway for trade between the Indian peninsula and these kingdoms, as also with China. The daily revenue from the western regions in the period 844-848 CE was estimated to be 200 maunds (eight tons) of gold.

Not only was there trade from ancient going to many areas of the globe, but other countries may have also been going to India. It is reported that marine archaeologists have found a stone anchor in the Gulf of Khambhat with a design similar to the ones used by Chinese and Japanese ships in the 12th-14th century CE, giving the first offshore evidence indicating India's trade relations with the two Asian countries. The stone anchor was found during an exploration headed by two marine archaeologists, A. S. Gaur and B. K. Bhatt, from the National Institute of Oceanography (NIO). "Though there are a lot of references and Chinese pottery (found from coastal sites) indicating trade relations between the two Asian nations (China and Japan) in the past, but this anchor from the offshore region is the first evidence from Indian waters. Similar type of anchors have been found from Chinese and Japanese waters," stated Mr. Gaur. [10]

Furthermore, another recent finding that shows the ancient advancement of Indian maritime capabilities is the evidence that Indian traders may have gone to South America long before Columbus discovered America. Investigation of botanical remains from an ancient site, Tokwa at the confluence of Belan and Adwa rivers, Mirzapur District, Uttar Pradesh (UP), has brought to light the agriculture-based subsistence economy during the Neolithic culture (3rd-2nd millennium BCE). They subsisted on various cereals, supplemented by leguminous seeds. Evidence of oil-yielding crops has been documented by recovery of seeds of Linum usitatissimum and Brassica juncea. Fortuitously, an important find among the botanical remains is the seeds of South American custard apple, regarded to have been introduced by the Portuguese in the 16th century. The remains of custard apple as fruit coat and seeds have also been recorded from other sites in the Indian archaeological context, during the Kushana Period (CE 100-300) in Punjab and Early Iron Age (1300-700 BCE) in UP. The factual remains of custard apple, along with other stray finds, favor a group of specialists to support with diverse arguments the reasoning of Asian-American contacts way before the discovery of America by Columbus in 1498. [11]

The art of boat making goes on in this small scale here in Varanasi on the banks of the Ganga where boats are used constantly in various ways

THE INDIAN NAVY AND SEA POWER

In the south especially there was an established navy in many coastal areas. The long coastline with many ports for trade for sending out ships and receiving traders from foreign countries necessitated a navy to protect the ships and ports from enemies. According to records, the Pallavas, Cholas, Pandyas, and the Cheras had large naval fleets of ocean bound ships because these rulers also led expeditions against other places, such as Malayasia, Bali, and Ceylon.

The decline of Indian maritime power commenced in the thirteenth century, and Indian sea power had almost disappeared when the Portuguese arrived in India. They later imposed a system of license for trade, and set upon all Asian vessels not holding permits from them.

The piratical activities of the Portuguese were challenged by the Zamorins of Calicut when Vasco da Gama, after obtaining permission to trade, refused to pay the customs levy. Two major engagements were fought during this period. First, the battle of Cochin in 1503, clearly revealed the weakness of Indian navies and indicated to the Europeans an opportunity for building a naval empire. The second engagement off Diu in 1509 gave the Portuguese mastery over Indian seas and laid the foundation of European control over Indian waters for the next 400 years.

Indian maritime interests witnessed a remarkable resurgence in the late seventeenth century, when the Siddhis of Janjira allied with the Moghuls to become a major power on the West Coast. This led the Maratha King Shivaji to create his own fleet, which was commanded by able admirals like Sidhoji Gujar and Kanhoji Angre. The Maratha Fleet along with the legendary Kanhoji Angre held sway over the entire Konkan Coast keeping the English, Dutch and Portuguese at bay. The death of Angre in 1729 left a vacuum and resulted in the decline of Maratha sea power. Despite the eclipse of Indian kingdoms with the advent of western domination, Indian shipbuilders continued to hold their own well into the nineteenth century. The Bombay Dock completed in July 1735 is in use even today. Ships displacing 800 to 1000 tons were built of teak at Daman and were superior to their British counterparts both in design and durability. This so agitated British shipbuilders on the River Thames that they protested against the use of Indian built ships to carry trade from England. Consequently, active measures were adopted to cripple the Indian shipbuilding industries. Nevertheless, many Indian ships were inducted into the Royal Navy, such as HMS Hindostan in 1795, the frigate Cornwallis in 1800, HMS Camel in 1801, and HMS Ceylon in 1808. HMS Asia carried the flag of Admiral Codrington at the battle of Navarino in 1827, the last major sea battle to be fought entirely under sail.

Two Indian built ships witnessed history in the making. The Treaty of Nanking, ceding Hong Kong to the British, was signed onboard HMS Cornwallis in 1842. The "Star Spangled Banner" national anthem of the USA was composed by Francis Scott Key onboard HMS Minden when the ship was on a visit to Baltimore. Numerous other ships were also constructed, the most famous being HMS Trincomalee, which was launched on 19 October, 1817, carrying 86 guns and displacing 1065 tons. This ship was latter renamed Foudroyant.

The period of 4000 years between Lothal and Bombay Dock, therefore, offers tangible evidence of seafaring skills the nation possessed in the days of sail. In the early seventeenth century, when British naval ships came to India, they discovered the existence of considerable shipbuilding and repair skills, as well as seafaring people. An ideal combination was thus available for supporting a fighting force in India. [12]

HOW THE BRITISH KILLED THE MARINE INDUSTRY OF INDIA

When the westerners made contact with India, they were amazed to see their ships. Until the 17th century, European ships were a maximum of 600 tonnes. But in India, they saw such big ships as the Gogha, which was more than 1500 tonnes. The European companies started using these ships and opened many new factories to make Indian artisans manufacture ships. In 1811, Lt. Walker writes, "The ships in the British fleet had to be repaired every 12th year. But the Indian ships made of teak would function for more than 50 years without any repair." The East India Company had a ship called Dariya Daulat which worked for 87 years without any repairs. Durable woods like rosewood, sal and teak were used for this purpose.

The French traveler Waltzer Salvins writes in his book *Le Hindu*, in 1811, "Hindus were in the forefront of ship-building and even today they can teach a lesson or two to the Europeans. The British, who were very apt at learning the arts, learnt a lot of things about ship building from the Hindus. There is a very good blend of beauty and utility in Indian ships and they are examples of Indian handicrafts and their patience." Between 1736 and 1863, 300 ships were built at factories in Mumbai. Many of them were included in the Royal Fleet. Of these, the ship called *Asia* was 2289 tonnes and had 84 cannons. Ship building factories were set up in Hoogly, Sihat, Chittagong, Dacca, etc. In the period between 1781 to 1821, in Hoogly alone 272 ships were manufactured which together weighed 122,693 tonnes.

In this connection, Suresh Soni, in his book *India's Glorious Scientific Tradition*, explains how India was deprived of its marine industry, but also from any notation in its ancient history of its ship-building ability. He writes:

"The shipping magnates of Britain could not tolerate the Indian art of ship manufacturing and they started compelling the East India Company not to use Indian ships. Investigations were frequently carried out in this regard. In 1811, Col. Walker gave statistics to prove that it was much cheaper to make Indian ships and that they were very sturdy. If only Indian ships were included in the British fleet, it would lead to great savings. This pinched the British shipbuilders and the traders. Dr. Taylor writes, 'When the Indian ships laden with Indian goods reached the port of London, it created such a panic amongst the British traders as would not have been created, had they seen the enemy fleet of ships on the River Thames, ready for attack.'

"The workers at the London Port were among the first to make hue and cry and said that 'all our work will be ruined and families will starve to death.' The Board of Directors of East India Company wrote that 'all the fear and respect that the Indian seamen had towards European behavior was lost when they saw our social life once they came here. When they return to their country, they will propagate bad things about us amongst the Asians and we will lose our superiority and the effect will be harmful.' At this, the British Parliament set up a committee under the chairmanship of Sir Robert Peel.

"Despite disagreement amongst the members of the committee on the basis of this report, a law was passed in 1814 according to which the Indians lost the right to become British sailors and it became compulsory to employ at least three-fourth British sailors on British ships. No ship, which did not have a British master was allowed to enter London Port and a rule was made that only ships made by the British in England could bring goods to England. For many reasons, there was laxity in enforcing these rules, but from 1863 they were observed strictly. Such rules which would end the ancient art of ship-building, were formulated in India also. Tax on goods brought in Indian ships was raised and efforts were made to isolate them from trade. Sir William Digby has rightly written, 'This way, the Queen of the western world killed the Queen of the eastern oceans.' In short, this is the story about the destruction of the Indian art of ship-building." [13]

Of course, let us not forget that not only was commerce between ancient India and other countries made through maritime capabilities, but also through land routes that extended to China, Turkistan, Persia, Babylon, and also to Egypt, Greece, and Rome, which continued to prosper.

These days, India is still very much in the ship building business, mostly in small and medium size ships. As of 2009 there were 27 major shipyards, primarily in Mumbai, Goa, Vishakhapatnam, and Cochin.

CONCLUSION

In conclusion, the fact is that the ancient Vedic civilization had a strong connection with the sea, and maritime abilities. Even in their language of Vedic Sanskrit, words such as *samudra, salil, sagar,* and *sindhu* indicated the sea or large rivers. The word *sindhuka* also meant sailor, which became the name Sindbad for the sailor in *Arabian Nights*. Also, the English word navigation actually originates from the Sanskrit word *Navagati*.

Further evidence has been shown, such as that presented at a 1994 conference on seafaring in Delhi where papers had been presented that shows how Indian cotton was exported to South and Central America back in 2500 BCE. Another report suggested Indian cotton reached Mexico as far back as 4000 BCE, back to the *Rig Vedic* period. According to Sean McGrail, a marine archeologist at Oxford University, seagoing ships called 'clinkers' that were thought to be of Viking origin, were known in India a good deal earlier. Thus, India's maritime trade actually flourished many years ago, along with many other of its advancements that are hardly recognized or accounted for today. [14]

This helps reveal that India's maritime trade actually flourished more and far earlier than most people realize. Though the talents and capabilities that came out of ancient India's Vedic civilization have often remained unrecognized or even demeaned when discussed. Nonetheless, the Vedic people were far more advanced in culture and developments then many people seem to care to admit, and it is time to recognize it for what it was.

CHAPTER NOTES

1. S. R. Rao, *Shipping in Ancient India*, in *India's Contribution to World Thought and Culture*, Published by Vivekananda Kendra Prakashan, Chennai, 1970, p. 83.
2. K. S. Ramachandran, *Ancient Indian Maritime Adventures*, in *India's Contribution to World Thought and Culture*, Published by Vivekananda Kendra Prakashan, Chennai, 1970, p. 74.
3. *Science and Technology in Ancient India*, by Editorial Board of Vijnan Bharati, Mumbai, August, 2002, p. 105.
4. Ibid., pp. 108-9.

5. Suresh Soni, *India's Glorious Scientific Tradition*, Ocean Books Pvt. Ltd., New Delhi, 2010, p. 68.

6. Ibid., p. 72.

7. Ibid., p. 73.

8. Niranjan Shah, *Little Known Facts About Shipping Activity in Ancient India*, in India Tribune, January 8, 2006.

9. Kamlesh Kapur, *Portraits of a Nation: History of India*, Sterling Publishers, Private Limited, 2010, pp. 414-15.

10. http://www.hindu.com/thehindu/holnus/000200903151560.htm.

11. http://www.ias. ac.in/currsci/ jan252008/ 248.pdf.

12. http://indiannavy.nic.in/maritime_history.htm.

13. Suresh Soni, *India's Glorious Scientific Tradition*, Ocean Books Pvt. Ltd., New Delhi, 2010, p. 74-75.

14. Dr. David Frawley and Dr. Navaratna S. Rajaram, *Hidden Horizons, Unearthing 10,000 Years of Indian Culture*, Swaminarayan Aksharpith, Ahmedabad, India, 2006, p. 79.

A view of the ghats along the Ganga at Dashashvamedha Ghat in Varanasi, one of India's oldest cities, where many river boats are used

CHAPTER FOURTEEN

Earliest Advanced Cities

Naturally, from a civilization that was so developed in all of the ways we have described so far, it would also be expected to have very organized and advanced cities. Indeed, this is the case. And one of the most noteworthy is the city of Dwaraka.

Dwaraka was the ancient city of Lord Krishna, according to the *Puranas*, which many had taken to be a mere myth, until the offshore explorations over the last 50 years proved that it really existed. However, even more recently, as explained by Kamlesh Kapur in, "In the first part of 2002, some divers from the National Institute of Ocean Technology were doing a routine check of the pollution of ocean waters. They took sonar photos. During the study of these photos, it was found that they had accidently stumbled onto the ruins of the city of Dwaraka, some thirty kilometers away from the western coast of India in the Gulf of Khambat (Cambay).

"According to the *Mahabharata*, Dwaraka was swallowed up by the sea a little after the war about 5,000 years ago. It is estimated that the vast city–which is five miles long and two miles wide–most likely predates the oldest known remains in the subcontinent. About 2,000 artifacts were found 40 meters under the ocean. The artifacts were spread over an area of 9 kilometers. There were remains of rectangular buildings, bathing facility, chiseled stone tools, broken pieces of potteries, jewelry, and human jaws and teeth. These artifacts were sent for further study to B. S. Institute of Paleobotany at Lucknow, India and National Geophysical Research Institute at Hyderabad, India. The carbon testing has determined the tentative age of some of these relics as 7500 years. This could be one of the oldest cities known. Some of the fragments of pottery, carved wood, bone and beads have been dated to more than 9,000 years old. Historians watched curiously as the scientists announced the discovery of an ancient metropolis 120 ft. under the sea in the Gulf of Khambat in Northwest India.

"... The time frame of the relics varying by several millennia clearly indicates that there must have been several settlements which were submerged under water besides Dwaraka. Because of this variation, it is also likely that Dwaraka was submerged in the deluge of 3000 BCE. According to Graham Hancock the discovery supports his theory that complex civilizations existed in the Ice Age. These civilizations were wiped out when the ice melted, submerging 15 million square miles of land." [1]

So, this sunken city in the Gulf of Cambay is said to be 9500 years old, making it one of the oldest cities to be found. It is thirty kilometers off the shore of northwestern India, wherein sonar has revealed large walled structures extending up to nine kilometers along the banks of an ancient riverbed. It is now forty meters under water. After dredging up some of the remains, they found over 2,000 artifacts, including stone tools, human bones, and collections of semi-precious stones.

Present day Dwaraka is situated on the mainland north of Mumbai (Bombay) and some distance south of the Indus river. Ancient Dwaraka is described in the Vedic texts as an island city off the coast of India that was very advanced and organized for its time. The *Bhagavata Purana* relates that the outer wall of the huge fortress covered as much as 96 square miles. Within the city were paved roads, gardens, and palatial buildings made of gold with rooms decorated with the finest of gems on the walls and floors. It was the heavenly city where Lord Krishna lived part of the time while on earth. It was also the capital of the Yadu dynasty, said to have had a population of one billion people. It is also recorded that it did sink into the ocean after Krishna departed from the planet about the time of 3100 BCE. This is near the era when the pyramids were supposed to have been built and when Egyptian culture made great progress.

A 3500 year old wall has been discovered not far off the island of Bet Dwaraka in the Gulf of Kutch. It was discovered on December 11, 1987, and belongs to the now sunken city of ancient Dwaraka. This 250 meter long wall runs along the coast and then circles around for another 50 meters. The length of the wall gives an idea of the large dimensions the city must have had. The wall can be seen above the water's surface during low tide, and gets submerged by as much as four meters of water during high tide. Also, artifacts such as seals with post-Harappan inscriptions, pottery, and stone anchors have been discovered in the area.

Due to the fact that the early settlements that are now underwater, such as those off the coast of Gujarat and Tamil Nadu, that date back to 7500 BCE, or even the dock at Lothal, which required a level of science or geometry to produce such architecture, this would indicate that these were ahead of the Mesopotamian civilization and puts doubt on the idea that Mesopotamia was the cradle of civilization.

MOHENJODARO AND HARAPPA

Much more interest and study has been placed on the cities of Mohenjodaro and Harappa. They were considered to be very organized for the age in which they existed, but their discovery did come as quite a surprise to those who found them. We can read in such places as *The First Cities* by Time-Life Books, in which Dora Jane Hamblin and other editors write: "Probably the first 'first city' in which a 20th Century visitor could have found his way around without the aid of a native guide was Mohenjo-Daro. It lay on the flat, hot flood plain of the Indus River, 300 miles north of today's Karachi in Pakistan. It and the other half-dozen other cities of the Indus Valley had already put to use the crisscross gridiron system of street layout–an urban convention long thought to have been invented by the Greeks of a later era."

Also, in *Prehistoric Civilization of the Indus*, Sir John Marshal, who excavated Mohenjodaro explains: "These discoveries establish the existence in Sind and the Punjab, during the fourth and third millennium B.C., of a highly developed city life; and the presence in many of the homes of wells and bathrooms as well as elaborate drainage system, betoken a social condition of the citizens at least equal to that found in Sumer, and superior to that prevailing in contemporary Babylonia and Egypt. Even at Ur, the houses are by no means equal in point of construction to those of Mohenjodaro."

In this way, the discovery of such a highly advanced metropolis was quite a surprise to such archeologists, who had hardly thought that such a civilization would exist in the Indian subcontinent as far back as 3000 to 4000 BCE. Only after their continued excavations when they found

Harappa to be of a similar setup, 400 miles away, did they realize that this was part of a network of rather modern cities of ancient times.

Before this, the impression of most scholars was that Mesopotamia and Greece were the first areas to use the technology of town-planning as they were seeing in the Indus Valley region. The point is that this region had already been using the checkerboard pattern of street layouts in town planning as far back as 6000 years ago, much earlier than Greece or the Middle East. And this requires much sophistication. Mohenjodaro had broad boulevards 30 feet wide, which ran north and south, with cross streets about every 200 yards which were somewhat smaller. The blocks had small curved connecting lanes. The avenues would have shops, businesses and food stands. Streets were often paved and lead from major boulevards to residential alleys. Thus, houses were away and protected from the noise of busy streets. These ancient cities were also known for their drainage systems to enhance an ideal of urban sanitation. The evidence lends to the idea that there was some central civic authority that oversaw its development and use. This would have been one of the first of such arrangements in the history of early civilizations. Each city covered around six or seven miles and could accommodate as many as 20,000 to 50,000 people. This was a large urban population at the time, but something that could be properly managed.

The most noteworthy of all of Mohenjodaro's monuments was the Great Bath. This was a complex brick structure, two stories high, and a triumph of engineering. The bathing pool was sunk into the paving of a courtyard approached from both north and south by flights of brick steps with wooden stair treads set into asphalt. [2]

Harappa was the other most important discovery of the Indus Valley Civilization. Based on the latest findings, we could say that the Harappan civilization was in its prime around the years 3000-2700 BCE. This means these cities were already developed and slowly faded away after the war of Kurukshetra, about 3067 BCE and after the age of Kali-yuga began, February 18, 3021 BCE.

The Indus civilization is one of the oldest of societies in the Asian Subcontinent, and one of the most organized and advanced as well. The ruins of the sites in this area show what is well-organized street layouts and town planning. There were three sections, which included the citadel in the western part of the town, which was for the priestly and the ruling class. To the east were the lower sections of town for farmers and merchants, and then the labor class. Houses were also made in certain patterns with one section for rooms, another for the bullock cart to enter, and a courtyard where the clay ovens were for cooking, and bath made of water-proof bricks. These oven baked and sun-dried bricks, a system that has been used for centuries, were also used for the fire altars, citadels, and the water reservoirs.

Connected with most houses was also the drainage system, made from clay pipes that carried the dirty water to the main sewer line. Stone wells also were used and the cities were made so that fresh water was available for everyone. In some places warehouses were also found, such as at the city of Dholavira. It was also there where the top layers of soil settlement were carbon dated back to 5,000 BCE, which means the town could date back another few thousand years.

Weights and measures had been found in the relics of the Indus-Sarasvati region, which indicates the need for exact calculating for trade, such as in gold, or especially in a variety of grains, including wheat, barley and millet. Cotton was also known to have been cultivated, and rice is known to date back to at least 7,000 years ago.

It is easy to understand the early advanced nature of the Harappan civilization when it took another 2000 years for the Roman Empire to reach the level of town planning and sanitation that had already been existing in the Harappan culture. Then the Lothal harbor, dating back to at least 2500 BCE, also shows engineering skill that requires an advanced level of mathematics for its construction, long before Pythagorus was around. This shows that the Vedic pundits did not wait to get their knowledge of mathematics from the Greeks or Sumerians. Let us remember that the *Shulbasutras*, which Seidenberg has already identified as the source of Greek and Babylonian mathematics, held the basis of mathematics and geometry for building altars and religious architecture that have been found in Harappa. The use of it for town planning was the secular application of such knowledge. This, therefore, was the real cradle of civilization as we know it.

The primary reason why the Indus Valley civilization has been so widely acclaimed is because of its ancient but advanced nature. Not only was it town-based, with city streets and obvious town planning, with residential and administrative quarters well marked out, but it also had granaries for storing grain that was brought in from surrounding areas. Thus, there was a high level of trading going on, and many of the people were also artisans or craftsmen, which indicates a high degree of occupational specialization. Also, buildings were constructed with baked bricks, and there was a well-developed sewage system in place, with an elaborate network of covered drains.

This was graphically described by A. L. Basham in his book *The Wonder That was India* (p. 16) where he says: "The houses had bathrooms, the design of which showed the Harappan, like the modern Indian, preferred to take his bath standing, by pouring pitchers of water over his head. The bathrooms were provided with drains, which flowed to sewers under the main streets, leading to soak pits. The sewers covered throughout their length by large brick slabs. The unique sewerage system of the Indus people must have been maintained by some municipal organization, and is one of the most impressive of their achievements. No other ancient civilization until that of the Romans has so efficient a system of drains."

More than this is that the people of that time had a standardization of weights and measures. The number of uniquely designed square seals with human and animal figures carved on them also seems to indicate that every family of traders had their own seals that allowed for authentication of goods that were traded. These Indus seals seem to indicate how extensive trading was during the day as they have been found all the way into the Persian Gulf and Sumer regions. [3]

An interesting thing about the seals of the Indus Valley is that they have been found all the way in Oman, Mesopotamia and in the Maldives. This would indicate the talents of the people as seafarers and traders over great distances.

From the earliest of excavations, starting in the 1920s of the Harappan and Mohenjodaro sites, archeologists have found that findings, through the carbon dating technique, date back to 3500 BCE.

SIZE OF THE HARAPPAN CIVILIZATION

Besides the most well known of the early cities of Mohenjodaro and Harappa, there is also the city of Mehrgarh in present day Afghanistan that is known to have begun as a small village in 7,000 BCE. Also off the coast from Surat is a large city that has been found that began as far back as 8,000 BCE. In fact, it was reported in Reuters, January 16, 2002, that, "Indian scientists have made an archeological find dating back to 7,500 BC suggesting the world's oldest cities came up about 4,000 years earlier than is currently believed."

The size of the Harappan civilization is known to have been as much as 300,000 square miles, bigger than the size of the state of Texas, with over 2500 sites from various periods that include such places as Lothal, Ganweriwala, Rakhigarhi, Dholavira, and Kalibangan, or even the largest center in the Kurukshetra region, all of which extend from the Himalayas in the north to the Godavari in the south, and from the Indus River valleys in the west, to the plains of the Ganga and Yamuna Rivers in the east. Additional sites have been found to extend it to the Amu Darya river in Afghanistan. [4] Two-thirds of these sites can be found along the Sarasvati River banks or near its delta region close to the Arabian Sea.

In this way, it becomes clear that this Indus Civilization was the most populous and largest of any culture of the third millennium, a huge center of many ideas and forms of knowledge that spread in all directions.

Excavations at Mehrgarh have shown that it dates back to a most early period before 6500 BCE. This places Mehrgarh in the same periods as the early settlements as Catal Huyuk in Anatolia, or Jarmo in Mesopotamia, and Jericho in Palestine. [5]

LOTHAL

Along with sophisticated city planning, some archeologists believe that Lothal, one of the Indus Valley sites, and also a port city, had the first dockyard, something connected with the maritime history of ancient India and the Sarasvati and Indus civilization. It could service boats of a capacity of 60-75 tons and 20-25 meters in length, and up to 20 or more boats. In those days, the people of ancient Gujarat traded with countries that are known today as Iraq, Qatar, Persia, and Egypt.

The brick-laid docks, wharfs, jetties and warehouses provided infrastructure facilities to the inland and maritime trade, while bullock carts provided transportation. This enabled customs officials to service traders in way that allowed for revenues from the imports and exports over waterways from various distances. Thus, we get an administrative setup of considerable sophistication.

Lothal was excavated by the Archeological Survey of India from February 13, 1955 to May 19, 1960. It is the world's earliest known dock connected to the ancient course of the Sabarmati River on the trade route between Harappan cities in Sindh and the Saurashtra peninsula when the Kutch desert of today was part of the Arabian Sea. So it was a thriving trade center in ancient times, trading in beads, gems and valuable ornaments from the far corners of West Asia and Africa. The beads and gems from Lothal were in great demand in the West. It also had a rich cotton and rice growing environment. To this day you can see some of its remnants that still provide a large collection of antiques in the archeology of India. The discovery of beads, semi-precious stones and copper objects attest to a prosperous economy in its day. A new technique of firing pottery under partly-oxidising and reducing conditions was improved by them, which became designated as black and red ware. Its scientists also used a shell compass and divided the horizon and sky into 8-12 whole parts, possibly pioneering the study of stars and navigation 2000 years before the Greeks. [6]

DISAPPEARANCE OF THE INDUS VALLEY CIVILIZATION

How the Indus Valley civilization disappeared had been in question for many years. Some have suggested that it was from wars with invading tribes, thus contributing to what has been called the Aryan Invasion. However, this theory has lost so much credibility over the years that few researchers accept it any longer. As many as 325 skeletons have been found and examined by anthropologists. They concluded that the skeletons do not belong to any of the postulated racial types such as Mongoloid, Nordics or Mediterranean. It has been explained that the cephalic index shows that the skeletons found in Mohenjodaro are like those of modern residents of Sindh, and those in Lothal are like modern residents of Gujarat. Thus, this leads to indicate there was no invasion nor war that killed off the residents at that time.

Furthermore, Prof. Kennedy of Cornell University, a renowned anthropologist, closely studied the same skeletons of those who are said to have been killed by weapons of invaders and has shown that none of them bear the marks of injury from any kind of weapon. Thus, there was some other cause besides an invasion for the disappearance of the Indus Valley civilization, or reason why they abandoned the area. [7]

In conclusion of all the research that has been done, along with the finding on the Sarasvati River, it is clear that, as stated in *Pride of India*: "The Indus Valley Civilization did not come to an end by an alien invasion, but it relocated itself. The drying up of the river was the natural cause for the decline and the demise of the Harappan civilization. The 'abrupt end to the civilization' theory in fact has come to an abrupt end and the invaders from Central Asia invented to fill this gap no longer have a role to play. In one stroke, scores of books on Indian history have become, to put it mildly, obsolete, and to put it plainly, wrong, as to the pre-historic period of Indian history. Therefore, 3500 BCE, the date of the Harappan finds, marks not the beginning of the 'Aryan Civilization' but the point of maturity of the Harappan Civilization." [8]

CHAPTER NOTES

1. Kamlesh Kapur, *Portraits of a Nation: History of India*, Sterling Publishers, Private Limited, 2010, pp. 85-6.

2. Niranjan Shah, *Gujarat Built World's First Naval Dockyard*, from India Tribune, May 8, 2010.

3. *Pride of India: A Glimpse into India's Scientific Heritage*, Samskriti Bharati, New Delhi, 2006, p. 75.

4. Georg Feuerstein, Subhash Kak & David Frawley, *In Search of the Cradle of Civilization*, by Quest Books, Wheaton, IL, 1995, p. 62.

5. Ibid., p. 144.

6. Niranjan Shah, *Gujarat Built World's First Naval Dockyard*, in India Tribune, May 8, 2010.

7. *Pride of India: A Glimpse into India's Scientific Heritage*, Samskriti Bharati, New Delhi, 2006, p. 78.

8. Ibid., p. 81.

CHAPTER FIFTEEN

India's Early Educational System and Universities

For the most part, India's early educational system was village based. It was the local rishis and Brahmanas who would teach the local students or seekers who were eligible. The place of education was called the *gurukula*, or place of the guru. The rishis who imparted knowledge utilized methods whereby the knowledge could be transmitted and remembered by the students who were qualified. The rishi teachers were like the father of the students, affectionate but effective, and of high moral and spiritual standards. By the respect the students had for him, he maintained authority. Yet, he would be sincere, honest, and true to both his work and to the students. However, he also followed the same serious disciplines that molded his own character and honor that the students would show him.

The first basis of the school was to mold young pupils into capable individuals who would be well aware of the principles of Vedic *Dharma*, the foundation for being honorable and respectable people. It was to build the character of the student, along with the physical, moral, intellectual, and spiritual potentials. As the student would study under the direction of the guru or teacher, he would also realize all of this knowledge through his own contemplation and insight. This is what enabled the knowledge to travel from one generation to the next. But this is also what enabled the student to acquire his own perfection and freedom, up to final liberation.

The Dharmic principles of education meant that everyone would act in harmony and peace with everything else, not only animate but inanimate things as well. In this way, the student imbibes a set a values, both cultivated and realized, that sustains the creation, sustains himself, and threatens no one. Plus, he can easily maintain himself, and live in harmony

165

with the world, and reach the ultimate purpose of human existence at the same time. Such a degree of sophisticated education was hardly found anywhere else.

So the main topic was *Atmavidya*, or knowledge of the self, after which all other topics could be easily mastered. After this came knowledge that included science, arts and crafts, music, math such as geometry and algebra, along with astronomy or Jyotish, logic, history, poetry, grammar, and knowledge of the Vedic texts.

Additional topics of education are further described by Kamlesh Kapur: "There were Gurukulas, Mathas and Ghatikkas offering educational facilities to the common people. In these schools and institutes, a variety of subjects were taught: languages, Sanskrit literature, grammar, mathematics, sciences, architecture, astronomy, political science, and administration were some of the subjects taught. Many schools trained soldiers in wielding weapons and training horses and elephants. Various occupational guilds were responsible for providing vocational training on an apprenticeship basis. Many craftsmen, artisans, architects, masons, sculptors, painters, stone cutters, carpenters, weavers, ship builders, scribes, and smiths were trained by their guilds. For their times, Southern Indian societies were well-organized and their economies were prosperous and well regulated." [1]

Techniques for passing the knowledge to the students included teaching and lecturing, recitation, dialogue, and then self-study.

"Thus, the main aim of the Vedic educational system was to produce a rational individual, free from passions, full of universal affection, continuously self-educating and striving to reach the highest goal. His rationalism, his attitude of universal love, his entire personality had their roots in experience. His learning must reveal itself through his thought, word and deed. He must cheerfully fulfill his obligations to his family, village, and country. [2] The ancient Indian system aimed at providing the student, in addition to a high degree of intellectual training, with the spiritual and ethical strength so that he would grow to be a full man." [3]

The most important purpose of education in ancient Bharatvarsha was for attaining liberation. However, that did not mean the neglect of the necessary crafts or skills needed for life, which were naturally handed down from generation to generation. But the most valued knowledge was that established by the *Vedas* for spiritual advancement. With what was established by the *Vedas*, the ancient education was more developed with guidance from the *Upanishads*, which made it more thoughtful or introverted and contemplative. Furthermore, such education was to provide emphasis on character building, learning good habits, following a proper daily routine by getting up early, performing daily rituals, and of course observing the basic moral standards like speaking the truth and living simply.

Vedic education was not limited to the spiritual aspect of life, but also would provide the means for self-reliance, self-control, individual development, knowledge of both civil and social life, physical development, along with preservation of cultural and national ideals.

For many years the tradition was based on oral teachings rather than the written word. This was partly because the education was determined by realization, not merely memorization, and sound had its own potency for invoking the energy of the knowledge it was describing in the vibration of the words. In this way, students were given verbal lessons upon which they would meditate and study, and learn and memorize them.

In the Vedic tradition, knowledge could be imparted or gained by three basic steps, which included hearing (*shravana*), meditation (*manan*) and realization (*nididhyasan*). However, hearing is divided into six categories, namely;

1. A formal ritual before studying the Vedic knowledge, or *upakrama*,
2. Recitation, or *abhyasa*,
3. An easy grasp of the knowledge, or *apurvata*,
4. Comprehending the goal, *phala*,
5. Reading of explanatory books, *arthavada*,
6. Reaching the full result or conclusion, *upapatti*.

At that time, there were three basic ways of education, which were: the *gurukula*, or the home and school of the guru; the *parishad* or an institution with several teachers; and the *sammelan*, a special conference by scholars who gathered for a specific purpose. These were all outside any external influence or control of the state or agency that dictated what the curriculum should be. The topics were determined completely by the rishis themselves to keep the education from any bias or leanings of any outside interests. [4]

To elaborate further, student life, called *brahmacharya* for the boys, was also based on discipline as outlined in the Vedic texts, with a systematic and organized lifestyle. This was meant for providing real education and culture for the development of all humanity. Students or disciples of the guru-teacher would perform duties or service to the teacher in exchange for the free education and food while staying under the shelter of the teacher. This may include helping clean and upkeep the ashrama, help graze the cows, go out for alms, or assist in rituals. However, the primary duty of the student was to study and learn.

Vedic education, contrary to what some believe, was available and free to everyone, regardless of caste or *varna*. Education for women generally had a different curriculum, such as learning handicrafts and household duties, but in the Vedic age they could still receive what they needed to become Rishikas, and be knowledgeable in Vedic spiritual wisdom and participate in Vedic rituals as well.

After the education is completed, the guru or teacher would provide the final instructions while the students would leave usually to enter householder life. Therefore, the teacher would give the final instructions that could make the student's family life useful and successful in every way. As explained in *History of Education in India*, the instructions would include:

"Always speak the truth, fulfill your duties, never ignore self-study. Do not break the ancestral and old traditions after giving *dakshina* (donations) to the *acharya*. Never go away from truth. Never leave *Dharma*. Do not ignore the useful works [or actions]. Do not miss the opportunity of becoming great. Never be careless in duties towards God and forefathers.

"Treat mother as Goddess, treat father as God. Treat the *acharya* (Teacher) as God (*Deva*). Treat the guest (*athithi*) as God (*Deva*). Always perform deeds free from faults. Imitate the good deeds that have been done and not others... Whatever gift you give, give it with full regard and respect and with pleasure and humility...

"If any doubt arises in your mind regarding religion or good conduct, then take advice from the Brahmanas, who are dispassionate, noble, and tender hearted, and fit the purpose and follow as they do. This is my instruction to you, you follow it." [5]

This shows some of the first systematized forms of higher education that had been known in human society in general. This assured everyone of an equal opportunity to use life in the best way possible for character building and community strengthening. This type of education went on for many years. Only later did the Vedic values begin to fade at which time people were given a more rigid class or caste orientation based on ancestral basis which carried over to occupational classifications. This also then made for the same kind of classifications on educational opportunities.

It was not only the schools or gurukulas that were the basis of education. Temples, however, also were known as cultural and educational centers for secular as well as spiritual knowledge. Donations to the temples were not only for the continued worship, but was for cultural preservation and education and care for the students, such as food and lodging. In the temples, students often would study only certain branches or one branch of the Vedic knowledge. Which branch or how many branches of the *Vedas* that were taught also depended on which area of the country the student lived. That is why names such as Dvivedi (for mastering two branches of the *Vedas*) or Trivedi (mastering three branches of the *Vedas*) would be given.

When it came to universities, kings would participate by giving donations of land and funds and general expenses for the continuation of the university. Thus government aid was not uncommon.

IMPORTANCE OF DHARMIC EDUCATION TODAY

Whenever I travel around India, I am often asked what to do about all of the corruption found in the country. I always answered that the best thing that I know of is to continue to teach the ethical and moralistic standards as found in Vedic *Dharma*. Fortunately for me, this was reaffirmed while I was in Bangalore in 2010 with my visit with the eminent M. Rama Jois, the retired Chief Justice of the Punjab and Haryana High Court. He told me that this was indeed the best way to relieve the country of all the corruption that we see, but he explained the best means to do that.

M. Rama Jois told me that before the independence of India in 1947, there used to be government pre-schools where the children would go to learn, not necessarily how to read and write, but about the basic rules of *Dharma*. Then the children would also hear of the examples of *Dharma* from the great epics, like the *Mahabharata* and *Ramayana* or *Puranas*, and about those great heroes who acted in various situations under the rules of *Dharma*. This way, before the children ever went to general school to learn reading and writing, etc., they were already educated in the proper content of character to know how to act as a proper human being, and know how to judge what is right or wrong in the various situations of life.

Unfortunately, it was after 1947 when the new administration of independent India decided that learning the ethics of *Dharma* was religious study, and that the new secular government could no longer support such pre-schools. Thus, all such education of basic moralistic principles under *Dharma* were no longer to be taught in the schools of India. And since that time, the materialistic selfishness, greed, and the insensitivity to the situation of others for the benefit of oneself, have all increased to the point where now it is found in almost all aspects of life.

As M. Rama Jois explains in his book *Dharma: The Global Ethic*, "All our present day problems are a direct result of disregarding *Dharma*, under the influence of a materialistic philosophy, in the belief that it alone can usher in happiness and secure the welfare of the people. Now it is becoming clear that human problems increase as we go on multiplying our lust and desire for material wealth and pleasure, and that the solution to all the problems, whether they be social, economic or political, and in particular the crash of our moral edifice which the world and our nation are facing, is *Dharma* alone. There is no alternative to *Dharma*. This is the eternal truth. This can be realized if we understand the real meaning of *Dharma*."

So, what is Dharma? I have already written more extensively about this, but to put it simply, the *Mahabharata* (Shanti Parva, 109.9-11) says: "*Dharma* has been explained to be that which helps the upliftment of living beings. Therefore, that which ensures the welfare of living beings is surely *Dharma*. The learned rishis have declared that which sustains is *Dharma*."

A little more clarity can also be provided by Madhavacharya, a Minister to Hakka and Bukka, founders of the Vijayanagar Empire, in his commentary on the *Parashara Smriti*: "*Dharma* is that which sustains and ensures progress and welfare of all in this world and eternal bliss in the next world. *Dharma* is promulgated in the form of commands (rules both positive and negative, Vidhi and Nishedha)."

The *Mahabharata* (Shanti Parva, 90.3) also says that, "The proper function of the king [or any ruler or politician] is to rule according to *Dharma* and not to enjoy the luxuries of life." Thus, a politician is not meant to take advantage of his position, but to execute his duties with the welfare of the people in mind, under the guidance of the rules of *Dharma*.

This means that *Dharma* is not the teaching of a religion, but it is the global ethical standard that we all need to learn. It is the very content that forms good character, proper intentions, the means for making fair and just decisions, and good and effective plans for our future.

The basic rules of *Dharma*, as explained in the *Manu-samhita* (10.63) are: "*Ahimsa* (non-violence), *Satya* (truthfulness), *Asteya* (not acquiring illegitimate wealth), *Shoucham* (purity), and *Indriyanigraha* (control of the senses) are, in brief, the common rules of *Dharma* for all classes of men."

These are the *Yamas* and *Niyamas*, which also includes *Santosha*–satisfaction or contentment of mind with what one has without undue endeavor; *Tapas*–voluntary austerity and tolerance in body, mind, and speech for a higher cause; *Swadhyaya*–self-analysis, introspection, scriptural research, and reflection to understand and perceive who and what is our real identity and how we are progressing; *Ishwara-pranidhana*–acceptance, devotion, and surrender to God, or the offering of the fruits of one's actions to God; and *Brahmacharya*–following the eternal principle of Brahma, or the control of sensual passions in thought, word, and deed, particularly in the student stage of life.

Therefore, by learning these rules, how to apply them in all aspects of life, and by hearing the examples of the great souls in India's history and great epics, a child would develop and build his character to be a truly strong, balanced and properly motivated individual who can continue to develop him or herself, and be a true contribution to the rest of society. When this kind of training is received at a young age, it can last for one's whole life. This is what makes a difference in all aspects of society.

Training in *Dharma*, which is certainly at the heart of India's Vedic tradition, can help provide for an orderly society. And an orderly society is the result and an expansion or even incarnation of *Dharma*.

This leads us to understand that the real happiness and prosperity of any nation is directly proportional to the number of men of character it has produced. This is why it is in the interest of the state or government to supply the means by which all children can understand these principles through appropriate education.

Being trained in and understanding the principles of *Dharma* do not mean this is promoting a particular religion. It can still be considered secular training, and not going against the Indian constitution. The *Yamas* and *Niyamas*, or the codes of *Dharma*, are basic moralistic principles. Religion means a mode of worship of God by believers of a particular faith, and calling God by a certain name, or using a particular book and set of rituals. Religion often divides or separates by its distinguishing characteristics between them, while *Dharma* unites by its unified code of conduct and seeing everyone equally. *Dharma* can be applied to all human beings. Thus, it sustains and harmonizes society, it does not create conflict. After all, regardless of whatever our theological beliefs may be, we can all agree on the need for kindness and honesty, self-control, compassion, and respect for one another, and the need for fellowship in society to maintain harmony and cooperation, and the ways to establish these things. And the education in the Dharmic principles, as in the *Yamas* and *Niyamas*, are merely codes of conduct to follow that will help everyone develop this content to their character. Therefore, it is this education that again needs to be offered and supplied to young students in India and elsewhere.

* * *

In summary, education in the Vedic sense means to establish and enliven the spiritual consciousness. It does not mean only learning a technology or a craft, or way to exist. It means to raise the total quality of the individual by raising the consciousness. This adds to the well-being of the whole society.

The ultimate means to accomplish this is to raise the person and society to understand and then attain spiritual consciousness. This is the inner experience of Vedic knowledge and the path of spiritual awakening. Then comes the next stage of direct spiritual perception. This is really the goal of life. It is not religious life, such as in following a dogma, but it is spiritual, the natural way of personal development to perceive the higher reality. It is not merely to live to work, and work to pave the way for one's existence. But it is a matter of enlivening the individual and society by recognizing one's real identity and how to live and relate according to that spiritual identity, and, thus, attain something that is far greater than whatever can be accomplished merely within this material existence in the limited situation in which we find ourselves.

THE EARLY UNIVERSITIES

One of the important aspects of education of the civilization at the time was its universities, which included the system of *gurukulas* and *mathas*. The most distinguished establishments included Takshashila, Nalanda, Vikramshila, Navadvipa, Kashi, Kanchi, Vallabhi, Gunasheela, Jagaddal, Mithila, Odantapura, and Ratnagiri.

Nalanda University, for example, was one of the prime educational facilities of the time, which flourished almost 800 years, from 500 to 1300 CE. It was maintained by the revenue from seven villages granted by the king for that purpose. You can still see some of the remnants of its structures today in the present state of Bihar.

Nalanda University is said to have had as many as 10,000 students and about 1500 teachers. Nalanda was but a small village in the beginning, but became a flourishing city and a Buddhist learning center. Lord Buddha gave many lectures here while staying in the Pravarik forest, and also in Rajgir. The Nalanda Vihara was established by Emperor Ashok, who also built a Sangharan for Buddhist nuns. It only became known as a university after the 3rd century CE. During that time, around 300 to 330 CE, Nagarjuna also studied there.

Some scholars feel that by 410 CE it became the center of Brahminical learning rather than Buddhist. By the time the Chinese traveler Huen Tsang arrived, it had become an important place for learning. It was known to teach Vedanta, Sankhya, Jyotish, Ayurveda, yoga, nyaya, various philosophies, along with physical education. It was known to have as many as 1510 teachers at that time. By the 7th century it had about 7,000 students, and 200 villages attached to the university. [6]

Kamlesh Kapur describes it more fully: "Nalanda University had a campus one mile in length and a half mile in width. There was a huge library called Dharma Gunj (mountain of knowledge). It had three wings–bearing the names Ratna-Sagara, Ratna-Nidhi and Ratna-Ranjana. One of these was nine stories high. Nalanda was graced by the presence of India's most brilliant philosophers–Hindu and Buddhist. Some of them were Nagarjuna, Aryadeva, Dharmapala, Silabhadra, Santarakshita, Kamalaseela, Bhaviveka, Dignaga, Dharmakirty, etc. The works they left behind are mostly available through Tibetan and Chinese translations. Xuanzang (Hiuen-Tsang) was a student at Nalanda. He subsequently became a teacher at this ancient university (Mahavihara). In his writings, he has given a vivid account of the life at this great center of learning in the 7th century A.D. Students from the foreign lands such as Tibet, China, Japan, Korea, Sumatra, Java, and Sri Lanka came here for higher learning. . . This was a residential university. The original manuscripts perished when the Muslim invaders under Bakhtiar Khilji set fire to Nalanda and beheaded the monks in 1037 A.D." [7] It is said that the library, with its thousands of manuscripts of knowledge, burnt for weeks.

Another of the first major universities was Takshashila (Taxila) around 800-540 BCE, which was in the northwest corner of the subcontinent, or now Rawalpindi, Pakistan. It provided a wide variety of subjects. It held conferences on medicine and attracted scholars of the day from as far away as Babylon, Syria, Arabia, Phoenicia, China, and Persia. Unfortunately, it had to withstand numerous attacks from Persians, Greeks, Parthians, Shakas, Kushans, and was ultimately razed to the ground by the Huns from Central Asia in 450 CE.

Of all the educational centers in ancient India, Takshashila was the most important. It had a great reputation throughout India and beyond. It attracted hundreds of scholars from such diverse places as Kashi, Rajgir, and Mithila, and also lured thousands of students to study there. According to the Valmiki *Ramayana*, Prince Bharat founded this city and then appointed his son Taksha as the ruler of the territory, after whom the city is named. Takshashila was the capital of Gandhar, 20 miles west of what is now Rawalpindi. It became the main center of learning and Brahminical culture. It was still quite famous up to the time of Alexander.

Unfortunately, due to its location it also was subject to many foreign invasions and disasters. Finally, it was conquered by the Persians in the 6th century BCE and by the Greeks, then the Sakas in the 2nd century BCE, then the Kushans in the 1st century BCE, and the Huns in the 5th century CE. The city was destroyed and rebuilt many times, but remained a cultural center that was influenced by these various cultures. [8]

THE LOSS OF GREAT VEDIC TEXTS AND
THE ATTACKS ON THE UNIVERSITIES

It is a shame that due to religious bias, when the Muslims invaded India with sword and fire in the 11th century, they attacked the ancient storehouses of knowledge, the universities, and aimed at burning all of the libraries that held the most valuable books of antiquity. This is one reason why today we do not have all of the Vedic texts, or the complete forms of some of them, as we could have. Had not this attack and destruction of the great libraries of the world not taken place, we would still have many of the original manuscripts that would have not only told of the world history, but would have revealed many things that today remain mysteries of the past.

Then after the destruction left by the Muslims, there came the oppression of the British and Portuguese colonial rule. It was the Christian missionaries of all denominations who were united in their attempts to destroy as many Vedic books as possible. Every Vedic text that was found was consigned to the flames, or were taken by the British in their attempt to monopolize the publishing of all such manuscripts. Thus, they could manipulate them in ways to try to make Indian natives feel less attracted or less trusting of their own culture.

Thankfully, there had been numerous copies of such Vedic texts that had been made so that many portions of the main manuscripts remain intact for the continuation of the culture and contemplation of the philosophy for which the tradition is known.

CHAPTER NOTES
1. Kamlesh Kapur, *Portraits of a Nation: History of Ancient India,* Sterling Publishers, Private Limited, 2010, pp. 627-8.
2. Chitambara Kulkarni, *Vedic Foundations of Indian Culture*, p. 119.
3. Ibid., p. 114.
4. R. N. Sharma & R. K. Sharma, *History of Education in India*, Atlantic Publishers and Distributors, New Delhi, 2004, p. 2.
5. Ibid., p. 17.
6. Ibid., p. 56.
7. Kamlesh Kapur, *Portraits of a Nations: History of India*, Sterling Publishers, Private Limited, 2010, p. 398.
8. R. N. Sharma & R. K. Sharma, *History of Education in India*, Atlantic Publishers and Distributors, New Delhi, 2004, pp. 54-5.

CHAPTER SIXTEEN

Principles of Vedic Economics

After one's education in the Vedic system, he or she would be an effective part of the wholesome system of economics in society. This was primarily a local, village-based economy. But also the higher vision and first principle of Vedic understanding is that we see everything as the energy of the Supreme Being. If we can see the Divine in all of life, meaning in all beings, we must understand that there is a way of conducting business between each other that upholds and advances our perception of this. Conducting business or managing economics in a way that deliberately cheats or exploits others will harden our hearts and our sensitivity so that we become unable to perceive the Divine in all living beings and even in ourselves. Otherwise, if we see another person as only another object to exploit for our own benefit, then such a negative attitude and consciousness will only reflect back on us like a dark cancer waiting to infect us with our own just deserts. And if this spreads throughout society, the pitfalls also become rampant.

The point is there must be integrity in all transactions and business relations. If we use the above mentioned principle, then by seeing the Divine in all living beings we must realize we are not merely doing business with another person, but we are also doing business with the Divine within that person. This means that the Supreme is also observing our every act, not only from within us but from within the person with whom we are dealing. If the relationship has integrity, then that is fine. We will continue in our spiritual development even while doing our business. But if there is dishonesty and cheating in our involvement, then the quick profits we make will only pave our way downward. This will not be helpful. So we must conduct ourselves, even in business, with the foundation of the Dharmic principles.

These days we have easily seen that companies with power may produce various foods, drugs, beverages or devices that are said to be of great benefit or are healthy for us, or help us solve our problems with no side effects or unexpected problems. Yet time and time again we learn that different kinds of products have indeed been pushed on the public that have caused harmful side effects, much to the dismay, suffering and frustration of the people. The company or even our government may deny any such possibility of injury. However, you must always bear in mind that a story presented as factual from an entity or company whose purpose is power, control or profits is often a story not to be trusted. This was meant to be avoided in a truly Vedic society.

For example, in today's world, the use of paper currency, which only represents a value rather than being a tangible item like gold or silver coins, may be convenient to the user. But those in positions to set the value on such currency can also more easily manipulate it. This creates abstractions in the link between the paper representation and the actual gold it is supposed to be representing. At other times the combined confidence that people and governments place in a currency may fluctuate greatly, making it especially vulnerable to times of political upheaval or war. Such currency can then become completely worthless.

The fluctuating character of this type of currency also helps separate society from nature. Nature requires balance in the environment to operate properly, while currency that only represents what is supposed to have tangible value is more easily tampered and takes us away from such balance. It is the adjustments in currency and interest values which often create stressful fluctuations for the ordinary consumers and for the general mass of people. People who are most implicated in these fluctuations are less likely to advance economically as those who are in positions to claim profits from the same adjustments or manipulations in the markets and economy. This is the difference between those involved in the global monopoly game, which is artificially propped up, and those that depend on real value, such as the gold standard or genuine real estate values.

In this way, the lack of true gold-standard currency is based on falsehood because the currency does not accurately represent the reserved gold. Or it is disconnected from any standard at all and becomes fiat money, which is fake money. Because the money value is inflated, prices on commodities rise. The only way to reduce inflation and have an honest currency is to use that which has intrinsic value, such as when trading something of equal value as in bartering or using real currency like gold and silver coins. That is an honest system.

Real prosperity flourishes on the natural gifts of nature, or God's gifts to us. Villages and towns and their local economy will flourish when there is plenty of grains, vegetables, herbs, trees full of fruits, rivers flowing with fresh and clean water, and hills full of minerals. When this is the situation, there will be plenty for everyone. If society has sufficient natural resources in this way, then why should it endeavor for huge industrial complexes that require the labor of numerous men by sending them into dark factories where they spend their lives in exchange for inflated dollars, and then have to pay a sizable portion of their earnings for government taxes?

Industry produces so many items that are in demand only because of the advertising they show to convince people that they need to purchase the item in order to be happy. Essentially, the more society depends on artificial necessities, the more vulnerable it becomes to artificial crises. Thus, civilization suffers and the economy slows whenever there is fear of the economic state of things, or when there is not enough oil, gas, electricity, or when the prices of such modern commodities become too high. When there is a loss of oil, gas, and other such necessities, or when there is an electrical blackout, so many activities are forced to stop. But these are only recent conditions of the past 100 years or so. These are not natural vulnerabilities. Plus, so many machines and appliances are but recent inventions, but now we have become so dependent on them that without them we think we can no longer function. Thus, people become trapped ever more deeply in the struggle to earn more money to buy more things that they are convinced they require to live happily and comfortably. In this way, they are tied and enslaved to a system whose goal is profits rather than really benefitting society or living in a balanced and wholesome economy. In such a system, humanity loses its sensitivity for their finer intellectual development and has no time and no taste for any spiritual pursuits, except possibly for the most elementary levels of moral standards.

Today's economic system is a means of keeping you under control, preoccupied by the bills you have to pay. This is an old system of stifling people's ability to make choices, sometimes against the present establishment, policies, or whatever it might be. It limits your ability to choose options of various lifestyles or alternative ways of doing things. It limits your field of possibilities. How? By forcing you to confine yourself to a system wherein you work for the almighty dollar to pay for the basic necessities of life. And you often are usually forced to do this by working for the profit of others in whatever business or industry that will hire you. And even if you are your own boss or a professional like a doctor or lawyer, you still have to be licensed and work within the system under the fear of losing your license if you do not cooperate or act as they expect. In other words, the time you have to think about and engage in alternative lifestyles, higher levels of philosophical thought, alternative forms of government, or spiritual practice, is quite limited when you have to make sure you have the money to pay for everything you need to exist. And these may include money for the payments on your mortgage or rent, your phone bill, your heat, your food, your tax payments, your car payments, property and health insurance for the unexpected, your children's care and education, your business license, and your electricity so that after a long and hard day at work when you want to simply come home and rest, you can do so with some pleasant or even brainless entertainment on your television. That can add up to a lot of money that you need to earn just to live.

Then, by plugging into the media, like television, that becomes the trigger in your mind for the kind of material desires that you wish to achieve. What you see on television and other forms of media then becomes the motivator for your preoccupation for the standards and desires for what are often unnecessary needs and wants you feel you cannot live without. Then you are psychologically locked into the present modern economical system, working mostly for someone else's profits, while getting a few things that make you feel you are accomplishing something. Yes, sir, you are trapped for your whole life without the time and means to change your participation in the system. Anyway, that is how it works for most people in the world today. That is called the middle class, or consumer class. While the poorer class cannot even do what has just been described.

For so many people, once they have a job that allows them to pay all of their bills and keep some apparent balance in their life, they do not want to change. They are afraid of change. They want to make sure they can continue with what they have and do not lose anything. It is the path of so-called security... which often leads to stagnation rather than to one's higher potential. This is what leads to the repetitious pattern that is often called "making a living but hardly living." Or it is having a JOB—Just Over Broke. But that is the nature of today's economic system for most people.

In this kind of economic system, it gives people opportunity for little else than the struggle to survive. This is why many people have to have two or even three jobs just to get by, under the fear that unless they have enough money to make all the payments they need to make, they may lose their house, or apartment, or car, or something else. There is an abundance of stress and anxiety in this kind of lifestyle, and some people begin to act in desperate ways, which leads to a rise in crime. It also keeps people away from attaining their spiritual potential, and society then becomes more godless and chaotic, misguided by leaders who either do not know what they are doing, or who purposefully keep people stifled by design. This is not the purpose of human existence.

The point is, as I previously mentioned, the more dependent you become to artificial necessities, the more vulnerable you become to artificial crisis, which is the basis of what we have today. Let's refer to one example, and that is years ago everything went on without the fiat money system that we have today. As it is now, the fiat money, which is not based on anything truly tangible, is falsely propped up until it cannot go on, like the pyramid scheme that it is, and then the media makes everyone think that everything will collapse without more centralization, more bank bail outs, and more financial contributions from participating countries to keep things afloat, based on the taxes that are forced out of the citizens to meet these debts and bail outs. Is this real? No, it is all fake. And that's the only thing that will fail, that which is fake, that which is false. Everything else will continue. But this is the system that keeps you slaves to your limited choices, and to the elite, those far above the middle classes who seem to make the decisions. Until the present system does collapse or change, and we can put something else in its place, we remain the slaves of those who keep this system going.

The Vedic system, however, was for freeing people from this repetitive cycle of working for few rewards and unnecessary requirements. It was to free you to work for your main necessities while still having the time and energy to reach your higher potentials through contemplation and inquiry and spiritual development, without being forced to work for the profits of someone else.

In the natural form of economy, which is the purpose of the Vedic system, the basic principle of economic development is land and its produce. Whoever controls land controls food. Whosoever controls food and fuel controls the world. This is why land should always be in the hands of local farmers, so everything is shared and all people can prosper. Once large industrial or national complexes take it, such large tracts of land are no longer in the hands of a local economy, but are controlled by large companies who have their own globalist concerns and plans for their own proceeds. Then land becomes another element to manipulate profits, resources, people, and even other communities and global markets. History has also shown that such companies are often connected with crooked politicians, or their networks that want more and more power.

However, by developing the land properly for vegetable and grain production, society can solve its eating problems. By producing enough cotton, wood, minerals, and additional resources from the land, humanity can work out its economic problems without depending on an artificial economic or political system.

Those who do become wealthy by honest means can more easily acknowledge his or her opulence as gifts from God. Thus, one's business, if done morally, can be a way of invoking the principle of *Dharma*. Such gifts or blessings also come in the form of one's own intelligence and ingenuity for devising wholesome ideas and needed products for the benefit of others, and from which one's business will expand. Thus, without the blessings of God in every way, we cannot progress or be happy. All things, from wealth, health, good birth, beauty, good education, etc., are all examples of gifts from God. Therefore, we all must acknowledge our gratefulness, especially those who have become more successful. When a family or society offers such acknowledgment, their success and happiness can increase in a balanced and moral way.

In conclusion to this line of thinking, we must recognize that one of the greatest forms of pollution in this world is that of competition-- competition for position, power and money. It is natural to work at devising better ways of doing business and producing more effective products. Whoever has what is best will more likely succeed. But competition based on envy, jealousy, and deviousness, or simply for more money, makes individuals and companies resort to dishonorable means to get ahead, to get more market share, more customers, and ways of making products more cheaply. This also adds to social stress by forcing people to increasingly think in terms of growing profits and income, and lowering expenses in any way possible. This takes away from the peace in the world, and often adds to the pollution in the environment by using resources in less eco-friendly ways.

Because we have forgotten our true spiritual nature, our real identity, we are stressed and crying over small and unimportant problems that have little to do with our real identity as spiritual beings. Because such difficulties are not connected to who we really are, they actually have little relevancy to our spiritual nature. But because we are so attached to our temporary and bodily identity, we are affected so much by these ephemeral and superficial troubles. This is not how we are meant to proceed through life. We should not get entangled in such a way in this illusion. It wastes our time and distracts us from the things that matter most.

We may have made so much technological progress and have numerous facilities added to our comforts of life, yet we can still see so many people suffering in this world. This is primarily because money, and people who are greedy for money, rule the world. Not everyone is cruel, but who cannot see how the misery of many people in this world is caused by the greediness of others? The corrupt politicians and rulers in various countries have created so much trouble that most all of the torment of people who are poor, starving, or even being slaughtered or tortured as political prisoners, or enslaved into prostitution to do the wicked bidding of others, has been due to the unending selfishness and greed for money and power. Do you think this is the way of a truly progressive world? We can plainly see that it is increasingly becoming more godless and thus more hellish. If this trend continues, society will lose its moral values and respect for life. People will become progressively more desperate and the world ever more lost.

A new influence must rise to purify this world from the rulership of money, dirty politics, and a false and misguided economic system. We must feel the influence of spiritual knowledge, for only then can society know what is real peace and happiness, and live together cooperatively. It is knowledge and awareness of our spiritual identity and our connection with the Supreme Spirit that will fill our hearts with the deep inner peace and contentment that we are looking for. If we can progress in this way, our own happiness and peace can spread to others. That is how we can become the peacemakers and help fill society with the tranquility of such self-sufficient happiness and contentment. Then our only concern will be how to relieve the suffering of others. The more people who reach this state of consciousness, the more society will be beautiful and the world will be wonderful. This was the purpose of the Vedic system. Then the tendency for war and the manipulation over others because of greed for money and power will cease, and the world will live in peace. We have to be strong enough to make such a change, and then put to use the principles of Vedic *Dharma* to create a balanced and spiritually uplifted society.

CHAPTER SEVENTEEN

Principles of Vedic Environmentalism

Some of the first means and activities for protecting the environment, whether through systems of water preservation, the development of rivers and canals, and for maintaining land and forests through systems of agriculture, have been recorded in ancient India. But this came about from the Vedic understanding of the purpose and usage of the environment.

The environment means nature, and whose nature is it? It is God's nature. Did anyone else create it? Did anyone else put it all together so that it operates the way it does? In fact, mankind is still trying to figure out all the intricacies of its functionality.

In all the inventions or devices we produce, all the ingredients and resources that we use are all given by God. The elements we need to make big buildings, bridges, ships, cars, or the fuel to operate them, are all being given by God, and we need to show the proper respect. To think we are the proprietors of everything is the illusion. It is our pride that makes us think we are so intelligent when actually the very brain with which we think is not created by us but has again been given by God.

As everything is created from the Supreme Creator, then we should certainly have a high regard for everything as the expansion of God's energies. This not only includes all of our fellow men, but all creatures, as well as all aspects of the planet. Violence toward the planet in the form of not caring for the environment, misusing and polluting our natural resources, not managing the land and forests properly, are all forms of disrespect toward God and the blessings that have been given us. Why should we expect God or the planet to continue giving us the necessities of life, or the means to acquire them, if we are going to ruin them, or do not know how to care for them properly? So we must never pollute our resources or waste the food we have.

We should also see that even the Earth is a living being, full of life. The globe is a mother to us since she supplies all that we need. All of our food, water, and resources for sustaining our own lives, as well as supplies for shelter and clothing, all come from her. How she reciprocates with us in regard to what she provides depends on how we treat, honor and care for her. The imbalance in nature, such as the green house effect, the changing climate and weather patterns, are reflections of the imbalance in the consciousness of humanity. The planet only reflects the mass consciousness of the humanity that populates it. Once there is balance and harmony in society's consciousness and the way we regard and treat the ecosystem, this will then be reflected in the balance in nature. Then many of the storms, natural upheavals and disasters will begin to cease.

The environment and the material creation are supplied with all the potencies to produce all the necessities that we require, not only for humans but also for all species. Human society should not consider itself as the only enjoyer of all of God's creation, and that no other creatures have a claim to it. Humanity is actually a minority species when we consider the many types of creatures that are sustained by the environment. If we manage the ecosystem properly, it will continue to produce everything we need. However, if people who have no genuine spiritual understanding start exploiting the Earth to take whatever they want in any way they want, then the supply of resources starts decreasing and the Earth, being a living organism, stops producing or responding to the needs of society as abundantly as it used to do. Then there will be shortages, droughts, and forest fires; subsequently the prices on commodities will increase. Gradually more people will become poor, and poverty and starvation will spread in parts of the world. Then we see fierce competition for whatever resources can be attained. When many people die while fighting over land and commodities, or temporary and ever-changing political stances, then all the bloodshed from the dead, dying or wounded is like offering Mother Earth blood sacrifices to drink. She is pained by this, as are so many other higher beings that watch the activities of humanity. Rather than respecting the Earth and cooperating to share her resources, when we fight over them it is most heartrending for Mother Earth. Thus, when the Earth and the Lord's environment are not properly appreciated and maintained, or are exploited by ungodly people, then scarcities and excess pollution is the result. However, nature itself can go on nicely except for the interference of ungodly men.

As a society controlled by godless men gathers all the resources from the land as fast as possible for power and quick profits, it may appear to be a mighty economic gain at first, but in time it is never enough. As demand grows, scarcity raises its angry head. When the environment is not respected and cared for properly, there are also changes in the various species that have existed for thousands of years, even extinctions. These are all signs of further unknown changes in the future that will be revealing themselves to us when it will be too late.

There may be times when the Earth needs to cleanse herself of unwanted activities or from the pain she suffers from society's wrong aims of life. She may move in various ways to adjust things so that humanity is not so out of balance and will be forced to reconfigure the value systems that are displayed by humanity and make them geared more toward the real goal of life. When Earth reacts in particular ways to relieve her from the weight of unwanted activities or segments of society, we should not miss the message. A society that is too spoiled often easily forgets the real reason why it is here.

The proper vision and Vedic understanding is that everything is the property of the Supreme Being. If we have any possessions or wealth, we should see that we are only borrowing them for a short time. We certainly cannot take them with us when we leave this body, and thus someone else will take it all when we are gone. The ultimate owner of everything is the Supreme Creator. Thus, the proper way to use anything is in the service or consciousness of God. The same goes for taking care of the environment. Everything belongs to God so, ultimately, we should take care of it as if we were being watched by God and only taking care of His property while, by God's good graces, it produces the resources we need to live. After all, as the Lord in our heart and as the Supersoul of every living being, He is observing everything we do.

All of one's land, home, wealth, and possessions belong to the Supreme Being though we wrongly think, "I am this body and all that belongs to it is mine." Thus, a person of wisdom should not see anything as separate from the Supreme Lord. In spiritual consciousness, such a person will see everything, whether it be fire, air, water, the earth, the sun and stars, all living beings, the trees and plants, the rivers and oceans, and, in fact, everything that exists as an expansion of the energies of the Supreme Lord. Even while actively engaged with so many objects and undertakings in this creation, a person who sees the whole world as the energy of the Supreme Being is indeed a great sage of wisdom.

Therefore, we should care for the environment as if it is not ours but God's property, and in this way assure ourselves that it will continue to provide all of our necessities for many years to come, and into many future generations. This is the Vedic view.

CHAPTER EIGHTEEN

India as the Source of Individual Freedom and Governance

You could say that it was the Vedic culture that is the origin of genuine democratic thought and governance. Villages especially were ruled by committees or *sanghas* that arranged a government through discussion, based on the principles outlined in the Vedic texts. The Vedic literature explains that democratic institutions are shaped by the spirit of tolerance and freedom of thought. Therefore, a unique feature of Vedic practice is that while Hindus worship God and call Him by different names, at the same time they revere everyone else's understanding of God as well. This is the foundation of real secularism and democracy.

As the President of India, A. P. J. Abdul Kalam, once correctly said: "In 3000 years of our history, people from all over the world have come and invaded us, captured our lands, conquered our minds. From Alexander onwards, the Greeks, the Turks, the Moguls, the Portuguese, the British, the French, the Dutch, all of them came and looted us, took over what was ours. Yet we have not done this to any other nation. We have not conquered anyone. We have not grabbed their land, their culture, and their history and tried to enforce our way of life on them. Why? Because we respect the freedom of others. That is why my first vision is that of FREEDOM."

This is the freedom which the Vedic culture always promoted, which is that of the individual and one's freedom of thought, and freedom to pursue one's happiness without infringing on others, and the means to follow one's own spiritual predilection. This was understood because the Vedic premise is that of the "Big Picture," which is that everyone is coming into this human form of life with different levels of consciousness, and, thus, different needs to continue in their own evolutionary development from whatever level they are on now. This is why the Vedic system offered many ways through which a person could be involved and yet progress to a higher level of consciousness, and, yet, have the freedom to do so in whatever way is best for him, without, again, infringing or inflicting one's own views on everyone else who may not necessarily be on the same level or have exactly the same outlook. This has always been what was viewed as a fair use of social norms and governance, as guided or curbed by the Vedic standards, and which also seems to be a rare commodity in many areas of the world today.

If anyone really understands the Vedic tradition and the latitude of philosophy and acceptance in the ways for making spiritual progress, he or she knows that a prime emphasis within it is the promotion of freedom for the individual. Part of the Vedic tradition is that everyone can pick up the process wherever they feel best, or where it is most appropriate for them to learn the lessons they most need to continue on their spiritual journey. Therefore, when it comes to any governing system, it also promotes and preserves the ideal of individual freedom.

This makes it clear that the basic principles of democracy were embedded in ancient Indian civilization and its religions long before they occurred in the West. Whereas democracy in Europe was born in the people's struggle against the dominance of the Church and its ruthless rulers. Democracy involves freedom of personal expression and liberty in one's pursuits, especially for one's happiness and personal development to attain one's highest potential. And all along, this has been the purpose of the Vedic system of personal and social development. The Vedic system has always offered lots of individual freedom for the individual to pursue such evolutionary progress. Other cultures and religions have often shown a very limited form of freedom, tolerance, and latitude for acceptance. The point is, that in the Vedic system, there are different paths to reach God, just as there are different ways or paths to reach the top of the mountain. This may be through Raja Yoga, Jnana Yoga, Karma Yoga, Bhakti Yoga, and Mantra Yoga and so on, all different *Dharmas* to reach self-realization, but all connected at the same time. However, as you go higher, differences between them are reduced. In this way, also, the closer one gets to the purpose of the Vedic system, or goal of life, everything becomes more clear, including the way we view each other and how we can assist each other along the way. Thus, this is the type of democracy that is naturally inherent in the Vedic system of governing society. Therefore, in conclusion, we can simply say that ancient India is where we can find the origination of democracy. So, yes, even today India is the seventh largest and second most populous country in the world, with more population, one constitution, one national elected parliament, etc., making it the largest democracy as well.

In this line of thinking, Dr. Will Durant states in *Case for India*: "Let us remember further that India was the motherland of our race, and Sanskrit, the mother of Europe's languages; that she was the mother of philosophy; mother of mathematics; mother through Buddha of the ideals embodied in Christianity; mother through the village community of self-government and democracy. Mother India is in many ways the mother of us all."

Professor Jabez T. Sunderland writes in *India Under Bondage*: "Ethnological, linguistic and other forms of historical research make it clear that the democratic and republican institutions of Europe and America, actually send their roots to Asia and especially to India. India is the natural home of liberty, of democratic government and of self-government. Where did our colonial town-meeting system come from? Our historians trace it to England, and beyond that to Germany. But they cannot stop with Germany. To find they are obliged to go to Asia and especially to the village republics of India. Thus, India proves to be, in a sense, the Mother of Republican America." [1]

We can find in the *Atharva Veda* the early principles to be followed by the king with respect for the will of the people, and to maintain the means for protecting *Sanatana-dharma* for everyone. However, Chanakya established the idea that if the king oppresses the people and disregards *Dharma*, the people can revolt, dislodge him from power and install another king. Thus the king could not be a dictator, but was subject to review as well. Villages were found to have their own democratic system with locally elected elders established to maintain law and order.

The Vedic civilization had great thinkers and was also the origin of many additional political ideas. For example, Kautilya, popularly known as Chanakya Pandit, in his *Artha Sashtra*, set up principles that are still used today by such organizations as NATO. He was the first to emphasize the need for the numerous kingdoms in Aryavrata (ancient India) to unite and operate with the interests of one community under a central governing authority. He set down the principles of the role of the leaders or king, advisors, and the basics of foreign policy, along with internal security and non-corrupt administration. But the main basis of the duties of a king or any ruler was outlined in the Vedic texts, some of which had more information than others, as we will see next.

INSIGHTS INTO THE PURPOSE AND FUNCTION OF LEADERSHIP ACCORDING TO MAHABHARATA AND OTHER TEXTS

Such texts as the *Mahabharata* has an abundance of information on the duties of government and the king or ruler. More than we could provide here. But by studying the following information, which is a concise and summarized explanation on how the government and its rulers should function, as provided in the Vedic texts, we will understand how they expected things should be done at the time, and how our present governments are inefficient in various methods of operation that they employ, or in what should be the idealistic foundation upon which they build the country. We should also be able to perceive how to improve them. Furthermore, these Vedic principles that are found in the ancient *Mahabharata* and other Vedic books are applicable for any leaders, whether they be local, state or national.

First, before any ruler should take any position of authority, there should be a proper constitution which the king or leader must follow and upon which the whole village or country, depending on the case, must base itself. This constitution must outline the real purpose of government and the ruler of the country, and from which should not be diverted, and, in this case, to protect *Dharma* and all those Truth seekers who follow the principles of *Dharma*. *Dharma* means the path that helps bring and maintain harmony, balance and peace, both individually and socially, and the Truth which can free us from illusion and bring us to the topmost reality.

PURPOSE OF GOVERNMENT

The government's purpose should first be outlined in order to establish the direction it will take for the citizens of the country. This is the reason for having a constitution. It is explained that the main objective of the constitution of the country must be for the protection of *Dharma* and the propagation of righteousness among the subjects according to the law of *Dharma*. The citizens must know how to live in an atmosphere of goodness or with a *sattvik* mindset [that which is in the mode of goodness and is beneficial for everyone].

A constitution must be written only after a thorough review of the Vedic texts which contain a universal standard for spiritual development and an uplifting society. Only with a constitution in which *Dharma* is protected can there be the manifestation of a progressive country. By progressive we mean in consciousness where humanity is reaching their highest potential in growth, maturity, morals, cooperation, and spiritual knowledge and awareness. In the Vedic standards this is called Ramarajya, or a kingdom like that of Lord Rama's rule of righteousness. This is considered a time when the ruler, namely Lord Rama, worked for everyone's ultimate benefit, and everyone cooperated together in progressive harmony. It is considered that when the constitution and the country are based on righteousness, the probability of it being affected by calamities, crime and discontent are low. But a country devoid of righteousness (*Dharma*) is lifeless, like a corpse, meaning that the deterioration of such a country and its society is practically guaranteed. Without the preservation of *Dharma* through educational programs, then the positive future of the state is destroyed. It may go through the motions of existence, but its real purpose, values, and heart are empty. The citizens themselves will become like hollow shells compared to what they could be if they could reach their true potential in a spiritually advanced society. This is the importance of following the path of *Dharma* and that the rulers observe and protect it.

HOW THERE BECAME A NEED FOR A KING

In ancient times, king Yudhishthira asked how there ever came to be a need to have a king. In a summarized version from the *Mahabharata*, it is explained in this way, that he asked: "How did the word 'RAJAN' come into use when a king is addressed? A king is like any other human being on the earth. His body and limbs are like those of anyone else. His understanding and his senses are similar to those of many others. He has the same joys and griefs, the same number of years to live on the earth, like anybody else. How then did it happen that he is considered different? This world is made up of men who are far superior to him in intelligence, bravery and all accomplishments. And yet, this one man rules the others: though they are superior to him. Why should it be the rule that one man is worshipped by all the others?"

Bhishma replied: "I will tell you. In the beginning [as in Satya-yuga] there was no king. There was no punishment. These two were not needed then. Men were all righteous and each man protected the other. As time passed on, however, the hearts of men began to be invaded by errors. Once error enters the heart, the mind gets clouded and the sense of right and wrong begins to wane. It was even so with the men of distant times.

"Covetousness was the first guest in their hearts. When covetous-ness came into life, men began to want things which did not · belong to them. The next passion to be born was lust. Lust can never exist alone. It has to have a companion and so wrath came into existence. As soon as these terrible passions found places in the hearts of men, righteousness had to beat a hasty retreat. Along with this confusion happened another great calamity. The *Vedas* disappeared. Righteousness was completely lost to the world. The gods were then overcome with fear. They went to Brahma Pitamaha [great father] and said: 'Look on the world you have created, my lord! It is threatened with destruction. Please save it and save us!'

"Brahma assured them that he would find a way. He then composed a treatise of a hundred thousand lessons. He treated [on the subjects] of *Dharma* [righteousness], *Artha* [economic development], *Kama* [sensual enjoyment] and *Moksha* [spiritual liberation]. He dealt with them in great detail. He formulated the rules for chastisement. The main features of this treatise on chastisement dealt with punishment of two kinds: open and secret punishment. It treated of conservation of wealth by traders and merchants, growth of penance of the ascetics, destruction of thieves and wicked men. There was a branch dealing with all the religious observances, and another dealt with the extensive subject of legislation and the behavior that is expected of counselors, of spies, of secret agents, envoys, and conciliation. All the many ways and means by which men may be prevented from deviating from the path of righteousness and honesty were described in it.

"After composing it, Brahma said: 'For the good of the world and for the establishment and propagation of *Dharma*, *Artha* and *Kama* I have composed this. Assisted by chastisement this will protect the world. Men are mostly led by chastisement and so this treatise will be called *Dandaneeti*.'

"It was studied and abridged by several of the gods, the first of them being Shankara. Finally, when it was to be given to the world, Sukra of great wisdom thought of the brevity of the life of men on earth and made the work much shorter. It contained just a thousand lessons. The gods then appeared before Vishnu and said: 'Lord! Indicate to us a man on the world who deserves to be superior to the rest'.

"Narayana said: 'I will enter the body of one man and he, as well as all those who are born in his line, will be lords of the world'.

"There was a king called Vena. From his right arm was born a man who was like a second Indra [King of heaven] in his looks and godliness. He was born with a coat of mail and all the weapons. He was proficient in all the arts and the *Vedas*. The rishis made him the ruler of the world. Sukra was his priest. There was current among men the feeling that he was the eighth son of Vishnu himself.

"His name was Prithu. He made the surface of the earth level. Vishnu and the deities assembled to crown Prithu king. The earth took a form and came to him with tributes of gems and jewels. Prithu milked the earth in the form of a cow and made her yield seven kinds of crops for the food of all living creatures. He made all men regard *Dharma* as the foremost of all things.

"Because he pleased all the people he was called 'RAJAN'. Because he healed the wounds of afflicted people he was called 'KSHAT-RIYA'. And again, because the earth became celebrated for the prevalence of virtue during his reign, she was called 'PRITHIVI'.

"Vishnu entered the body of that monarch. A pure man, when his *punya* [good karmic merit] becomes exhausted, descends from heaven to earth and is born as a king. Such a person is indeed great and is a portion of Vishnu on earth. He has a heritage of divine intelligence and he is superior to all the others. He is established by the gods and he is not to be slighted. This is the reason why the world cannot command him but he can command the world. This is why the multitude has to obey his words of command though he is like anybody else."

In this regard, even the great Greek philosopher Plato recognized that the ideal ruler or administrator is the philosopher king. In such ancient cultures found in North and South America, or Egypt and Japan and many others, it was the sun that was worshiped and was considered the ultimate ruler. The king was considered the earthly representative of the sun, and his dynasty was the solar dynasty.

It is a fundamental principle of government that the authority of the ruler is ultimately derived from God. The form of government that is the oldest, most prevalent down through the ages, and most widely found around the globe is that of the divine monarchy. These were found in India, China, Japan, Mexico, Peru, Babylonia, Mesopotamia, Sumer, Ur, Egypt, Ethiopia, the Sudan, in ancient Greece, as well as in Scandinavia and Celtic Europe. In all these civilizations the king was spoken of as divine representatives.

Thereafter, Yudhishthira asked: "What are the principal duties of the subjects?"

Bhishma responded: "Their first duty is to elect a [properly qualified] king and perform his coronation. For the sake of the treasury, the subjects should give one fiftieth of their animals and precious metals and a tenth part of their grains. From among them they should choose those who are proficient in the use of weapons, and help the king in the maintenance of the army. A fourth part of the merits of the people will go to the king and a fourth part of their evil also. A disciple behaves with humility in the presence of his preceptor. Even so a subject should humble himself before his king. A king who is honored by his subjects will naturally be respected and feared by his foes." [2]

Here it is established how there became the position of a king, and why all citizens should respect him. Plus, how one-fourth of the credit of the citizens' pious acts go to the king, along with one-fourth of their impious actions. That is why if the king is unworthy and the majority of the citizens are engaged in impious, mean, evil, or sinful actions, as we find so much of in this age, the Vedic texts say that such a king can have nothing but a dark future ahead of him in his next life.

ANARCHY WITHOUT A PROPER RULER

As the morality of humanity declined through the ages, the need for proper rulers became increasingly evident. As it is further explained, when there is no ruler or proper administrator over a country, there will be anarchy in the region. In this regard the *Ramayana* (2.67.18) says: "In a state without a king the wealthy are insecure. Even farmers and cowherds cannot sleep peacefully with their doors open."

So the above description is a sure sign of improper leadership, or when a ruler has no ability to handle the situation in the appropriate way. When there is an abundance of crime and thievery, then the wealthy are especially vulnerable because those with less or who are in need will look at them with envy. Of course, the poor are even more vulnerable because they have little means to defend themselves from marauders and vandals who come through to do as they wish. Thus, the property of the weak will be forcefully taken away by those who are more powerful or clever. And the abduction of women will become common. Without good leadership, then even the police will not come forward to protect the people in an efficient manner. Furthermore, on a social level, religious principles will disappear, relationships like marriage will begin to become extinct, and crime and chaos will manifest even in the areas of business, banking, agriculture, and health care or pharmaceuticals. Even a simple and peaceful life will be increasingly difficult to find. This is further elaborated in the *Ramayana* (2.67.17):

"In a state where anarchy prevails a group of young women embellished with gold ornaments do not go to the garden in the evening for recreation." This may have been the sign of anarchy in the times of the *Ramayana*, but where I live in Detroit a group of women simply do not go out at night without risking their safety, embellished with gold or not. And in Africa and other parts of the world, the same situation is there that if any women are seen, they are vulnerable to rape, torture and murder. Is this not anarchy? So, according to these descriptions from the Vedic texts, a country with a crooked ruler where anarchy prevails is as good as a country with no ruler at all.

"No soul is peaceful in a state without a ruler. In such a state men exploit one another like fish who swallow each other." (*Ramayana* 2.67.31)

So a good government and qualified leader is essential for a progressive society. But who is a good leader?

WHO CAN RULE THE COUNTRY

In the Vedic system, a king is called a Raja. This means one who shines. But it also means one who rids his subjects of obstacles. This indicates that only one who ideally considers the welfare of his subjects should be a king or ruler.

If the ideal king follows the laws of *Dharma*, then the people will also follow (from *Mahabharata*, abbreviated as *Mb*.12.75.4) This also means that if the king is unrighteous, he will have little ability to lead people and keep them from crime and dishonesty. They will follow his own character. Thus, as rulers become more and more crooked, the same character will naturally trickle down to the general populace. This illustrates why corruption is so rampant today. The only way to escape from this situation is to have moralistic and righteous leaders, if there are any who can be found.

Crowning an ideal person as a king is the chief duty of a nation because eventually if a state is without a proper administrator, it becomes weak and subject to the attack of its enemies. (*Mb*.12.67.2) This means that a dynamic country and the code of punishment for wrongdoers can only blossom with strong leadership. When the code of punishment deteriorates or when rulers begin to behave unjustly, then corruption will spread unabated. Consequently people will become unhappy and social unrest will increase.

The nurturing of the subjects, displaying the means to endow them with happiness and contentment, protecting the righteous, and giving the citizens the means of prosperity and to punish the wrongdoers, are the chief duties of a king. (*Vishnusmriti*)

"The kingdom of that monarch who looks on while a Shudra [those who are unqualified or ill-trained for positions of rulership] settles the law, will sink (low), like a cow in a morass. That kingdom where Shudras are very numerous, which is infested by atheists and destitute of the twice-born (inhabitants) [those born a second time by spiritual knowledge], soon entirely perishes, afflicted by famine and disease." (*Manu-samhita*, 8.21-22)

RECOGNIZING THE CHARACTER OF A PROPER LEADER

The prime protector of the citizens in the Sanskrit language is called a Kshatriya. This word means warrior, but primarily as one who protects people from *kshat* or unhappiness, or one who removes problems and difficulties.

Such a Kshatriya is said to display the characteristics of bravery, courage, vigilance, charity, the ability to display his prowess, and not retreating from battle. (*Mb*. 6.42.43)

A proper Kshatriya has the ultimate duty to protect all beings (*Mb*.12.120.3) along with fostering the righteous, destroying those who are cruel, and not fleeing from the enemy. (*Mb*.12.14.16)

Kshatriyas should take up their weapons only to protect others, such as individuals and the community at large. (*Ramayana* 3.10.3)

However, a Kshatriya who does not display his strength according to his capacity due to fear of losing his life deserves to be called a thief. (*Mb*.5.134.2)

A Kshatriya must exhibit the appropriate conduct toward his subordinates. He can exercise control of the other classes in society and is thus called a statesman. He thus must exhibit impartiality in executing his duties without favoritism or disdain toward anyone. He must have consideration for the benefit of all. He naturally must personally follow the laws as set by others. He must be able to punish evildoers regardless of their own status or position in society. He must be willing to seek counsel from others who are able to advise him.

A Kshatriya's own spiritual progress is determined by his ability to protect the saintly and destroy evildoers.

Philosophers have stated that a warrior who is brave enough to be killed on the battlefield acquires the state of an ascetic who has been devoted to the practice of yoga. In other words, he attains heaven after this earthly life.

Again it is emphasized that only the rulers who can always protect the righteous and drive away the evildoers should be crowned as king. The entire universe lives on his support. (*Mb*.12.78.44) The strength of the downtrodden and the desolate lies in the king. (*Ramayana* 7.59) This means that those who are poor depend on the king for their welfare. Without that they are forever doomed to poverty and without condolence.

A QUALIFIED KING MUST BE SELF-CONTROLLED

In a summarized version of the *Mahabharata*, it is described: "A wise man should learn good behavior, good words and good acts from every side, as a gleaner collects grains of corn from the field abandoned by the reapers. Virtue is preserved by truthfulness; learning by application; beauty by cleansing the body; high lineage by good character. Mere lineage, in the case of one whose behavior is not good, cannot command respect. A king or a man who envies another's wealth, beauty, might, high lineage, happiness, good fortune and honor, suffers from an incurable disease. Good behavior is essential to man. Intoxication of wealth is much more to be censured than wine; for a man intoxicated with prosperity can never be brought to his senses unless and until he meets with a fall.

"Like the moon during the lighted fortnight, calamities increase for him who is a slave to his senses. The king who wishes to control his counselors before controlling his own self, or the king who wishes to subdue his adversaries before controlling his counselors, fights a losing battle, losing his strength. A king should first subdue his own self, regarding it as his foe. He will then never fail to subdue his counselors and later his enemies. Great prosperity waits upon him who has subjugated his senses, or controlled his soul, or who is capable of punishing all offenders, or who acts with discernment, or who is blessed with patience.

"One's body is the chariot: the soul within is the driver; and the senses are its steeds. Drawn by those excellent steeds when they are well trained, the wise man pleasantly goes through the journey of life in peace. The horses, however, if unbroken and incapable of being controlled, lead the unskilled driver to destruction in the course of the journey. Many evil-minded kings, because of their want of mastery over the senses are ruined by acts of their own, lust for kingdom being the cause of their sin." [3]

THE STRENGTHS AND CHARACTERISTICS RULERS SHOULD HAVE

"Kings are said to have five different kinds of strength. Of these the strength of arms is considered to be the most inferior kind. The acquisition of good counselors is regarded as the second kind of strength. The acquisition of wealth is the third kind of strength. The strength of birth which one naturally acquires from one's sires and grandsires is the fourth kind of strength. That, however, by which all these are won, and which is the foremost of all kinds of strength, is called the strength of the intellect.

"Illustrious and mighty kings have ruled this mighty earth so full of wealth and glory and joy. All of them have become victims of the Universal Destroyer. They went away leaving behind them their kingdoms and their immense pleasures. The son, brought up with anxious care, when dead, is taken up and carried away by men to the burning grounds. With disheveled hair and with piteous cries they cast the body into the funeral pyre as though it were a piece of wood. Others enjoy the wealth of a dead man while birds and fire feast on the elements of his body. Only two things go with him to the other world: his merits and his sins. Throwing away the body, relatives, friends, and sons retrace their steps like birds abandoning the tree without flowers or fruits. The man cast into the funeral pyre is followed only by his own actions. Therefore should men, carefully and gradually, earn the merit of righteousness." [4]

Yudhishthira further asked: "How should a king behave?"

Bhishma answered: "Righteousness is the watchword of a king. Nothing is greater than that in this world. A righteous king can easily conquer the entire world. His counselors should all be pure in heart and pure in mind. Malice should have no place in the heart of a king. His senses should be perfectly under control. He should use his intelligence and he will then be glorious: swelling in greatness like the ocean fed with the waters of a thousand rivers." [5]

"Poison kills but one man: so does a weapon. But wicked counsels destroy an entire kingdom with kings and subjects. The highest good is righteousness. The one supreme peace is forgiveness. Supreme contentment is knowledge. Supreme happiness is benevolence. A king can easily become great by doing just two things: refraining from harsh speech and disregarding those that are wicked. Three crimes are considered to be terrible: theft of another's property, outrage of another man's wives and breach with friends. Three things destroy the soul: lust, anger and covetousness. Three are essential: a follower, one who seeks protection and one who has come to your abode. These should be protected. A king, although powerful, should never confer with these four: men of small sense, men that procrastinate, men who are indolent, and men who flatter. Five things have to be worshiped: father, mother, fire, the preceptor, and the soul. Six faults should be avoided by a king who wishes to be great: sleep, drowsiness, fear, anger, indolence, and procrastination. These six should not be forsaken: truth, charity, diligence, benevolence, forgiveness, and patience. A king should renounce the seven faults [which are women, dice, hunting, harshness of speech, drinking, severity of punishment, and waste of wealth]. Eight things glorify a king: wisdom, high birth, self-restraint, learning, prowess, moderation in speech, gifts given with discrimination, and gratitude. This human body is a house with nine doors, three pillars, and five witnesses. It is presided over by the soul. The king who knows this is wise. These ten do not know what virtue is: the intoxicated, the inattentive, the raving, the fatigued, the angry, the starving, the dejected, the covetous, the frightened and the lustful." [6]

FURTHER DESCRIPTIONS OF THE CHARACTER AND DUTIES OF A KING

Here is the advice given for one to be a proper Dharmic king:

Bhishma was immensely pleased with the humility and eagerness of Yudhishthira. He smiled at him and said: "My child, I am only too eager to tell you all that you want to know. A king's first duty is to worship the gods and the Brahmanas [those spiritually advanced individuals who are meant to work selflessly for the spiritual upliftment of all others]. A king should essentially be a man of action. You might have heard from many that destiny rules a king. It is a fallacy in reasoning if you think so. Destiny does play a part. I grant that. But without action a king can never help destiny to play her part. Destiny is powerful but action is equally powerful. Both are potent. But to me, it seems that action is the more potent of the two. It is action which shapes the destiny.

"The next equally important duty of a king is Truth. If you want to inspire confidence in the minds of your subjects, you should always be truthful.

"All accomplishments find a home in a king. His behavior should be above reproach. Self-restraint, humility and righteousness are qualities which you have to look for in a king if he has to be successful. He should have his passions under perfect control.

"Justice should be the second nature of a king. There are three more things which a king should cultivate. He should know how to conceal his own weaknesses carefully. By weakness is meant the weaknesses in his kingdom. He should take the trouble to find out the weaknesses in his enemies and he should be very careful to be secretive about his plans.

"A king's conduct should be straight forward. Another danger for a king is mildness. He should not be too mild. He will then be disregarded. The subjects will not have enough respect for him and his words. Again, he should avoid the other extreme. He should not be too fierce because then the subjects will be afraid of him, and that is not a happy state of affairs.

"A king should know the art of choosing servants. He should have compassion as part of his mental make-up, but he should guard against too forgiving a nature. The lowest of men will take advantage of him and his nature if they are considered weak.

"Alertness is a great necessity for a king. He should study his foes and his friends too, incessantly."

"Skill, cleverness and truth are all three necessary in a king. Old and fallen buildings and living-houses should be renovated by him if he has to win the good opinion of his subjects. He should know how to use his powers in inflicting corporal punishments and fines on miscreants." [7]

A KING MUST PROTECT HIS SUBJECTS

Time and again the *Mahabharata* and other Vedic texts stress that a ruler must be able to protect and care for the citizens. This is done in a variety of ways, which are briefly explained in the many quotes that follow. But if a ruler cannot look after his subjects with concern and firmness, then it is obvious that such a person is unfit to continue in any position of leadership. As it is described:

"Having thus arranged all the affairs (of) his (government), he shall zealously and carefully protect his subjects. That (monarch) whose subjects are carried off by robbers (Dasyu) from his kingdom, while they loudly call (for help), and he and his servants are quietly looking on, is a dead and not a living (king). The highest duty of a Kshtriya is to protect his subjects, for the king who enjoys the rewards is bound to (discharge that) duty. (*Manu-samhita* 8.142-144)

"A king should protect his subjects just as a pregnant women nurtures the foetus in her womb." (*Mb*.12.56.44) In this way, as a pregnant woman sacrifices her own interests for the sake of the child in her womb, so also a king should be able to give up his own interests to address the needs of the citizens.

"Just as a father helps his son rise over a crisis, so also a king should deliver his subjects from difficulties." (*Bhagavata Purana* 11.17.45)

"If a king is too gentle, then people disobey him. And if he is authoritarian they fear him. Hence, depending on the situation he should be authoritarian or gentle." (*Mb*.12.140.65)

"Keeping the subjects happy on this earth itself is the code of righteousness (*Santana-dharma*) of a king." (*Mb*.12.57.11)

"Punishing evildoers, honoring the righteous, enriching the treasury lawfully, deciding the cases of petitioners, and protecting the nation are the five sacrificial fires (*yajnas*) or spiritual duties of a king." (*Atrismruti* 28)

"The king who nurtures his subjects on the best possible way is certainly knowledgeable in righteousness. Why does such a king require penance? Why at all does he need to perform sacrificial fires?" (*Mb*.12.69.73)

The feeble and downtrodden, blind, dumb, crippled, orphaned, old, widowed, diseased and distressed should be provided with food, clothing, medicines, shelter, etc. (*Mb*.12.86.24)

Provisions of facilities such as lakes and water canals, distribution of seeds, control of rodents, elephants, and those things which destroy harvests, augmenting farming by developing meadows for cattle to graze, etc., are all part of the assortment of ways meant to be overseen by the king and his government for the protection and continued development of the citizens.

"A king must consider that his first duty is to his subjects. He should guard them as a mother guards the child in her womb. Will any mother have thoughts of pleasing herself when her child is in her womb? All her thoughts will be bent only on the child and its welfare. Even so, a king should subordinate his desires and wishes to those of his subjects. Their welfare should be his only concern."

"The best king is one whose subjects live in freedom and happiness as they do in their father's house. Peace will be theirs, and contentment. There will then be no wickedness, no pretense, no dishonesty, and no envy.

"The very core of a king's duty is the protection of his subjects and their happiness. It is not easy. To secure the happiness of his people he should use diverse methods." [8]

TAXES

One of the primary functions of a ruler is to oversee and design the development of his country, and one of the means he uses for this is taxes. But how he collects tax must be systematic and with proper consideration of his subjects. As it is described: "Just as a bumble-bee sucks nectar from flowers without harming them, so also a king should collect money from his subjects without hurting them." (*Mb*.5.34.17)

"Just as a bumble-bee sucks nectar from flowers delicately without harming the plant so also a king should collect money by levying taxes on his subjects, without hurting them. One who milks a cow does not milk it dry but takes care to see that some milk is left for its calf. Similarly, a king should levy taxes on the people carefully after considering that they will be sufficiently provided for." (*Mb*.12.88.4)

"Like a leech, a king should gently take money from the state by levying taxes. A tigress lifts its cubs with its teeth yet does not harm them. Similarly a king should levy taxes on his subjects without causing them distress." (*Mb*.12.88.5)

"O king, it is the ruler's great folly if despite taking one sixth of the income of his subjects he does not nurture them like his children." (*Ramayana* 3.6.11)

"It is said that a king who without protecting his subjects takes one sixth of their income (in the form of taxes) acquires their sins." (*Mb*.1.213.9)

"A king should become a gardener, not a coal manufacturer. A gardener takes care of plants to obtain flowers and fruits from them. Similarly a king should guide his subjects towards prosperity and then secure one fourth of their income from them in the form of taxes. A coal trader uproots a tree and then chars it completely. A king should not uproot his subjects likewise plundering their wealth totally." (*Mb*.)

"Just as one who cuts off the udders of a cow with the hope of getting milk never acquires it, so also a state in which taxes are levied

inappropriately, thus harassing the subjects, does not prosper."
(*Mb*.12.71.16)

"Most of the authors of the *Smritis* have stated that taxes should not
be levied upon the Brahmanas (priests) who have mastered the *Vedas*. This
is because the king gets one sixth of the merits acquired by a Brahmana
following the righteous path." (*Vishnu Dharmasutra* 3.26-27)

The point is that it is the duty of the king to support and look after
the worldly and spiritual needs of learned Brahmanas, ascetics and scholars
and teaching institutions. This would augment a king's prestige. The king
would treat them with great respect since they are meant to assist in the
preservation of *Dharma* and social balance whereby the whole society can
work in harmony and continue their spiritual development by which all can
be content and happy.

Therefore, the king must also adopt the attitude that he is the
servitor of the citizens. A crooked government must fear the citizens who
will sooner or later revolt against a dishonest leader. Otherwise, what value
is there in the citizens paying high taxes to a crooked leader who is not
ruling them properly, and not being able to protect them, either militarily,
economically, educationally, etc? A leader is meant to get a salary from the
taxes collected only when he or she can do the proper job. Otherwise the
taxes collected for such purposes are wasted.

USE OF THE TREASURY

The main purpose of how a king is meant to use the treasury is also
explained: "The treasury of a king is meant for the protection of the army,
his subjects and of righteousness (*Dharma*). If it is used for these purposes,
it will prove beneficial. On the other hand, if the treasury is misused, it will
prove disastrous. Should the king use the royal treasury for his wife and
children and to fulfill his own sensual pursuits, it will bring him
unhappiness and he will attain hell." (*Shukraniti* 4.2.3-5)

The ruler must use only his personal account for any of his own
interests, but must never divert any administrative accounts and finances for
inappropriate purposes. Not only will he accrue the bad karma that will take
him to hell, but often his own life, private and political, along with the
future of his subjects and country, becomes doomed in due time.

"The king should remember that his treasury should always be full. Supervision of the work of all his officers should be done by the king himself. He should never trust the guardians of the city or fort implicitly." [9]

DEFENDING THE COUNTRY–BEING AWARE OF THE ENEMY

In protecting the citizens from obstacles, overseeing the safety of the country from enemies is certainly a prime concern that must be addressed by the ruler. Herein it is further advised:

"O king, it is neither written on one's countenance nor engraved in words that so-and-so is an enemy or a friend. The one from whom one experiences harassment is termed as an enemy." (*Mb*.2.55.10)

"Despite being feeble those who are cautious are not slain by the enemy, as against this is a powerful one who is not vigilant about the enemy is annihilated even by a weak enemy." (*Mb*.12.138.198)

"Even if an enemy is weak when its strength rises, even a powerful man cannot afford to ignore it." (*Mb*.5.9.22)

"Even if one is powerful one should not consider a weak enemy inferior because though a flame is small it is sufficient to burn, and even a minute quantity of poison is enough to snuff out life." (*Mb*.12.58.17)

"In this world there is nothing more dangerous than being inadvertent. All wealth deserts such a careless individual and then he has to face catastrophes." (*Mb*.10.10.19)

DEALING WITH AN ENEMY

Once an enemy has been recognized, there are specific ways of dealing with them, according to one's position: "One should befriend an enemy by conciliation with a false air of friendship but should fear him constantly like a snake that has entered the house." (*Mb*.12.140.15)

"One should speak (to the enemy) meekly but should actually be heartless. One should speak with a smile but never reveal one's true nature by performing a harsh act." (*Mb*.1.140.66)

"One should win the enemy's trust by convincing him with valid reasons and after sometime when his position becomes unstable, one should attack him." (*Mb*.12.140.44)

Lord Vishnu told the deities before the churning of the ocean of milk, "O deities, to accomplish a great task, you may even have to befriend the enemy. Do that and once you accomplish your mission, just as a rattlesnake swallows rodents, destroy the demons." (*Bhagavata Purana* 8.6.20)

"A king who does not annihilate his enemy will not gain fame on this earth, will not acquire wealth, and his subjects too will remain insecure. Even Indra was accorded the status of Mahendra after he slew the demon Vritrasura." (*Mb*.12.15.15)

"A person who foolishly disregards a flourishing enemy is totally vanquished by it, akin to an ailment in its terminal stage." (*Mb*.2.55.16)

"One should not let an enemy realize one's weaknesses. However, one should certainly find out the enemy's weaknesses. Just as a tortoise keeps all parts of its body hidden beneath its shell, a king should keep all the strategies of the state a secret and should be careful about his weaknesses." (*Mb*.12.140.24)

"One who trusts an enemy and sleeps peacefully after making a truce with the latter is akin to a man sleeping on a treetop who wakes up only after he falls down." (*Mb*.12.140.37)

"One does not acquire the great Lakshmi bestowing governance (Rajalakshmi) without striking the enemy at its strategic points, exhibiting tremendous valiance, and without slaying the enemy like a fisherman kills his catch." (*Mb*.12.140.50)

"When the enemy becomes weak, wise men do not hesitate even for a moment to destroy it. An enemy should be slain specially when it is facing a calamity. If a clever one annihilates an enemy in such circumstances, not only is he called righteous but he also becomes famous." (*Mb*.8.90.71) An enemy in this regard is also considered to be an enemy of *Dharma*, the destruction of which becomes necessary before it destroys all means of peace and stability in society. Thus, *Dharma*, the means to have a balanced and peaceful country, must be defended at all times.

Sri Krishna to Yudhisthira explains: "O Dharmaraja, vanquisher of enemies, so long as you continue to reconcile with them (the enemies of the Kauravas) they will continue to rule your kingdom." (*Mb*.5.73.8)

"Despite being intelligent, if a king does not attack his enemies, then like a non-venomous snake he will always fall prey to his enemy." (*Mb*.12.58.16)

"If one finds an enemy who deserves to be killed, then one should never let him go." (*Mb*.5.38.29)

"Just as a debt keeps growing even if a fraction of it is unpaid, if the lives of your enemies are spared, then because they have been insulted, in the future they will generate terror just as neglected diseases become dreadful later." (*Mb*.12.140.59)

"Even if the enemy who charges with a weapon on the battlefield is a scholar of the Vedanta, a king who observes righteousness (*Dharma*) should wage a righteous war and defeat him." (*Mb*.12.56.29)

"One should speak to him (the enemy) sweetly both when contemplating an attack on him and also during the attack. In fact, even after the attack one should show sympathy and grief and shed tears as well." (*Mb*.1.140.56)

"One should not fight several enemies alone. One should resort to the four methods of reconciliation, compromise with money, breaking the amity of allies and punishment appropriately and annihilate them one by one. Even if very powerful, the wise should never make the folly of fighting several enemies simultaneously." (*Mb*.3.52.22)

"Do not attempt to swim across when the opposite bank is beyond one's reach. Never seize anything that will later be snatched away by someone else. Never dig at something which cannot be uprooted. Never strike one who cannot be beheaded." (*Mb12.140.69*)

"A king should first win over his own mind, then it becomes easier to gain victory over his enemy. How will one who has not won over his own mind vanquish his enemies?" (*Mb*.12.69.4)

"A king should be wise in dealing with six problems. The first is making peace with a foe who is stronger. The next consideration is making war on one who is equal to him in strength. Invading the country of one who is weaker is his next problem. He should use his discrimination when he makes a decision about these things. He should be prepared to seek protection in his fort if his position is weak. The most important work of a king is to cause dissensions among the chief office-bearers in his enemy's country. He should have clever spies at his service and find out the secrets of the enemy. He should bribe and cajole the officers of the enemy and win them over to his side.

"A king should be pleasant in speech. He should have about him men who are all like him in nature and in noble qualities. The only difference between the king and his officers should be the white umbrella [his insignia as a king]. [10]

"He [the king] must produce disloyalty among the people in a hostile country and he must have friends and allies there.

"He should amass troops, and this should be done in secret. A king can never protect his kingdom by candor and by simplicity. A king should be both candid and crooked. He must employ crookedness and wrong acts when he wants to subdue the enemy. All these things should be concealed behind a candid and open exterior." [11]

The king is expected to have control over his mind and senses if he is to have control over his enemies and subjects. He must rise above the influence of the six defects, namely desire, anger, greed, pride, and the desires for fame and happiness. Otherwise both the king and his kingdom are doomed. We have often seen that rulers who exhibit weaknesses, whether toward women, liquor, gambling, or hunting and other vices which stem from desire; or other unbalanced mindset regarding criticism, misappropriation of money, or being overly cruel with punishment, etc., all of which originate from excessive anger and pride, lead to a downfall or disaster. Thus he must avoid these issues and weaknesses in order to rule pleasantly over his subjects.

In this age of Kali-yuga, rulers in any part of the world fail to lead properly because they are filled with their own weaknesses and unable to control their own minds and senses properly. The leader must be focused without the distractions of the senses, or the tendency to give privileges to political groups because of an attraction to the money they offer. When the senses of a ruler are controlled, then the state can become prosperous in all aspects and as a result, wealthy. When the ruler is not able to control his senses, then the citizens suffer the results of a leader who is too easily swayed and distracted with the result of a lack of impartial justice and leadership. Thus, the government itself becomes the home of corruption and thieves. When the leader becomes a thief, then the citizens become beggars.

The following also explains that any response by a king to an enemy or someone in the world who should be curbed should be done after a well thought out plan, rather than merely by an emotional reaction, which is often based on an impulsive and prideful basis rather than wisdom and focus.

[As Bhishma said to Yudhisthira] "Great men do not express hostility towards those who insult them all at once. Nevertheless they display their prowess gradually, with time." (*Mb*.12.157.10) In other words, they make a plan for dealing with it at a later time in a more efficient manner.

THE ARMY

The army is, of course, the main agency through which the king handles enemies. Herein are a few statements in how the army must be guided, not necessarily by the king himself, but through farsighted military leaders.

"A military organization functions best if it is well guided. The army is blind and ignorant. Hence farsighted leaders should guide it appropriately." (*Mb*.2.20.16)

"Soldiers brimming with enthusiasm for battle is the prime sign of achieving victory." (*Mb*.6.3.75)

Even though there would be fights between tribes and kingdoms, in the Vedic times strict principles were used, such as the war would be waged only in certain areas, the warriors would stop fighting at night, only to begin the next morning after a conch was blown by both sides. No civilians would be pulled into the battle, and women and children were never attacked. People engaged in farming or trade, artisans, manufacturers and similar professions would not be forced into the military campaign. Noncombatants were never killed and habitations other than forts were never attacked. The civilians were never plundered, women's chastity was never violated, and Brahmanas, priests, temples and cows were also never touched. Many of these rules are still utilized by international organizations and the Red Cross. Unfortunately, in these days of terrorism, and when children are forced into brutal military service by tyrants, and when women and girls are raped as a matter of routine, we can see how far society has fallen away from such discipline and codes of honor, and into a truly demonic mentality.

DUTIES OF A KING IN DISTRESS

There are times and circumstances in which a ruler will find himself in a weaker position than another, or in comparison with an enemy. Thus, the situation may dictate a different strategy for the survival of the country, or for maintaining peace among neighboring countries. In this regard, Bhishma explained: "I will tell you about the duties of a king when in distress. A foe then becomes a friend, and a friend will most probably turn out to be a foe. Circumstances will so conspire that the course of human actions becomes uncertain. This is where intelligence comes to one's rescue. It helps you to decide whether one should make war on the foe or make peace with him. It all depends on the time and place, and, at times, it is even necessary to make friends with the enemy. You should make friends with intelligent men who are desirous of your welfare. If your life cannot otherwise be saved, then you should certainly make peace with the enemy. If you are foolish enough not to consider this, then you will never succeed in achieving things for which everyone strives so hard. A king, who makes a truce with the enemy, and quarrels with his erstwhile friends after considering the situation to the utmost, its pros and its cons, will certainly be able to succeed.

"Friends should be examined to the utmost before accepting them as friends. Foes should be well studied and their strength and weakness known. Friends appear as foes, and foes assume the guise of friends. When friendly compacts are undertaken, it is not possible to be sure if the feelings of the other are really friendly or if it is just selfishness which prompts him to accept the pact. The words 'friend' and 'foe' are, after all, relative terms. A man considers another to be his friend so long as he is assured that his interests are safe; so long as he is sure that it is profitable for him to do so. If he is sure that this state of things will continue as long as the other man is alive, he allows the friendship to continue for life.

"Self-interest [the instinct to survive] is the most powerful factor in the life of everyone. The entire world is pivoted round only this one factor and it ever revolves around it. No one is dear to another unless there is some gain involved. No affection is evident unless there is a motive of self-interest. One man is popular because he is very liberal-minded, another because he speaks sweetly, and a third because he is very religious. Generally it is the rule rather than the exception that a man is dear because of the purpose he serves: nothing more. The friendship terminates as soon as the reason for the friendship dies.

"An intelligent man should know when to make peace with a foe. Remember, when two persons who were once enemies become friends it is obvious that each is only biding his time when he can get the better of the other. The wiser of the two will necessarily succeed. The policy is that, while you are afraid of the other man, you should appear as though you are not. You should appear as though you trust him implicitly and all the time you should be mistrusting him. When the time demands it you should make peace with your foe and at the earliest opportunity you must wage war. This rule should apply even for a friend." [12]

A KING SHOULD TRUST NO ONE

Unfortunately, a king or ruler, due to his position, must be careful regarding who he trusts. There may be so many who are envious, or who are enemies set to take over the ruler's position, or who are enemies who wish to take control over the country. Thus, placing trust in the wrong people can have devastating effects. Thus, confidentiality must be observed in many areas of the ruler's activities. Future plans must not be jeopardized by allowing too many or the wrong people to know too much.

"A king should be careful not to place implicit confidence in anyone. His innermost thoughts must be concealed from even his nearest and dearest and he should not tell anyone about his decisions." [13]

"One should always attempt to make others trust in oneself. However, one should not trust others." (*Mb*.12.138.195)

"One should acquire the trust of others but should never trust anyone. O King, never trust even one's own son completely." (*Mb*.12.85.33)

"One should not undertake a mission depending on another's strength as opinions of two people generally do not match." (*Mb*.2.56.8)

In determining what kind of person a king can trust, Yudhishthira asked: "Nothing, not even the smallest act can be accomplished by a single man. He has to have assistance. This is all the more true when one thinks of ruling a kingdom. So much of it depends on the minister of the king. Tell me, what are the characteristics of a minister and his duties? Which kind of man deserves the king's entire confidence?"

Bhishma replied: "A king has friends and these can be classified into four types. The first is the man whose object coincides with that of the king. The second is the man who is devoted to the king. The third is one related to the king by birth. The fourth is one whom the king has placated by gifts. There is a fifth and that is a righteous man who firmly serves one and not both sides. He belongs to the side where there is righteousness. To this man the king should never confide plans which are in danger of being disapproved. A king who wants to be successful has to be righteous and unrighteous too according to circumstances. And so, he cannot be too careful in regard to these friends. A wicked man may appear to be honest and an honest man is likely to become dishonest. No man can always be of the same mind all the time. No one should be trusted completely. Entire reliance on the ministers is not wise. And again, a want of trust is also wrong. A king's policy, therefore, should be trust as well as mistrust.

"A king should fear his kinsmen as he would death himself. A kinsman can never bear to see the prosperity of the king. At the same time, a king without kinsmen is unfortunate indeed. The policy is: mistrusting them at heart, but behaving with them as though he trusts them completely." [14]

A KING SHOULD TAKE COUNSEL

The power of government should be overseen and monitored by different people or organizations because if only one person or class controls it, it will create a monopoly that generates fear and suspicion in the general mass of people. Furthermore, a ruler is never meant to make unilateral decisions without counsel as this leads to tyranny and dictatorship.

[Rama asked Bharat] "Do you take decisions by yourself or do you seek the counsel of several others? Does your policy get published much before it is implemented?" (*Ramayana* 2.100.18)

A ruler, no matter how clever or intelligent he may be, is never meant to make decisions on his own without consulting his ministers. It has been seen time and time again that any leader who draws his own designs without consultation with his advisors is soon on his way to ruin.

As it is explained: "The one who judges the strength of the enemy and that of his own state, who contemplates intelligently on the present status, growth and destruction of his army and that of the enemy's army and suggests the required measures for the welfare of his master can truly be called a minister." (*Ramayana* 6.14.22)

"A king should be proficient in the art of choosing honest men to hold important offices." [15]

CHARACTER OF THE LEGISLATORS

Yudhishthira asked: "What should be the characteristics of the legislators, the ministers of war, the courtier, and the counselors of a king?"

Bhishma responded: "The legislators should be men who are modest, self-restrained, truthful and sincere, and they should have the courage to speak what is proper. The ministers for war should be those who are always by the side of the king. They should be very brave. They should belong to the higher caste, and be learned and affectionate to a fault as far as the king is concerned. A courtier should be of high lineage. He should always be honored by the king. He should be a man who has the king's interests always at heart. He should never abandon the king whatever the circumstances may be.

"The officers of the army should again be of high lineage, born in the country of the king; possessed of wisdom, great learning, and beauty of form and features. They should be of excellent behavior, and they should be devoted to the king." [16]

THE NEED FOR SECRECY

"Both poison and a weapon kill only one person at a time, but discrepancy in a king's plan becomes the cause for destruction of all the subjects along with the king." (*Mb*.5.33.45)

"Just as a peacock maintains silence in autumn, so also a king should always keep his policies a secret." (*Mb*.12.120.7)

[Sage Narada explains to Yudhisthira] "The main cause for victory of a king is secret counsel." (*Mb*.2.5.27)

SPIES

A ruler must hear of the intentions and actions of the people, both within and outside his country, and of both honest and dishonest people. Not that this is expected to take away the rights of the people, but only so the king will understand how things are going on amongst his subjects. By understanding the intentions of the citizens, a king can propose proper plans to his legislators for counsel. Herein it is explained: "A king keeps an eye on his subjects through his spies." (*Mb*.5.34.34)

"It is said that spies are the support of a state and secret counsel is its strength." (*Mb*.12.83.51)

A KING SHOULD UNDERSTAND
CHARACTERISTICS OF A WISE MAN AND FOOL

The *Mahabharata* also explains how a king should understand the characteristics of both a wise man and a fool. This would also have an affect on the character of the king. This is from the Vidura-neeti section of the *Mahabharata* in which Vidura addresses King Dhritarasthra.

Vidura said: "I will tell you what a wise man should be like. A man should aspire for the higher things, ideals, in life. The assets of such a man are self-knowledge, exertion, forbearance and steadiness in virtue. Such a man is wise. Neither anger, nor joy, nor pride, nor false modesty, nor vanity, can distract him from his purpose. His actions are always done with the thought that they should serve both the worlds. Desire does not tinge his actions. Honest deeds delight him and he loves what is good. He is unaffected either by honors or by slights. Like a lake in the course of the river Ganga, he is calm, cool and unagitated.

"On the other hand, the qualities of a fool are also easy to enumerate. Scripture is a closed book as far as he is concerned. He is vain: he is proud and, when he wants to have something, he will never hesitate to employ unfair means. He has a knack of desiring what he has no right to desire. Those who are powerful make him envious. Let me tell you about a peculiar attribute of sin. One man commits a sin and several reap the fruits resulting from his sin. But in the end, the sin attaches itself ONLY to the one man, while those many who enjoyed the fruits of his sin escape unscathed!

"A wise king should discriminate the TWO with the help of the ONE. He must control the THREE by means of the FOUR. He has to conquer the FIVE. Know the SIX. Abstain from the SEVEN and be happy. By ONE is meant the intellect: by TWO, right and wrong: by THREE friend, stranger and enemy; by FOUR is meant gift, conciliation, disunion and severity: by FIVE the senses: by SIX, treaty, war, etc: by SEVEN, women, dice, hunting, harshness of speech, drinking, severity of punishment, and waste of wealth. This means that one should know how to discriminate between right and wrong by the use of the intellect. Friend, foe or stranger can be won over by one of the four: gift, etc. The senses must be under control and a king should be familiar with treaty, etc., which are essential. The seven have naturally to be avoided if a king aspires to be wise." [17]

DEALING WITH CRIMINALS

There is definitely a need for a king and ruler in any position to take a stern stance on criminals. Outlaws and wrongdoers are a prime source for fear and disruption in the lives of honest citizens. So, they must be dealt with firmly. However, the king must also be of sound character or he will not possess a mental disposition in which he will be able to take a proper or powerful stand against such criminals. This is why from the very start, a suitable king must be put into office and not someone who is ill-suited for the position.

"After he be punished or pardoned, the thief is freed from the (guilt of) theft; but the king, if he punishes not, takes upon himself the guilt of the thief." (*Manu-samhita* 8.316)

"But men who have committed crimes and have been punished by the king, go to heaven, being pure like those who performed meritorious deeds." (*Manu-samhita* 8.318)

If one who has acted unrighteously is slain, then it does not amount to unrighteousness [for the slayer]. (*Ramayana* 2.96.24)

No sin arises out of killing a terrorizing enemy. On the contrary, pleading before it for mercy or tolerance is unrighteous and a stigma on one's reputation. (*Mb*.5.3.21)

One who has to protect his subjects should not hesitate if sometimes he is compelled to be a little cruel or to perform slightly wrong actions in order to protect them. (*Ramayana* 1.25.18)

PURPOSE OF PUNISHMENT

Without punishment in the universe, the subjects would have become extinct, just as big fish in the water swallow the small ones, powerful people would have destroyed the weak. (*Mb*.12 15.30)

Due to fear of punishment some animals do not devour each other. If people are not protected by the experience of punishment, then they would bring about darkness through the destruction of each other. (*Mb*.12.15.7)

It is punishment alone which disciplines all subjects and protects everyone. It remains vigilant even when all are asleep. That is why learned men have opined that punishments are what maintains *Dharma*. (*Mb*.12.15.2)

Everyone keeps themselves under control because of the threat of punishment. A basically pure individual is rarely found. It is the fear of punishment that makes one act properly and perform the task allotted to him. (*Mb*.12.15.34)

If there was no protection by the means of punishment, then everything would be reduced to ashes, all rules would be violated and no one would own anything. (*Mb*.12.15.8)

Learned men consider that it is punishment that brings unethical people onto the righteous path and punishes those who are uncivilized because of its two characteristics of control and meting out punishment. (*Mb*.12.15)

When the punishing authority is highly efficient, people are very cautious. Hence, a king should keep all beings in his control through the code of punishment. (*Mb*.12.140.8)

"Punishment should be given to offenders according to the immensity of the offence. The wealthy should be fined and their property should be confiscated, while loss of liberty should be the punishment for the poor offender. Wicked conduct should be punished by inflicting corporal punishment." [18]

CONSEQUENCES FOR THE KING

A ruler can never do whatever he wants, whether it be in acting overly harsh, or in not being firm and decisive enough, or in being too liberal and soft. There are always consequences if a ruler does not act appropriately or if he neglects his duties. If he proves to be unfit, he is and must be rejected by the people. But there are also karmic consequences for someone who is a ruler but does not govern the people with a spiritual regard. For example, it is explained that a king who levies taxes on his subjects without teaching them about righteousness (*Dharma*) has to suffer for their sins and loses his opulence. (*Bhagavata Purana* 4.21.24)

This is why, especially in this age of Kali-yuga, it is said that hardly any ruler attains anything but a dark future after death. Unable to direct his subjects properly, or even being infected with crooked desires himself, a ruler is forced to endure a hellish afterlife because of not being able to lead his subjects properly or allow them to be trained in the ways of *Dharma*. Such understanding of *Dharma* is what frees them from sinful life, and which also frees the king from accepting one-sixth of the reactions of his subjects.

"An arrogant king in whose kingdom innocent people are tormented by evildoers loses his fame, longevity, fortune, and a meritorious place after death." (*Bhagavata Purana* 1.17.10)

"Undoubtedly a king who does not perform his duties toward his subjects regularly goes to hell, a place which is devoid of air." (*Ramayana* 7.53.6)

"A king who (duly) protects (his subjects) receives from each and all the sixth part of their spiritual merit; if he does not protect them, the sixth part of their demerit also (will fall on him). Whatever (merit a man gains by) reading the *Vedas*, by spiritual practice, by charitable gifts, (or by) worshiping (God), the king obtains a sixth part of that in consequence of his duly protecting (his kingdom)." (*Manu-samhita* 8.304-5)

"A king who protects the created beings in accordance with the sacred law and smites those worthy of corporal punishment, daily offers (as it were) sacrifices at which a hundred thousands (are given as) fees." (*Manu-samhita* 8.306)

"A king who does not afford protection, (yet) takes his share in kind, his taxes, tolls and duties, daily presents and fines, will (after death) soon sink into hell. They declare that a king who affords no protection, (yet) receives the sixth part of the produce, takes upon himself all the foulness of his whole people. Know that a king who heeds not the rules (of the law), who is an atheist, and rapacious, who does not protect (his subjects, but) devours them, will sink low (after death)." (*Manu-samhita* 8.307-9)

"The subjects reject a king whose administration is faulty." (*Yogavasistha* 6.84.27)

"None, not even his kith and kin rush to the rescue of a king who behaves cruelly (with his ministers, etc.), pays them very low emoluments, behaves arrogantly, is conceited and secretly harms people in times of a calamity." (*Ramayana* 3.33.15)

"Even if the one who harasses living beings is cruel and a sinner becomes the master of all the three regions, he does not remain in power for long." (*Ramayana* 3.29.3)

"The king who does not organize a network of spies (to get news about the kingdom), or does not grant the subjects an opportunity to express their woes to him, who is controlled by others (whether by women for sense enjoyment or by political groups), is rejected by the people just as elephants abandon a river seeing the mud in it." (*Ramayana* 3.33.5)

The *Manu-samhita* (7.46-52) also explains: "For a king who is attached to the vices springing from love of pleasure, loses his wealth and his virtue, but (he who is given) to those arising from anger (loses) even his life. Hunting, gambling, sleeping by day, censoriousness, (excess with) women (or illicit sex), drunkenness (intoxication), (an inordinate love for) dancing, singing, and music, and useless travel are the tenfold set (of vices) springing from love of pleasure. Telling of tall tales, violence, treachery, envy, slandering, (unjust) seizure of property, reviling, and assault are the eightfold set (of vices) produced by wrath. That greediness which all wise men declare to be the root even of both these (sets), let carefully conquer; both sets (of vices) are produced by that. Drinking (intoxication), playing dice (gambling), (illicit connection with) women, and hunting (unnecessary killing and eating of animals), these four in succession, he must know to be the most pernicious in the set that springs from love of pleasure. Doing bodily injury, reviling, and the seizure of property, these three he must know to be the most pernicious in the set produced by wrath. A self-controlled (king) should know that in this set of seven, which prevails everywhere, each earlier-named vice is more abominable (than those named later)."

CONCLUSION
POLITICS AND LEADERSHIP IN THE VEDIC WAY

In applying the Vedic principles to our lives, it will also change the way we view politics and the system of leadership we choose. There will be certain standards that we will want to maintain.

Many civilizations on the planet that have prided themselves for being advanced are not genuine civilizations. This means that they are not as civilized as they think. A true civilized society will hold love, compassion, cooperation, wisdom, and freedom as its basis and foundation, and not mere technological, economic or military superiority to dominate others. This sort of emphasis in advancement does not solve all the problems of life. It does not promote true peace in the world, nor does it make a society truly civilized. It mostly perpetuates the differences between the members of society as well as the selfish idea that the privileged can control all situations by the notion that might is right, and thus continue to dominate the weak.

Society must pick a true leader, and not merely elect the lesser of the evils among the candidates running for office. But, they must know what is a real leader. A real leader must also know the Universal Spiritual Truths. Then such a leader can make programs that use a foundation that is universally applicable to everyone. In this way, the leader must use a complete philosophy for his or her politics. Otherwise an imperfect leader will not be able to create an ideology that is acceptable to everyone, but he will continue to speculate on what might work and suggest ideas that are untried, untrue and that continue to create confusion. This goes on while hiding the real agenda, which is often to trick people into working hard to pay large amounts in taxes that are funneled away from truly benefitting the people and the planet. If the leader is a fool, the government becomes a fool's paradise. If the leader is a thief, the citizens become paupers.

A real leader must be ethically fit and strong in order to subdue disturbances properly. Before a leader can affect the world, he must take care of things locally, in his own domain. He must first curb whatever sufferings his own subjects and citizens endure. They are supporting him, it is their taxes he is overseeing, and thus they should be the first to reap the rewards of proper leadership and government funding. So first, all thieves, rapists, kidnapers, murderers, and dacoits of all kinds must be stopped and apprehended. This will help create peace for all honest citizens. Also, programs that benefit the people, such as securing employment opportunities, natural resources and the environment, must be established or people will lose hope for the future.

Dishonest miscreants and criminals in society flourish because of cowardly and impotent heads of state. If such leaders cannot manage their position properly, criminals make use of the situation to terrorize honest citizens. But, when heads of state are strong enough to curb all sorts of criminals in any part of the country, then they will not be able to flourish. When miscreants are punished in an exemplary and immediate manner, then good fortune follows. Crime goes down, the expense for law enforcement decreases, and then the citizens in general do not need to live in fear. This will affect their confidence in government and the way they contribute to the country. However, when laws are passed that protect criminals and force honest citizens to become incapable of defending themselves, or where law enforcement is slow and ineffective, then thieves and rogues become prominent in society due to an incapable government. Such a country soon becomes a dangerous place in which to live. Misfortune is then bound to follow.

Thus, a leader's priority is first to his or her land and citizens. Only after his own area is secure and beneficial programs are firmly established should there be any engagement for large expenditures or military action outside of defending his own jurisdiction, beyond his borders, and only then if such military ventures do not unnecessarily tax the economy. Once local problems are solved and adjusted, the leaders and people will have a stronger base from which to tackle challenges and difficulties in other parts of the world.

If a ruler or government is effective in curbing crime in its own country, keeping the citizens free from disturbances of cheating businessmen, corrupt politicians, terrorists, thieves, etc., by virtue of such a strong leader, he can more easily collect taxes. More citizens will be honest and willing to pay. However, if a leader or government cannot protect the citizens from such dacoits in public or government affairs, such an ineffective leader should not be so ostentatious as to think he deserves the right to continue to collect heavy taxes from his subjects, or even continue in his position. If the leader is ineffective and allows criminals to occupy his jurisdiction, then he will share in the reactions of the evil deeds that are conducted under his regime, and his future will become very dark. Thus, a bad ruler perpetuates the spoiling of the whole country.

What is worse is when rogues themselves are elected to office. Then such cheaters, taking advantage of their situation and position, will enjoy life by living off the high taxes that are taken from the citizens. Or, they will engage in political or financial intrigue that will put large profits into their pockets at the taxpayers' expense. This in turn makes the people more dishonest by trying to hide their income from being taxed by crooked politicians. Then, as this criminal mentality spreads, trickling down from the politicians, the whole country becomes increasingly corrupt.

The hierarchies and regimes that operate according to self-serving methods that are in fact vicious and unjust, especially toward honest people, cannot remain in place. The ultimate force of Truth in the world will see them fall sooner or later. We must bring forth the power of transformation, not by force or manipulation but by making a stand for what is right through genuine concern and spiritual love.

However, it is not enough that leaders try to provide peace through military domination or force. There needs to be funds that will support educational projects that will spread genuine spiritual knowledge that can invoke a real change of consciousness in humanity at large. This does not mean simply to spread a particular religion, but to spread that spiritual information that can be applied by anyone, anywhere, regardless of religious affiliations. By providing the means for a genuine change of consciousness, and an uplifting growth in perceptivity of our spiritual unity, there can be peace by the deliberate choice of society as opposed to mere military might. There can be harmony through intellectual and spiritual growth. Otherwise, real peace will not be possible. It will only be a strained peace since the underlying cause for disunity and trouble remains, waiting for the opportunity for conflict to break out again.

Naturally, there may be times when military force is needed to put an end to unnecessary conflict or to subdue criminals, but it can never be a means to lasting peace.

Our disrespect toward one another is nothing but a reflection of our disrespect toward God, or at the very least our disconnection from God. Whereas the more our relation with God is established in a mature manner, the more we can see God in everything and everyone. In such a state of mind, war, being a vehicle in which we try to kill as many of the enemy as possible, is like blaspheme in itself. As we continue to lose our connection with God we lose our moral values, our civility, our care and concern for each other, and then the basis for quarrel and war escalates.

A ruler should be the representative of perfect morality. He should exhibit exemplary behavior in his actions, directions and speech. Thus, as it is most beneficial for society in general to work toward spiritual advancement, so it is also beneficial for a ruler to work in ways that enhance his or her own spiritual development. He or she should see to it that everyone has an equal opportunity to do the same. This is proper leadership.

Furthermore, proper leadership should arrange things in such a way so there is cooperation between God, nature and humanity. If we act in a way that pleases God, then He will oversee us and supply what we need. But, that also means we should respect and honor the blessings the Supreme has given us and continues to give us, and exhibit thankfulness by honoring and cooperating with nature. Thus, we will not spoil or overuse our natural resources, and there will be harmony between humanity and all aspects of nature. If our land is full with natural assets, the nation and world can be economically well to do. If we do not honor our resources, or if we spoil them through pollution, or overuse them through bad management or leadership, there will be scarcity and high prices. This gives way to apprehension, fear and difficulties for people who must conduct their lives at increasing expense. Thus, the economic status of the country and the confidence of the people in the leaders and the future of the country will begin to plummet. This is why there must be proper cooperation between God, mankind and nature, which is another aspect of understanding the principles of Vedic culture.

If people cannot progress spiritually and see things according to such universal Vedic standards, they will not make any advancement toward the higher goal of human life. This is beyond moralistic principles and is the foundation of real spiritual perception and realization. It is a duty of the government that the facilities are provided so this can go on nicely.

CHAPTER NOTES

1. Niranjan Shah, *India is Mother of Self-government and Democracy*, India Tribune, November 7, 2009.

Mahabharata is abbreviated as *Mb* throughout the article.

2. *Mahabharata*, translated by Kamala Subramaniam, published by Bharatiya Vidya Bhavan, Bombay, 1982, pages 710-12

3. Ibid., pages 354-355

4. Ibid., page 357

5. Ibid., page 714

6. Ibid., page 354

7. Ibid., pages 708-709

8. Ibid., pages 709

9. Ibid., page 709

10. Ibid., page 709

11. Ibid., pages 709-10

12. Ibid., pages 715-16

13. Ibid., page 709

14. Ibid., page 712-13

15. Ibid., page 709

16. Ibid., page 714

17. Ibid., page 353

18. Ibid., page 714

CHAPTER NINETEEN

Developments in Military and Martial Arts

The earliest form of military science, if we want to call it that, is outlined in the standard Vedic text called the *Dhanurveda*. However, this has been lost. Nonetheless, much of this knowledge can still be found in such books as the *Mahabharata*, *Agni Purana*, and so on that describe military techniques. This was based firstly on the several arrays of military forces for defensive measures and for attacks on the enemy. These were for arranging the army in *Uras* or center-based, *Kakshas* or flanks, *Pakshas* or wings, *Praligraha* or reserves, *Koti* or vanguards, *Madhya* or back centered, and *Prishtha* or back line behind the *Madhya* but in front of the reserves.

Some arrays, called *vyuhas*, are named for the object they resemble. These are the *Madhyabhedi*, or one which breaks the center; *Antarbhedi*, or that which penetrates between the divisions; *Makaravyuha*, the army drawn up like a *makara* creature; *Syenavyuha*, like a hawk with spread out wings; *Sakalavyuha*, or shaped like a wagon; *Aradhachandra*, a half-moon; *Sarvatobhadra*, or hollow square; *Gomutrika*, or echelon; and so on. Then there were other arrangements for other parts of the forces, such as elephants, calvary, infantry called *Danda* or staff; *Bhoja* or column; *Mandala* or hollow circle; and *Asanhata* or detached arrangements for these.

The use and training of weapons was a most important part of the military, which during those days comprised the use of bow and arrows while riding horses. Archery also included the shooting of not just a single arrow but included the shooting of several arrows at once. Besides the bow and arrow, several other weapons where also implemented. These included thrown missiles called *Yantramuktas*; those hurled by hand, *Hastamuktas*;

weapons to be held, or *Muktamuktas*, like javelins, tridents, or swords, maces, etc.; then natural weapons like fists, fingers, feet, and so on.

However, there were also weapons based on some explosive projectile, called a *vajra* or thunderbolt. Some suspect this to relate to explosives like gunpowder. The Vedic Aryans were well aware of the ingredients of gunpowder, such as sulphur, charcoal, saltpeter, which had been described in some of their medical treatises, and all of which were easily acquired locally. In fact, Greek writers describe the fire-arms used by the Hindus. In a letter to Aristotle, Alexander describes the terrific flashes of flame which showered on his army in India. In this regard, there were weapons called *Shatagnis*, a machine which shoots out pieces of iron to kill numbers of men at once. It appears that rockets and cannons were an early Indian invention before they became popular in other areas.

The *Brahmastra* was another weapon mentioned repeatedly in the Vedic texts. These were types of mantra weapons that were then attached to arrows that would produce the effect of a nuclear blast when they landed or hit their target. However, the energy of the blast could be contained to affect only the target, not like the nuclear bombs of today which destroy everything in the area.

Another interesting science was that of *Vimana Vidya*, the science of what we now call airplanes. The knowledge itself has disappeared, except for a few texts that still reflect what was once known. But many of the Vedic books speak of Vimanas that could fly through the sky, and which were also used for military purposes. Thus, the Vedic Aryans knew of airplanes that could be used for various purposes, and could navigate the skies and even fight battles in the skies.

INDIAN MARTIAL ARTS

India is also known for its distinguished and fierce forms of martial arts, which is one of the earliest developments that have been in existence for thousands of years. In fact, many of the forms of martial arts that have come out of the orient were first influenced by the techniques from India. Some of the styles of martial arts from India traveled to the orient, to places like Tibet, then China, and later to Japan, along with Buddhism when it first arrived in those areas.

The martial arts in India were called *shastravidya* and *dhanurvidya*. *Vidya* means knowledge, and *shastra* based on *astra* in this case means weapon, and *dhanur* relates to the bow (*dhanushya*) for archery. The *Dhanurveda* was an *upaveda* for the knowledge of military fighting or weaponry.

Many of the Vedic texts contain references to fighting. The *Bhagavata Purana*, *Vishnu Purana*, *Mahabharata*, and others contained descriptions of personal fighting and combat that took place, and descriptions of the weapons that were used, including trees, swords, bows and arrows, rocks, fists, etc., and even related the techniques that were used as well, such as kicks, knee strikes, hand strikes, or even headbutts. The *Agni Purana* especially had a section (chapters 248-251) that was considered a manual on *dhanurveda* and discussed the usage of various weapons.

Only later, around the 3rd century BCE, were elements from the *Yoga Sutras* of Patanjali used in martial arts. Even dance moves from such styles as Kathakali, which is also well known in Kerala, were incorporated into martial arts. We can also find references to fighting styles in the Tamil Sangam texts that date back to the 2nd century BCE. Amongst these, the *Akananuru* and *Purananuru* relate the use of spears, swords, knives, shields, bows, etc.

What also developed was the knowledge of *Marma* points, or pressure points that could be used in martial arts as well. These were explained in such texts as the *Sushruta Samhita*, a medical treatise by the sage Shusruta in the 4th century, which identified 107 such points over the human body, of which 64 could be lethal when struck properly with the fist or a weapon.

In the 8th century, there was the *Kuvalaymala* by Udyotanasuri that was taught at various educational institutions for non-warrior students to learn the art of using swords and shields, daggers, knives, sticks, lances, and so on.

Indian wrestling dates to the earliest of times and was found in many parts of India, and still influences numerous aspects of martial arts today. Of course, today much of the serious training and preservation of combat methods are practiced and taught in special ashramas of Kerala. But in the early days, such training of various styles could be found in a wide variety of places. In fact, the interesting thing is that there is not just one location where such martial techniques were developed, but various methods and styles originated in different locations of ancient India.

For example, what is called Kalaripaayattu is a well known system of martial arts in India, but mostly of Kerala origin. The name is based on where it is taught, which is the *kalari* or training hall. This technique uses much footwork, with kicks and unarmed combat, but also with various weapons, such as sticks, canes, swords and shields, knives, spears, etc. The origins for this technique can be traced back to at least the 4th century CE. However, tradition says that it began as far back as the time of Lord Parashurama thousands of years ago. He was also known as the great axe wielder and to have taught forms of martial arts.

From Tamil Nadu, especially around Madurai, we have the Silambam style, which is primarily with the use of weapons, along with positions and movements based on animals like the snake, tiger, eagle, etc. This can be traced back to at least the era of the Pandya kings, and to the *Silapathiharam* (a Tamil romance called *The Ankle Bracelet*) that relates the sale of *Silambam* sticks and swords back in the 2nd century CE. However, tradition also says that the sage Agastya developed and taught this technique. Many people still practice this as a form of exercise.

One of the oldest forms of martial arts is that of the *lathi*, or long stick. It was practiced primarily in Bengal and in the Punjab and is still used today in many areas. Also from the Punjab comes Gatka style martial art, which was created by the Sikhs and uses weapons like the stick and *kirpan* or knife, both long and short. These are used in the form of attacks or defense positions determined by the placement of the hands and feet. From the area around Kolhapur in Maharashtra we get what is called Mardani Khel. From Bihar we find Pari-Khanda fighting created by the Rajputs, with the use of the sword and shield. From the area of Varanasi we get the Musti Yuddha system, based on being unarmed and using techniques of kicks, punches, along with strikes from the elbows and knees. You do not see this technique much, but it was more popular in the middle ages. From Himachal Pradesh, such as around Kullu and Manali, we also see the style called Thoda, which relies primarily on archery, said to date back to the times of the *Mahabharata*, such as in battles between the Pandavas and Kauravas. Thoda referred to the blunt piece of wood on the tip of the arrow meant for wounding its target. From Manipur we find the Thang Ta style, also called Huyen Lallong, or the Cheibi Gad-ga style, which uses primarily swords and spears and leather shields as the means for defense.

In this way, there are many techniques and styles of martial arts that came out of various areas of Bharatvarsha and spread elsewhere.

A demonstration of some seriously skilled martial artists, two against one, using swords and shields, in Imphal, Manipur

CHAPTER TWENTY

Airplanes or Vimanas

In supplying information about the advancements of Vedic science, the subject of Vedic airplanes, *vimanas*, is almost in a classification of its own. Some of this information is so amazing that for some people it may border science fiction. Nonetheless, as we uncover and explain it, it provides serious food for thought.

First of all we need to understand that the Vedic conception of universal time is divided into different periods. For example, a period called one day of Brahma is equivalent to 4,320,000,000 of our years on earth. Brahma's night is equally as long and there are 360 of such days and nights in one year of Brahma. Each day of Brahma is divided into one thousand cycles of four *yugas*, namely Satya-yuga, Treta-yuga, Dvapara-yuga, and finally the Kali-yuga, which is the *yuga* we are presently experiencing. Satya-yuga lasts 1,728,000 years, and is an age of purity when all residents live very long lives and can be fully developed in spiritual understanding and mystical abilities and remarkable powers. Some of these abilities, or mystic *siddhis*, include changing one's shape, becoming very large or microscopically small, becoming very heavy or even weightless, securing any desirable thing, becoming free of all desires, or even flying through the sky to wherever one wanted to go on one's own volition. So at that time, the need for mechanical flying machines was not necessary.

As the *yugas* continued, the purity of the people, along with their mystical abilities, decreased by 25% in each age. The age of Treta-yuga lasts 1,296,000 years. During that age, the minds of humanity became more dense, and the ability for understanding the higher spiritual principles of the Vedic path was also more difficult. Naturally, the ability to fly through the sky by one's own power was lost. After Treta-yuga, Dvapara-yuga lasts 864,000 years, and Kali-yuga lasts 432,000 years, of which 5,000 have now already passed. At the end of Kali-yuga, the age of Satya-yuga starts again and the *yugas* continue through another cycle. One thousand such cycles is one day of Brahma. Now that we are in Kali-yuga, almost all spiritual understanding disappears, and whatever mystical abilities that remain are almost insignificant.

It is explained that it was not until the beginning of Treta-yuga that the development of *vimanas* took place. In fact, Lord Brahma, the chief demigod and engineer of the universe, is said to have developed several *vimanas* for some of the other demigods. These were in various natural shapes that incorporated the use of wings, such as peacocks, eagles, swans, etc. Other *vimanas* were developed for the wiser human beings by great seers of Vedic knowledge.

In the course of time, there were three basic types of *vimanas*. In Treta-yuga, men were adept in mantras or potent hymns. Thus, the *vimanas* of that age were powered by means of knowledge of mantras. In Dvapara-yuga, men had developed considerable knowledge of tantra or ritual. Thus, the *vimanas* of Dvapara-yuga were powered by the use of tantric knowledge. In Kali-yuga, knowledge of both mantra and tantra are deficient. Thus, the *vimanas* of this age are known as kritaka, artificial or mechanical. In this way, there are three main types of *vimanas*, Vedic airplanes, according to the characteristics of each *yuga*.

Of these three types, there is listed 25 variations of the *mantrika vimanas*, 56 variations of the *tantrica vimanas*, and 25 varieties of the *kritakaah vimanas* as we find today in Kali-yuga. However, in regard to the shape and construction, it is explained that there is no difference between any of these *vimanas*, but only in how they were powered or propelled, which would be by mantras, tantras, or mechanical engines.

The controversial text known as *Vimaanika Shastra*, said to be originally by Maharshi Bharadwaja, also describes in detail the construction of what is called the mercury vortex engine. This is no doubt of the same nature as the Vedic Ion engine that is propelled by the use of mercury. Such an engine was built by Shivkar Bapuji Talpade, based on descriptions in the *Rig Veda*, which he demonstrated in Mumbai (Bombay), India in 1895. I more fully explained this in Chapter Three of *Proof of Vedic Culture's Global Existence*. Additional information on the mercury engines used in the *vimanas* can be found in the ancient Vedic text called the *Samarangana Sutradhara*. This text also devotes 230 verses to the use of these machines in peace and war. We will not provide the whole description of the mercury vortex engine here, but we will include a short part of William Clendenon's translation of the *Samarangana Sutradhara* from his 1990 book, *Mercury, UFO Messenger of the Gods*:

"Inside the circular air frame, place the mercury-engine with its electric/ultrasonic mercury boiler at the bottom center. By means of the power latent in the mercury which sets the driving whirlwind in motion, a man sitting inside may travel a great distance in the sky in a most marvelous manner. Four strong mercury containers must be built into the interior structure. When those have been heated by controlled fire from iron containers, the *vimana* develops thunder-power through the mercury. At once it becomes like a pearl in the sky."

This provides a most simplistic idea of the potential of the mercury engines. This is one kind of a propulsion mechanism that the *vimanas* of Kali-yuga may use. Other variations are also described. Not only do these texts contain directions on how to make such engines, but they also have been found to contain flight manuals, aerial routes, procedures for normal and forced landings, instructions regarding the condition of the pilots, clothes to wear while flying, the food to bring and eat, spare parts to have, metals of which the craft needs to be made, power supplies, and so on. Other texts also provide instructions on avoiding enemy craft, how to see and hear what occupants are saying in enemy craft, how to become invisible, and even what tactics to use in case of collisions with birds. Some of these *vimanas* not only fly in the sky, but can also maneuver on land and fly into the sea and travel under water.

There are many ancient Vedic texts that describe or contain references to these *vimanas*, including the *Ramayana*, *Mahabharata*, *Rig Veda*, *Yajur Veda*, *Atharva Veda*, the *Yuktilkalpataru* of Bhoja (12th century CE), the *Mayamatam* (attributed to the architect Maya), plus other classic Vedic texts like the *Satapatha Brahmana*, *Markandeya Purana*, *Vishnu Purana*, *Bhagavata Purana*, the *Harivamsa*, the *Uttararamcarita*, the *Harsacarita*, the Tamil text *Jivakacintamani*, and others. From the various descriptions in these writings, we find *vimanas* in many different shapes, including that of long cigars, blimp-like, saucer-shapes, triangular, and even double-decked with portholes and a dome on top of a circular craft. Some are silent, some belch fire and make noise, some have a humming noise, and some disappear completely.

These various descriptions are not unlike the reports of UFOs that are seen today. In fact, David Childress, in his book *Vimana Aircraft of Ancient India & Atlantis*, provides many reports, both recent and from the last few hundred years, that describe eye witness accounts of encounters with UFOs that are no different in size and shape than those described in these ancient Vedic texts. Plus, when the pilots are seen close up, either fixing their craft or stepping outside to look around, they are human-like, sometimes with an Oriental appearance, in clothes that are relatively modern in style. In other reports, we have read where the craft may have alien type beings on board along with ordinary humans navigating the craft.

Does this mean that these are ancient *vimanas* that still exist today? Are they stored in some underground caverns somewhere? Or are they simply modern-built, using the ancient designs as described in the Vedic texts? The UFOs that have been seen around the world may not be from some distant galaxy, but may be from a secret human society, or even military installation.

In any case, many of the early Vedic texts do describe interplanetary travel, and the vehicles that can do it, the likes of which are found in no other literature, and certainly not in such detail as that in the Vedic tradition. So they must have known about flying machines, otherwise how could they have written about them?

CHAPTER TWENTY-ONE

Additional Developments From Ancient India

VAISHESHIKA ATOMIC THEORY

India was also known for its atomic theory that it had developed, way before any such thoughts had appeared in Greece. As explained by B. V. Subbarayappa in his *India's Contributions to the History of Science* in the volume *India's Contribution to World Thought and Culture*, he explains: "In the history of the evolution of physical ideas, the Indian Vaisheshika system deserves special mention. This system, which is supposed to have been propounded by a sage called Kanada, Kanabhuj or Kanabhaksha, even in its sutra form, seems to be very old, probably pre-Buddhistic. In ten chapters, the *Vaisheshika Sutras* deal with a number of physical concepts, such as those concerning substance, the five elements, motion, attributes, space, time and atomism. The point worthy of note is that the system had assumed a definite shape by about the sixth century B. C. When even the pre-Socratic thinkers were gradually generating their views on the physical world. There is considerable resemblance between the ideas contained in a cryptic form in the *Vaisheshika Sutras* and those later propounded by some of the leading Greek thinkers including Aristotle. The concepts of substance, element-theory of matter, and the atomism are cases in point. It is not unlikely that the Vaisheshika school with its systematic formulations might have attracted and stimulated the attention of like-minded people from far and wide including the Greek thinkers." [1]

This was the Vedic concept of the atomic nature of things, based on the atom. Kanada propounded that the *Parmanu* (atom) was the essential, indestructible particle of matter, which could be divided no further. However, when two *Parmanus* of one substance combined, a *dwinuka* or binary molecule would form. It was different combinations of atoms that made the five primary elements of earth, fire, water, air, and ether, and from there made different forms and bodies.

These types of ideas were the first in regard to atomic theories, and only after coming in contact with India did such theories about the atom begin to appear in Greek science.

CHESS CAME FROM INDIA

Dr. Will Durant, famous author on civilization, wrote in *Our Oriental Heritage*: "It is true that even across the Himalayan barrier India has sent to us such questionable gifts as grammar and logic, philosophy and fables, hypnotism and chess, and above all, our numerals and our decimal system."

Yes, it seems that chess also was an invention that came from India. This appeared during the Gupta empire, where its early form in the 6th century was known as *chaturanga*, which translates as four divisions of the military; namely infantry, cavalry, elephantry, and chariotry, represented by the pieces that would evolve into the modern pawn, knight, bishop, and rook. In this way, the game was a battle simulation game. In Persia, around 600 CE, the name *chaturanga* and the rules were developed further, and players started saying "Sh'h!" (which means King in Persian) when they were attacking the opponent's king piece. And then "Sh'h m't!" meant that the King was finished, such as when now saying "Check mate!" These phrases persisted as the game moved from one region to another.

By 1100-1200 CE, the game became known in central Europe, and was well established across all of Europe by 1400 CE with the rules of the game which we use today. Russia's great interest in chess is more recent, dating from the Communist revolution of 1917.

Dr. Stanley Wolpert, professor of history at UCLA, also recognizes, as he writes in the publication *India*, that it is thanks to India for the game of chess. Dr. A. L. Basham, professor of history and author of *The Wonder That was India*, also summarizes in the same way: "As well as her special gifts to Asia, India has conferred many practical blessings on the world at large; notably rice, cotton, the sugar cane, many spices, the domestic fowl, the game of chess, and most important of all, the decimal system of numeral notation." [2]

OTHER GAMES

There were many games that were developed and continue to be played in India from long ago. These include Kabbadi, Kho-Kho, AtyaPatya, Malkhamb, Gulli-danda, and so on. There was also Ludo (Snakes and Ladders). Even playing cards were played in India from many years ago. This game was known as Kridapatram in ancient times, and later as Ganjifa in medieval times. The Muslim historian Abul Fazal, author of *Ain-e-Akbari*, mentioned that the game of cards was of Indian origin and was already a popular pastime in Indian courts when the Muslims arrived there.

CHAPTER NOTES
1. B. V. Subbarayappa, *India's Contributions to the History of Science*, published in *India's Contribution to World Thought and Culture*, by Vivekananda Kendra Prakashan, Chennai, 1970, p. 59.
2. Niranjan Shah, *The Game of Chess Originated in India*, in India Tribune, December 5, 2009.

CHAPTER TWENTY-TWO

The Early Homeland of Humanity

Genetic studies, at least at this point in time, seem to have established that the home or place of early development of *Homo sapiens* was Africa around 150,000 years ago. Recent discoveries indicate other areas of the planet where *Homo sapiens* have appeared many years ago as well. But for now we will focus on the "Out of Africa" premise. It is figured that 80,000 years ago a number of them left Africa to travel along the coast to South Asia, especially to ancient India, to settle and gradually spread out from there to colonize different parts of the world. According to this premise, all non-Africans descended from this area of the world, which means that Europeans were the descendants of these early South Asians. This also indicates that the Indian population is mostly of the same indigenous origin and not based on some invasions or migrations or divisions that came into the area much later as some people believe. [1]

Additional genetical research has shown similar conclusions, that the gene flow into the region has been most limited, meaning there was not a flow into the area. If anything, it shows the gene flow has been on an outward basis, meaning that from the earliest settlements in ancient India, people migrated from it in different directions.

With the use of genetics, it has been found that modern Europeans are descended from South Asians. Therefore, in their early travels, they are most likely to have taken two routes, which included a southern course through West Asia and the Mediterranean, or north through Central Asia and into West Europe, all of which began up to 50,000 years ago. [2]

All of this certainly puts a damper on the Aryan Invasion Theory that many people are finally starting to reject because of overwhelming evidence to the contrary.

One of the world's foremost human geneticists, Luiga Luca Cavalli-Sforza, Emeritus Professor at Stanford University, and his colleagues have done research which provide the conclusions that show there is no racial divisions in the tribal and caste populations of India. Their observations were:

"Taken together, these results show that Indian tribal and caste populations derive largely from the same genetic heritage of Pleistocene southern and western Asians and have received limited gene flow from external regions since the Holocene."

What this means is that the people of India, whether it be tribals, Dravidians, northern Aryans, etc., are all mainly of indigenous origin, going back past the last Ice Age to 50,000 years or more, without a genetic contribution from any invaders or from outside. This has helped nullify the Aryan Invasion Theory, but also helped put aside the idea that was used by the British that the Dravidians of the south, who were the original residents of India, had been oppressed by the invading Aryans of the north. Of course, this idea was rooted not in reality, which we can presently see, but was based on the politics of missionary colonialism. This was to help divide the people into antagonistic groups that fought each other under the labels of Aryans and Dravidians, which then helped facilitate the British in their occupation of India and their conversions to Christianity. This had also become the political manifesto of Dravidian politicians as part of their caste-based politics, especially in Tamil Nadu.

For years, the Hindu population had looked to the Brahmanas for social and spiritual guidance, but these Brahmana priests were also seen as obstacles to the British missionary agenda to convert the society. Thus, the purpose of promoting the non-existent differences between Aryans (Brahmanas) and Dravidians was to turn the people against those who had always been the primary preservers and protectors of Hindu culture and tradition. The main reason why this contention still continues is because humanities education in India is still dominated by Christian institutions of the colonial era. [3]

Furthermore, Stephen Oppenheimer, in his *Out of Eden*, gives another approximate date of when modern humans lived in South Asia as being at least 70,000 years ago. This makes it even more clear that if the modern humans, for the most part, developed first in Africa, as the evolutionists like to say, and then left for South Asia, then all non-African humans living in the world today are descendants of these ancient people of South Asia, namely India. Or, as N. S. Rajaram sums up, "This means, all modern humans of the world–Europeans, Chinese, Southeast Asians, American Indians, Australian aborigines, and so forth–each and every group of them is descended from South Asians who were the first people to leave Africa and survive outside of Africa... Further, Indians have received hardly any gene flow from outside in the past ten thousand years (since the Holocene or since the last Ice Age ended)." [4] This again is another final nail in the coffin of the Aryan Invasion Theory.

THE FLOW FROM THE EAST TO THE WEST

The point is, if we analyze the history of the Vedic tradition, we can begin to see that ever since the earliest of times, there has been a steady flow of people, population, and later philosophy and science from the East to the West. We can see that all cultures, whether it be the early Egyptian, Babylonian, Sumerian, or even the Jewish, Persian, and Greek received the light of spirituality and science from the East. However, Indian and Vedic traditions also traveled eastward, which can easily be recognized when we look at the cultures of Burma, Thailand (the rulers of which still call themselves by the name of Rama), Cambodia (the rulers who still use the Indian name of Varma), and further to Laos, Vietnam, and Indonesia. Look at locations such as Angkor Wat and Angkor Thom (of which the Sanskrit name origins are Nagara-vati and Nagara-dhama), the area of which was once ruled by Jayavarman II, or the Sanskrit name origins of Cambodia (Kambuja-desha), or Vietnam (Champa), or Jaya and Sumatra in Indonesia, all of which clearly show the Vedic influence. [5]

One of the earliest migrations from India was around the date of 4600 BCE or earlier. This is when an Indian ruler known as Mandhata conducted a series of campaigns in the northwest of India against a people known as the Druhyas, who are recorded in ancient texts such as the *Rig Veda* as being a very ancient people. The Druhyas were greatly defeated. This is what forced them to leave India, which is what preceded a large migration into Central Asia and on into Europe. This could have also been the root of many of the similarities in linguistics, myths and traditions recognized between India and Europe. This is also the way that places like China, Japan and the other areas of the Far East received Buddhism from India many centuries ago. In fact, this and other situations that occurred is quite likely to be why we can see such strong relations between the Sanskrit language of Lithuania and India. In fact, we could do a separate study on Lithuania and Russia, in its old languages and culture, to recognize how many carry-overs there are between the region of India and the other. I have friends who are always telling me about the many ways Vedic culture and Sanskrit language can be identified in Russia and Lithuania and other countries of the area. This would seem to indicate that Bharatvarsha, ancient India, had also extended into or included the northern area of Russia as well.

On this point Shrikant Talageri goes on to explain: "The major reference in the *Puranas* is in the time of Mandhata, when the Druhyus had occupied the Punjab and were driven out from there by Mandhata for the sake of his maternal relations (the Purus). The Druhyu king of the time was Angara, and the next Druhyu king Gandhara retired to the northwest and gave his name to the Gandhara country [Afghanistan]." [6]

Thus, the main section of Druhyus were then settled in what became Afganistan. The *Puranas* then mention only four or five kings after Gandhara. And then the *Puranas* make the most amazing and clear declaration of the emigration of major sections of these Druhyus from Afghanistan to strange and distant lands in the north. The evidence provided by this unique statement is so absolute that no honest scholar can deny that it constitutes evidence of the migration of Indo-Europeans from India to Europe via Central Asia. [7]

Also, what became known as the Battle of Ten Kings is described in the seventh book of the *Rig Veda* by the sage Vasistha when the Vedic king Sudas battled with a confederation led by the Druhyus and other people from the area west and northwest of India. As described by N. S. Rajaram: Among the people defeated and driven out by Sudas were the Prithu-Parthavas, the Parsus, the Alinas and several others mentioned in the *Rig Veda*. The Prithu-Parthavas of course are known as the Parthians whose descendants founded a great empire in Iran; the Parthians in fact called themselves Parthava. The Parsus became the Persians and the Alinas are the Hellenes or the ancient Greeks, according to some scholars.

In the *Rig Veda* and the battle of ten kings, it is described that Sudas drove half of his enemies out of the area. Thus, the Anus and Druhyus went farther to the west, which gave rise to the Persian and Parthian cultures, and possibly even seeded the Greek, Mittani, Kassite, and Hittite cultures.

According to Shrikant Talageri, it was the Druhyus who became known as Druids, who themselves claim a history in Europe that goes back to 3900 BCE, having their origin in the East in Asia. The Druids are also known to have a priestly class and an organized society similar to the *Varnashrama* system of Vedic culture, along with many other similarities. [8]

"Other opponents of Sudas included Pakthas and Balhanas. Their descendants are known today as Pathans (or Pakthoons) and Baluchis of the Bolan Pass. Talageri notes several others. Thus, many of the so-called Indo-European peoples of the ancient world can be traced to India in very ancient times. This incidentally also helps explain why people from India to Iceland speak languages similar to one another and have also related mythologies." [9]

As Talageri goes on to describe: "Among the speakers of the Indo-European languages, a great historical occurrence took place when a major part of the India-Europeans of south-eastern Uttar Pradesh migrated to the west and settled down in the northwestern areas–Punjab, Kashmir and the further north-west, where they differentiated into three groups: the Purus (in the Punjab), the Anus (in Kashmir) and the Druhyus (in the northwest and Afghanistan)....

"The Purus developed the Vedic culture of the Punjab... Meanwhile, major sections of Anus spread out all over Western Asia and developed into the various Iranian cultures. The Druhyus spread out into Europe in two installments: the speakers of the proto-Germanic dialect first migrated northwards and then westwards, and then later the speakers of the proto-Hellenic and proto-Italo-Celtic dialects moved into Europe by a different, more southern, route." [10]

Anyway, this is a summarization of one of the processes that is likely to have started the early form of immigration from India to the northwest regions. Since the Vedic civilization had already been flourishing well before 4000 BCE, it is not logical that there would have been any other expansion but to the west, and also toward the east and southeast from India.

EXPANSION OF THE VEDIC PEOPLE

The Vedic Empire during the *Rig Veda* times had the basic boundaries of the Indus River on the west, the Sarayu on the east, and the Vindhya Mountains to the south, and all the way to the Arabian Sea to the west. However, evidence can be seen how the Vedic people had already expanded well beyond these lines and into Gandhara, Afghanistan, Iran, and further into Central Asia. The west was easy to traverse, with long plains where the horse provided natural transportation. To the east and southeast, once the Vedic people reached the Bay of Bengal, the route of ocean travel was used for contacting other people to spread or even reawaken the Vedic traditions.

The Iranians themselves speak of their homeland as outside of Iran. Being descendants of the Anus, their ancient home must be in the Sarasvati region, as the *Vedas* speak of no other homeland outside India. With the Persians, their early lands were considered to be Afghanistan, Tajikastan and Eastern Iran. The *Rig Veda* also mentions the Parshus (Persians), Parthavas (Parthians) and Pakthas (Pathans).

As the plateau of Iran became the center of a new culture populated by the migrants from north India, the Vedic people also spread over to the Caspian Sea. From there they could go on to the Black Sea and over to what became Eastern Europe. As migration increased, another route taken was through the mountains of Iran to Anatolia and over to Greece and Mesopotamia. These routes had also been used by those who became the Armenians, Scythians, Celts, and Druids, as well as earlier groups such as the Hittites and Mittani. Those tribes of the Sarasvati region who became familiar with maritime trade probably also moved on to Sumeria and Elam, or even to Egypt where they influenced the cultures and Aryanized them with their philosophy and traditions. [11] This is also why there have been some scholars, such as L. A. Waddell and others, who have felt that Sumeria was but a branch or a part of Vedic culture.

The Hittites seemed to have appeared in Anatolia at about 2200 BCE where they dominated the region through most of that second millennium BCE. They faded away as the Assyrians gained prominence. The Mittani also prevailed over the area of Syria, while the Kassites were in Babylonia during this same time period, after also appearing here in the late third millennium. It was the elites of these clans that also ruled over the non-Aryan people of these areas. This is why the Vedic gods were known in these areas, such as Indra, Varuna and Mitra as a form of Surya the sun god. [12]

THE PERSIANS

The Anus were the ancestors of the Persians, offshoots that became known later as the Mlecchas. Thus, the Persians were originally a Vedic people that came out of the Punjab. They still continued with variations of the Vedic traditions, but then the appearance of Zoroaster brought about a new religion. The *Mahabharata* (Adi Parva 85.34) refers to the Mlecchas as offshoots of the Anus, but later the term included many people living outside the Vedic principles. In the *Brahmanas* (*Shatapatha Brahmana* 3.2.1.24) the term was used for those who lived in the west of ancient India, like the Mid-East and further. [13]

After the appearance of Zoroaster, the Persians became more separate from their Vedic connection. The conventional dating for Zarathustra or Zoroaster is about 600 BCE, but it is more likely that he appeared much earlier around 1400 BCE. Vedic Aryan culture had crossed into Southwest Asia and Iran many years before that. But it was Zarathustra who established his own religion that, for all intents and purposes, was in direct contrast from the Vedic culture in many ways.

It is said that the Zoroastrian religion was started in Balkh with the patronage of King Vistaspes in northeastern Afghanistan. This is not far from India. The name of Balkh, or what is known as Bactria, is also found in the *Atharva Veda* (5.22) in which the practices of the people are regarded as unorthodox, or non-Vedic. However, there were naturally religious, language and cultural similarities with the Vedic traditions. For example, they also had a sacred fire and priest (Atar, Atarva like the Vedic Athar, Atharvan), along with the sacred plant called Haoma, like the Vedic Soma, and similar gods like Mithra (Mitra), Airyaman (Aryaman), and Vayu, and Vedic Yama is known as Yima. However, there are some specific differences that helped turn the Zoroastrian religion away from their Vedic similarities. These include that the name of the Divine is called Ahura (Asura) and the demonic is called Daeva (Deva), and Indra is considered a demon, whereas this is just the opposite in the Vedic culture. [14]

THE GREEKS

We all know of the great connections between Greece and India. The Greeks are generally known as Yavanas. The *Mahabharata* (Adi Parva 85.34) describes the Yavanas to be descendants of Turvasha, which shows the Greeks as one of the five Vedic tribes that came out of ancient India. The *Vishnu Purana* (4.3.18-21) also lists them among those who were defeated by Sagara, along with the Persians, Scythians and Kambojas (meaning the Yavanas, Shakas and Pahlavas).

THE PRE-CHRISTIAN RELIGIONS IN EUROPE

As we study the expansion of the Vedic people, we can also understand how variations of Vedic *Dharma* were kept as part of their culture. We only have to be educated in the Vedic tradition to see this connection. As the Vedic Aryans moved into Europe, we can see that they kept Gods like Zeus, Thor, or Jupiter and others so that, though the names had been changed, they still filled the functions of corresponding Vedic Gods. They maintained a pluralistic tradition, using images, and worshiping many gods, for particular requests or purposes. This was still the foundation as supplied by the Vedic tradition.

In the *Annals and Histories of Tacitus*, the Germans also claimed to be descendants of Mannus, the son of Tuisto, who is regarded as the Sky God. Tuisto is the same as the Vedic Tvashtar, the Vedic father-sky God, or the father of Manu, Vivasvan the Sun God, and also father of Yama, the brother of Manu. (*Rig Veda*, 10.17.1-2)

The Celts also called themselves "Tuatha De Danaan," which meant they were children of Danu, the Mother Goddess. [15]

All of this gives us insight into understanding how the Vedic culture of Bharatvarsha was indigenous to India, and spread out from there in various directions to accept alternate forms in what became different traditions, the roots of which can be traced back to the Vedic philosophy and its center of Bharatvarsha, ancient India.

CHAPTER NOTES

1. Dr. David Frawley and Dr. Navaratna S. Rajaram, *Hidden Horizons, Unearthing 10,000 Years of Indian Culture*, Swaminarayan Aksharpith, Ahmedabad, India, 2006, pp. 22-23.

2. Ibid., p.123.

3. N. S. Rajaram, *Sarasvati River and the Vedic Civilization*, Aditya Prakashan, New Delhi, 2006, p. 57-58.

4. Ibid., p. 82.

5. Dr. David Frawley and Dr. Navaratna S. Rajaram, *Hidden Horizons, Unearthing 10,000 Years of Indian Culture*, Swaminarayan Aksharpith, Ahmedabad, India, 2006, p.120.

6. F. E. Pargiter, *Ancient Indian Historical Tradition*, Motilal Banarsidass, Delhi, 1962, p. 262.

7. Shrikant Talageri, *The Aryan Invasion Theory: A Reappraisal*, Aditya Prakashan, New Delhi, 1993, p. 327.

8. N. S. Rajaram, *Sarasvati River and the Vedic Civilization*, Aditya Prakashan, New Delhi, 2006, p. 72.

9. Ibid., p. 74.

10. Shrikant Talageri, *The Aryan Invasion Theory: A Reappraisal*, Aditya Prakashan, New Delhi, 1993, p. 367.

11. David Frawley, *The Rig Veda and the History of India*, Aditya Prakashan, New Delhi, 2001, p. 231.

12. Ibid., pp. 231-2.

13. Ibid., p. 224.

14. Ibid., p. 219.

15. Peter Ellis, *The Druids*, p. 118.

CHAPTER TWENTY-THREE

The Aryan Invasion Theory

The Aryan Invasion Theory (AIT) is the idea that the Vedic people were not indigenous to the area of northern India, but were invaders from the Caucasus Mountain region that descended on India around 1500 BCE, and then wrote the Vedic literature and forced the natives to accept their culture. In writing this chapter I want to emphasize that this book is not about the Aryan Invasion Theory (AIT), but we should at least include one chapter on it to show its place in discovering the real history of the development of ancient India and the origins of Vedic culture. In doing so, I acknowledge there have already been volumes written on this controversial topic, and on where the original homeland of the Indo Aryans might be. So anyone can read any of those books until one is nauseated with various viewpoints, but that is not what we are going to do here. Going into a long dissertation about how all the theories were developed and what evidence they found is the last thing I want to do. For all but the specialist researchers and readers, it would make for an extremely tedious book, at least more so than some may feel it is already. So, we are only going to summarize some of the most recent and concluding research that is available today.

Let us remember that the idea that the Vedic Aryans came from outside of ancient India and entered the region to start what became the Vedic civilization is a foreign idea. There was never any record, either historical, textual or archeological, that supports this premise for an Aryan invasion. There also is no record of who would have been the invaders. The fact is that it is a theory that came from mere linguistic speculation which happened during the nineteenth century when very little archeological excavation had yet been done around India.

There have been many researchers who have tried to study the linguistics of the people to gather an indication of where the original homeland of the Vedic Aryans was actually located. This was done to either try to uphold or refute the idea of the Aryan Invasion Theory. In my book, *Proof of Vedic Culture's Global Existence*, I dealt with linguistics and word similarities to a degree, but this topic, in spite of all the research, study, and books written on whatever findings were made, has done little to absolutely establish with clarity the original home of the Vedic Aryans.

Some scholars have always felt that the linguistic evidence is not sufficient to draw definite conclusions where the homeland of the Vedic Aryans was located.

Linguistics amongst some scholars have always been a speculative process, at best arriving at various conjectures about the origins of particular cultures and languages. Others have been even more dismissive of the idea of reconstructing a hypothetical language based on words that remain present in spoken languages thousands of years later. Thus, in trying to understand the Vedic Aryans and where their homeland may have been by analyzing some hypothetical Proto-Indo-European language that still has not been identified seems rather doubtful. At best, it may provide some basic hypothesis, which in reality may be most misleading. This also seems to say that there is little reason to hold the field of linguistics in such a high degree of respect, considering all the books that have been written that seem to use this process to determine so many conclusions, or conjectures, on the homeland of the Vedic Aryans.

As a further comment to this issue, G. P. Singh relates, "They (proponents of the Aryan Invasion Theory) are divided in their opinion regarding the exact location of the said common home, the reason for which is not far to discover. The speakers of Aryan languages have been clubbed together as an Aryan race which never existed as such. The philological and ethnological explanations regarding the identification of an Aryan language with an Aryan race are conflicting. The similarities of a few words do not necessarily constitute a proof of common origin of their speakers, rather they indicate commingling and sociocultural contacts and fellowship. The theory of a common home of members of a so-called Aryan family whether in Asia or Europe cannot be accepted merely on the evidence of linguistic paleontology... The Aryan invasion of India is a myth and not the truth. The Aryans were neither invaders nor conquerors. They were not the destroyers of the Harappan civilization but one of its authors." [1]

This does not mean, however, that we cannot still use linguistics to help recognize the many similarities of cultures by the closeness of words, in both spelling and meaning, that are used in the languages of various traditions, or where and how far the Vedic and Sanskrit influence has traveled, and how various cultures may have shared traditions with each other. But to supply proof of where the Vedic people originated, that is not possible. Plus, today we have so much more research and archeological evidence that tells far more than the study of linguistics, which will certainly lead us to the correct conclusion about this matter.

Up till today, there is still no culture from the time of ancient India that can be said to have originated outside and then invaded or brought the Vedic culture to the interior of India. More evidence will be given as we discuss this topic. But for now, what this means is that if we look at the ancient ruins, or agricultural practices, artifacts, or social activities, it can be recognized that they were all based on indigenous techniques and traditions. They are not linked to anything that would have come from outside of India, although just the opposite is the case. Moreover, we can see a migration from India to the west or even eastward.

Traditionally, as we find in the *Manu-samhita* (2.17-18), Vedic culture was founded by the sage Manu between the banks of the Sarasvati and Drishadvati Rivers. And the Sarasvati River was the main river in the *Rig Veda*, which, according to modern land studies, was a massive and important river at the time (before 1900 BCE). Only after this did the emphasis shift to the sacred Ganga (Ganges) River. This would indicate that the Vedic tradition is indeed a product of the area of ancient India.

There was also no real divide between north and south India in terms of the so-called invading Aryans in the north and the Dravidians of the south. As explained by David Frawley, "Dravidian history does not contradict Vedic history either. It credits the invention of the Tamil language, the oldest Dravidian tongue, to the rishi Agastya, one of the most prominent sages in the *Rig Veda*. Dravidian kings historically have called themselves Aryans and trace their descent through Manu (who in the *Matsya Purana* is regarded as originally a south Indian king). Apart from language, moreover, both north and south India share a common religion and culture." [2]

A recent landmark global study in population genetics by a team of internationally reputed scientists (as reported in *The History and Geography of Human Genes*, by Luca Cavalli-Sforza, Paolo Menozzi and

Alberta Piazzo, Princeton University Press) reveals that the people who inhabited the Indian subcontinent, including Europe, concludes that all belong to one single race of Caucasian type. This confirms once again that there really is no racial difference between north Indians and south Indian Dravidians.

Other scholars and researchers are also giving up the idea of the Aryan Invasion Theory. As further explained in the book *Origin of Indian Civilization*, based on the results of the conference of the same name, it was described that, "While not in complete agreement, yet for Professor Witzel and Eltsov to acknowledge that the Harappan and Vedic civilizations were concurrent, is an important landmark in the debate on the Indic civilization. Prof. Witzel also stated for the first time to many in the audience that he and his colleagues no longer subscribe to the Aryan Invasion Theory (AIT). Prof. Witzel of Harvard agreed with the scholars present that the Aryan invasion theory is a nineteenth-century concept and a spent force today. He said, 'nobody in the right mind believes in something like Aryan Invasion Theory.'" [3]

THE DEVELOPMENT OF THE ARYAN INVASION THEORY

Before the 1857 uprising it was recognized that British rule in India could not be sustained without a large number of supporters and collaborators from within the Indian population. Recognizing this, it was influential men like Thomas Babbington Macaulay, who, as Chairman of the Education Board, sought to set up an educational system modeled after the British system, which, in the case of India, would serve to undermine the Hindu tradition. While not a missionary himself, Macaulay came from a deeply religious family steeped in the Protestant Christian faith. His father was a Presbyterian minister and his mother a Quaker. He believed that the conversion of Hindus to Christianity held the answer to the problems of administering India. His idea was to create a class of English educated elite that would repudiate its tradition and become British collaborators. In 1836, while serving as chairman of the Education Board in India, he enthusiastically wrote his father about his idea and how it was proceeding:

"Our English schools are flourishing wonderfully. The effect of this education on the Hindus is prodigious... It is my belief that if our plans of education are followed up, there will not be a single idolator among the respectable classes in Bengal thirty years hence. And this will be effected without any efforts to proselytise, without the smallest interference with religious liberty, by natural operation of knowledge and reflection. I heartily rejoice in the project."

So the point was that religious conversion and colonialism were to go hand in hand. European Christian missions were an appendage of the colonial government, with missionaries working side by side with the government. In this case, we could ask if over the years much has really changed in the purpose of the Christian missions in India.

The key point here is Macaulay's belief that "knowledge and reflection" on the part of the Hindus, especially the Brahmanas, would cause them to give up their age-old belief in anything Vedic in favor of Christianity. The purpose was to turn the strength of Hindu intellectuals against their own kind by utilizing their commitment to scholarship in uprooting their own tradition, which Macaulay viewed as nothing more than superstitions. His plan was to educate the Hindus to become Christians and turn them into collaborators. He persisted with this idea for fifteen years until he found the money and the right man for turning his utopian idea into reality.

He needed someone who would translate and interpret the Vedic texts in such a way that the newly educated Indian elite would see the superiority of the Bible and choose that over everything else. Upon his return to England, after a good deal of effort he found a talented but impoverished young German Vedic scholar by name Friedrich Max Muller who was willing to take on the arduous job. Macaulay used his influence with the East India Company to find funds for Max Muller's translation of the *Rig Veda*. Though an ardent German nationalist, Max Muller agreed for the sake of Christianity to work for the East India Company, which in reality meant the British Government of India. He also badly needed a major sponsor for his ambitious plans, which he felt he had at last found.

The fact is that Max Muller was paid by the East India Company to further its colonial aims, and worked in cooperation with others who were motivated by the superiority of the German race through the white Aryan race theory.

This was the genesis of his great enterprise, translating the *Rig Veda* with Sayana's commentary and the editing of the fifty-volume *Sacred*

Books of the East. In this way, there can be no doubt regarding Max Muller's initial aim and commitment to converting Indians to Christianity. Writing to his wife in 1866 he observed:

"It [the *Rig Veda*] is the root of their religion and to show them what the root is, I feel sure, is the only way of uprooting all that has sprung from it during the last three thousand years."

Two years later he also wrote the Duke of Argyle, then acting Secretary of State for India: "The ancient religion of India is doomed. And if Christianity does not take its place, whose fault will it be?" This makes it very clear that Max Muller was an agent of the British government paid to advance its colonial interests. Nonetheless, he still remained an ardent German nationalist even while working in England. This helps explain why he used his position as a recognized Vedic and Sanskrit scholar to promote the idea of the "Aryan race" and the "Aryan nation," a theory amongst a certain class of so-called scholars, which has maintained its influence even until today.

MAX MULLER DENIES HIS OWN THEORY

It was in the nineteenth century when Max Muller tried to date the *Vedas* to 1200 BCE. Then he accepted the *Sutra* literature to the sixth century BCE and assigned a duration of just 200 years to each of the periods of Vedic literature, namely the *Aranyakas*, *Brahmanas* and *Vedas*. But when his contemporary scholars, like Goldstucker, Whitney and Wilson, raised a fuss about this, he had to regress and stated (in his Preface to the *Rgveda*): "I have repeatedly dwelt on the merely hypothetical character of the dates, which I have ventured to assign to the first periods of Vedic literature. All I have claimed for them has been that they are minimum dates, and that the literary productions of each period which either still exist or which formerly existed could hardly be accounted for within shorter limits of time than those suggested."[4]

This indicates his admission that he really did not know and he was expressing nothing but conjecture. This is not exactly a scholarly action. But still being pressed by his contemporaries, he finally admitted it in a publication in 1890 (*Physical Religion*) and reflected the responsibility by saying no one can figure it out: "If now we ask how we can fix the dates of these periods, it is quite clear that we cannot hope to fix a *terminum a qua*. Whether the Vedic hymns were composed [in] 1000 or 1500 or 2000 or 3000 BC, no power on earth will ever determine." [5]

Although Max Muller was the one who cleverly came up with the Aryan Invasion Theory, he later worked to bring out the *Sacred Books of the East* series, which helped promote the spiritual wisdom of the East to the general public in Europe. Later, though a German by birth, he was living comfortably in England when in 1872, after the German nationalists finally achieved unification, he marched into a university in German occupied France (Strasbourg) and denounced the German doctrine of the superior Aryan race. It was at this time that he began to clarify that by Aryan he meant language and not a race. This was in stark contrast with his previous views, which had all been well documented, and which kept following him since politicians and propagandists kept using his conclusions as authority for their own race ideas. At last, he stated clearly in 1888:

"I have declared again and again that if I say Aryan, I mean neither blood nor bones, nor skull nor hair; I mean simply those who speak the Aryan language... To me an ethnologist who speaks of Aryan blood, Aryan race, Aryan eyes and hair is as great a sinner as a linguist who speaks of a dolicocephalic dictionary or of brachycephalic grammar." [6]

Just as he had previously been a proponent of the Aryan race theory for the first 20 years of his life, he remained an opponent of it for the remaining 30 years of his life. However, in spite of this fact, we still find Indian scholars who still hold onto Muller's previous views, however inaccurate they may have been, in their own conclusions on India's history.

THE DAMAGE DONE BY THE ARYAN INVASION THEORY

The premise of the Aryan Invasion Theory (AIT) was used as a perfect tool, especially by the British, to divide the Hindu society and the state of India. The North Indian "Aryans" were then pit against the South Indian "Dravidians," along with high-caste against low-caste, mainstream Hindus against tribals, Vedic orthodoxy against the indigenous orthodox sects, and later to neutralize Hindu criticism of the forced Islamic occupation of India, since "Hindus themselves entered India in the same way as Muslims did." Even today, the theory has still been used as the basis for the growth of secularist and even Marxist forces.

The problem with all of this is that people of Indian descent, especially the youth, when they hear all of this Aryan Invasion theory nonsense, they begin to lose faith in their own country, culture and history, and especially in the Vedic tradition and epics. They think it is all just stories, fiction, or even a lie. But that is not the case at all, which is why it is important to show where this theory came from, what its purpose was, and why we should throw it away and take a second and much deeper look at what the Vedic tradition has to offer, and how it was actually the source of much of the world's advancement in so many areas.

Even in India today it is often the case that schools teach the Western views of Indian history and even use European translations of the great Vedic texts. Children are taught that their culture is inherently inferior to the Western developments, and that Hinduism is archaic, outdated, with nothing to offer people today. Therefore, in this view, Indian students should no longer value their own culture and instead look toward the West for everything they need. But this notion is absolutely false. They do not known how much the Western youth looks toward India for its spiritual inspiration, and are using the ancient Indian and Vedic traditions, such as yoga, Jyotish, Vastu, Ayurveda, and the Vedic philosophy to reach their highest potential and well-being. They would not do that if they were not experiencing the benefits of it. In fact, it is all becoming increasingly popular because there is more curiosity, inquiry, and need to find something of substance rather than being content with the shallow nature of Western society and its values.

Part of the problem today is in the educational system of India, and everywhere for that matter, that still often projects the idea that the native Indians were undeveloped and pushed out of the area that was taken over by the invading Aryans, who then pushed their language, culture, and religion onto the people who remained. Those who went south to avoid the invading Aryans were called the Dravidians. The British missionaries, even as early as 1840, went on to use this theory as a means to persuade people of South India to reject the Vedic tradition, since it had been forced on them by invaders, and accept Christianity. By using the typical "divide and rule" policy that the British were known for, they helped create a schism in the people of India which gave them better means to control and manipulate them under the guise of giving them back the respect they had always deserved. Of course, if they became Christian they would deserve even more respect, as portrayed by the missionaries. So, the Aryan Invasion Theory, which had originally been developed by a Christian certainly continued to serve the Christian interests well, unbeknownst to the people who falsely accepted the Dravidian identity. In this regard, Chandrasekharendra Saraswati summed it up very nicely: "Their conclusions would permit them to regard the ancient rishis as primitive men inferior to the moderns... their analysis of our religious texts was motivated by the desire to show Christianity as a better religion." [7]

Thus, the real truth was kept hidden so their agenda could be served. But was not that the whole purpose behind the Aryan Invasion Theory from the start? After all, as N. S. Rajaram has succinctly related, "English translations of the *Rigveda*... represent a massive misinterpretation built on the preconception that the *Vedas* are the primitive poetry of the nomadic barbarians. Nothing could be further from the truth." [8]

Even of late, there have been leaders in Tamil Nadu who have promoted this Dravidian identity, and gave reasons why they should reject Hinduism, which is but an imposition on the natives. Of course, now, through the use of genetics, it has been proven that there never was any division, except in name only, between the Vedic Aryans and the native Dravidians. They were all part of the same native and indigenous fabric of ancient Indian civilization. Any other divisions were all but hypothetical and theory only. But this was part of the damage that such mental speculation had caused. And it still goes on. That is why books and information such as this needs to be spread, so that the truth of the matter can finally be displayed for all to see, and the unity to help preserve and protect the truth of the depth and profound nature of the Vedic civilization can be properly understood.

OBJECTIONS TO THE ARYAN INVASION THEORY

As archeologists B. B. Lal explains, it was Mortimer Wheeler who, after reporting a few skeletons being found at Mohenjodaro, said that the people of Mohenjodaro had been massacred in the invasion of the region. However, the skeletons had been found at different stratigraphic levels of the site–some from intermediate levels, late levels, and also from the deposits that had accumulated at the site after its desertion. This showed that Wheeler was wrong in his assessment. Recent skeletons would have been no where but the uppermost levels.

Thus, the conclusion would have to be that no evidence whatsoever of an invasion has been found at any of the hundreds of Harappan sites. Furthermore, at most of these sites, there is ample proof of continuity of habitation. An outside invasion also means the presence and entry of a new people, but no such evidence exists. A detailed study of human skeletal remains by Hemphill and his colleagues (1991) showed that no new people arrived between 4500–800 BCE, during which the "Aryan invasion" was said to have happened (around 1500 BCE). Therefore, no evidence for an invasion exists, and certainly not by any Aryans.

Furthermore, when new invaders arrive, place names of some towns and rivers remain from the previous people who occupied the area. But no Dravidian names exists for any such objects in the entire area once occupied by the Harappans. [9]

Another point is that before the *Vedas* were written, it had been an oral tradition. However, an oral tradition of this kind of philosophy and culture cannot be maintained by a people in constant movement for decades if not centuries over many thousands of miles, which is what the Aryan Invasion Theory proposes. Such a tradition as the Vedic culture could be preserved only by a sedentary people where the older generation would have the necessary time to pass the communal lore to the younger generation. [10]

In fact, as we have established in *Proof of Vedic Culture's Global Existence*, the Vedic texts make no mention of any migration at all. Surely, if that had happened there would have been some narration of it, or history of a previous location. But nothing exists like that, nor any language previous to the Vedic culture that existed in the Gangetic plains as would be expected.

There are many reasons why common sense can tell you that there could not have been any invasion into Aryavrata (India) by Vedic Aryans from outside. The question is that if the Aryans were supposed to be rambling barbarians, as viewed by some, yet were able to develop such a sophisticated language (Sanskrit) and compositions (the *Vedas*), then how did they not leave in the countries they left behind a rich culture that shows their previous developments? What happened to their descendants who should have kept the remnants of their culture and language? Why were not similar developments made by those who remained in Eastern Europe? And what happened to the pre-Sanskrit language and culture of the area that the Aryans invaded, if that is what happened? No answers have been found regarding these points.

Furthermore, as Dr. B. B. Lal relates, "Let it be squarely stated that the earliest book of the Aryans, the *Rig Veda*, does not mention any of the species of cold-climate trees enumerated. On the other hand, all the trees mentioned in the *Rig Veda*, such as the *Ashvatha* (Ficus religiosa L.), *Khadira* (Acadia catechu Wild), *Nigrodhas* (Ficus benghalenis L.), do not belong to a cold climate but to a tropical one. Likewise, the *Rig Vedic* fauna, comprising such species as the lion, elephant, peacock, also belong to a tropical climate. Further, during the *Rig Vedic* period the Sarasvati was a mighty river, but it gradually dried up. The evidence of archeology, hydrology and radiocarbon dates shows that the Sarasvati dried up around 2000 BCE. All this proves that the *Rig Veda* antedated the magic figure. Again, the *Rig Vedic* geography covers the area from the Ganga-Yamuna on the east to the west of the Indus. Likewise, the archeological evidence shows that prior to 2,000 BCE it was the Harappan Civilization that flourished in this region. Thus, the textual and archeological data combine to establish a perfect spatial-cum-chronological oneness between the *Rig Vedic* and Harappan cultures. And since, as demonstrated in this book, the Harappans were 'the sons of the soil', it squarely follows that the *Rig Vedic* people were indigenous." [11]

We also need to understand from what frivolous basis came the term "Aryan race." The people who created this term, and the Aryan Invasion Theory itself, were not biologists, archeologists, or scientists, though some of them later adopted this. But they were only linguists of questionable qualifications. Even in 1929, Sir Julian Huxley, one of the great natural scientists of the twentieth century related (in *Oxford Pamphlet*, No. 5, OUP: p.9):

"In 1848, the young German scholar Friederich Max Muller (1823-1900) settled in Oxford... About 1853 he introduced into the English language the unlucky term *Aryan* as applied to a large group of languages.

"Moreover, Max Muller threw another apple of discord. He introduced a proposition that is demonstrably false. He spoke not only of a definite Aryan language and its descendants, but also of a corresponding 'Aryan race.' The idea was rapidly taken up both in Germany and in England." [12]

Part of the problem was a misinterpretation of the word *aryan*. With the AIT, it was meaning a race of people, or even a separate language. But the word *arya* was always meant to be used as an honorific title for someone who lead a pure life, who was on the path for attaining a pure and spiritual consciousness. *Arya* actually means clear as in light consciousness, not as a light-skinned person of another separate race. An Aryan in this case meant an ethical, social and spiritual ideal of a well-governed life, for someone who was noble, straightforward in his dealings, was courageous, gentle, kind, compassionate, protector of the weak, eager for knowledge, and displayed respect for the wise and learned. Thus, everything that was opposite of this, such as mean, cruel, rude, false, ignoble, was considered *non-aryan*.

Huxley, regarding the scientific view at the time (1939), said the following: "In England and America the phrase 'Aryan race' has quite ceased to be used by writers with scientific knowledge, though it appears occasionally in political and propagandist literature... In Germany, the idea of the 'Aryan race' received no more scientific support than in England. Nevertheless, it found able and very persistent literary advocates who made it appear very flattering to local vanity. It therefore steadily spread, fostered by special interests."

In this regard, N. S. Rajaram explains: "Those 'special conditions' were the rise of Nazism in Germany and British imperial interests in India. While both Germany and Britain took to the idea of the Aryan race, the courses taken by this racial theory in the two countries were quite different. Its perversion in Germany leading eventually to Nazism and its horrors is too well known to be repeated here. The British, however, put it to more creative use for imperial purposes, especially as a tool in making their rule acceptable to Indians. A BBC report admitted (6 October, 2005):

"It [AIT] gave a historical precedent to justify the role and status of the British Raj, who could argue that they were transforming India for the better in the same way that the Aryans had done thousands of years earlier." [13]

This was the way the British could justify their presence in India as a new and improved brand of Aryans that were doing the same thing that the present Indians who were the previous invading Aryans had done in the past. Thus, the Aryan Invasion Theory was perpetuated by special interests rather than by true historical evidence. In such a case, when the truth finally becomes apparent, such false notions have to dwindle and fade. That is why I have written about how those who believe in the false history of India are but a dying breed. The modern archeologists simply do not believe or see enough evidence to accept the Aryan Invasion Theory. Thus, it becomes self-evident that the Vedic culture was part of the indigenous tradition of India all along, and not brought to India by any outside invaders.

MISLEADING DATES OF THE ARYAN INVASION THEORY

When the idea for the Aryan invasion was developed by Max Muller, he was formulating dates based on his familiarity and loyalty to the Biblical tradition, which tries to establish that the world was created in 4004 BCE. Therefore, whatever dates he came up with had to fit into this scheme of things. So, as we know, he decided that the Aryans had to have invaded India in 1500 BCE, and then developed the *Rig Veda* thereafter in 1200 BCE. This means that such calculations are based on faith in the Bible, and, accordingly, a group of linguistically unified people must have been existing around the Caspian Sea before invading India. It is this Biblical reference that formed the foundation of these dates of Max Muller's for the Aryan Invasion Theory and when the *Rig Veda* may have been written. These were merely assumptions, many of which have been left uncontested, especially outside of India, up until a few decades ago.

Furthermore, Dr. Narahari Achar, a physicist from the University of Memphis clearly showed with astronomical analysis that the *Mahabharata* War took place in 3067 BCE, seriously challenging the outside "Aryan" origin of Vedic people. [14] Therefore, if we accept the year 3102 BCE as the date for the beginning of Kali-yuga, and 3067 BCE as the time for the *Mahabharata* war, this surely means that human society itself had been in existence for many, many years before the Christian date of 4004 BCE as the date for the creation of the world. This would make the 4004 BCE date of creation and the stories that go with it complete fiction.

The real problem with this is that these dates of 1500 BCE for the invasion of the Aryan forces and 1200 BCE for the creation of the *Rig Veda* have been propagated in both school and college books for many years as if they are the substantiated truth. However, even Muller admitted many times later in his life that these dates were arbitrary in nature, or merely guesses grounded on his own view of things, which were precarious opinions based on his allegiance to the Bible. He had written in admission, "I need hardly say that I agree with everyone of my critics. I have repeatedly dwelt on the entirely hypothetical character of the dates that I venture to assign [to the Vedic literature]. ... Whether the Vedic hymns were composed 1000, 1500 or 2000 or 3000 BC, no power on earth will ever determine."

As we have seen, it is the findings in archeology and the statements and history within the *Rig Veda* that have contradicted the dates of the fictional Aryan Invasion and the idea of an invasion itself. For example, the *Rig Veda* has described the ancient and glorious Sarasvati River, which is known to have dried up around 1900 BCE, and was probably already in the process of drying up back in 3000 BCE. This could not have been written by any invaders who entered India around 1500 BCE. How could they have described worshiping a river that had already ceased to exist 500 hundred years earlier? This is impossible. It would be like a haunting ghost story, still talking about things that had disappeared many generations ago.

This indicates that the *Rig Veda* had to have been in existence while the Sarasvati River was in her prime. This also means that the dates that many Western scholars have assigned for the formation of the *Rig Veda* are also in error by probably 2000 years or more. Of course, it was Max Muller who was paid by the British Government to write a negative interpretation of the *Vedas* to undermine the view Hindus themselves had for their own scripture, so he may have also been under pressure for his employment if he did not provide such viewpoints. Nonetheless, he had his own ambitions, as was outlined in a letter to his wife in 1866 about his edition of the *Rig Veda* having "a great extent on the fate of India and the growth of millions of souls in that country. It is the root of their religion and to show them what that root is, I feel sure, is the only way of uprooting all that has sprung from it in the last three thousand years."

Well, his purpose did not work, but certainly created a major distraction in finding the truth of the matter, which, fortunately, there have been many scholars that have now shown the inaccuracy of the views that had originated from Max Muller's hypothesis and guesswork.

THE SARASVATI RIVER IN THE RIG VEDA

The Sarasvati River is mentioned in the *Rig Veda* over 60 times, with three hymns that make Sarasvati the subject, namely in book 6, hymn 61, and book 7, hymns 95 & 96. The most noted verse from the *Rig Veda* that refers to the mighty Sarasvati river and its civilization is 7.95.1.1-2, which states:

> *pra kshodasa dhayada sasra*
> *esha sarasvati dharunamayasi puh*
> *prababadhana rathyeva yati*
> *vishva apo mahina sindhuranyaha*

"Pure in her course from the mountains to the ocean, alone of streams Sarasvati hath listened."

Thus, it stands to reason that the Sarasvati acquired this state of reverence during its prime and not after it started drying up. In other verses that describe her, we find it said in the *Rig Veda* (7.36.6) she is the holiest and greatest of all rivers, the best of the seven rivers, and Mother of the rivers and the Sindhu River. Then again she is the best of the seven rivers (6.61.9-10), and is fed by three, five or seven streams (6.61.12), and nourishes all of the Vedic people, and flows through the mountains and crushes boulders like the stems of lotus flowers (6.61.2), and that Sarasvati was the best of mothers, the best river and best goddess (6.41.16).

For further insight into this, we can see how the *Rig Veda* described the Sarasvati River. Some of the Sanskrit words used to describe the Sarasvati in the *Rig Veda* are *naditama*, *ambitama*, and *devitama*, which mean best river, best mother and best goddess (2.41.16); it is swollen and fed by three or more rivers *pinvamana sindhubhih* (6.52.6); it is endless, swift moving, roaring, most dear among her sister rivers; together with her divine aspect, it nourishes the tribes (6.61.8-13). In 7.95.2 it is said *giribhyah a samudrat*, it flows in a pure course from the mountains to the ocean. Then 7.96.2 and 10.177 mentions to pray to the river goddess for sustenance and good fortune, and 10.64.9 calls upon her (and Sarayu and Indus) as great and nourishing. Thus, the descriptions indicate a live and flowing river of great importance, flowing from the Himalayas to the ocean. [15]

The *Rig Veda* (10.75.5) also indicates where the Sarasvati was located by listing the main northern rivers in order from the east, in which case places the Sarasvati between the Yamuna and the Shutudri (modern Sutlej), as found in the verse:

imam me gange yamune sarasvati shutudri stomam parushnya
asiknya marudvridhe vitastya arjikiye shrinuhya sushomaya

"Ganga, Yamuna, Sarasvati, Shutudri (Sutlej) Parushni (Ravi) Asikni, Manuvridha, Vitasta, Arjikiye, Shrinuhya, and Sushomaya."

Many great Vedic rishis were also mentioned in the *Rig Veda* as having a connection with the Sarasvati River, such as Vasistha and Jamadagni (7.96.3), Gritsamada (2.41.16), and Bharadvaj (6.61). Also kings like Divodas (6.61) and Bharatas such as Devavat and Devashravas (3.23) are mentioned in connection with the Sarasvati. Also of the *Rig Veda* are the clan of the Purus who resided along the Sarasvati, in which it says, "Sarasvati, on both whose plant-laden banks the Purus dwell." (7.96.2) [16]

The importance of the Sarasvati, as herein demonstrated, cannot go unnoticed. Besides references to the Sarasvati River in the *Rig Veda*, we can find some in the *Atharva Veda* as well. One reference (6.30.1) refers to Indra ploughing the banks of the Sarasvati to cultivate barley, which was not only one of the items for offering into the fire during the *yajna* ritual, but was also one of the earliest staple foods.

During sacrifices, we find (*AV* 5.27.9) Sarasvati as the goddess was invoked along with goddesses Ida, Mahi and Bharathi. Then in hymns (*AV* 7.68 and 18.1.41) she is called to accept oblations during the ritual. We also find (*AV* 7.57.1) where Vamadeva was shaken due to the apathy and derogatory words of the people, and invokes Sarasvati to reduce tension and cleanse the mind. In a similar way, we find (*AV* 19.40.1) where Sarasvati is praised in order to overcome frailties of the mind.

PROOF OF THE SARASVATI RIVER

While surveying the course of the Sarasvati River, geologist Sir Auriel Stein (1862-1943) concluded that there was indeed such a river that had dried up when the course of the Sutlej changed, and discontinued being the main contributory of the Sarasvati River. Thus, as the Sarasvati began to dry, the cities and residents that depended on the river also had to move. With the satellite images made through earth sensing satellites from 1978 by NASA (National Aeronautics and Space Administration) and the ISRO (Indian Space Research Organization) that revealed the ancient river courses, these show that the Sarasvati was a channel that ranged from six to eight kilometers wide, and up to 14 kilometers in some parts. Thus, the greatness of the Sarasvati River, as described in the *Rig Veda*, was verified.

This was further confirmed by an aerial survey conducted by the American Landsat satellite in 1990 that showed a dried tract of 1000 miles where the Sarasvati would have flowed from the Himalayas to the Sourashtrian coast. This changed the way many researchers viewed this issue. This was later followed up in 1996 by the Indian remote sensing satellite of the Indian Space Research Organization, the color images of which also clearly showed marks of a palaeochannel as wide as 3 km to 12 km in the same stretch.

Furthermore, in 1998, there were 24 wells dug by the Central Ground Water Commission along the dry bed, all of which produced potable water but one. Also in 1998, after the Pokhran atomic test, the Baba Atomic Research Center (BARC) drilled down 70 meters for sub-soil water to confirm that the aquifers had not been affected by radioactive material and found that the water was of Himalayan origin from as far back as 14,000 years.

This discovery of the Sarasvati also solved the reason why there were alluvial deposits in the Gulf of Cambay, discovered in 1869 by archeologist Alex Rogue. It was odd because there was no known river that flowed from the Himalayas at the time. [17]

THE DEMISE OF THE SARASVATI

The *Rig Veda* describes the Sarasvati River as a mighty flowing river. So if we know that it dried up completely around 2000 BCE, and had to have been in the process of drying by 3000 BCE or before, then the *Rig Veda* had to have been written before it started to dry up. There is nothing in the *Rig Veda* about the Sarasvati diminishing in any way. However, we do find in the *Mahabharata* where the Sarasvati was decreasing to a shorter course, such as in 3.130.3; 6.7.47; 6.37.1-4; 9.34.81; and 9.36.1-2.

The *Mahabharata* (*Shalya Parva*, 36-55) also describes the Sarasvati in relation to Balarama's pilgrimage, which He took to occupy Himself rather than participate in the war at Kurukshetra with His brother Lord Krishna. It states that the Sarasvati was still significant in its holiness, but from its origin it flowed only for a forty-day journey by horse into the desert where it disappeared. All that was left were the holy places that used to be on its banks (as also mentioned in 3.80.84; 3.88.2; & 9.34.15-8). The *Mahabharata* also describes the geographical location of the river, saying that it flows near Kurukshetra (3.81.125). Similar information along with the place where the Sarasvati disappears, Vinashana, is found in the *Manusamhita* (2.21).

All of this also indicates that the *Rig Veda* had to have existed well before 2000 BCE because it is described therein that the Sarasvati was a mighty flowing river during the *Rig Vedic* times, before it finally dried in 2000 BCE. According to the *Rig Veda* (10.75.5-6), the Vedic people occupied the area from the Ganga in the east to the Indus in the west. And as we have established in *Proof of Vedic Culture's Global Existence*, the Harappan civilization was a part of the Vedic culture in the form of its continuance and diversity, or regional variations. In fact, the *Rig Veda* was already in existence before the Harappan Civilization came into its prime.

From other research we have found that the whole of the Sarasvati River had dried by about 2000 to 1800 BCE, and was at best a few small lakes. But the site of the Harappan Civilization called Kalibangan, that sits along the bank of the Sarasvati, after hydrological investigations (Raikes 1968), reveals that it was abandoned because of the drying up of the river. And this happened because of the rise of the Bata-Markanda Terrace in the Himalayas (Puri and Verma 1998). Even the *Panchavimsha Brahmana* (15.10.16) mentions the drying up of the Sarasvati. Radiocarbon dates also show that Kalibangan was abandoned around 2000 BCE. [18]

Research explains that the demise of the Sarasvati River was caused by the lack of water it had previously received from the Yamuna, which had changed its course to flow eastward into the Ganga. Then the Sutlej also turned southwest, while the glacial melt also decreased, all of which greatly weakened the flow of the Sarasvati. This resulted in the Sarasvati disappearing into the desert at a place called Vinashana, or Samantapanchaka in the *Mahabharata*, before it reached the sea. [19]

This, along with the world drought that was known to have happened around 2200 to 1900 BCE, contributed to drying up the Sarasvati and Drishavati rivers and to the disappearance of the Harappan or Indus Valley Civilization. It also created the Thar desert. After this many people were forced to abandon this area and whatever towns and cities flourished there at that time. This massive worldwide drought not only impacted the Harappan civilization, but is also known to have affected or ended the civilizations of not only Egypt, but also of the Sumer-Akkad regions in Mesopotamia. All of this caused a deterioration of the Vedic bond in this area, and a rise in small political groups known as Janapadas, which is described in the Buddhist and Jain literature. Sanskrit also lost influence while Prakrits, regional languages, like Pali and Ardhamagadhi were used, as we find in the Buddhist and Jain texts of that era.

As further explained by N.S. Rajaram, it was sometime around 3000 BCE when the Yamuna River changed its course and started its flow into the Ganga River. This may have been due to earthquakes or something similar. That, of course, weakened the flow of the Sarasvati River, wherein it soon disappeared into the desert at a place called Vinashana. Some archeologists have identified this place as Kalibangan in Rajasthan, which is also where Harappan and pre-Harappan settlements have been found, as well as signs of possible earthquakes in the area. This corresponds to descriptions found in the *Jaiminiya Brahmana* and the *Mahabharata*.

The lower part of the Sarasvati River was still fed by the Sutlej and other rivers for some time, which continued to flow through the Thar desert and support some of the Harappan settlements in Rajasthan, Sindh and Cholistan to the Rann of Kutch. However, the Sutlej later also changed course, so this stretch of the river also dried up in stages from 2200 to 1900, when it is known to have disappeared completely, putting an end to whatever was left of the Harappan society in that area. This means that the Harappan civilization came to an end by natural causes, not any invaders, and then moved farther east into the Gangetic plains. Some Harappan people may have also moved westward into West Asia where the contributed to the growing tribes there. Some of the Kassite rulers seemed to have been of Indian origin who established an empire there.

Since Mohenjodaro and Harappa were first discovered in 1922, numerous other settlements have been uncovered, which now number over 2500, which stretches from Baluchistan to the Ganga and beyond, and down to the Tapti Valley. All of this covers nearly a million and a half square miles, all of which have been researched by archeologists. And 75% of all of these are concentrated around the dried up Sarasvati River bed. However, this also means that it was not an invasion that forced the abandonment of these towns and cities, but it was the drying up of the Sarasvati River, which was a catastrophe that lead to an outflow of people going in different directions from here to resettle elsewhere, especially into the Gangetic plain, but also including westward into Iran, Mesopotamia and other areas.

Even a most recent study, as reported in *The Daily Mail* in London, combining the latest archaeological evidence with state-of-the-art geoscience technologies provides evidence that climate change was a key ingredient in the collapse of the great Indus or Harappan Civilization almost 4000 years ago.

Liviu Giosan, a geologist with Woods Hole Oceanographic Institution (WHOI) and lead author of the study published the week of May 28, 2012, in the *Proceedings of the National Academy of Sciences*, "We reconstructed the dynamic landscape of the plain where the Indus civilization developed 5200 years ago, built its cities, and slowly disintegrated between 3900 and 3000 years ago. Until now, speculations abounded about the links between this mysterious ancient culture and its life-giving mighty rivers... We considered that it is high time for a team of interdisciplinary scientists to contribute to the debate about the enigmatic fate of these people," Giosan explained.

As the report related, the research was conducted between 2003 and 2008 in Pakistan, from the coast of the Arabian Sea into the fertile irrigated valleys of Punjab and the northern Thar Desert. The international team included scientists from the U.S., U.K., Pakistan, India, and Romania with specialties in geology, geomorphology, archaeology, and mathematics. By combining satellite photos and topographic data collected by the Shuttle Radar Topography Mission (SRTM), the researchers prepared and analyzed digital maps of landforms constructed by the Indus and neighboring rivers, which were then probed in the field by drilling, coring, and even manually-dug trenches. Collected samples were used to determine the sediments' origins, whether brought in and shaped by rivers or wind, and their age, in order to develop a chronology of landscape changes.

The new study suggests the same conclusions as had previously been arrived at by other researchers, that the decline in monsoon rains led to weakened river dynamics, and played a critical role both in the development and the collapse of the Harappan culture, which relied on river floods to fuel their agricultural surpluses.

From the new research, a compelling picture of 10,000 years of changing landscapes emerges. Before the plain was massively settled, the wild and forceful Indus and its tributaries flowing from the Himalaya cut valleys into their own deposits and left high "interfluvial" stretches of land between them. In the east, reliable monsoon rains sustained perennial rivers that crisscrossed the desert leaving behind their sedimentary deposits across a broad region.

The new research argues that the Sarasvati (Ghaggar-Hakra) was primarily a perennial monsoon-supported watercourse, and that aridification reduced it to short seasonal flows. Therefore, the conclusion of their research, in this regard, is that the slow drying of the Sarasvati River was the primary reason for the movement of the Indus Valley Civilization from the region, not invaders who took over the area. By 3900 years ago, their rivers drying, the Harappans had an escape route to the east toward the Ganges basin, where monsoon rains remained reliable. [20]

LOCATION OF VINASHANA

It is said that the place of Vinashana is where the Sarasvati River stopped flowing. However, not everyone is sure of exactly where it was located. Some historians and archaeologists locate it near Bharner, others near Kalibanga, and others in Rajasthan. But the popular convention of the lists of holy places in the *Puranas* locates it in the Kurukshetra region, Samanta-panchaka. Whereas the *Padma Purana* (18.247) seems to locate the site of Vinashana as far downstream as Pushkaranya. The *Skanda Purana* (Nagara Khanda, 164.39) appears to say that the flow of the Sarasvati went underground after it reached Pushkararanya in her westward flow.

As related in *New Discoveries About Vedic Sarasvati*, "Pushkararanya of Kurukshetra was the forest area located close to present Jind or Jayantika. Still this place is famous as Pokharan. There is a pond, which is known even today as a pond where Duryodhana hid himself after being defeated by Bhima in mace fighting. So it is crystal clear from this reference that Vinashana is located in Haryana itself and not Rajasthan."

"Sridharasvani (c1400 AD) cited by C. Rayachaudhuri [21] in his gloss on *Bhagavata Purana* (1.9.1) locates Vinashana in Kurukshetra itself. The fact is that during the age of composition of the *Brahmanas* and *Sutras*, when the sacrificial cult was at its climax, the name of Vinashana stuck to one particular locality, which almost constantly remained humming with all sorts of sacrificial activity. As we have already described, Beri, close to Bisan, being such a holy place, the geographical identification of Vinashana of the Kurukshetra region with the area of Bisan near Beri of Rohtak will not be a farfetched one." [22]

The *Bhagavata Purana* (10.79.23) further describes Vinashana as the place where Balarama went to forestall the mace duel between Bhima and Durodhana, which gives more credence to the whereabouts of Vinashana, since the mace duel took place in the region of Kurukshetra. Plus, modern Bisan in Rohtak is a place close to Pokaran in Jind where Duryodhana, according to tradition, is said to have hid himself after his defeat in the duel. This is also in the region where Bhisma fell after the 18 days of battle in the war of Kurukshetra, which is a famous place near Kurukshetra.

THE ARGUMENT OF NO HORSE IN HARAPPA

In analyzing the culture of the Harappans, one of the arguments has been that there was no horse, and that no horse bones have been found there. This is to justify the idea that the horse was not indigenous to the region and was brought into the area by invading Aryans. However, when we research the Harappan seals, we find what is called the Horse Seal, which means the horse had been a part of the Harappan culture. Furthermore, horse bones have been found at all levels at several Harappan sites. Furthermore, when deciphering the seals, the word *ashva* (a Sanskrit word for horse) is a commonly occurring word on the seals. Therefore, the idea of a horseless Harappan culture is a fallacy that has been proved wrong by evidence. [23] Horse remains have also been found in places like Koldihwa and Mahagara in the interior of India dating back to 6500 BCE.

As further elaborated by B. B. Lal: "A study of the horse anatomy shows that there were two types of horses in the ancient world that we still find today. There is an Indian type that has seventeen ribs and a West and Central Asian horse that has eighteen ribs. The *Rig Vedic* horse, as described in the Ashwamedha or horse offering of the *Rig Veda*, has thirty-four ribs (seventeen times two for the right and left side). (*Rig Veda* 1.162.18) This shows that the *Rig Vedic* horse did not come from Central Asia but was the South Asian breed. The *Rig Vedic* horse is born of the ocean, which indicates southern connections. (*Rig Veda* 1.163.1)"

As further explained, "Relative to the idea some people have that there are no horse remains at Harappa, Sir John Marshall who excavated Harappa and Mohenjodaro gave measurements of the horse remains he had found at Mohenjodaro (see his *Mohenjodaro Indus Civilization*, Vol.II, pages 653-4). Clay horse figurines, like the terracotta horse, have also been found from Lothal. In this regard, noted archeologist B. B. Lal states [24] :

"Even the much touted argument about the absence of the horse from the Harappan Civilization has no validity in the light of the new evidence regarding its presence. The noted international authority on the palaeontology of the horse, Sandor Bokonyi of the Archaeological Institute, Budapest, after duly examining the faunal remains concerned, had declared as far back as 1993 that 'the domestic nature of Surkotada horse (a Harappan site in Kachchh) is undoubtful'" [25]

Furthermore, Sir John Marshall, Director General of the Archaeological Survey, when excavating Harappa and Mohenjodaro, recorded the presence of what he called the "Mohenjodaro horse:"

"It will be seen that there is a considerable degree of similarity between these various examples, and it is probable the Anau horse, the Mohenjo-daro horse, and the example of Equus caballus of the Zoological Survery of India, are all of the type of the 'Indian country bred,' a small breed of a horse, the Anau horse being slightly smaller than the others." [26]

This is quite prominent evidence for the existence of the horse. However, the idea that if the horse was not already present in the Harappan area, that it was brought into ancient India by invading Aryans, then it would have to be proved, which is not actually possible because the *Rig Veda* (1.162.18) also describes the horse as having 34 ribs, with a similar description in the *Yajur Veda*, while the Central Asian horse as 36 ribs. This shows that the native Indian horse has been in India for many hundreds of years. This should clearly nullify the whole argument of no horse in the

Harappa region, along with another factor used to try to justify the Aryan Invasion Theory.

The thing about the horse is that it was a greatly prized and valuable animal. So, there may not be many circumstances that would allow for horse bones to be found. However, the Sanskrit word for horse, *ashva*, is found 215 times in the *Rig Veda*. Also, many personalities had names connected with the word as well. Thus, the horse was highly valued.

The conclusions of whether the inhabitants of Harappa were Vedic Aryans or not were based on excavations in 1930-40 when they were not so complete, and when they found few remains of horses at the Harappan Indus sites, which gave way for the argument of no horse in Harappa. However, now that numerous sites along the Indus and the dried Sarasvati River have been excavated more thoroughly, bones of domesticated horses have been found at various locations. Dr. S. R. Rao, the renown archeologist, informs us that horse bones have been found from the "Mature Harappan" and "Late Harappan" levels of these sites. Many other scholars have also unearthed numerous bones of horses of both domesticated and combatant types. Thus, if any scholar still clings to the idea that the Indus Valley inhabitants can not be connected to or were not a part of the Vedic Aryan culture because of no horse remains, then they have not updated their research. This also clarifies the fact that this civilization was indeed a part of the Vedic culture.

Besides the evidence for horse bones being found at places already mentioned, Edwin Bryant describes additional places where the bones of horses have been found. "The report claiming the earliest date for the domesticated horse in India, ca. 4500 BCE, comes from a find from Bagor, Rajasthan, at the base of the Aravalli Hills (Ghosh, 1989). In Rana Ghundai, Baluchistan, excavated by E. J. Ross, equine teeth were reported from a pre-Harappan level (Guha and Chatterjee 1946, 315-316). Interestingly, equine bones have been reported from Mahagara, near Allahabad, where six sample absolute carbon 14 tests have given dates ranging from 2265 BCE to 1480 BCE. (Sharma et al. 1980, 220-221). Even more significantly, horse bones from the Neolithic site Hallur in Karnataka (1500-1300 BCE) have also been identified by the archaeozoologist K. R. Alur (1971, 123). These findings of the domestic horse from Mahagara in the east, and Hallur in the south, are significant because they would seem inconsistent with the axiom that the Aryans introduced the domesticated horse into the Northwest of the subcontinent in the later part of the second millennium BCE...

"In the Indus Valley and its environs, Sewell and Guha, as early as 1931, had reported the existence of the true horse, *Equua caballus* Linn from Mohenjo-Daro itself, and Bholanath (1963) reported the same from Harappa, Ropar, and Lothal. Even Mortimer Wheeler (1953) identified a horse figurine and accepted that 'it is likely enough that camel, horse and ass were in fact all a familiar feature of the Indus caravan.' Another early evidence of the horse in the Indus Valley was reported by Mackay, in 1938, who identified a clay model of the animal at Mohenjo-Daro, Piggott (1952, 126, 130) reports a horse figurine from Periano Ghundai in the Indus Valley, dated somewhere between Early Dynastic and Akkadian times. Bones from Harappa, previously thought to have belonged to the domestic ass, have been reportedly critically reexamined and attributed to a small horse (Sharma 1992-93, 31). Additional evidence of the horse in the form of bones, teeth, or figurines has been reported in other Indus sites such as Kalibangan (Sharma 1992-93, 31); Lothal (Rao 1979), Surkotada (Sharma 1974), and Malvan (Sharma 1992-93, 32). Other later sites include the Swat Valley (Stacul 1969); Gumla (Sankalia 1974, 330); Pirak (Jarrige 1985); Kuntasi (Sharma 1995, 24); and Rangpur (Rao 1979, 219)." [27]

In spite of these considerable findings of the horse in ancient India, many archeologists ignored them and kept pointing back to the idea that the true domesticated horse was never known to the Harappans. This only kept the confusion of the real date for the Harappans and history of the Indus Valley Civilization in circulation, when actually it was something that would help show that it was an indigenous society.

THE URBAN OR RURAL ARGUMENT

Another argument had been that the Harappan society was not part of the Aryan Civilization because Harappa was urban while the Aryans were rural pastoralists. Therefore, they had to be two separate societies. However, B. B. Lal explains: "Just as there were cities, towns and villages in the Harappan ensemble (as there are even today in any society) there were both rural and urban components in the Vedic times." [28]

S. P. Gupta also shares a similar thought on this that helps make it more clear that the Harappan or Indus Civilization was merely an outgrowth and a part of the Vedic culture: "Once it becomes reasonably clear that the *Vedas* do contain enough material which shows that the authors of the hymns were fully aware of the cities, city life, long-distance overseas and overland trade, etc... it becomes easier for us to appreciate the theory that the Indus-Sarasvati and Vedic civilizations may have been just the two complementary elements of one and the same civilization. And this, it is important to note, is not a presupposition against the cattle-keeping image of the Vedic Aryans. After all, ancient civilizations had both the components, the village and the city, and numerically villages were many times more than the cities. In India presently there are around 6.5 lakhs of villages but hardly 600 towns and cities put together.... Plainly, if the Vedic literature reflects primarily the village life and not the urban life, it does not at all surprise us." [29]

DECIPHERING THE INDUS SEALS

Many scholars have suggested that the final clue in understanding the location of the Indo-Aryans would be if and when the Indus Seals could be deciphered. With the book of N. Jha and N. S. Rajaram, *The Deciphered Indus Script: Methodology, Readings, Interpretations*, it would seem that a big step in that direction has been made, if not completed.

With this new information, it would seem to corroborate the notion that in reality the Vedic Age was developed before the Indus Valley Civilization. Many scholars previously have tried to separate the two completely, saying that the Indus Valley Civilization, such as places like Harappa and Mohenjodaro were not a part of the Vedic culture, but that is not accurate. They indeed were a part of it, and their seals represented a form of the Vedic language. This would also indicate that a largely indigenous civilization must have been flourishing a thousand years before what became the development of Dynastic Egypt and Mesopotamia.

The Sarasvati-Indus Valley Civilization was probably in its prime about 3100 to 1900 BCE. But if we accept the dates that were given by Muller and his followers, that Vedic culture did not start until 1500 BCE, then that is why many are those that say Harappa and Mohenjodaro could not have been part of the Vedic Aryans. This brings us to what is called

"Frawley's Paradox", for as David Frawley points out, it gives us a history without a literature for the Harappans, and a literature without history, archeology or geography for the Aryans. This makes no sense. How can there be one without the other for any developed civilization?

Therefore, it becomes more apparent that the Vedic literature is far older than most thought, and the Harappans were a part of the Vedic culture. And the Indus seals help make that clear. It is generally accepted that the year 3067 is when the war at Kurukshetra took place. The Vedic Aryans were already well established and were a part of that war. This means that most if not all of the *Rig Veda* hymns had already been developed by 3500 BCE, not later, though they may have been written or compiled later. The Harappans had to have participated to some degree in that war. This was also about the time when the Indus seals had been formed. In fact, as N. S. Rajaram explains, "the *Mahabharata*, in the Shanti Parva, contains a description of the etymological texts whose contents are recorded on the seals, as well as the Vedic symbolism relating to the images on them... This is what holds the key not only to the decipherment [of the seals], but also to an understanding of the culture and civilization of the Harappans." [30]

In the deciphering of the Indus script, it was found that there are close connections between the structure of the Indus script and the rules of grammar and phonetics described in such primary works on Vedic Sanskrit as the *Rik-Pratishakhya* of Shaunaka, and the *Nighantu* by Yaska. This helped pave the way for understanding the seals. Many of the words on the seals can be traced back to the *Nighantu*.

Actually, several investigators before the publication of the work of N. Jha in 1996 recognized that the language on the Indus script had to be Vedic Sanskrit. N. S. Rajaram himself had concluded the writings were connected with the *Sutras*, based on short statements or meanings. In this way, the Indus seals have provided further insights into the original location and time period of the Vedic culture.

GENETICS SHOW AN EAST TO WEST MOVEMENT

From the scientific perspective, Dr. Chandrakant Panse presented a paper that explained that the tissue antigens of the north and south Indians were completely distinct from those of the Europeans. "The stark lack of similarities in the gene pools of the Indian subcontinent and Europe, vividly evident in the mtDNA and the MHC complex, destroys any Aryan invasion notions, and confirms the genetic uniformity of people of the Indian subcontinent." [31]

Another aspect for the dismissal of the Aryan Invasion Theory based on genetics was reported in *The Hindu* newspaper on June 24, 2006. The report was that Chairman of the Indian Council of Historical Research, D. N. Tripathi, in Bangalore explained that geneticists from Pakistan had collected samples for genetics analysis of the people of the Indian subcontinent and sent them to cellular and molecular biology laboratories in the U.S. From the DNA tests of the blood samples from the people in the Indian subcontinent, the scientists concluded that the human race spread out of Africa 60,000 years before Christ. They had settled in the subcontinent region. However, from these tests, the geneticists concluded that people living in both the northern and southern regions of India, and those in the West Asian region were from the same gene pool. This indicated that the human race had its origins in Africa and not Europe or Central Asia, as claimed by a few historians, and then went primarily to and spread out from ancient India. [32]

When asked about the argument of many historians that the lineage of people in north India is traced to the Aryans outside of India who later entered or invaded India, Professor Tripathi said that test results had proved this wrong. "We have the results of studies. The conclusion of some historians that Aryans came here 1500 years before Christ does not hold water."

As further explained in this regard by N. S. Rajaram, "A particular trait that we choose as characterizing a population group is called a genetic marker. One such marker that has proven useful is the M17 genetic marker. It is common in India and in adjacent regions, but becomes increasingly rare as we move westward into Europe. This, combined with the fact that Indian carriers of M17 are genetically more diverse than European carriers shows that the Indian population is older than the European." [33]

"Noting that the mtDNA is carried by the female line, while Y-chromosome is passed on through the male line, what this means is that the Indian population is largely indigenous in origin and has received negligible external input (gene flow) since the end of the last Ice Age

(Holocene). This means that various migration theories like the Aryan invasion in 1500 BCE simply cannot be true." [34]

Furthermore, the Oxford geneticist Stephen Oppenheimer is quite clear on this and, while focusing on the M17 marker, explains: "... South Asia is logically the ultimate origin of M17 and his ancestors; and sure enough we find highest rates and greatest diversity of the M17 line in Pakistan, India and eastern Iran, and low rates in the Caucasus. M17 is not only more diverse in South Asia than in Central Asia, but diversity characterizes its presence in isolated tribal groups in the south, thus undermining any theory of M17 as a marker of a 'male Aryan invasion' of India."

"One age estimate for the origin of this line in India is as much as 51,000 years. All this suggests that M17 could have found his way initially from India or Pakistan, through Kashmir, then via Central Asia and Russia, before finally coming to Europe." [35]

He also explains that the eastward movement of those people with the M17 marker traveled from India westward through Kashmir, Central Asia, up into Russia and then into Europe after 40,000 BP (38,000 BCE). Thus, as we have been saying, all migration in this regard has been from the east westward. [36]

So the conclusion is that there could have been no thing called the Aryan Invasion as some propose, and that the tribal people of India are ancestrally no different than the rest of the Indian population. Therefore, anyone saying something different is only proposing such for some special interest or divisive purpose, and, thus, they should not be trusted. There are many of us who have known this, but it can take a long time to continue gathering enough evidence to present it in a way that establishes the truth. Furthermore, the divisions in India known as the northern Aryans and the southern Dravidians is also a fallacy based on conjecture, used now only to facilitate "special interests" that need to divide people for political, financial or other reasons.

In this way, we can understand that the idea that the Vedic culture and people of the area now called India have not developed out of invaders who are said to have brought the culture to the region. The idea that the Vedic and Dharmic culture was brought out of the Caucasus and into ancient India cannot be taken seriously without losing one's credibility. If anything, it is the Europeans who are descendants of the migrants from

India, going back as far as 40,000 years, making them a younger population than the much older Indian population.

All of this also pushes the dates back much farther by several thousand years than the foolishly proposed guestimate of 1500 BCE.

CONCLUSION:
THERE NEVER WAS ANY ARYAN INVASION

Though there have been many scholars and researchers who have written and provided evidence that establishes that there never was an Aryan invasion, and that the Vedic people and its culture were indeed originally from the area of India, Nicholas Kazanas, the Greek professor, was the most recent to provide evidence and articles that were published in academic journals, thus forcing the academics to take another look at this issue. The theory of the Aryan invasion still has held much influence, if not bias and prejudice, at the way academics view the history of India, which is something that should have changed and been corrected years ago. Thus, after years of promoting the Aryan Invasion Theory, and then rejecting it after having done his own research, Kazanas concludes:

"The Aryan Invasion Theory, despite its 150-year-long life, has no real support anywhere except continued prejudice. It has now been substituted in a similar shameless frame of mind, by 'migration' of an alleged complex and, to the archaeologist or anthropologist, incomprehensible nature; this is a deception, since the aryanisation of North India on so an enormous a scale could not possibly have been effected without conquest and coercion–for which there is no testimony of any sort. Why this preposterous proposition should have acquired the status of historical fact among serious Indologists is for me a mystery. There may have been racist prejudice as many writers aver (Shaffer 1984; Leach 1990; Frawley 1991, 1994; Feuerstein 1995; Trautman 1997; Bryant chs 1-2, 13; many Indian writers like Talageri 2000, and Indian-American Kak 2000); this was perpetuated by mechanical repetition rather than logical consideration. Renfrew too was right perhaps in seeing nothing in the *Rig Veda* demonstrating that the Indoaryans 'were intrusive to the area: this comes rather from a historical assumption about the 'coming of the Indoeuropeans' (1989: 182)...

"In sharp contrast, all the primary materials of a historian agree in showing no evidence at all for any entry. On the contrary, such testimony as had been preserved, early historical documentation and later traditions testify that Indoaryans are indigenous to Saptasindhu [land of seven rivers in Northern India]. These traditions (corroborated by foreign writers of the 4th cent BC) affirm that the Indoaryans have been in Saptasindhu since at least the 4th millennium [BCE]; this is now fully supported by Archaeoastronomy which places the great Bharata war at 3067, a *Brahmana* text c 3000 – 2900 and the *Vedanga Jyotish* c 1800. Given that archaeologists, anthropologists et all, specializing in the prehistory of that area, affirm unequivocally since 1980 that the local culture has an uninterrupted continuity since c 7000 (except for a break in the skeletal record c 4500), we can say that the Indoaryans have been in North India since that time. There is also the fact that the *Rig Veda* knows nothing of elements in the Indus-Sarasvati-Civilization whereas the later texts have these elements; moreover even in very late hymns the Sarasvati is a large river supporting the Aryans on its banks: therefore the *Rig Veda* must belong to a period before 3000." [37]

This is an important point, that the Vedic texts make no mention of any entry into the region by outside invaders, or that they were a part of a culture of invaders. Plus, due to their content, it can be discerned that they had to have been existing before 3000 BCE.

In the *Rig Veda* (and later Indic texts) there is no hint of any invading Aryas coming into the Sarasvati or Saptasindhu, the area of the seven rivers in North India and Pakistan. A. B. Keith [38] wrote, "It is certain... that the *Rig Veda* offers no assistance in determining the mode in which the Vedic Aryans entered India... the bulk at least [of the *Rig Veda*] seems to have been composed rather in the country round the Sarasvati River." [39]

The Vedic texts further refer to people being exiled or driven away from the area of northern India, such as in the *Aitareya Brahmana* (8.33.6 or 8.18) which tells of how the sage Vishvamitra exiled his 50 disobedient sons so that, in later periods, most of those people called the Dasyus are known as the descendants of Vishvamitra. Therefore, the *Rig Veda* provides no reference for an Aryan entry or displacement of the natives, but points out how Aryans and Dasyus went westward from the area of Northern India. [40]

Therefore, the idea that the Indoaryans migrated into the vast area of the Sarasvati region, including the Punjab, Gujarat, Haryana, and so on, back in 1700 to 1500 BCE at which time the local natives learned the complicated language of the Vedic Aryans, after which numerous mountains, rivers, etc., suddenly had Sanskrit names is something you might find in a fairy tale rather than real history. There is no real explanation for this to have happened [except that they were an indigenous people]. [41]

Because of these factors, there have been those who always spoke against the idea of an Aryan Invasion. Vivekananda was one such strong opponent of the Aryan Invasion Theory. He boldly challenged in this way (5:534-535): "And what your European pundits say about the Aryans swooping down from some foreign land, snatching away the lands of the aborigines and settling in India by exterminating them, is all pure nonsense, foolish talk! In what *Veda*, in what *Sukta* do you find that the Aryans came into India from a foreign country? Where do you get the idea that they slaughtered the wild aborigines? What do you gain by talking such nonsense? Strange that our Indian scholars, too, say amen to them; and all these monstrous lies are being taught to our boys!... Whenever the Europeans find an opportunity, they exterminate the aborigines and settle down with ease and comfort on their lands; and therefore they think the Aryans must have done the same!... But where is your proof? Guess work? Then keep your fanciful ideas to yourself. I strongly protested against these ideas at the Paris Congress. I have been talking with the Indian and European savants on the subject, and hope to raise many objections to this theory in detail, when time permits. And this I say to you–to our pundits–also, 'You are learned men, hunt up your old books and scriptures, please, and draw your own conclusions.'"

Dayananda Sarasvati (February 12, 1824 to September 26, 1883), the founder of the Arya Samaj (1875), was another who had strong words against it: "No Sanskrit book or history records that the Aryas came here from Iran... How then can the writings of foreigners be worth believing in the teeth of this testimony."

We cannot forget Aurobindo who had voiced his opinion about this many times, such as: "The indications in the *Veda* on which this theory of a recent Aryan invasion is built are very scanty in quantity and uncertain in significance. There is no actual mention of any such invasion." [42]

Jim Shaffer, a western archeologist, was another to strongly protest the idea of an Aryan invasion. In his article, *The Indo-Aryan Invasions: Cultural Myth and Archaeological Reality*, he explains how he thinks after all of his work and research: "Current archaeological data do not support the existence of an Indo-Aryan or European invasion into South Asia at any time in the pre- or protohistoric periods. Instead, it is possible to document archaeologically a series of cultural changes reflecting indigenous cultural development from prehistoric or historic periods... The Indo-Aryan invasion as an academic concept in 18th- and 19th-century Europe reflected the cultural milieu of that period. Linguistic data were used to validate the concept that in turn was used to interpret archaeological and anthropological data. What was theory became unquestioned fact that was used to interpret and organize all subsequent data. It is time to end the 'linguistic tyranny' that has prescribed interpretive frameworks of pre- and protohistoric cultural development in South Asia." [43]

After having done extensive research into the issue at hand, Nicholas Kazanas explains how he came to his own conclusions: "Having held and taught for more than 18 years, but without investigating, the received doctrine that the Indo-European branches dispersed from the South Russian or Pontic Steppe (as per Mallory 1997, 1989; Gimbutas 1985, 1970; and others), and that the Indo Aryans had entered Saptasindhu c1500 [BCE], I began to examine these mainstream notions thoroughly and in c1997 abandoned them. I decided that no evidence of any kind supported them; on the contrary, the evidence showed that by 1500 [BCE] the Indo Aryans were wholly indigenous and that the elusive Indo-European homeland was very probably Saptasindhu and the adjacent area—the Land of Seven Rivers in what is today N-W India and Pakistan; this area could well have extended as far northwest as the Steppe.

"Apart from the recent genetic studies, which at the time were not so well-known nor so secure, the decisive evidence for me now is the antiquity of Sanskrit, indicated by its inner coherence and its preservation of apparently original PIE [Proto-Indo-European] linguistic features (like the *dhatu*, five families of phonemes, etc) and cultural elements. The Vedic language as seen in the *RV* alone, despite much obvious attrition and several innovations, has preserved many more features from the putative PIE [Proto-Indo-European] language and wider culture. This was due to its well attested and incomparable system of oral tradition which preserved the ancient texts fairly intact and continued even into the 20th century. An oral tradition of this kind cannot be maintained by a people on the move for decades if not centuries over many thousands of miles, as the AIT proproses. Such a tradition could be preserved only by a sedentary people where the older generation would have the necessary leisure to pass the communal lore to the younger one." [44]

Kazanas also brings up the argument that even if the Vedic Aryans had been maintaining their language and literacy during an invasion or migration into the Saptasindhu region, why then is there no mention of it in any of the Vedic literature? Why was there no mention of their travels, mishaps, dangers in meeting alien people, etc? The reason is simple: they did not migrate, but were the original inhabitants of the area.

The only reason that has kept this defective and deformed doctrine alive is the personal and political interests that had an agenda to fulfill for their own purposes. There have been those, as there still are, who have a purpose in demeaning and belittling the Indian Vedic tradition and its early history. Even, as odd as it may seem, many Indian scholars also dumb-down the profound history and nature and the early advanced developments that came out of ancient India. Hopefully they will stop doing this and actually take a deep interest and research into their own culture to see what it really had to offer, and still does offer the world of today. Why not? What do they have to lose? That is the telltale question.

Therefore, as Nicholas Kazanas summarizes, which I quote because I could not say it better than he does, "Let us hope that the noxious AIT and all notions rooted in it will sooner than later end up in the only place they should be–the dustbin of history." [45]

SCHOLARS WHO BELIEVE IN THE FALSE HISTORY OF INDIA ARE A DYING BREED

Now that India has been free for a number of decades from British rule, researchers, historians, and archeologists can all begin to take a new look at the true history of India. We can have a more unbiased view of the numerous new findings that keep cropping up that give an increasingly accurate understanding of how ancient and how advanced was the Indian Vedic civilization. Now more than ever there is a serious lack of support and opposing evidence for the theories that were made popular by the British, such as the Aryan Invasion Theory, or that it was the invading Muslims who gave India the great contributions to Indian art, music, or even architecture. With the newer and more accurate historical findings, many of these ideas are falling apart like a house of cards.

These days there is much more evidence being presented by newer, younger and bolder researchers that show the falsity of these antiquated ideas. Furthermore, there are also more questions that are no longer answered by the old beliefs about India's history and the Aryan Invasion Theory. The theories of the old scholars are being overturned.

We also see that new students of archeology and history are hesitant to accept these ideas in the face of the newer findings and evidence that keep being discovered, such as the latest discovery (January, 2002) that ancient Indian civilization could date back to 9,000 years ago.

I have even talked to some students who are informed about the truth of Indian history and archeology who confronted their professors about the outdated inaccuracies and overtly misleading information that they were teaching in schools and universities. One professor admitted that it was wrong, but she had to teach it because it was in the book the college was using and that is what she had to teach.

I have even had friends discuss with educated Muslims the idea that many ancient buildings of India were not built by the Muslim invaders who have been given the credit, but were only captured them, and they readily agreed that anyone who really knew their history would admit this was the case. There was no argument with this. India had the mathematics (*Shulba Shastras*) and architectural treatises and abilities, along with knowledgeable craftsmen, to have built such structures, while the invading Muslims did not bring such knowledge and facility. In fact, the chronicle of Al Biruni, who accompanied Mahmoud Ghazni, relates the surprise and awe of the Muslim invaders to see such buildings. Thus, such structures had to have already been in existence.

It is interesting that the common laypersons are quicker to see the logic in the new research findings and in considering these new architectural discoveries than the academic scholars. The academicians who cling to such old ideas tend not to write more books justifying what they teach, but seem to spend more time on trying to debunk, criticize or discredit the new findings or theories that seem more relevant and able to answer or put to rest the age-old questions. Just a few of these questions include: Where is the pre-Aryan language that existed if the people of India were not part of the Vedic culture? What existed in India before the Vedic culture, if it was brought by invaders? If the Vedic Aryans invaded the Indus region after 1500 BCE, then how is it that the *Vedas* glorify the greatness of the Sarasvati River which is known to have dried up no later than 1800 BCE? How did the Vedic Aryans know of the Sarasvati River at all, unless they were already there and a part of the advanced Vedic culture from thousands of years ago? How is it that Arabic and European countries were able to make advancements in mathematics only after they learned the numeric system that originated in India, now called the Arabic numerals, with its unique symbol of zero? Why, when we seriously look at the way the area of India, the Middle East and Europe developed, it appears that the advanced nature of society came from India rather than from outside? When we read in the *Puranas* of the advanced organizational nature of the Vedic cities and their fabulous palaces and buildings such as in Dwaraka as found in the *Bhagavata Purana*, why should we think that India had no amazing structures before the Muslim invaders entered the country? Should we think that ancient Indians only lived in forests and tents? That is what it seems many academicians would have us believe. Anyway, these and other questions have not and can not be answered by the old ideas on India's history such as the Aryan Invasion Theory.

So it is unfortunate that many of these academics still hold on to these ideas as the basis of their views. The reason why some of these academics take this so personally is that they have the most to lose. The basis of their job, or their own identity, and their value to society and the whole basis of everything they thought they knew about history becomes threatened if it is proved that what they have been teaching is false.

The fact of the matter is, unfortunately, and as we can plainly see, much historical analysis is but a big ego trip; theories and opinions meant to do little more than support the premise of the superiority of one culture over another. There is a need to take a new look at reason and cultural development without this sort of interference of ego.

Now more than ever before truth is prevailing, and the corruption of the British and Muslim theories and stories that have been put forth to demean India and the Indian race and its Vedic culture is being recognized on an increasing scale. For this reason, the academics that still cling to such theories as the Aryan invasion are a dying breed. Maybe then we can be free from their closed-minded prejudice that came from the theories and attempted validations meant to do nothing but support the premise of the superiority of the European and Caucasian races over the darker skinned Indian people.

Eventually, truth prevails. And after a few hundred years of ideas that were purposely contrived to demean the culture and history of India, we are now learning that the truth is quite different, and India was more advanced than the old British theories give it credit. And we can see that these old theories are falling by the way side.

The threat to the Aryan Invasion Theory is coming as a surprise only to those who have not kept up with, or outrightly rejected, all the new evidence that is continually being uncovered, and all the new questions that cannot be substantiated by such concepts as the Aryan Invasion Theory. Thus, it is a revolution that is going in like a needle and out like a plow to propose that the Aryan Invasion is but a fictional account, and that the Muslims who invaded India merely captured the major monuments of India without really building them.

As time goes on, more and more evidence will accumulate to show the truth of India's Vedic history. As the evidence mounts, the old theories will slip away and anyone still clinging to such ideas as the Aryan invasion or the false history of India's architectural wonders will only look foolish. It is taking some time to reveal this truth, but out of all the cultures of the world, it is India that has best withstood the tests of time and remains the oldest living culture in the world. And this is not due to remaining dependent on the views of outsiders who think they know India's culture and history better than Indians, or those who still are influenced by the stories of India from invaders and dominators who disliked or even despised India and its people.

Now is the time for those of us connected with, or who appreciate India's historical and Vedic culture to unite and work to reveal the true and advanced nature of India's timeless Dharmic tradition, and its advancements, which were already in existence before the credits of its wonders were attempted to be taken by outsiders.

CHAPTER NOTES

1. G. P. Singh, *Facets of Ancient Indian History and Culture.*
2. David Frawley, *The Myth of the Aryan Invasion of India*, Voice of India, New Delhi, 2002, p. 43.
3. Bal Ram Singh, Editor, *Origin of Indian Civilization*, Center for Indic Studies, Dartmouth, USA, 2010, p. 15.
4. B. B. Lal, *Origin of Indian Civilization*, Edited by Bal Ram Singh, Center for Indic Studies, Dartmouth, USA, 2010. p. 23-24.
5. Ibid., p. 24.
6. Max Muller, *Biographies of Words and the Home of the Aryas*, by London, 1888, p. 120.
7. Chandrasekharendra Saraswati, *The Vedas*, Bharatiya Vidya Bhavan, Bombay, 1988, p. 16.
8. N. S. Rajaram, *The Politics of History*, Voice of India, New Delhi, 1995, p. xvi.
9. B. B. Lal, *Origin of Indian Civilization*, Edited by Bal Ram Singh, Center for Indic Studies, Dartmouth, USA, 2010. p. 26.
10. Kazanas, *Origin of Indian Civilization*, Edited by Bal Ram Singh, Center for Indic Studies, Dartmouth, USA, 2010, p. 57.
11. B. B. Lal, *The Home land of the Aryans, Evidence of Rig Vedic Flora and Fauna and Archeology*, Aryan Books International, Delhi, pp. 85-88.
12. N. S. Rajaram, *Origin of Indian Civilization*, Edited by Bal Ram Singh, Center for Indic Studies, Dartmouth, USA, 2010, p. 166-67.
13. Ibid., p. 167.
14. *Origin of Indian Civilization*, Edited by Bal Ram Singh, Center for Indic Studies, Dartmouth, USA, 2010, p. 17.
15. Kazanas, *Origin of Indian Civilization*, Edited by Bal Ram Singh, Center for Indic Studies, Dartmouth, USA, 2010, p. 54.
16. Dr. David Frawley and Dr. Navaratna S. Rajaram, *Hidden Horizons, Unearthing 10,000 Years of Indian Culture*, Swaminarayan Aksharpith, Ahmedabad, India, 2006, p. 64-65.
17. *Pride of India: A Glimpse into India's Scientific Heritage*, Samskriti Bharati, New Delhi, 2006, p. 78-79.
18. B. B. Lal, *Origin of Indian Civilization*, Edited by Bal Ram Singh, Center for Indic Studies, Dartmouth, USA, 2010, p. 34.
19. Dr. David Frawley and Dr. Navaratna S. Rajaram, *Hidden Horizons, Unearthing 10,000 Years of Indian Culture*, Swaminarayan Aksharpith,

Ahmedabad, India, 2006, p70-71)

20.   http://www.dailymail.co.uk/sciencetech/article-2151143/Climate-change-wiped-worlds-great-civilisations-4-000-years-ago.html.

21. C. Rayachaudhuri, *Studies in Indian Antiquities*, Calcutta, 1958, p. 134.

22. Dr. Ravi Prakash Arya, *New Discoveries About Vedic Sarasvati*, Indian Foundation for Vedic Science, Rohtak, Haryana, India, 2005, p. 26.

23. N. Jha and N. S. Rajaram, *The Deciphered Indus Script*, Aditya Prakashan, New Delhi, 2000, p. 162.

24. Dr. David Frawley and Dr. Navaratna S. Rajaram, *Hidden Horizons, Unearthing 10,000 Years of Indian Culture*, Swaminarayan Aksharpith, Ahmedabad, India, 2006, p.106.

25. B. B. Lal, *Homeland of the Aryans: Evidence of Rig Vedic Flora and Fauna and Archaeology*, pp. 80-81.

26. Sir John Marshall, *Mohenjo-Daro and the Indus Civilization*, Vol. II, p. 654.

27. Edwin Bryant, *The Quest for the Origins of Vedic Culture*, Oxford University Press, 2001, p. 170-171.

28. B. B. Lal, *Colonialism, Nationalism, Ethnicity, and Archaeology*, Parts 1 and 2, *Review of Archaeology* 18, no. 2:1-14 and 35-47, 1997, p. 285.

29. S. P. Gupta, *The Indus Sarasvati Civilization*, Pratibha Prakashan, 1996, p. 147.

30. N. Jha and N. S. Rajaram, *The Deciphered Indus Script*, Aditya Prakashan, New Delhi, 2000, p. 31.

31. Chandrakant Panse, *DNA, Genetics and Population Dynamics: Debunking the Aryan Invasion Propaganda*, Professor of Biotechnology, Newton, Massachusetts. Paper presented at the Third Annual Human Empowerment Conference at Houston, Texas, September, 2005.

32. http://www.thehindu.com/2006/06/24/stories/2006062412870400.htm.

33. N. S. Rajaram, *Origin of Indian Civilization*, Edited by Bal Ram Singh, Center for Indic Studies, Dartmouth, USA, 2010, p. 171.

34. Ibid., p. 173.

35. Stephen Oppenheimer, *Out of Eden: The Peopling of the World*, Constable, London, 2003, p. 152.

36. Stephen Oppenheimer, *The Real Eve: Modern Man's Journey Out of Africa*, Carroll & Graf, 2003, p. 152.

37. Nicholas Kazanas, *Indo-Aryan Origins and Other Vedic Issues*, Aditya Prakashan, New Delhi, 2009, p. 62-3.

38. A. B. Keith, *The Age of the Rigveda, Cambridge History of India*, Vol. I, 1922, pp. 77-113.

39. Nicholas Kazanas, *Indo-Aryan Origins and Other Vedic Issues*, Aditya Prakashan, New Delhi, 2009. p. 9.

40. Nicholas Kazanas, *Indo-Aryan Origins and Other Vedic Issues*, Aditya Prakashan, New Delhi, 2009, p. 10-11.

41. Ibid., p. 243.

42. Shri Aurobindo, *The Secret of the Veda*, Shri Aurobindo Ashram, Pondicherry, 1971, p. 24.

43. Jim Shaffer, *The Indo-Aryan Invasions: Cultural Myth and Archaeological Reality* (in *The People of South Asia*, 77-90. Ed. John Lukacs, Plenum Press, New York, 1984, p. 88.

44. Nicholas Kazanas, *Indo-Aryan Origins and Other Vedic Issues*, by Aditya Prakashan, New Delhi, 2009, p. 302.

45. Ibid., p. 328.

CHAPTER TWENTY-FOUR

How the Sciences Faded From India

This does not mean that the advancements that had been developed in India simply vanished or were merely neglected, but this refers to how India lost the recognition from both within and outside for the great accomplishments it gave to the world, for which it was once well known.

Some people may naturally wonder why, if ancient India had developed so many of the early forms of sciences, knowledge or skills that we use today, did they seem to fade away in further development and research in India. Why did they not continue to be on the cutting edge of scientific, mathematical, medical, engineering, or philosophical advancement? Some of the reasons are explained by Dr. Kshetraprasad Sensharma in his contribution to *Science and Technology in Ancient India*: "Maintenance of secrecy, foreign invasions, easy availability of the means of subsistence, lack of royal patronage, and the apathy of the Indian people due to general introverted tendencies–all these gradually stemmed the flow of scientific research in ancient India, and in time reduced it to an antique. Even then, we must certainly remember with pride that the scientific research of ancient India is indeed an essential chapter of Indian culture in the evolution of national pedigree." [1]

However, there have been not only causes from inside India, but some strong opposing outside forces as well. For example, during the colonization of India, a trend was set by the British in a systematic manner to discard all traditional systems of knowledge in India and to look at traditional practices with contempt. Unfortunately, this trend continued further after independence, and can still de detected even today. This resulted in the neglect of all the traditional knowledge systems, practices and indigenous science and technology systems of India. This was manifested in various policies and programs of government including monetary allocation, as well as the attitude of the people.[2]

Furthermore, one of the bands of scholars whose primary interest was the converting of Hindus to the one "true faith" by any means necessary were those at the University of Oxford who started the Boden Professorship of Sanskrit. The special objective of this foundation, as described by Sir Monier Williams, was stated like so: "I must draw attention to the fact that I am only the second occupant of the Boden Chair, and that its founder, Colonel Boden, stated most explicitly in his will (dated August 15, 1811) that the special object of his munificent bequest was to promote the translation of scriptures into Sanskrit; so as to enable his countrymen to proceed in the conversion of the natives of India to the Christian Religion..."[3]

Another such agenda that started long ago and continues in various ways to this day is through the educational system that was initiated by the British. This was the brainchild of T. B. Macaulay. Macaulay came from a deeply religious Protestant family, so his motivation was to convert numerous Hindus to Christianity, which he thought would also help the administrative problems that the English were facing. His plan was to create an educational system that would make an educated elite that would naturally be English by their own choice, and thus give up their own Hindu traditions. Then they would also work and cooperate more efficiently with the English administration. This conversion would then also facilitate the British colonialism by making Indians, especially the Brahmanas, collaborators loyal to their new masters. This may have been an ambitious goal at the time, but this English education has remained a factor in the Indian educational system ever since. In recognition of this goal, Macauley wrote to his father in 1836 while serving as chairman of the Education Board in India:

"Our English schools are flourishing wonderfully. The effect of this education on the Hindus is prodigious... It is my belief that if our plans of education are followed up, there will not be a single idolater among the respectable classes in Bengal thirty years hence. And this will be effected without any efforts to proselytize, without the smallest interference with religious liberty, by natural operation of knowledge and reflection. I heartily rejoice in the project."[4]

T. B. Macaulay was quite specific on his design for the educational system in India. He had written a few articles on it, namely *T. B. Macaulay on India 2-2-1834*, and another *T. B. Macaulay on India 9-3-1843*, which we can find in Shri Dharampal's book *Despoliation and Defaming of India–The Early Nineteenth Century, British Crusade*. There in the first article, Macaulay describes his utter contempt for Sanskrit literature:

"It is, I believe, no exaggeration to say, that all the historical information which has been collected from all the books written in Sanskrit language is less valuable than what may be found in the most paltry abridgements used at preparatory schools in England. In every branch of physical or moral philosophy, the relative position of the two nations is nearly the same." [5]

He went on to make his thoughts on the matter even more clear: "To sum up what I have said, I think it clear that we are not fettered by the Act of Parliament of 1813, that we are not fettered by any pledge expressed or implied; that we are free to employ our funds as we choose; that we ought to employ them in teaching what is best worth knowing; that English is better worth knowing than Sanskrit or Arabic; that the natives are desirous to be taught English, and not desirous to be taught Sanskrit or Arabic; that neither as the languages of law; nor as the languages of religion have the Sanskrit and Arabic any peculiar claim to our engagement; that it is possible to make natives of this country thoroughly good English scholars, and that to this end our efforts ought to be directed.

"In one point I fully agree with the gentlemen to whose general views I am opposed. I feel with them, that it is impossible for us, with our limited means, to attempt to educate the body of the people. **We must at present do our best to form a class who may be interpreters between us and the millions whom we govern; a class of persons, Indian in blood and colour, but English in taste, in opinions, in morals, and in intellect.** To that class we may leave it to refine the vernacular dialects of the country, to enrich those dialects with terms of science borrowed from the Western nomenclature, and to render them by degrees fit vehicles for conveying knowledge to the great mass of the population." [6]

This is in reference that Macaulay figured that the British would not be able to educate all Indians in the ways of the British, but could indeed create a class of them who would be English in taste, opinions, morals and intellect, and then engage them in influencing the rest of India, thus helping the English in their job of overseeing the rest of India, and, of course, converting them.

Years later, in 1843, Macaulay never deviated from his disdain of Vedic culture and his desire to bring all Hindus to Christianity in whatever way it would take. This becomes clear in his article *T. B. Macaulay on India 9-3-1843*:

"Through the whole Hindoo Pantheon you will look in vain for anything resembling those beautiful and majestic forms which stood in the shrines of ancient Greece. All is hideous, and grotesque, and ignoble. As this superstition is of all superstitions the most inelegant, so is it of all superstitions the most immoral. Emblems of vice are objects of public worship. Acts of vice are acts of public worship. The courtesans are as much a part of the establishment of the temple, as much ministers of the god, as the priests. Crimes against life, crimes against property, are not only permitted but enjoined by this odious theology." [7]

In this way, we can clearly see the basis which was Macaulay's whole motivation on India. By his use and development of the British educational system, his plan was to exterminate India's Vedic culture, and make the people of India forget all its advancements, sciences, and contributions to world progress, and make them but slaves to the Western straightjacket of conformity to its materialistic values and ways of thinking. How could there be anything else from someone who had so little understanding of India's tradition, and who had such an egoistic and proud view of his own superiority?

For me, it has always been my perception that the lack of understanding of the real philosophy, the actual traditions and purpose of the Vedic culture, or the distancing from it, or the misinterpretation of it, as the primary reason for any misconception and any misuse of the Vedic way of life. Everything within the tradition has a purpose and intention and expected result for why something is done. But if that is not understood properly, nor taught in the correct way to others, it is like anything else that can be misperceived and then misdirected in the actions that follow. And the British system of education was a great means of making Indians forget their culture and all that they once were, and how India was once the wealthiest area in the world and a center for great learning. Moreover, it was also a means to make the Indian people feel backwards and unworthy, and that only by accepting the Western values could they again become truly progressive and part of the civilized world. Of course, the question of what was truly civilized could lead to a whole conversation by itself. And this was only one of a number of obstacles that India had to encounter.

In this way, we can see that there had been an ongoing endeavor to stifle India's means of continued advancements, of its ingenuity, of its inventiveness and freedom of thought, and make it but a puppet, a slave, a servant to the desires of those who wanted to continue its exploitation of all its resources. This is why India was not been able to regain its position and high standards of development as it once had in the past.

Nonetheless, we should also understand that the status of India does not lie only in the accomplishments of the past, though they should not be forgotten, but also in the achievements of the present and future. There have been numerous Indians who have been highly accomplished with inventions and developments that raised the status of India and its civilization throughout the ages, recently as well. Even today the students of India are some of the brightest in the world, when given a chance to become fully educated. And I have seen even here in America that most of the top performing students in any given class are Indians, or are the champions of spelling contests, and so on.

So with the freedom from the pressure of invaders that has been given to India at the time of Independence, we can see how the people of Indian descent can truly reach their real potential when given the opportunity. But now they must also help develop and guide India into the future so that it is a country that can overcome the obstacles of the past, and show others by example of how to arrange and manage themselves and their resources so that everyone can benefit and reach the epitome of civilized culture. That may not be so easy with the problems of increased population, or increased pollution that destroys many of the rivers and water supply, or the lack of infrastructure that decreases the means for proper harvest and distribution of produce and food, and the corruption that has become widespread, and so on. But if India has been able to overcome so many of the problems of the past, by using the natural ingenuity of the younger generations, and the continued respect for its ancient traditions that lead to the right mindset and consciousness that paved the way for the early advancements that lead the world, they should be able to pave their way into the future.

In this way, the developments that originated in India, Bharatvarsha, never left India, but the credit for them was no longer given, and such achievements were no longer recognized as the heritage of ancient India or its Vedic culture. So it is time that the world give its rightful recognition and acknowledgment of what ancient India has given to the world. However, we can only guess at how much more advanced the world could have been, and how many more developments may have originated out of Vedic culture if it had been allowed to continue, uninterrupted by the invaders over the past 1000 years or so, whether they be the Muslims, Moghuls, the British, the Portuguese, or so on. They cared little for the culture and even preferred to destroy it, and had even less concern for the people. And if you do not know what I am talking about, then read my book *Crimes Against India*. Is that civilized? Is that progressive when they could have gained much more if they had worked in cooperation with the people of India? Nonetheless, there are still many scholars and researchers that are again reviving this insight, and serious spiritual organizations that are working to keep the Vedic spiritual traditions very much alive. After all, it still has much more to offer humanity, as anyone can see if they investigate it.

CHAPTER NOTES
1. Dr. Bijoya Goswami, *Science and Technology in Ancient India*, edited by Dr. Manabendu Banerjee, Sanskrit Pustak Bhandar, Calcutta, 1994, p. 94.
2. Dr. Shamasundar, Preface to *Medicine and Surgery in Ancient India*, A Yugayatri Publication, Bangalore.
3. Kailash Chandra Varma, *Some Western Indologistss and Indian Civilization*, in *India's Contribution to World Thought and Culture*, Published by Vivekananda Kendra Prakashan, Chennai, 1970, p. 167.
4. Rajaram and Frawley, *Vedic Aryans and the Origins of Civilization*, Voice of India, New Delhi, 1995, p. 31.
5. Shri Dharampal, *Despoliation and Defaming of India–The Early Nineteenth Century, British Crusade*, p. 194.
6. Ibid., pp. 201-2.
7. Ibid., p. 204.

CHAPTER TWENTY-FIVE

Bharatvarsha
Home of the Greatest Philosophies
and Spiritual Culture

Besides all of the scientific, mathematical, architectural, agricultural, and medical developments that came out of the Vedic culture of ancient India, it also provided the greatest and deepest level of philosophical thought and spiritual processes that the world had yet to see. In fact, most of the world's religions either adapted or were influenced by the spiritual understandings that came out of the Vedic culture. It was and has continued to be one of the main spiritual forces and deepest and most profound traditions in the world. It has never been spread by force, fear, intimidation, or war, but only through the grace of the attraction to its spiritual upliftment that it offers everyone. It has never been a dogma or belief system inflicted on anyone, but presents a more tolerant, open and accepting process with a wide latitude of philosophical outlooks within it that allow anyone to participate and be a part of it.

This can only be the outcome of a great civilization, a deep understanding of human nature, a profound view of the internal quest of all of humanity that drives them to understand more about themselves and where they came from. It is this insight and realizations of the great rishis and spiritual authorities of ancient India, Bharatvarsha, that lead to the teachings of the true nature of the soul, of God, reincarnation or rebirth, karma, *Dharma*, and the yogic practices that provided everyone with the means to have the same spiritual experiences and insights, and freedom for God-realization. It was not that it was unattainable for a mere few, but it was the teachings with which everyone could take advantage of and make progress from whatever was their situation or level of consciousness. The fact remains even today that when we look around, few are those religions that have anywhere near a similar outlook of equality and fairness and allowance for everyone to participate.

There have, of course, been social injustices that have appeared, but this has not been from the Vedic system itself, but from a misunderstanding of the Vedic teachings, or a deliberate manipulation of them for the corrupt and advantageous agenda of a few, which has unfortunately spread over a wider spectrum with time. This has to be corrected, and the best way to do that is simply by re-educating people in the true teachings and knowledge of the Vedic philosophy and culture as it once was and still is meant to be. This higher truth is still attainable by everyone if they want it. The ways to do so simply have to be supplied and taught through the right means, and many are those who are still doing that.

This is why, practically speaking, one of the greatest heritages we have from the Vedic tradition is its library of texts, or whatever we have left of them, that can still provide humanity with some of the greatest and most profound spiritual insights ever known to man. People, especially the younger people of today, often do not understand or realize how important this is and how fortunate we are that we still have such texts to study and perceive the spiritual depth that they have to offer. These include, for example, the main Vedic texts of the *Vedas*, namely the *Rig*, *Atharva*, *Yajur* and *Sama Vedas*, the *Brahmanas*, *Aranyakas*, the *Upanishads*, the *Vedanta Sutras*, the *Itihasas* or histories, like the *Ramayana* and *Mahabharata* which includes the *Bhagavad-gita*, and then the *Puranas*, which relate the history of the universe from the perspective of different days of Brahma or periods of creation, and which also elaborate on all of the original spiritual teachings found in the *Vedas*. Of course, many are those who do not have time to read them all, but there are those of us who can help spread the core teachings in a simple way that is easy to grasp.

The *Puranas*, for example, preserved the Vedic heritage by remolding or elaborating on the essential spiritual truths in the early Vedic *samhitas*, and presented it in relevant teachings and histories, stories and customs that could be used for a later age and a broader geographical area. Therefore, in this day and age, a more understandable and comprehensive way of learning the Vedic philosophy is through the teachings in the *Puranas*, the *Bhagavata Purana* being one of the most important.

There also are many other texts as well, all of which make for a

The ancient 5,000-year-old cave of Vyasadeva where it is said he wrote the Mahabharata and Bhagavata Purana, in Mana near Badrinatha in the Himalayas. A Deity of Vyasadeva is inside sitting in meditation.

The ornate stone sculptures of Lakshmi-Narayana last hundreds of years. These are on the exterior of the Hoysala Shiva Temple in Halebid, South India

complete Vedic library of the various ways of understanding who we are and the Absolute Truth, and the ways and paths of self-realization, and much more. I have provided a much more detailed analysis of these texts in other publications of mine, such as in *The Heart of Hinduism*.

The Vedic culture has provided humanity with the largest amount of spiritual information of any culture today, and remains a tradition that is still practiced in this day and age. In other words, though everything goes through transition, it has not changed that much. Though many other cultures have ceased to exist, only leaving us with their architecture and pyramids, the Vedic culture continues to live by the knowledge it has presented, and numerous temples where these traditions are still alive in which we can still see, witness and participate in them.

Furthermore, these Vedic texts, being in Sanskrit, have also provided humanity with one of the most self-preserving languages the world has ever known. It is certainly the most spiritual of languages, considered traditionally to be part of the spiritual sound vibration that pervades both the material creation and exists eternally in the spiritual dimension. Therefore, it has the potential to invoke both the Supreme Being, the internal knowledge of the soul, and raise the consciousness to perceive the divine realms.

The authority of Vedic knowledge is that it is stated to be non-human, or provided from nonmaterial origins, meaning the spiritual domain, or by Divine Intervention or arrangement. The Sanskrit word for this is *apaurusha*, meaning that it is knowledge from beyond time and space, or beyond the physical dimensions of matter.

The conclusion is that no other civilization, either ancient or modern, has presented and passed along such a deep spiritual and philosophical tradition for the ultimate benefit of humanity, nor provided so many deeply insightful teachers and spiritual authorities for such a long time. It still provides the mainstream of philosophical principles in India, which has spread around the globe at various times and in various ways.

The greatness and sophistication of the Vedic tradition has been noted by numerous writers, scholars and deep thinkers from the time of its discovery. Many examples could be given, which can include such people as Philip Rawson, in *The Art of Southeast Asia*: "The culture of India has been one of the world's most powerful civilizing forces. Countries of the Far East, including China, Korea, Japan, Tibet and Mongolia owe much of what is best in their own cultures to the inspiration of ideas imported from India. The West, too, has its own debts... No conquest or invasion, no forced conversion imposed." [1]

Victor Cousin (1792-1867), the noteworthy French philosopher was well aware of the preeminence of the Vedic philosophy years before it actually took hold in Europe. He said, "When we read with attention the poetical and philosophical monuments of the East–above all those of India, which are beginning to spread in Europe–we discover there many a truth, and truths so profound, and which make such a contrast with the meanness of the results at which European genius has sometimes stopped, that we are constrained to bend the knee before the philosophy of the East and to see in this cradle of the human race the native land of the highest philosophy." [2]

Henry David Theoreau (1817-1862) we all know was most impressed with India's spiritual tradition, especially with the *Bhagavad-gita*. He had said: "In the morning I bathe my intellect in the stupendous and cosmogonal philosophy of the *Bhagavad Gita*, since whose composition years of the gods have elapsed and in comparison with which our modern world and its literature seems puny and trivial."

Later, the likes of Romain Rolland (1866-1944) who was famous as a French novelist, biographer, playwright, and musicologist, also paid tribute to the land of India: "If there is one place on the face of earth where all dreams of living men have found a home from the very earliest days when man began the dream of existence, it is India." [3]

As most people know, the philosopher Schlegel was a great admirer of Vedic philosophy. There are many quotes from him. Here, from the *History of Literature* (p. 126), he speaks of the grand nature of Vedic Indian thought compared to that found in Europe at the time: "Even the loftiest philosophy of the Europeans, the idealism of reason, as is set forth by Greek philosophers, appears in comparison with the abundant light and vigour of Oriental idealism like a feeble promethean spark in the full flood of heavenly glory of the noonday sun–faltering and feeble and ever ready to be extinguished."

Count Bjornstjerna also relates in *Theogony of the Hindus* (p. 27): "In this respect, the Hindus were far in advance of the philosophers of Greece and Rome, who considered the immortality of the soul as problematical."

Most people have also agreed that the origins of most deep spiritual philosophy, and even the core teachings within most religions, can be found within the Vedic tradition, which was the first to present many of the views of spiritual understanding that later traveled around the world. For example, Dr. Enfield, in his *History of Philosophy* (Vol. I p. 65), expresses, "We find that it [India] was visited for the purpose of acquiring knowledge by Pythagoras, Anaxarchus, Pyrrho, and others who afterwards became eminent philosophers in Greece." Mr. Pococke in his *India in Greece* (p. 353) also relates, "Certain it is that Pythagoras visited India, which I trust I shall make self-evident." In this same view, Schlegel points out in *History of Literature* (p. 109): "The doctrine of the transmigration of souls was indigenous to India and was brought into Greece by Pythagoras."

Arthur Schopenhauer (1788-1860) also mentions the greatness of the Vedic philosophy as found in the *Upanishads*, as quoted by Nehru (*Discovery of India*, p. 92):

"From every sentence (of the *Upanishads*) deep, original and sublime thoughts arise, and the whole world is pervaded by a high and holy and earnest spirit... In the whole world there is no study... so beneficial and as elevating as that of the *Upanishads*... (They) are products of the highest wisdom... It is destined sooner or later to become the faith of the people." In this way, it seems that he felt that as people rediscover the depths of Vedic spiritual philosophy, they will again accept it more enthusiastically and with greater appreciation all over the world.

He also said, "In the whole world there is no study so beneficial and so elevating as that of the *Upanishads*. It has been the solace of my life, it will be the solace of my death."

Annie Besant had appreciated the Vedic culture for many years. As she had stated in her publication, *India: Eassays and Lectures*, "Among the priceless teachings that may be found in the great Indian epic *Mahabharata*, there is none so rare and priceless as the *Gita*... This is the India of which I speak–the India which, as I said, is to me the Holy Land. For those who, though born for this life in a Western land, and clad in a Western body, can yet look back to earlier incarnations in which they drank the milk of spiritual wisdom from the breast of their true mother–they must feel ever the magic of her immemorial past, must dwell ever under the spell of her deathless fascination; for they are bound to India by all the sacred memories of their past and with her, too, are bound up all the radiant hopes of their future, a future which they know they will share with her who is their true mother in the soul-life." [4]

Annie Besant later said in a lecture at the Grand Theatre in Calcutta on the 15th of January, 1906: "India is the mother of religion. In her are combined science and religion in perfect harmony and that is the Hindu religion, and it is India that shall be again the spiritual mother of the world."

Of course, many know the quote by Dr. Annie Besant as written in the cover notes from the book, *Hindus, Life-Line of India*, by G. M. Jagtiani. Her words put great emphasis on the value of India, its history, the Vedic culture, and its importance to the world. She says: "After a study of some forty years and more of the great religions of the world, I find none so perfect, none so scientific, none so philosophic, and none so spiritual as the great religion known by the name of Hinduism. The more you know it, the more you will love it; the more you try to understand it, the more deeply you will value it. Make no mistake; without Hinduism, India has no future. Hinduism is the soil into which India's roots are struck, and torn of that she will inevitably wither, as a tree torn out from its place. Many are the religions and many are the races flourishing in India, but none of them stretches back into the far dawn of her past, nor are they necessary for her endurance as a nation. Everyone might pass away as they came and India would still remain. But let Hinduism vanish and what is she? A geographical expression of the past, a dim memory of a perished glory, her literature, her art, her monuments, all have Hindudom written across them. And if Hindus do not maintain Hinduism, who shall save it? If India's own children do not cling to her faith, who shall guard it? India alone can save India, and India and Hinduism are one."

Aldous Huxley (1894-1963) was another with great appreciation for the *Bhagavad-gita*, which he expressed as, "The *Bhagavad Gita* is the most systematic statement of spiritual evolution of endowing value of mankind. The *Gita* is one of the clearest and most comprehensive summaries of the spiritual thoughts ever to have been made." [5]

Max Muller, in spite of his initial agenda, was also not one without the highest praise for the *Vedas*, which he expressed towards the end of his life: "I shall say even more, and I have said it before, namely, that supposing that the Vedic hymns were composed between 1500 and 1000 B.C., we can hardly understand how, at so early a date, the Indians had developed ideas which to us sound decidedly modern...

"I maintain that for a study of man, or, if you like, for a study of Aryan humanity, there is nothing in the world equal in importance with the *Veda*. I maintain that to everybody who cares for himself, for his ancestors, for his history, or for his intellectual development, a study of Vedic literature is indispensable; and that, as an element of liberal education, it is far more important and far more improving than the reigns of Babylonian and Persian kings, aye even the dates and deeds of many of the kings of Judah and Israel.

"It is curious to observe the reluctance with which these facts are accepted, particularly by those to whom they aught to be most welcome. I mean the students of anthropology. Instead of devoting all their energy to the study of these documents, which have come upon us like a miracle, they seem only bent on inventing excuses why they need not be studied. Let us not be supposed that, because there are several translations of the *Rig Veda* in English, French and German, therefore all that the *Veda* can teach us has been learned. Far from it... We are still on the mere surface of Vedic literature, and yet our critics are ready with ever so many arguments why the *Veda* can teach us nothing as to a primitive state of man... We mean by primitive the earliest state of man of which, from the nature of the case, we can hope to gain any knowledge; and here, next to the archives hidden away in the secret drawers of language, in the treasury of words common to all Aryan tribes, and in the radical elements of which each word is compounded, there is no literary relic more full of lessons to the true anthropologist, to the true student of mankind, then the *Rig Veda*." [6]

In speaking about Schopenhauer's appreciation for Vedanta, Max Muller also related, "I am neither afraid or ashamed to say that I share his enthusiasm for the Vedanta, and feel indebted to it for much that has been helpful to me in my passage through life... the *Upanishads* are the sources of the Vedanta philosophy, a system in which human speculation seems to me to have reached its very acme... I spend my happiest hours in reading Vedantic books. They are to me like the light of the morning, like the pure air of the mountains–so simple, so true, if once understood." [7]

Count Bjornstierna in his book *The Theogony of the Hindus* (p. 168) rightly states, "No nation on earth can vie with the Hindus in respect of the antiquity of their religion. It is there (Aryavarta) we must seek the cradle for the Brahmin religion but for the cradle of high civilization of the

Hindus, which gradually extended itself in the west to Ethiopia, to Egypt, to Phoenicia, in the east to Siam, to China and to Japan, in the south to Ceylon, to Java and to Sumatra, and in the north to Persia, to Chaldia and to Colchis, whence it came to Greece and to Rome and at length to the remote abode of the Hyperboreans."

This was reiterated even more recently by N. S. Rajaram, wherein he states: "The seeds of both Eastern and Western rationalism can be found in the Vedic tradition. The *Vedas*, and more particularly the *Rig Veda*, belong to an earlier layer of civilization before the rise of Egypt, Sumeria and the Indus Valley. This was the world of the primeval Aryas–a culture, not a race–the soil from which grew the mighty Indo-European tree. This appears to be the verdict of science." [8]

THE REAL TREASURE OF INDIA

As we have seen herein, India was once known for her vast resources and great wealth, but her greatest treasure was, of course, her Vedic spiritual philosophy, which had no comparison anywhere. This was the preceptor of all other forms of religious thought. Unbounded love for humanity and all of God's creatures are the results of the noblest influence of true religion, which found their highest expression in ancient India, and even today, as long as the people do not continue to lose interest in their own tradition.

The Vedic spiritual knowledge and path of realization are precepts that are ever true, or genuine, universal spiritual truths, applicable at any time and in any place. Its principles circumscribe the planet and govern all humanity, in fact, every soul in all species. Thus, it takes into its fold all people from everywhere, no matter whether they be Indians, Arabs, Europeans, Americans, Africans, or whatever.

Unlike other religions, it is not a dogma that must be accepted without question to be a believer. It is not a confession of weakness or admission of hopelessness without a savior, or an absolute reliance on an external power for our salvation. But it is an assertion of confidence that with proper knowledge, right guidance, uplifted attitude and determination to follow the spiritual path, we can all reach a level of directly perceiving the Divine, or at least our higher identity. It is not a matter of depending on the good grace's of an institution or church or any place of worship to develop a relationship with God, but it is a matter of merely reawakening the relationship that we already have with God through the means that are provided, such as the Vedic texts, guru, *sadhus* or sages, temples, worship, meditation, hearing and chanting, or any of the processes that help spiritualize our consciousness. In this way, it is a scientific process of following the formula for attaining our own spiritual experiences and reawakening the link between the soul and Supersoul, between the infinitesimal and the Infinite.

This is the difference between the Vedic spiritual path of *Sanatana-dharma*, which never feared nor was contrary to science, nor was it ever guilty of the terrors of something like the Inquisition that demanded surrender to a particular belief system, and tortured you to death in the most inhumane way if you did not do so. It never shed the blood of a Galileo, or a Copernicus or a Bruno. Yet, we can see that portions of Christian or Muslim and Buddhist ethics are but repeated portions of the much older Vedic tenants. This and similar observations have been done time and again throughout the study of comparative religion, which I have presented in numerous ways in previous books of mine. But we can see it again briefly in the way the Swedish Count Bjornstjerna, when comparing the Scandinavian *Eddas* with the *Vedas*, said in his *Theogony of the Hindus* (pp. 107-108): "All these questions are so exceedingly similar to those which the angels make to Brahma and the answers similar to those of Brahma in the *Vedas*, that we can scarcely question the derivation of the *Edda* from the *Veda*."

With a little research we can see that the theology of the Greeks, Egyptians and the Assyrians is wholly founded on the Hindu philosophy. As Professor Max Muller said: "The poetry of Homer is founded on the mythology of the *Vedas*," [9] and without the *Veda*, he continues, "The science of mythology would have remained mere guesswork and without a safe basis" [10]

Herewith we can begin to understand that the gods and goddesses of Greece and other places are but copies of the Vedic originals, though the names have been changed according to the region. This perception is nothing new, though the more recent comparisons have become more sophisticated, but we can see such realizations of the preceding nature of the superior Vedic tradition as far back as this description, given in the

Daily Tribune by Mr. W. D. Brown, who says so eloquently, "By careful examination the unprejudiced mind cannot but admit that Hindu is the parent of the literature and theology of the world. The researches and investigations made in Sanskrit language, which was once spoken in that country, by scholars like Max Muller, Jaccolliot, Sir William Jones and others, have found in the ancient records of India the strongest proofs that thence were drawn many or nearly all the favorite dogmas which latter theologians have adopted, and the strongest proofs show to the thoughtful student that the ancient Hindus were neither the practicers of idolatry nor the unlearned, uncivilized, barbaric race they have usually been thought [to be], but a people enjoying a measure of inspiration that might be envied by more pretentious nations. And I have not the least doubt that these translations of ancient Hindu literature will confound the so-called modern civilizations, that they will look upon India as a century flower once more coming into full bloom, wafting forth its delicious fragrance, and will beg for a slip from its branches." [11]

CHARACTER OF HINDUS

Because of the refined and sophisticated nature of the culture and the level of mind it promoted, the typical Hindus who had grown up in such an environment were also known for their polished character and personality. Even today when I travel around India, I often find a level of an accommodating nature in the personality of Indian Hindus that is hardly found elsewhere, at least in those areas where the Vedic tradition is still held in high esteem. Of course, this implies that those who have no regard for the Vedic principles often show less than respectable traits, and certainly less than favorable regard toward others, which I have also observed in my travels in India. But the high character of Indians was also observed years ago.

Professor Max Muller, for example, in his *India, What can it Teach Us?* (p.57) mentions how truthful the Hindus were, which was a prominent feature in their national character. But many others had also recognized how Hindus years ago were known for their generosity, tolerance, intelligence, courtesy, gentleness, sobriety, love of knowledge, and feeling of honor for their character.

Mr. Elphinstone also related how, "The villagers are inoffensive, amiable people, affectionate to their family, kind to their neighbours and towards all but Government, honest and sincere." [12]

In this same line of thinking and same time period in 1813, when evidence was given before the British Parliament, Mr. Mercer said: "They (Hindus) are mild in their disposition, polished in their general manners; in their domestic relations, kind and affectionate." [13]

One interesting narrative is presented by Max Muller wherein he explains: "During the last twenty years, however, I have had some excellent opportunities of watching a number of native scholars under circumstances where it is not difficult to detect a man's true character, I mean in literary work, and, more particularly, in literary controversy. I have watched them carrying on such controversies both among themselves and with certain European scholars, and I feel bound to say that, with hardly one exception that they have displayed a far greater respect for truth, and a far more manly and generous spirit than we are accustomed to even in Europe and America. They have shown strength, but no rudeness; nay, I know that nothing has surprised them as much as the course invective to which certain Sanskrit scholars have condescended, rudeness of speech being, according to their view of human nature, a safe sign not only of bad breeding but of want of knowledge. When they were wrong they have readily admitted their mistake; when they were right they have never sneered at their European adversaries. There has been, with few exceptions, no quibbling, no special pleading, no untruthfulness on their part, and certainly none of that low cunning of the scholar who writes down and publishes what he knows perfectly well to be false, and snaps his fingers at those who still value truth and self-respect more highly than victory or applause at any price. Here, too, we might possibly gain by the import cargo." [14]

INDIANS DO NOT APPRECIATE THEIR OWN CULTURE AS MUCH AS THEY SHOULD

After all this appreciation for what the Vedic tradition has given to us, what is the future for it? The problem is that Vedic culture, over the past several generations, seems to be fading from India, or even shifting from India to the West. Why? In spite of India being the homeland of such a great philosophy and culture, Indians do not seem to be that interested in what they can find in their own backyard. Thus, when nondharmic politicians of India work against the Hindu culture, when those of foreign religions work to establish themselves and their religion in India, when churches out-number the temples in areas, the Hindus do little about it. They are less appreciative of their own tradition than they are of what comes from the West.

This reminds me of a news item I read wherein one wealthy girl in Delhi was saving her money to try and find the best yoga teacher that she could, by traveling to California and looking there. The funny part of this is that she was ignoring what treasures she could find in her own backyard of India, the homeland of yoga. Does she think yoga originated in California? Furthermore, she seems to overlook the fact that so many Westerners save their money so they can also find the best yoga teacher they can by traveling to India. In fact, when I look at various yoga conferences in India, I see far more Westerners who attend than Indians. It seems that Westerners are displaying more value, in many ways, for what comes from India than Indians. So is it that Vedic culture is shifting to America? Or will India again begin to value what has existed for thousands of years in their own homeland?

However, even M. K. Gandhi spoke of this and possibly answered this question years ago. He once said, "Just as in the West they have made wonderful discoveries in material things, similarly, Hinduism has made still more marvelous discoveries in things of religion, of the spirit, of the soul. But we have no eye for those great and fine discoveries. We are dazzled by the material progress that Western science has made... After all, there is some thing in Hinduism that has kept it alive up till now. It has witnessed the fall of Babylonian, Syrian, Persian and Egyptian civilization... Yes, I see here ancient India still living. True, there are dung heaps, too, here and there, but there are rich treasures buried under them. And the reason why it has survived is that the end which Hinduism set before it was not development along material but spiritual lines."

CHAPTER NOTES
1. Philip Rawson, *The Art of Southeast Asia*, Thames and Hudson, New York, 1990, p. 7.

2. Mark Healey, *The Bhajan Belt: Serenity in the Catskill*, New York Times, Escapes section, October, 18, 2002.

3. Purnima Voria, *The Economic Times*, September 26, 2010.

4. Annie Besant, *India: Essays and Lectures*, Vol. IV, The Theosophical Publishing Co., London, 1895, p. 11.

5. T. C. Galav, *Philosophy of Hinduism–An Introduction*, p. 65.

6. Max Muller, *India: What can it Teach Us?*, first published in 1883, published by Rupa & Co., New Delhi, 2002, pp. 79-81.

7. Jawaharlal Nehru, *Discovery of India*, Signet Press, Calcutta, 1946, p. 92.

8. N. S. Rajaram, *Sarasvati River and the Vedic Civilization*, Aditya Prakashan, New Delhi, 2006, p. 86.

9. Count Bjornstierna, *Theogony of the Hindus*, p. 131.

10. Max Muller, *Chips from A German Workshop*, Vol. III, p. 79.

11. Mr. W. D. Brown, in *Daily Tribune*, Salt Lake City, Sunday Morning, February 20th, 1884.

12. Mr. Elphinstone, *Modern India and the Indians*, p. 33.

13. *Mill's History of India*, Vol. I, p. 523.

14. Max Muller, *India: What can it Teach Us?*, p. 63.

CONCLUSION

Vedic Culture: Ain't Dead Yet

By this time, at the end of this book, I would hope that you would see some of what is so ancient, so advanced, so profound, and so deep about the Vedic culture and its philosophy and how that philosophy has been applied to the way society can use it for its benefit, advancement, its insights into life and the spiritual world, and in the way it can help humanity reach its highest potential on every level.

Plus, for me it has been the path that has made all the difference in my life. It has taken me to an adventure that I never would have known existed, especially in my search for true meaning in life, and in reaching my highest potential, and in being able to perceive the highest dimensions of reality, beyond mere sense perception. For me, I can never accept something without proof, without reaching it by practical experience. In other words, dogma alone has no place for me, I must be able to directly perceive whatever is being spoken about or taught. And it is the spiritual processes that have been described in the Vedic texts that have enabled me to have that experience.

I hope that reviewing the information in this book will stir some pride and exhilaration about the Vedic tradition in those who already follow it, and more curiosity among those who do not or are just looking into it. We need to recognize what it has given to humanity and also realize how much it can continue to give if we understand its true purpose and the profound nature that it has always held within it. I would hope that the politicians and government of India should see the past developments that were given to mankind. It was by these which society has developed great inventions based on these ancient advancements that came from the Vedic sages and rishis, and the advanced nature of its texts, the thinking and realizations that went into its early writings, and the means and methods by which it proposed for mankind to attain higher levels of consciousness, something that is sorely lacking in today's society.

Let us continue to be participants in the traditions, practices and views that the timeless Vedic philosophy and culture have given us so that we can continue to use it for attaining our highest capacity, to attain loftier perceptions of who we are, of what is this universe and material creation, and what is our purpose here.

Let us not merely be witnesses like a journalist who is only reporting what is going on, but let us be participants who are directly involved in the experiences we can attain by the instructions and guidance that Vedic culture has given us. Let us not merely wait until the only way we can observe the Vedic culture is by visiting museums that display past achievements, historical accomplishments, ancient relics or sites that are no longer really understood but only questioned regarding their significance.

Today, we can see this culture as a living tradition, very much alive and kicking, asking for everyone to dive in and see what can be attained through it. But we can also see that there are those, whether they be atheistic politicians, secular educational institutions, outright materialists who cannot see anything beyond the tip of their nose, or even other religions who are systematically trying to destroy whatever remains of the Vedic culture until future generations can only admire or reminisce about it by attending museums or reading encyclopedias. This itself is also a fanaticism and arrogance that would stifle and keep hidden what has always been a contribution from ancient India for bringing humanity up to its highest possibility and standards. We have seen the demise or even destruction of such civilizations as Egypt, Greece, Persia, the Celts, the Maya, the Inca, along with various indigenous tribes, and so on, by the same kinds of people and thoughtlessness and condemnation towards anything but their own religion or culture. This is but the attitude of subjugation and the desire to overpower all others, rather than to empower and enrich them through understanding and cooperation. Are we to let the same thing happen to the culture of ancient India and its Vedic tradition?

Let us all work together to understand and experience the depth of what the Dharmic tradition has to offer, and then preserve, protect, promote, and perpetuate this grand way of life so that everyone can live equally, not merely by philosophical views, but by direct realization and perception, which is always what the Dharmic path has tried to direct us to do.

The arati ritual is thousands of years old, as done in most Vedic temples in India and around the world, as seen here as it is offered to the Deities of Sri Sri Radha-Shyamasundara (Krishna) in Vrindavana, where Lord Krishna performed many pastimes 5000 years ago

*The Deities of Sri Sri Radha Govinda at one of the most popular temples
for the past several hundred years in Jaipur, originally from Vrindavana*

As it has been said before, in this case by Max Muller, "And as it was a hundred years ago, so it is now; or at least, so it may be now. There are many bright dreams to be dreamt about India, and many bright deeds to be done in India, if only you will do them. Though many great and glorious conquests have been made in the history and literature of the East, since the day when Sir William Jones landed at Calcutta, depend upon it, no young Alexander here need despair because there are no kingdoms left for him to conquer on the ancient shores of the Indus and the Ganges." [1]

In this way, there are many avenues of understanding that yet remain open for investigation, enquiry, research, and study for the explorer who arrives in India. But these are the paths not only for the outer perception, whether it be green valleys, high mountains, deserts and populated cities, and many holy sites, but also the pathways inward to the soul, the infinitesimal force of life, the cause of our existence, and further into the Infinite. This is the path that has motivated mankind from the beginning of time. And this is the path that continues to motivate any deep thinker to this day. And this philosophical search has also been the loftiest aspect of ancient India's contribution to mankind for thousands of years, which has also produced the fertile soil from which so many other developments originated, as we have explained in this book.

All foreign travelers and writers who had visited India over the years, whether it be Strabo, Megasthanes, Huien Tsiang, Marco Polo, Pliny, Ibn Batuta, Al Beruni, and others, many of whom we have mentioned herein, have all expressed their appreciation of India's progressive development. Let us make sure that we can again say this, perhaps with new or additional travelers of the future, 100 years or 1000 years hence.

SANATANA-DHARMA: THE ETERNAL RELIGION

Why is this called the eternal spiritual process? When it comes to understanding the meaning of *Sanatana-dharma*, we have to be aware of its Sanskrit definition. The root of the word *dharma* comes from *dhri*, which means to uphold or maintain. The Sanskrit says *dharayati iti dharmaha*, which translates as *dharma* is that which upholds. However, not only what is supported is *Dharma*, but that which does the supporting is also *Dharma*, *dhriyate iti dharmaha*. So *Dharma* consists of both the force that sustains as well as what is sustained. It can also be said that there is the path of *Dharma* as well as its conclusion, the object of *Dharma*, or what we are seeking, the goal of life. So, *Dharma* is the means as well as the goal.

Dharma is also said to be the force which maintains the universe. Where there is *Dharma* there is harmony and balance individually, socially, and inter-galactically. So the path of *Dharma* brings about the harmony and contentment that is also another aspect of what we are seeking. In this way, we want harmony inwardly, in our own consciousness, but we also cannot have individual peace unless there is harmony or cooperation socially, amongst the masses. So where there is no *Dharma*, there is disharmony and a state of being that is out of balance. And socially it means that without *Dharma*, there is a lack of cooperation, along with escalating quarrel and fighting. This often manifests as a lack of distribution of resources, whereas some parts of the world may experience abundance of water, food or fuel, yet other parts are starving. Or by dishonest manipulation of supply and demand some necessities become priced so high that they are out of reach for the poor. When we act against the law of *Dharma*, we disrupt the very harmony and cooperation that we want. In other words, we create a life for ourselves in which there is stress, confusion, discontent, and frustration. And when we feel that way, that becomes our contribution to the general social condition. It is the exact opposite of what we wish to attain. Thus, to live a life outside of *Dharma* means to work against ourselves.

Furthermore, if we live on the basis of lust and greed, to accumulate possessions, money, and sensual pleasure by the demands of the mind and senses, it will become most difficult to follow the path of *Dharma*. Of course, when this is the case, we often see that such people become increasingly discontent and out of balance, enamored by the illusory happiness in material existence. Doing what should not be done is called *vidharma*, which is a type of *adharma* or nondharmic activity. The conclusion, therefore, is that if we want happiness and peace we must learn how to live according to the path of *Dharma*.

The practice of *Dharma* should be done not out of compulsion but out of love due to the perception of the Supreme in all living beings. With this motivation, *Dharma* can assist in preventing injury to others and treating each other respectfully. *Dharma* also means righteous conduct. This includes following social laws and proper moral activity and behavior. It encourages truthfulness of thought, word and deed. The point of which is to reach the goal of *Dharma*.

Dharma also means truth. So we follow the path of *Dharma* to free ourselves from illusion and reach the ultimate Truth, which is the topmost reality, the spiritual strata. The Absolute Truth means the final philosophical goal and end of all knowledge, or Vedanta, which is God, the Supreme Being, the Ultimate Reality. So, when we want to attain liberation from material existence, after realizing the futility of its temporary nature, and wish to reach God, or at least a higher level of reality, then it becomes much easier to follow the path of *Dharma* and overcome the temptations of the temporary material world. Then we can let go of the illusory objects that are, in fact, hurdles on the path to Truth and God, and happiness in general.

The more we are attracted to the material existence and in accumulating the illusory objects to satisfy our mind and senses, in essence, the more hurdles we are bringing into our life. And we must overcome these obstructions at some point to reach the Absolute Truth. Therefore, life lived according to the law of *Dharma* means the freer we become from false obstacles, from stress, from false hangups and mood swings, and inner conflicts. Thus, the freer we are to experience our real selves as spiritual beings. And the more society chooses to follow the path of *Dharma*, the more easily we can attain an existence of cooperation and harmony instead of one of wars, conflict, terror and killing. So whatever we do, even if it is doing business, making money, politics, etc., it should be done on the basis of *Dharma*. Then things will progress in the proper way. Following *Dharma* will bring both material well-being as well as final liberation from material existence. Thus, one can attain all that this world can offer through the path of Vedic *Dharma*.

On a national, ethnic, or racial level, *Dharma* is an instrument of unity, not divisiveness. That which helps unite everyone and develop love and universal brotherhood is *Dharma*. That which causes discord or disharmony or provokes hatred is *adharma*. That which works against or tries to destroy *Dharma* is also *adharma*. With this understanding we can perceive that certain religions that exist on this planet that encourage divisiveness between those that are "saved" and those that are supposedly going to hell, or which primarily focus on differences between their sect and others, are actually *adharmic*. Those religions that do not teach that we are all spiritual beings, all children of the same God, all equal in the eyes of God, are *adharmic*. They may merely be limited in their depth of knowledge and awareness, but until they adopt the *dharmic* principles they will continue to produce disagreements, restlessness, harsh attitudes, and even hatred amongst people in the name of religion. The reason is that they are absent of real transcendental knowledge and deep spiritual insights. Since such religions lack *Dharma*, they will not be able to deliver one to *Dharma*, or to the Absolute Truth, the spiritual world. Thus, lack of peace and harmony amongst various religions will be commonplace until this is remedied. In this way, the path of *Dharma* is more than a religion or belief system. It is the means to directly perceive and live according to that higher reality and spiritual unity between us all.

So we can see that the path of *Dharma* is more of a way of life. Some people may say that Vedic *Dharma*, or Hinduism, is another religion. Yet, if we understand this principle of *Dharma*, we can see that it is not merely another religion or "ism". It is a way of life that is lived with every moment and every breath. It is a matter of raising our consciousness to the highest level possible. It is a matter of understanding and living according to the Universal Spiritual Truths and principles that apply to everyone, at any time, anywhere. Through this process, we reach our fullest potential, which in the end is on the spiritual platform.

In this way, when one comes to the level of *Dharma*, then all of his or her actions are in accordance with the *Dharma*, the path of harmony and balance, in tune with the Divine. For example, in Vedic culture we can find the artful expression of dance. This is just one of many art forms in the Vedic tradition. But on the path of *Dharma* it is an expression of one's emotional outlet toward God, Ishwara or Krishna. An emotional outlet in this manner means you express yourself to God, you release your love for God, and your thoughts and consciousness become more absorbed in God. So this is also like yoga, a form of dedicated meditation. In this way, the attitude within the dance is unique. It is not merely an emotional release for satisfying one's own mind, but it is an expression of longing toward becoming united with God. That is yoga. This is *Dharma*. So in this sense, *Dharma* means the freedom to naturally express our inner proclivity, which is to get closer to or connect with the Absolute Truth, and worship this Truth, this Ishvara or God.

Therefore, on the path of *Dharma* the dances, the movements, the costumes and jewelry, are all used to either relate the pastimes of God or to enhance our attachment to God. So these are all expressions of *Dharma*, our eternal nature to love God and be loved by God, which can be used in all aspects of life. Thus, *Dharma* is also protected by continuing the tradition. For this reason there needs to be a class of men who are dedicated to protect the *Dharma*. It is only one who has the *Dharma* that can protect it. That is why it is also said: *Dharma Rakshati Rakshita*, if we take care of *Dharma*, *Dharma* will take care of us.

Now when we add the word *Sanatana* to *Dharma*, it expands the meaning and purpose. *Sanatana* means eternal. So *Sanatana-dharma* can mean the ancient path that has existed from time immemorial. It also means that it is the eternal path which has been given to humanity and comes from beyond the material dimension. Thus, *Sanatana-dharma* is the inter-dimensional path of progress for all living beings.

It can also be said to be the unceasing and imperishable path of the soul. *Sanatana-dharma* also means the eternal path and our eternal nature. *Dharma* means the ultimate nature of the living being, the spirit soul. And the nature or *Dharma* of the soul is to love and be loved, to serve its most lovable object and to receive love. Just like the *Dharma* or nature of sugar is to be sweet, we know that if it is not sweet or if it is salty, then it is not sugar. The *Dharma* of fire is to give light and heat. If it does not do that, then it cannot be fire. So the *Sanatana-dharma* or eternal nature of the soul is that it is a spiritual being that is naturally connected to God and feels the greatest joy in its constitutional position as a servant of God. The soul needs to love. It cannot do without it. And our nature as human beings reflects the nature of the soul because we are always looking for love. Although when such love is interpreted through the mind and senses, it is often accepted as the satisfaction of the mind and body. This only brings temporary happiness because it is merely a reflection of what we really want and need. So for the soul, the most lovable object is the Lord and the most pleasing things are spiritual relations and exchanges between all of us in connection with the Supreme. This is what will give the epitome of bliss that we long for in loving relationships, whether here in this world or in the spiritual realm. If any religion cannot do that, or if it does not emphasize that, then its knowledge and teachings are incomplete.

So, *Sanatana-dharma* means both the ultimate spiritual truth and the means to attain it. And that truth is the divine knowledge of the soul. Thus, if there is to be any eternality in our relationships, or any spiritual connection with anything we do, it has to be based on that divine knowledge of the soul, the ultimate reality. That is the path of *Sanatana-dharma*, to realize our spiritual identity and then know how to act accordingly. By understanding this, it is clear that the Vedic tradition, as *Sanatana-dharma*, is eternal since the beginning of time, and even before that, and it will continue until the end of time and even beyond that. There is no end to it, and there is no end to us on the path of *Sanatana-dharma*, the Vedic tradition. It is only up to us to preserve, protect, promote and perpetuate it so that it does not fade away from our awareness of it and that it remains accessible for all of humanity.

CHAPTER NOTES
1. Max Muller, *India: What can it teach us?*, first published in 1883, published by Rupa & Co., New Delhi, 2002, p. 25.

GLOSSARY

Acharya--the spiritual master who sets the proper standard by his own example.

Advaita--nondual, meaning that the Absolute Truth is one, and that there is no individuality between the Supreme Being and the individual souls which merge into oneness, the Brahman, when released from material existence. The philosophy taught by Sankaracharya.

Agastya Muni--a sage who was the knower of the *Vedas*.

Ahimsa--nonviolence.

Akarma--actions which cause no *karmic* reactions.

Ananda--spiritual bliss.

Ananta--unlimited.

Arati--the ceremony of worship when incense and ghee lamps are offered to the Deities.

Archa-vigraha--the worshipable Deity form of the Lord made of stone, wood, etc.

Aryan--a noble person, one who is on the Vedic path of spiritual advancement.

Asana--postures for meditation, or exercises for developing the body into a fit instrument for spiritual advancement.

Asat--that which is temporary.

Ashrama--one of the four orders of spiritual life, such as *brahmacari* (celibate student), *grihastha* (married householder), *vanaprastha* (retired stage), and *sannyasa* (renunciate); or the abode of a spiritual teacher or *sadhu*.

Astanga-yoga--the eightfold path of mystic yoga.

Asura--one who is ungodly or a demon.

Atma--the self or soul. Sometimes means the body, mind, and senses.

Avatara--an incarnation of the Lord who descends from the spiritual world.

Avidya--ignorance or nescience.

Aum--*om* or *pranava*

Ayodhya--the birthplace of Lord Rama in East India.

Ayurveda--the original holistic form of medicine as described in the Vedic literature.

Badrinatha--one of the holy places of pilgrimage in the Himalayas, and home of the Deity Sri Badrinatha along with many sages and hermits.

Bhagavan--one who possesses all opulences, God.

Bhajan--song of worship.

Bhakti--love and devotion for God.

Bhakti-yoga--the path of offering pure devotional service to the Supreme.

Brahma--the demigod of creation who was born from Lord Vishnu, the first created living being and the engineer of the secondary stage of creation of the universe when all the living entities were manifested.

Brahmacari--a celebate student, usually five to twenty-five years of age, who is trained by the spiritual master. One of the four divisions or *ashramas* of spiritual life.

Brahmani--consort of Brahma.

Brahmajyoti--the great white light or effulgence which emanates from the body of the Lord.

Brahmaloka--the highest planet or plane of existence in the universe; the planet where Lord Brahma lives.

Brahman--the spiritual energy; the all-pervading impersonal aspect of the Lord; or the Supreme Lord Himself.

Brahmana or brahmin--one of the four orders of society; the intellectual class of men who have been trained in the knowledge of the *Vedas* and initiated by a spiritual master.

Brahmana--the supplemental books of the four primary *Vedas*. They usually contained instructions for performing Vedic *agnihotras*, chanting the *mantras*, the purpose of the rituals, etc. The *Aitareya* and *Kaushitaki Brahmanas* belong to the *Rig-veda*, the *Satapatha Brahmana* belongs to the *White Yajur-veda*, and the *Taittiriya Brahmana* belongs to the *Black Yajur-veda*. The *Praudha* and *Shadvinsa Brahmanas* are two of the eight *Brahmanas* belonging to the *Atharva-veda*.

Brahmarsis–great rishis or sages who are also knowledgeable brahmanas.

Brahmastra--a nuclear weapon that is produced and controlled by *mantra*.

Brahmeshvara--a name of Shiva.

Brahminical--to be clean and upstanding, both outwardly and inwardly, like a *brahmana* should be.

Buddha--Lord Buddha or a learned man.

Causal Ocean or Karana Ocean--is the corner of the spiritual sky where Maha-Vishnu lies down to create the material manifestation.

Chaitanya Mahaprabhu--the most recent incarnation of the Lord who appeared in the 15th century in Bengal and who originally started the *sankirtana* movement, based on congregational chanting of the holy names.
Chakra--a wheel, disk, or psychic energy center situated along the spinal column in the subtle body of the physical shell.
Chandra--the moon.
Cit--eternal knowledge.
Darshan--the devotional act of seeing and being seen by the Deity in the temple.
Dashavatara--the ten incarnations of Lord Vishnu: Matsya, Kurma, Varaha, Narasimha, Vamana, Parashurama, Rama, Krishna, Buddha, and Kalki.
Deity--the *arca-vigraha*, or worshipful form of the Divinity in the temple.
Dham--a holy place.
Dharma--the essential nature or duty of the living being.
Diksha--spiritual initiation.
Dualism--as related in this book, it refers to the Supreme as both an impersonal force (Brahman) as well as the Supreme Person.
Dwaita--dualism, the principle that the Absolute Truth consists of the infinite Supreme Being along with the infinitesimal, individual souls.
Ganges--the sacred and spiritual river which, according to the *Vedas*, runs throughout the universe, a portion of which is seen in India. The reason the river is considered holy is that it is said to be a drop of the Karana Ocean outside of the universe that leaked in when Lord Vishnu, in His incarnation as Vamanadeva, kicked a small hole in the universal shell with His toe. Thus, the water is spiritual as well as being purified by the touch of Lord Vishnu.
Garbhodakasayi Vishnu--the expansion of Lord Vishnu who enters into each universe.
Gayatri--the spiritual vibration or *mantra* from which the other *Vedas* were expanded and which is chanted by those who are initiated as *brahmanas* and given the spiritual understanding of Vedic philosophy.
Goloka Vrindavana--the name of Lord Krishna's spiritual planet.
Gopuram--the tall ornate towers that mark the gates to the temples, often found in south India.
Gosvami--one who is master of the senses.
Grihastha--the householder order of life. One of the four *ashramas* in spiritual life.

Guru--a spiritual master.

Hatha-yoga--a part of the yoga system which stresses various sitting postures and exercises.

Impersonalism--the view that God has no personality or form, but is only an impersonal force (Brahman) which the individual souls merge back into when released from material existence.

Impersonalist--those who believe God has no personality or form.

Japa--the chanting one performs, usually softly, for one's own meditation.

Japa-mala--the string of beads one uses for chanting.

Jiva--the individual soul or living being.

Jnana--knowledge which may be material or spiritual.

Jnana-kanda--the portion of the *Vedas* which stresses empirical speculation for understanding truth.

Jnana-yoga--the process of linking with the Supreme through empirical knowledge and mental speculation.

Jnani--one engaged in *jnana-yoga*, or the process of cultivating knowledge to understand the Absolute.

Kali-yuga--the fourth and present age, the age of quarrel and confusion, which lasts 432,000 years and began 5,000 years ago.

Kalki--future incarnation of Lord Vishnu who appears at the end of Kali-yuga.

Kalpa--a day in the life of Lord Brahma which lasts a thousand cycles of the four *yugas*.

Kama--lust or inordinate desire.

Karanodakasayi Vishnu (Maha-Vishnu)--the expansion of Lord Krishna who created all the material universes.

Karma--material actions performed in regard to developing one's position or for future results which produce *karmic* reactions. It is also the reactions one endures from such fruitive activities.

Karma-kanda--the portion of the *Vedas* which primarily deals with recommended fruitive activities for various results.

Karma-yoga--system of yoga for using one's activities for spiritual advancement.

Kirtana--chanting or singing the glories of the Lord.

Krishna--the name of the original Supreme Personality of Godhead which means the most attractive and greatest pleasure. He is the source of all other incarnations, such as Vishnu, Rama, Narasimha, Narayana, Buddha,

Parashurama, Vamanadeva, Kalki at the end of Kali-yuga, etc.

Krishnaloka--the spiritual planet where Lord Krishna resides.

Kshatriya--the second class of *varna* of society, or occupation of administrative or protective service, such as warrior or military personnel.

Ksirodakasayi Vishnu--the Supersoul expansion of the Lord who enters into each atom and the heart of each individual.

Kuruksetra--the place of battle 5,000 years ago between the Pandavas and the Kauravas ninety miles north of New Delhi, where Krishna spoke the *Bhagavad-gita*.

Lila--pastimes.

Lilavataras--the many incarnations of God who appear to display various spiritual pastimes to attract the conditioned souls in the material world.

Mahabharata--the great epic of the Pandavas, which includes the *Bhagavad-gita*, by Vyasadeva.

Maha-mantra--the best *mantra* for self-realization in this age, called the Hare Krishna *mantra*.

Mahatma--a great soul or devotee.

Mahat-tattva--the total material energy.

Mahavira--Great Hero, referring to the last of the great Jain teachers, or *tirthankaras*.

Maha-Vishnu or Karanodakasayi Vishnu--the Vishnu expansion of Lord Krishna from whom all the material universes emanate.

Mandapa or *Mandapam*--the front hallway of a Vedic temple.

Mandir--a temple.

Mantra--a sound vibration which prepares the mind for spiritual realization and delivers the mind from material inclinations. In some cases a *mantra* is chanted for specific material benefits.

Maya--illusion, or anything that appears to not be connected with the eternal Absolute Truth.

Mayavadi--the impersonalist or voidist who believes that the Supreme has no form, or that any form of God is but a product of *maya*.

Meenakshi--Parvati as Fish-Eyed.

Mleccha--a derogatory name for an untouchable person, a meat-eater.

Moksha--liberation from material existence.

Murti--a Deity of the Lord or an image of a demigod or spiritual master that is worshiped.

Narasimha--Lord Vishnu's incarnation as the half-man half-lion who killed the demon Hiranyakashipu.

Narayana--the four-handed form of the Supreme Lord.

Nirvana--the state of no material miseries, usually the goal of the Buddhists or voidists.

Om or *Omkara--pranava*, the transcendental *om mantra*, generally referring to the attributeless or impersonal aspects of the Absolute.

Paramatma--the Supersoul, or localized expansion of the Lord.

Parampara--the system of disciplic succession through which transcendental knowledge descends.

Prema--matured love for Krishna.

Puja--the worship offered to the Deity.

Pujari--the priest who performs worship, *puja*, to the Deity.

Purusha or *Purusham*--the supreme enjoyer.

Radha--Krishna's favorite devotee and the personification of His bliss potency.

Rajarsi--a Raja or great *rishi* or sage.

Raja-yoga--the eightfold yoga system.

Rajo-guna--the material mode of passion.

Ramachandra--an incarnation of Krishna as He appeared as the greatest of kings.

Ramanuja--Vaishnava philosopher.

Ramayana--the great epic of the incarnation of Lord Ramachandra.

Rasa--an enjoyable taste or feeling, a relationship with God.

Sadhana--a specific practice or discipline for attaining God realization.

Sadhu--Indian holy man or devotee.

Samadhi--trance, the perfection of being absorbed in the Absolute.

Samsara--rounds of life; cycles of birth and death; reincarnation.

Sanatana-dharma--the eternal nature of the living being, to love and render service to the supreme lovable object, the Lord.

Sangam--the confluence of two or more rivers.

Sannyasa--the renounced order of life, the highest of the four *ashramas* on the spiritual path.

Sarasvati--the goddess of knowledge and intelligence.

Sattva-guna--the material mode of goodness.

Satya-yuga--the first of the four ages which lasts 1,728,000 years.

Shabda-brahma--the original spiritual vibration or energy of which the *Vedas* are composed.

Shaivites--worshipers of Lord Shiva.

Shakti--energy, potency or power, the active principle in creation. Also the active power or wife of a deity, such as Shiva/Shakti.

Shastra--the authentic revealed Vedic scripture.

Shiva--the benevolent one, the demigod who is in charge of the material mode of ignorance and the destruction of the universe. Part of the triad of Brahma, Vishnu, and Shiva who continually create, maintain, and destroy the universe. He is known as Rudra when displaying his destructive aspect.

Sikha--a tuft of hair on the back of the head signifying that one is a Vaishnava.

Skanda--son of Shiva and Parvati, leader of the army of the gods; also known as Karttikeya and Subramanya or Murugan.

Smaranam--remembering the Lord.

Smriti--the traditional Vedic knowledge "that is remembered" from what was directly heard by or revealed to the *rishis*.

Sravanam--hearing about the Lord.

Srimad-Bhagavatam--the most ripened fruit of the tree of Vedic knowledge compiled by Vyasadeva.

Sruti--scriptures that were received directly from God and transmitted orally by *brahmanas* or *rishis* down through succeeding generations. Traditionally, it is considered the four primary *Vedas*.

Stupa–a Buddhist hemispherical or dome monument that often housed ashes or relics of great Buddhist teachers.

Sudra--the working class of society, the fourth of the *varnas*.

Surya--Sun or solar deity.

Svami--one who can control his mind and senses.

Treta-yuga--the second of the four ages which lasts 1,296,000 years.

Upanishads--the portions of the *Vedas* which primarily explain philosophically the Absolute Truth. It is knowledge of Brahman which releases one from the world and allows one to attain self-realization when received from a qualified teacher. Except for the *Isa Upanishad*, which is the 40th chapter of the *Vajasaneyi Samhita* of the *Sukla* (*White*) *Yajur-veda*, the *Upanishads* are connected to the four primary *Vedas*, generally found in the *Brahmanas*.

Vaikunthas--the planets located in the spiritual sky.

Vaishnava--a worshiper of the Supreme Lord Vishnu or Krishna and His expansions or incarnations.

Vaisya--the third class of society engaged in business or farming.

Vanaprastha--the third of the four *ashramas* of spiritual life in which one retires from family life in preparation for the renounced order.

Varna--sometimes referred to as caste, a division of society, such as *brahmana* (a priestly intellectual), a *kshatriya* (ruler or manager), *vaisya* (a merchant, banker, or farmer), and *sudra* (common laborer).

Varnashrama--the system of four divisions of society and four orders of spiritual life.

Vedanta-sutras--the philosophical conclusion of the four *Vedas*.

Vedas--generally means the four primary *samhitas; Rig, Yajur, Sama, Atharva*.

Venktateshvara--Vishnu as Lord of the Venkata Hills, worshiped in Tirumala.

Vidya--knowledge.

Vikarma--sinful activities performed without scriptural authority and which produce sinful reactions.

Vishnu--the expansion of Lord Krishna who enters into the material energy to create and maintain the cosmic world.

Vrindavana--the place where Lord Krishna displayed His village pastimes 5,000 years ago, and is considered to be part of the spiritual abode.

Vyasadeva--the incarnation of God who appeared as the greatest philosopher who compiled the main portions of the Vedic literature into written form.

Yajna--a ritual or austerity that is done as a sacrifice for spiritual merit, or ritual worship of a demigod for good *karmic* reactions.

Yantra--a machine, instrument, or mystical diagram used in ritual worship.

Yoga--linking up with the Absolute.

Yuga-avataras--the incarnations of God who appear in each of the four *yugas* to explain the authorized system of self-realization in that age.

References

Amongst all the books that were researched and quoted, the following are the main books used:

Adams, Alexander, *Millennia of Discoveries*, Vantage Press, New York, 1994

Airavata dasa, *Vedic Economy*, Bhaktivedanta Institute of Vedic Studies, Mayapur, 1997

Arya, Dr. Ravi Prakash, *India: The Civiliser of the World*, Published by Dilip and Dipika Doctor of International Vedic Vision, in association with India Foundation for Vedic Science, Haryana, India, 2005.

Arya, Dr. Ravi Prakash, *New Discoveries About Vedic Sarasvati*, Published by Dilip and Dipika Doctor of International Vedic Vision, in association with India Foundation for Vedic Science, Haryana, India, 2002.

Arya, Dr. Ravi Prakash, *Vedic Meteorology, Vedic Science of Weather Modification*, Published by Dilip and Dipika Doctor of International Vedic Vision, in association with India Foundation for Vedic Science, Haryana, India, 2006.

Bakhle, Dr. S. W., *Afro-Hindu Vision*, Editor Dr., S.W. International Center for Cultural Studies, Nagpur, 1999

Bakhle, Dr. S. W. Editor, *Cultural Studies*, International Center for Cultural Studies, Nagpur, 2000

Banerjee, Dr. Manabendu and Dr. Bijoya Goswami, Editors, *Science and Technology in Ancient India*, Published by Sanskrit Pustak Bhandar, Calcutta, 1994

Basham, L. A., *The Wonder That was India*, Grove Press, Inc., New York, 1954,

Bharati, Vijnan, Editor, *Science and Technology in Ancient India*, Mumbai, 2002

Bryant, Edwin, *The Quest for the Origins of Vedic Culture: The Indo-Aryan Migration Debate*, Oxford University Press, New York, 2001

Champion, Selwyn, & Dorothy Short, *Readings From World Religions*, Fawcett World Library, New York, New York, 1951

Childe, V. Gordon, *The Aryans*, Dorset Press, New York, 1987

Cobo, Father Bernabe, *History of the Inca Empire*, University of Texas Press, Austin, Texas, 1979

Cobo, Father Bernabe, *Inca Religion and Customs*, University of Texas Press, Austin, Texas, 1990

Coomaraswamy, Ananda K., *History of Indian and Indonesian Art*, Dover Publications, New York, 1965

Cremo, Michael A., *The Forbidden Archeologist*, Bhaktivedanta Book Publishing, Inc., Los Angeles, 2010.

Cremo, Michael and Richard Thompson, *Hidden History of the Human Race*, Govardhan Hill Publishing, Badger, CA. 1994

Dani, Mrs. Lata, *Indo-Aztec Cultural Affinities*, International Center for Cultural Studies, Nagpur, 1998

Deshpende, G. K., *Bharat (India) As Seen and Known by Foreigners*, Swadhyaya--Mandal, Killa Pardi, District Surat, 1950

Deshpande, Dr. Leela, *Indo-Inca Cultural Panorama*, International Center for Cultural Studies, Nagpur, 2000

Dhanesvara Das, *Spiritual Economics*, ISBN: 1451589719, 2009-10

Didolkar, Dr. V. K., *Metallurgy in Samskrita Literature*, Samskrita Bharati, New Delhi, Oct. 2000

Doane, T. W., *Bible Myths and Their Parallels in Other Religions*, reprinted by Health Research, P. O. Box 70, Mokelumne Hill, CA 95245, 1985

Fell, Barry, *America B.C., Ancient Settlers in the New World*, Pocket Books, New York, 1976

Feuerstein, Georg, Subash Kak, & David Frawley, *In Search of the Cradle of Civilization*, Quest Books, Wheaton, Illinois, 1995

Frawley, David, *Gods, Sages and Kings*, Passage Press, 1991

Frawley, Dr. David, & Dr. Navaratna S. Rajaram, *Hidden Horizons: Unearthing 10,000 Years of Indian Culture*, Swaminarayan Aksharpith Amdavad, Ahmedabad, India, 2006

Frawley, David, *The Myth of the Aryan Invasion of India*, Voice of India, New Delhi, 1994

Frawley, David, *The Rig Veda and the History of India*, Aditya Prakashan, New Delhi, 2001

Gharge-Deshmukh, Sarjerao Ramrao, and Pratibha Deshmukh, *Ramayana: A Fact or Fiction?*, Pune, October, 2003,

Hancock, Graham, *Underworld: The Mysterious Civilization*, Crown Publishers, New York,

Higgins, Godfrey, Rowland Hunter, *The Celtic Druids*, St. Paul's Churchyard, Hurst & Chance, St. Paul's, Churchgate & Radgway & Sons, Picadilly, 1929

Jacolliot, Louis, *Revisiting the Roots of Judeo - Christianity*, re-edited by Dr. Ravi Prakash Arya, Published by Dilip and Dipika Doctor of International Vedic Vision, in association with India Foundation for Vedic Science, Haryana, India, 2005

Jha, N. and N. S. Rajaram, *The Deciphered Indus Script*, Aditya Prakashan, New Delhi, 2000

Jones, Prudence & Nigel Pennick, *A History of Pagan Europe*, Routledge, New York, 1995

Kanjilal, Dileep Kumar, *Vimana in Ancient India*, Sanskrit Pustak Bhandar, 38, Bidhan Sarani, Calcutta, India, 1985

Karnik, Ravindranath Ramchandra, *Ancient Indian Technologies as Seen by Maya, The Great Asura*, Published by the organizers of The Second International Seminar on Mayonic Science and Technology, Thiruvanathapuram, Keral India, 1997

Kazanas, Nicholas, *Indo-Aryan Origins and Other Vedic Issues,* Aditya Prakashan, New Delhi, 2009

Kapur, Kamlesh, *Portrait of a Nation: History of Ancient India*, Sterling Publishers Private Limited, New Delhi, 2010.

Keay, John, *India A History*, Grove Press, New York, 2000

Krishnamurthy, K.H., *Medicine and Surgery in Ancient India*, A Yugayatri Publication, Bangalore

Kulke, Hermann and Dietmar Rothermund, *A History of India*, Dorset Press, New York, 1986

Lakshmikantham, V. & J. Vasundhara Devi, *The Origin and History of Mathematics*, Published by Dilip and Dipika Doctor of International Vedic Vision, in association with India Foundation for Vedic Science, Haryana, India, 2004.

Lal, Chaman, *Hindu America*, Chaman Lal, New York, 1966

Lomperis, Timothy J., *Hindu Influence on Greek Philosophy*, Minerva Associates (Publications) PVT. LTD., Calcutta, 1984

Mallory, J.P, *In Search of the Indo-Europeans*, Thames & Hudson, New York, 1989

Mann, Charles C., *1491: New Revelations of the Americas Before Columbus*, Vintage Books, New York, July, 2011

Michell, George, *The Hindu Temple*, University of Chicago Press, Chicago, 1977

Morris, Charles, *The Aryan Race: It's Origins and Achievements*, S. C. Griggs and Company, 1888

Muller, F. Max, *India, What can it teach us?* Published by Rupa & Co., New Delhi, reprint in 2002

Olmstead, A. T., *History of the Persian Empire*, University of Chicago Press, Chicago, 1948

Pargiter, F. E., *Ancient Indian Historical Tradition*, Motilal Banarsidass, Delhi, 1962,

Parrinder, *World Religions, From Ancient History to the Present*, Facts on File Publications, New York, 1971

Pathak, A.R., *Indo-Kenyan Cultural Ethos*, International Center for Cultural Studies, Nagpur, 2000

Pathak. P.V., *The Afghan Connection*, Prajna Prakashan, Maharashtra, 1999

Peet, Preston, Editor, *Underground! The Disinformation Guide to Ancient Civilizations, Astonishing Archaeology and Hidden History*, The Disinformation Company, New York, 2005

Pitale, Dr. R. L., Editor, *Indo-Native American Cultural Similarities*, International Center for Cultural Studies, Nagpur, 1999

Pococke, E., *Indian Origin of Greece and Ancient World*, (E. Pococke's Thesis re-edited and revised) by Dr. Ravi Prakash Arya, Published by Dilip and Dipika Doctor of International Vedic Vision, New York, in association with India Foundation for Vedic Science, Haryana, India, 2003.

Rajaram, N. S., *Sarasvati River and the Vedic Civilization: History, Science and Politics*, Aditya Prakashan, New Delhi, 2006

Rajaram, Navaratna S. and David Frawley *Vedic Aryans and The Origins of Civilization*, Published by World Heritage press, Quebec, Canada, and Voice of India, 2/18, Ansari Road, New Delhi 110 002, 1995, 1997

Rohl, David M., *Pharaohs and Kings: A Biblical Quest*, Crown Publishers, Inc., New York, 1995.

Roy, Raja Ram Mohan, *Vedic Physics*, Golden Egg Publishing, Toronto, 1999

Sarda, Har Bilas, *Hindu Superiority*, Ajmer, 1906

Sardesai, D. R., *India The Definitive History*, Westview Press, Perseus Books Group, Philadelphia, PA, 2008

Schoch, Robert, M. Ph.D., *Voices of the Pyramid Builders*, Tarcher/Putnam, New York, 2003

Sethna, K. D., *The Problem of Aryan Origins (From the Indian Point of View)*, Published by Rakesh Goel for Aditya Prakashan, 4829/1 Prahlad Lane, 24 Ansari Road, New Delhi, 1992

Sharma, R. N. & R. K. Sharma, *History of Education in India*, Atlantic Publishers and Distributors, New Delhi, 2004

Sharma, Bhu Dev, and Nabarun Ghose, Editors, *Revisiting Indus-Sarasvati Age and Ancient India*, Editors Published by World Association for Vedic Studies, c/o Dr. Deen B. Chandora, 4117 Menloway, Atlanta, GA. 30340. 1998.

Singh, Bal Ram, Editor, *Origin of Indian Civilization*, Center for Indic Studies, Dartmouth, USA, 2010.

Soni, Suresh, *India's Glorious Scientific Tradition*, Ocean Books Pvt. Ltd., New Delhi, 2010,

Sonnerat, Pierre, *Voyages aux Indes Orientales et la Chine*, Paris, 1782.
Talageri, Shrikant G., *The Aryan Invasion Theory: A Reappraisal*, Published by Pradeep Kumar Goel for Aditya Prakashan, F-14/65, Model Town II, Delhi 110 009, 1993

Subramaniam, Kamala, *Mahabharata* translation, published by Bharatiya Vidya Bhavan, Bombay, 1982,

Tirthaji, Sri Bharati Krishna Maharaja, *Vedic Mathematics*, Motilal Banarsidass, Delhi, 1965

Thompson, Richard L., *Vedic Cosmography and Astronomy*, Bhaktivedanta Book Trust, Los Angeles, 1989

Vaishnav, Dr. Y. D., *Whence & Whither Humanity*, Published by Vasant Mahadeo Kelkar, OMSS, Tara Enterprises, 41 Leah Pareppany, New Jersey, 07054

Waddell, L. A., *Egyptian Civilization*, Christian Book Club, Hawthorne, CA

Waddell, L. A., *The Indo-Sumerian Seals Deciphered*, Omni Publications, Hawthorne, California, 1980

Woolley, C. Leonard, *The Sumerians*, W. W. Norton & Co., New York, 1965

India's Contribution to World Thought and Culture, Published by Vivekananda Kendra Prakashan, Chennai, 1970.

Pride of India: A Glimpse into India's Scientific Heritage, Samskriti Bharati, New Delhi, 2006,

Science and Technology in Ancient India, by Editorial Board of Vijnan Bharati, Mumbai, August, 2002, Foreword by B. V. Subbarayappa.

Other Books that Were Also Included:

Agni Purana, translated by N. Gangadharan, Motilal Banarsidass, Delhi, 1984

Bhagavad-gita As It Is, translated by A. C. Bhaktivedanta Swami, Bhaktivedanta Book Trust, New York/Los Angeles, 1972

Brahma Purana, edited by J.L.Shastri, Motilal Banarsidass, Delhi 1985

Brahmanda Purana, edited by J.L.Shastri, Motilal Banarsidass, 1983

Brahma-samhita, translated by Bhaktisiddhanta Sarasvati Gosvami Thakur, Bhaktivedanta Book Trust, New York/Los Angeles,

Brahma-Sutras, translated by Swami Vireswarananda and Adidevananda, Advaita Ashram, Calcutta, 1978

Brahma-Vaivarta Purana, translated by Shanti Lal Nagar, edited by Acharya Ramesh Chaturvedi, Parimal Publications, Delhi, 2005.

Caitanya-caritamrta, translated by A. C. Bhaktivedanta Swami, Bhaktivedanta Book Trust, Los Angeles, 1974

Garuda Purana, edited by J. L. Shastri, Motilal Barnasidass, Delhi, 1985

Hymns of the Rig-veda, tr. by Griffith, Motilal Banarsidass, Delhi, 1973

Kurma Purana, edited by J. L. Shastri, Motilal Banarsidass, Delhi, 1981

Narada Purana, tr. by Ganesh Vasudeo Tagare, Banarsidass, Delhi, 1980

Narada Sutras, translated by Hari Prasad Shastri, Shanti Sadan, London, 1963

Padma Purana, tr. by S. Venkitasubramonia Iyer, Banarsidass, Delhi, 1988

Ramayana of Valmiki, tr. by Makhan Lal Sen, Munshiram Manoharlal Publishers, New Delhi, 1976.

Rig-veda Brahmanas: The Aitareya and Kausitaki Brahmanas of the Rigveda, translated by Arthur Keith, Motilal Banarsidass, Delhi, 1971

Srimad-Bhagavatam, translated by A. C. Bhaktivedanta Swami, Bhaktivedanta Book trust, New York/Los Angeles, 1972

Twelve Essential Upanishads, Tridandi Sri Bhakti Prajnan Yati, Sree Gaudiya Math, Madras, 1982. Includes the *Isha, Kena, Katha, Prashna, Mundaka, Mandukya, Taittiriya, Aitareya, Chandogya, Brihadaranyaka, Svetasvatara,* and *Gopalatapani Upanishad* of the Pippalada section of the *Atharva-veda.*

The Upanisads, translated by F. Max Muller, Dover Publications; contains Chandogya, Kena, Aitareya, Kausitaki, Vajasaneyi (Isa), Katha, Mundaka, Taittiriya, Brihadaranyaka, Svetasvatara, Prasna, and Maitrayani Upanisads.

Varaha Purana, tr. by S.Venkitasubramonia Iyer, Banarsidass, Delhi, 1985

Vayu Purana, translated by G. V. Tagare, Banarsidass, Delhi, India, 1987

Vedanta-Sutras of Badarayana with Commentary of Baladeva Vidyabhusana, translated by Rai Bahadur Srisa Chandra Vasu, Munshiram Manoharlal, New Delhi, 1979

Vishnu Purana, translated by H. H. Wilson, Nag Publishers, Delhi

Yajurveda, translated by Devi Chand, Munshiram Manoharlal, Delhi, 1980

INDEX

ABOUT THE AUTHOR

Stephen Knapp grew up in a Christian family, during which time he seriously studied the Bible to understand its teachings. In his late teenage years, however, he sought answers to questions not easily explained in Christian theology. So he began to search through other religions and philosophies from around the world and started to find the answers for which he was looking. He also studied a variety of occult sciences, ancient mythology, mysticism, yoga, and the spiritual teachings of the East. After his first reading of the *Bhagavad-gita*, he felt he had found the last piece of the puzzle he had been putting together through all of his research. Therefore, he continued to study all of the major Vedic texts of India to gain a better understanding of the Vedic science.

It is known amongst all Eastern mystics that anyone, regardless of qualifications, academic or otherwise, who does not engage in the spiritual practices described in the Vedic texts cannot actually enter into understanding the depths of the Vedic spiritual science, nor acquire the realizations that should accompany it. So, rather than pursuing his research in an academic atmosphere at a university, Stephen directly engaged in the spiritual disciplines that have been recommended for hundreds of years. He continued his study of Vedic knowledge and spiritual practice under the guidance of a spiritual master. Through this process, and with the sanction of His Divine Grace A. C. Bhaktivedanta Swami Prabhupada, he became initiated into the genuine and authorized spiritual line of the Brahma-Madhava-Gaudiya *sampradaya*, which is a disciplic succession that descends back through Sri Caitanya Mahaprabhu and Sri Vyasadeva, the compiler of Vedic literature, and further back to Sri Krishna. Besides being *brahminically* initiated, Stephen has also been to India several times and traveled extensively throughout the country, visiting most of the major holy places and gaining a wide variety of spiritual experiences that only such places can give.

Stephen has put the culmination of over forty years of continuous research and travel experience into his books in an effort to share it with those who are also looking for spiritual understanding. More books are forthcoming, so stay in touch through his website to find out further developments.

More information about Stephen, his projects, books, free ebooks, and numerous articles and videos can be found on his website at: www.stephen-knapp.com or at http://stephenknapp.wordpress.com.

Stephen has continued to write books that include in *The Eastern Answers ot the Mysteries of Life* series:
The Secret Teachings of the Vedas;
The Universal Path to Enlightenment;
The Vedic Prophecies: A New Look into the Future;
How the Universe was Created and Our Purpose In It.

He has also written:
Toward World Peace: Seeing the Unity Between Us All;
Facing Death: Welcoming the Afterlife;
The Key to Real Happiness;
Proof of Vedic Culture's Global Existence;
Vedic Culture: The Difference It Can Make In Your Life;
Reincarnation and Karma: How They Really Affect Us;
Power of the Dharma: An Introduction to Hinduism and Vedic Culture;
The Eleventh Commandment: The Next Step in Social Spiritual Development;
The Heart of Hinduism: The Eastern Path to Freedom, Empowerment and Illumination;
Seeing Spiritual India: A Guide to Temples, Holy Sites, Festivals and Traditions;
Crimes Against India: And the Need to Protect its Vedic Tradition;
Yoga and Meditation: Its Real Purpose and How to Get Started;
Avatars, Gods and Goddesses of the Vedic Tradition;
The Soul: Understanding Our Real Identity;
Prayers, Mantras and Gayatris: A Collection for Insight, Protection, Spiritual Growth, and Many Other Blessings;
Krishna Deities and Their Miracles: How the Images of Lord Krishna Interact With Their Devotees;
Defending Vedic Dharma: Tackling the Issues to Make a Difference; and
Destined for Infinity, an exciting novel for those who prefer lighter reading, or learning spiritual knowledge in the context of an action oriented, spiritual adventure.

Bhakti-Yoga: The Easy Path of Devotional Yoga;
Casteism in India;
A Complete Review of the Vedic Literature;
The Power of the Maha-Mantra.

More books and articles are always in the making, so stay tuned for whatever may develop next.

If you have enjoyed this book, or if you are serious about finding higher levels of real spiritual Truth, and learning more about the mysteries of India's Vedic culture, then you will also want to get other books written by Stephen Knapp, which include:

The Secret Teachings of the Vedas
The Eastern Answers to the Mysteries of Life

This book presents the essence of the ancient Eastern philosophy and summarizes some of the most elevated and important of all spiritual knowledge. This enlightening information is explained in a clear and concise way and is essential for all who want to increase their spiritual understanding, regardless of what their religious background may be. If you are looking for a book to give you an in-depth introduction to the Vedic spiritual knowledge, and to get you started in real spiritual understanding, this is the book!

The topics include: What is your real spiritual identity; the Vedic explanation of the soul; scientific evidence that consciousness is separate from but interacts with the body; the real unity between us all; how to attain the highest happiness and freedom from the cause of suffering; the law of karma and reincarnation; the karma of a nation; where you are really going in life; the real process of progressive evolution; life after death—heaven, hell, or beyond; a description of the spiritual realm; the nature of the Absolute Truth—personal God or impersonal force; recognizing the existence of the Supreme; the reason why we exist at all; and much more. This book provides the answers to questions not found in other religions or philosophies, and condenses information from a wide variety of sources that would take a person years to assemble. It also contains many quotations from the Vedic texts to let the texts speak for themselves, and to show the knowledge the Vedas have held for thousands of years. It also explains the history and origins of the Vedic literature. This book has been called one of the best reviews of Eastern philosophy available.

This book is 230 pages, $19.95, ISBN: 1466267704, ISBN-13: 978-1466267701.

The Universal Path to Enlightenment
The Way to Spiritual Success for Everyone

Although all religions and spiritual processes are meant to lead you toward enlightenment, they are not all the same in regard to the methods they teach, nor in the level of philosophical understanding they offer. So an intelligent person will make comparisons between them to understand the aims and distinctions of each religion, and which is the most elevating.

This book presents a most interesting and revealing survey of the major spiritual paths of the world and describes their histories, philosophical basis, and goals. It will help you decide which path may be the best for you.

You Will Learn

- the essential similarities of all religions that all people of any culture or tradition can practice, which could bring about a united world religion, or "THE UNIVERSAL PATH TO ENLIGHTENMENT."
- how Christianity and Judaism were greatly influenced by the early pre-Christian or "pagan" religions and adopted many of their legends, holidays, and rituals that are still accepted and practiced today.
- about evidence that shows Jesus traveled to India to learn its spiritual knowledge, and then made bhakti-yoga the basis of his teachings.
- the philosophical basis and origin of Christianity, Judaism, Islam, Hinduism, Buddhism, Zoroastrianism, Jainism, Sikhism, and many others.
- and, most importantly, what is the real purpose that you should strive for in a spiritual process, and how to practice the path that is especially recommended as the easiest and most effective for the people of this age.

This book is $19.95, 6"x9" trim size, 340 pages, ISBN: 1453644660.

The Vedic Prophecies:
A New Look into the Future

The Vedic prophecies take you to the end of time! This is the first book ever to present the unique predictions found in the ancient Vedic texts of India. These prophecies are like no others and will provide you with a very different view of the future and how things fit together in the plan for the universe.

Now you can discover the amazing secrets that are hidden in the oldest spiritual writings on the planet. Find out what they say about the distant future, and what the seers of long ago saw in their visions of the destiny of the world.

This book will reveal predictions of deteriorating social changes and how to avoid them; future droughts and famines; low-class rulers and evil governments; whether there will be another appearance (second coming) of God; and predictions of a new spiritual awareness and how it will spread around the world. You will also learn the answers to such questions as:

* Does the future get worse or better?
* Will there be future world wars or global disasters?
* What lies beyond the predictions of Nostradamus, the Mayan prophecies, or the Biblical apocalypse?
* Are we in the end times? How to recognize them if we are.
* Does the world come to an end? If so, when and how?

Now you can find out what the future holds. The Vedic Prophecies carry an important message and warning for all humanity, which needs to be understood now!

Order your copy: ISBN: 1461002249, $20.95, 328 pages.

How the Universe was Created
And Our Purpose In It

This book provides answers and details about the process of creation that are not available in any other traditions, religions, or areas of science. It offers the oldest rendition of the creation and presents insights into the spiritual purpose of it and what we are really meant to do here.

Every culture in the world and most religions have their own descriptions of the creation, and ideas about from where we came and what we should do. Unfortunately, these are often short and generalized versions that lack details. Thus, they are often given no better regard than myths. However, there are descriptions that give more elaborate explanations of how the cosmic creation fully manifested which are found in the ancient Vedic *Puranas* of India, some of the oldest spiritual writings on the planet. These descriptions provide the details and answers that other versions leave out. Furthermore, these Vedic descriptions often agree, and sometimes disagree, with the modern scientific theories of creation, and offer some factors that science has yet to consider.

Now, with this book, we can get a clearer understanding of how this universe appears, what is its real purpose, from where we really came, how we fit into the plan for the universe, and if there is a way out of here. Some of the many topics included are:

Comparisons between other creation legends.

Detailed descriptions of the dawn of creation and how the material energy developed and caused the formation of the cosmos.

What is the primary source of the material and spiritual elements.

Insights into the primal questions of, "Who am I? Why am I here? Where have I come from? What is the purpose of this universe and my life?"

An alternative description of the evolutionary development of the various forms of life.

Seeing beyond the temporary nature of the material worlds, and more.

This book will provide some of the most profound insights into these questions and topics. It will also give any theist more information and understanding about how the universe is indeed a creation of God.

This book is $19.95, 6" x 9" trim size, 308 pages, ISBN: 1456460455.

Proof of Vedic Culture's Global Existence

This book provides evidence which makes it clear that the ancient Vedic culture was once a global society. Even today we can see its influence in any part of the world. Thus, it becomes obvious that before the world became full of distinct and separate cultures, religions and countries, it was once united in a common brotherhood of Vedic culture, with common standards, principles, and representations of God.

No matter what we may consider our present religion, society or country, we are all descendants of this ancient global civilization. Thus, the Vedic culture is the parent of all humanity and the original ancestor of all religions. In this way, we all share a common heritage.

This book is an attempt to allow humanity to see more clearly its universal roots. This book provides a look into:

- How Vedic knowledge was given to humanity by the Supreme.
- The history and traditional source of the Vedas and Vedic Aryan society.
- Who were the original Vedic Aryans. How Vedic society was a global influence and what shattered this world-wide society. How Sanskrit faded from being a global language.
- Many scientific discoveries over the past several centuries are only rediscoveries of what the Vedic literature already knew.
- How the origins of world literature are found in India and Sanskrit.
- The links between the Vedic and other ancient cultures, such as the Sumerians, Persians, Egyptians, Romans, Greeks, and others.
- Links between the Vedic tradition and Judaism, Christianity, Islam, and Buddhism.
- How many of the western holy sites, churches, and mosques were once the sites of Vedic holy places and sacred shrines.
- The Vedic influence presently found in such countries as Britain, France, Russia, Greece, Israel, Arabia, China, Japan, and in areas of Scandinavia, the Middle East, Africa, the South Pacific, and the Americas.
- Uncovering the truth of India's history: Powerful evidence that shows how many mosques and Muslim buildings were once opulent Vedic temples, including the Taj Mahal, Delhi's Jama Masjid, Kutab Minar, as well as buildings in many other cities, such as Agra, Ahmedabad, Bijapur, etc.
- How there is presently a need to plan for the survival of Vedic culture.

This book is sure to provide some amazing facts and evidence about the truth of world history and the ancient, global Vedic Culture. This book has enough startling information and historical evidence to cause a major shift in the way we view religious history and the basis of world traditions.

This book is $20.99, 6"x9" trim size, 431 pages, ISBN: 978-1-4392-4648-1.

Toward World Peace:
Seeing the Unity Between Us All

This book points out the essential reasons why peace in the world and cooperation amongst people, communities, and nations have been so difficult to establish. It also advises the only way real peace and harmony amongst humanity can be achieved.

In order for peace and unity to exist we must first realize what barriers and divisions keep us apart. Only then can we break through those barriers to see the unity that naturally exists between us all. Then, rather than focus on our differences, it is easier to recognize our similarities and common goals. With a common goal established, all of humanity can work together to help each other reach that destiny.

This book is short and to the point. It is a thought provoking book and will provide inspiration for anyone. It is especially useful for those working in politics, religion, interfaith, race relations, the media, the United Nations, teaching, or who have a position of leadership in any capacity. It is also for those of us who simply want to spread the insights needed for bringing greater levels of peace, acceptance, unity, and equality between friends, neighbours, and communities. Such insights include:

- The factors that keep us apart.
- Breaking down cultural distinctions.
- Breaking down the religious differences.
- Seeing through bodily distinctions.
- We are all working to attain the same things.
- Our real identity: The basis for common ground.
- Seeing the Divinity within each of us.
- What we can do to bring unity between everyone we meet.

This book carries an important message and plan of action that we must incorporate into our lives and plans for the future if we intend to ever bring peace and unity between us.

This book is $6.95, 90 pages, 6" x 9" trim size, ISBN: 1452813744.

Facing Death
Welcoming the Afterlife

Many people are afraid of death, or do not know how to prepare for it nor what to expect. So this book is provided to relieve anyone of the fear that often accompanies the thought of death, and to supply a means to more clearly understand the purpose of it and how we can use it to our advantage. It will also help the survivors of the departed souls to better understand what has happened and how to cope with it. Furthermore, it shows that death is not a tragedy, but a natural course of events meant to help us reach our destiny.

This book is easy to read, with soothing and comforting wisdom, along with stories of people who have been with departing souls and what they have experienced. It is written especially for those who have given death little thought beforehand, but now would like to have some preparedness for what may need to be done regarding the many levels of the experience and what might take place during this transition.

To assist you in preparing for your own death, or that of a loved one, you will find guidelines for making one's final days as peaceful and as smooth as possible, both physically and spiritually. Preparing for deathcan transform your whole outlook in a positive way, if understood properly. Some of the topics in the book include:

- The fear of death and learning to let go.
- The opportunity of death: The portal into the next life.
- This earth and this body are no one's real home, so death is natural.
- Being practical and dealing with the final responsibilities.
- Forgiving yourself and others before you go.
- Being the assistant of one leaving this life.
- Connecting with the person inside the disease.
- Surviving the death of a loved one.
- Stories of being with dying, and an amazing near-death-experience.
- Connecting to the spiritual side of death.
- What happens while leaving the body.
- What difference the consciousness makes during death, and how to attain the best level of awareness to carry you through it, or what death will be like and how to prepare for it, this book will help you.

Published by iUniverse.com, $13.95, 135 pages, ISBN: 978-1-4401-1344-4

Destined for Infinity

Deep within the mystical and spiritual practices of India are doors that lead to various levels of both higher and lower planes of existence. Few people from the outside are ever able to enter into the depths of these practices to experience such levels of reality.

This is the story of the mystical adventure of a man, Roman West, who entered deep into the secrets of India where few other Westerners have been able to penetrate. While living with a master in the Himalayan foothills and traveling the mystical path that leads to the Infinite, he witnesses the amazing powers the mystics can achieve and undergoes some of the most unusual experiences of his life. Under the guidance of a master that he meets in the mountains, he gradually develops mystic abilities of his own and attains the sacred vision of the enlightened sages and enters the unfathomable realm of Infinity. However, his peaceful life in the hills comes to an abrupt end when he is unexpectedly forced to confront the powerful forces of darkness that have been unleashed by an evil Tantric priest to kill both Roman and his master. His only chance to defeat the intense forces of darkness depends on whatever spiritual strength he has been able to develop.

This story includes traditions and legends that have existed for hundreds and thousands of years. All of the philosophy, rituals, mystic powers, forms of meditation, and descriptions of the Absolute are authentic and taken from narrations found in many of the sacred books of the East, or gathered by the author from his own experiences in India and information from various sages themselves.

This book will will prepare you to perceive the multi-dimensional realities that exist all around us, outside our sense perception. This is a book that will give you many insights into the broad possibilities of our life and purpose in this world.

Published by iUniverse.com, $16.95, 255 pages, 6" x 9" trim size, ISBN: 0-595-33959-X.

Reincarnation and Karma: How They Really Affect Us

Everyone may know a little about reincarnation, but few understand the complexities and how it actually works. Now you can find out how reincarnation and karma really affect us. Herein all of the details are provided on how a person is implicated for better or worse by their own actions. You will understand why particular situations in life happen, and how to make improvements for one's future. You will see why it appears that bad things happen to good people, or even why good things happen to bad people, and what can be done about it.

Other topics include:
- Reincarnation recognized throughout the world
- The most ancient teachings on reincarnation
- Reincarnation in Christianity
- How we transmigrate from one body to another
- Life between lives
- Going to heaven or hell
- The reason for reincarnation
- Free will and choice
- Karma of the nation
- How we determine our own destiny
- What our next life may be like
- Becoming free from all karma and how to prepare to make our next life the best possible.

Combine this with modern research into past life memories and experiences and you will have a complete view of how reincarnation and karma really operate.

Published by iUniverse.com, $13.95, 135 pages, 6" x 9" trim size, ISBN: 0-595-34199-3.

Vedic Culture
The Difference It Can Make In Your Life

The Vedic culture of India is rooted in Sanatana-dharma, the eternal and universal truths that are beneficial to everyone. It includes many avenues of self-development that an increasing number of people from the West are starting to investigate and use, including:

- Yoga
- Meditation and spiritual practice
- Vedic astrology
- Ayurveda
- Vedic gemology
- Vastu or home arrangement
- Environmental awareness
- Vegetarianism
- Social cooperation and arrangement
- The means for global peace
- And much more

Vedic Culture: The Difference It Can Make In Your Life shows the advantages of the Vedic paths of improvement and self-discovery that you can use in your life to attain higher personal awareness, happiness, and fulfillment. It also provides a new view of what these avenues have to offer from some of the most prominent writers on Vedic culture in the West, who discovered how it has affected and benefited their own lives. They write about what it has done for them and then explain how their particular area of interest can assist others. The noted authors include, David Frawley, Subhash Kak, Chakrapani Ullal, Michael Cremo, Jeffrey Armstrong, Robert Talyor, Howard Beckman, Andy Fraenkel, George Vutetakis, Pratichi Mathur, Dhan Rousse, Arun Naik, and Stephen Knapp, all of whom have authored numerous books or articles of their own.

For the benefit of individuals and social progress, the Vedic system is as relevant today as it was in ancient times. Discover why there is a growing renaissance in what the Vedic tradition has to offer in *Vedic Culture*.

Published by iUniverse.com, 300 pages, 6"x 9" trim size, $22.95, ISBN: 0-595-37120-5.

The Heart of Hinduism:
The Eastern Path to Freedom, Empowerment and Illumination

This is a definitive and easy to understand guide to the essential as well as devotional heart of the Vedic/Hindu philosophy. You will see the depths of wisdom and insights that are contained within this profound spiritual knowledge. It is especially good for anyone who lacks the time to research the many topics that are contained within the numerous Vedic manuscripts and to see the advantages of knowing them. This also provides you with a complete process for progressing on the spiritual path, making way for individual empowerment, freedom, and spiritual illumination. All the information is now at your fingertips.

Some of the topics you will find include:
- A complete review of all the Vedic texts and the wide range of topics they contain. This also presents the traditional origins of the Vedic philosophy and how it was developed, and their philosophical conclusion.
- The uniqueness and freedom of the Vedic system.
- A description of the main yoga processes and their effectiveness.
- A review of the Vedic Gods, such as Krishna, Shiva, Durga, Ganesh, and others. You will learn the identity and purpose of each.
- You will have the essential teachings of Lord Krishna who has given some of the most direct and insightful of all spiritual messages known to humanity, and the key to direct spiritual perception.
- The real purpose of yoga and the religious systems.
- What is the most effective spiritual path for this modern age and what it can do for you, with practical instructions for deep realizations.
- The universal path of devotion, the one world religion.
- How Vedic culture is the last bastion of deep spiritual truth.
- Plus many more topics and information for your enlightenment.

So to dive deep into what is Hinduism and the Vedic path to freedom and spiritual perception, this book will give you a jump start. Knowledge is the process of personal empowerment, and no knowledge will give you more power than deep spiritual understanding. And those realizations described in the Vedic culture are the oldest and some of the most profound that humanity has ever known.

Published by iUniverse.com, 650 pages, $35.95, 6" x 9" trim size, ISBN: 0-595-35075-5.

The Power of the Dharma
An Introduction to Hinduism and Vedic Culture

The Power of the Dharma offers you a concise and easy-to-understand overview of the essential principles and customs of Hinduism and the reasons for them. It provides many insights into the depth and value of the timeless wisdom of Vedic spirituality and why the Dharmic path has survived for so many hundreds of years. It reveals why the Dharma is presently enjoying a renaissance of an increasing number of interested people who are exploring its teachings and seeing what its many techniques of Self-discovery have to offer.

Herein you will find:

- Quotes by noteworthy people on the unique qualities of Hinduism
- Essential principles of the Vedic spiritual path
- Particular traits and customs of Hindu worship and explanations of them
- Descriptions of the main Yoga systems
- The significance and legends of the colorful Hindu festivals Benefits of Ayurveda, Vastu, Vedic Astrology and gemology,
- Important insights of Dharmic life and how to begin.

The Dharmic path can provide you the means for attaining your own spiritual realizations and experiences. In this way it is as relevant today as it was thousands of years ago. This is the power of the Dharma since its universal teachings have something to offer anyone.

Published by iUniverse.com, 170 pages, 6" x 9" trim size, $16.95, ISBN: 0-595-39352-7.

Seeing Spiritual India
A Guide to Temples, Holy Sites, Festivals and Traditions

This book is for anyone who wants to know of the many holy sites that you can visit while traveling within India, how to reach them, and what is the history and significance of these most spiritual of sacred sites, temples, and festivals. It also provides a deeper understanding of the mysteries and spiritual traditions of India.

This book includes:

- Descriptions of the temples and their architecture, and what you will see at each place.
- Explanations of holy places of Hindus, Buddhists, Sikhs, Jains, Parsis, and Muslims.
- The spiritual benefits a person acquires by visiting them.
- Convenient itineraries to take to see the most of each area of India, which is divided into East, Central, South, North, West, the Far Northeast, and Nepal.
- Packing list suggestions and how to prepare for your trip, and problems to avoid.
- How to get the best experience you can from your visit to India.
- How the spiritual side of India can positively change you forever.

This book goes beyond the usual descriptions of the typical tourist attractions and opens up the spiritual venue waiting to be revealed for a far deeper experience on every level.

Published by iUniverse.com, 592 pages, $33.95, ISBN: 978-0-595-50291-2.

Crimes Against India:
And the Need to Protect its Ancient Vedic Traditions

1000 Years of Attacks Against Hinduism and What to Do about It

India has one of the oldest and most dynamic cultures of the world. Yet, many people do not know of the many attacks, wars, atrocities and sacrifices that Indian people have had to undergo to protect and preserve their country and spiritual tradition over the centuries. Many people also do not know of the many ways in which this profound heritage is being attacked and threatened today, and what we can do about it.

Therefore, some of the topics included are:

- How there is a war against Hinduism and its yoga culture.
- The weaknesses of India that allowed invaders to conquer her.
- Lessons from India's real history that should not be forgotten.
- The atrocities committed by the Muslim invaders, and how they tried to destroy Vedic culture and its many temples, and slaughtered thousands of Indian Hindus.
- How the British viciously exploited India and its people for its resources.
- How the cruelest of all Christian Inquisitions in Goa tortured and killed thousands of Hindus.
- Action plans for preserving and strengthening Vedic India.
- How all Hindus must stand up and be strong for Sanatana-dharma, and promote the cooperation and unity for a Global Vedic Community.

India is a most resilient country, and is presently becoming a great economic power in the world. It also has one of the oldest and dynamic cultures the world has ever known, but few people seem to understand the many trials and difficulties that the country has faced, or the present problems India is still forced to deal with in preserving the culture of the majority Hindus who live in the country. This is described in the real history of the country, which a decreasing number of people seem to recall.

Therefore, this book is to honor the efforts that have been shown by those in the past who fought and worked to protect India and its culture, and to help preserve India as the homeland of a living and dynamic Vedic tradition of Sanatana-dharma (the eternal path of duty and wisdom).

Available from iUniverse.com, 370 pages, $24.95, ISBN: 978-1-4401-1158-7.

The Eleventh Commandment
The Next Step in Social Spiritual Development

A New Code to Bring Humanity to a Higher Level of Spiritual Consciousness

Based on the Universal Spiritual Truths, or the deeper levels of spiritual understanding, it presents a new code in a completely nonsectarian way that anyone should be able and willing to follow. We all know of the basic ten commandments which deal mostly with moralistic principles, but here is the Eleventh Commandment that will surely supplant the previous ones and provide a truly spiritual dimension to everything we do. It increases our awareness of the spiritual nature all around and within us.

Herein is the next step for consideration, which can be used as a tool for guidance, and for setting a higher standard in our society today. This new commandment expects and directs us toward a change in our social awareness and spiritual consciousness. It is conceived, formulated, and now provided to assist humanity in reaching its true destiny, and to bring a new spiritual dimension into the basic fabric of our ordinary every day life. It is a key that unlocks the doors of perception, and opens up a whole new aspect of spiritual understanding for all of us to view. It is the commandment which precepts us to gain the knowledge of the hidden mysteries, which have for so long remained an enigma to the confused and misdirected men of this world. It holds the key which unlocks the answers to man's quest for peace and happiness, and the next step for spiritual growth on a dynamic and all-inclusive social level.

This 11th Commandment and the explanations provided show the means for curing social ills, reducing racial prejudices, and create more harmony between the races and cultures. It shows how to recognize the Divine within yourself and all beings around you. It shows how we can bring some of the spiritual atmosphere into this earthly existence, especially if we expect to reach the higher domain after death. It also explains how to:

- Identify our real Self and distinguish it from our false self.
- Open our hearts to one another and view others with greater appreciation.
- Utilize higher consciousness in everyday life.
- Find inner contentment and joy.
- Attain a higher spiritual awareness and perception.
- Manifest God's plan for the world.
- Be a reflection of God's love toward everyone.
- Attain the Great Realization of perceiving the Divine in all beings.

The world is in need of a new direction in its spiritual development, and this 11th Commandment is given as the next phase to manifest humanity's most elevated potentials.

This book is $13.95, Size: 6" x 9", Pages: 128, ISBN: 0-595-46741-5.

Yoga and Meditation Their Real Purpose and How to Get Started

Yoga is a nonsectarian spiritual science that has been practiced and developed over thousands of years. The benefits of yoga are numerous. On the mental level it strengthens concentration, determination, and builds a stronger character that can more easily sustain various tensions in our lives for peace of mind. The assortment of *asanas* or postures also provide stronger health and keeps various diseases in check. They improve physical strength, endurance and flexibility. These are some of the goals of yoga.

Its ultimate purpose is to raise our consciousness to directly perceive the spiritual dimension. Then we can have our own spiritual experiences. The point is that the more spiritual we become, the more we can perceive that which is spiritual. As we develop and grow in this way through yoga, the questions about spiritual life are no longer a mystery to solve, but become a reality to experience. It becomes a practical part of our lives. This book will show you how to do that. Some of the topics include:

- Benefits of yoga
- The real purpose of yoga
- The types of yoga, such as Hatha yoga, Karma yoga, Raja and Astanga yogas, Kundalini yoga, Bhakti yoga, Mudra yoga, Mantra yoga, and others.
- The Chakras and Koshas
- Asanas and postures, and the Surya Namaskar
- Pranayama and breathing techniques for inner changes
- Deep meditation and how to proceed
- The methods for using mantras
- Attaining spiritual enlightenment, and much more

This book is 6"x9" trim size, $17.95, 240 pages, 32 illustration, ISBN: 1451553269.

Avatars, Gods and Goddesses of Vedic Culture

The Characteristics, Powers and Positions of the Hindu Divinities

Understanding the assorted Divinities or gods and goddesses of the Vedic or Hindu pantheon is not so difficult as some people may think when it is presented simply and effectively. And that is what you will find in this book. This will open you to many of the possibilities and potentials of the Vedic tradition, and show how it has been able to cater to and fulfill the spiritual needs and development of so many people since time immemorial. Here you will find there is something for everyone.

This takes you into the heart of the deep, Vedic spiritual knowledge of how to perceive the Absolute Truth, the Supreme and the various powers and agents of the universal creation. This explains the characteristics and nature of the Vedic Divinities and their purposes, powers, and the ways they influence and affect the natural energies of the universe. It also shows how they can assist us and that blessings from them can help our own spiritual and material development and potentialities, depending on what we need.

Some of the Vedic Divinities that will be explained include Lord Krishna, Vishnu, Their main avatars and expansions, along with Brahma, Shiva, Ganesh, Murugan, Surya, Hanuman, as well as the goddesses of Sri Radha, Durga, Sarasvati, Lakshmi, and others. This also presents explanations of their names, attributes, dress, weapons, instruments, the meaning of the Shiva lingam, and some of the legends and stories that are connected with them. This will certainly give you a new insight into the expansive nature of the Vedic tradition.

This book is: $17.95 retail, 230 pages, 11 black & white photos, ISBN: 1453613765, EAN: 9781453613764.

The Soul
Understanding Our Real Identity
The Key to Spiritual Awakening

This book provides a summarization of the most essential spiritual knowledge that will give you the key to spiritual awakening. The descriptions will give you greater insights and a new look at who and what you really are as a spiritual being.

The idea that we are more than merely these material bodies is pervasive. It is established in every religion and spiritual path in this world. However, many religions only hint at the details of this knowledge, but if we look around we will find that practically the deepest and clearest descriptions of the soul and its characteristics are found in the ancient Vedic texts of India.

Herein you will find some of the most insightful spiritual knowledge and wisdom known to mankind. Some of the topics include:

*   How you are more than your body
*   The purpose of life
*   Spiritual ignorance of the soul is the basis of illusion and suffering
*   The path of spiritual realization
*   How the soul is eternal
*   The unbounded nature of the soul
*   What is the Supersoul
*   Attaining direct spiritual perception and experience of our real identity

This book will give you a deeper look into the ancient wisdom of India's Vedic, spiritual culture, and the means to recognize your real identity.

This book is 5 ½" x 8 1/2" trim size, 130 pages, $7.95, ISBN: 1453733833.

Prayers, Mantras and Gayatris
A Collection for Insights, Spiritual Growth, Protection, and Many Other Blessings

Using mantras or prayers can help us do many things, depending on our intention. First of all, it is an ancient method that has been used successfully to raise our consciousness, our attitude, aim of life, and outlook, and prepare ourselves for perceiving higher states of being.

The Sanskrit mantras within this volume offer such things as the knowledge and insights for spiritual progress, including higher perceptions and understandings of the Absolute or God, as well as the sound vibrations for awakening our higher awareness, invoking the positive energies to help us overcome obstacles and oppositions, or to assist in healing our minds and bodies from disease or negativity. They can provide the means for requesting protection on our spiritual path, or from enemies, ghosts, demons, or for receiving many other benefits. In this way, they offer a process for acquiring blessings of all kinds, both material and spiritual. There is something for every need.

Some of what you will find includes:

- The most highly recommended mantras for spiritual realization in this age.
- A variety of prayers and gayatris to Krishna, Vishnu and other avatars, Goddess Lakshmi for financial well-being, Shiva, Durga, Ganesh, Devi, Indra, Sarasvati, etc., and Surya the Sun-god, the planets, and for all the days of the week.
- Powerful prayers of spiritual insight in Shiva's Song, along with the Bhaja Govindam by Sri Adi Shankaracharya, the Purusha Sukta, Brahma-samhita, Isha Upanishad, Narayana Suktam, and Hanuman Chalisa.
- Prayers and mantras to Sri Chaitanya and Nityananda.
- Strong prayers for protection from Lord Narasimha. The protective shield from Lord Narayana.
- Lists of the 108 names of Lord Krishna, Radhika, Goddess Devi, Shiva, and Sri Rama.
- The Vishnu-Sahasranama or thousand names of Vishnu, Balarama, Gopala, Radharani, and additional lists of the sacred names of the Vedic Divinities;
- And many other prayers, mantras and stotras for an assortment of blessings and benefits.

This book is 6"x9" trim size, 760 pages, ISBN:1456545906, or 978-1456545901, $31.95.

Krishna Deities and Their Miracles
How the Images of Lord Krishna Interact With Their Devotees

This book helps reveal how the Deities of Krishna in the temple are but another channel through which the Divine can be better understood and perceived. In fact, the Deities Themselves can exhibit what some would call miracles in the way They reveal how the Divine accepts the Deity form. These miracles between the Deities of Krishna and His devotees happen in many different ways, and all the time. This is one process through which Krishna, or the Supreme Being, reveals Himself and the reality of His existence. Stories of such miracles or occurrences extend through the ages up to modern times, and all around the world. This book relates an assortment of these events to show how the images in the temples have manifested Their personality and character in various ways in Their pastimes with Their devotees, whether it be for developing their devotion, instructing them, or simply giving them His kindness, mercy or inspiration.

This book helps show that the Supreme Reality is a person who can play and exhibit His pastimes in any manner He likes. This is also why worship of the Deity in the temple has been and remains a primary means of increasing one's devotion and connection with the Supreme Being.

Besides presenting stories of the reciprocation that can exist between Krishna in His Deity form and the ordinary living beings, other topics include:

The antiquity of devotion to the Deity in the Vedic tradition.

Historical sites of ancient Deity worship.

Scriptural instructions and references to Deity veneration.

The difference between idols and Deities.

What is darshan and the significance of Deities.

Why God would even take the initiative to reveal Himself to His devotees and accept the position of being a Deity.

This book will give deeper insight into the unlimited personality and causeless benevolence of the Supreme, especially to those who become devoted to Him.

This book is 210 pages, 6"x9" trim size, $14.95, ISBN-10: 1463734298, ISBN-13: 978-1463734299.

Defending Vedic Dharma
Tackling the Issues to Make a Difference

The Vedic Culture and its philosophy is one of the most deeply spiritual and all encompassing traditions in the world. It has been a major contributor to philosophical thought and the development of civilization. This book takes some of the issues of the day and describes what they are and the remedies for dealing with them in order to make a difference in how we participate in Vedic culture, how we can make it more effective in our lives, and how it can be perceived in a more positive way. All of this makes a difference in the objectives of preserving, protecting, promoting, and perpetuating the Vedic spiritual path.

So this book shows some of the many uplifting and insightful qualities we can find in the Vedic tradition, of which everyone should be aware and can appreciate.

Some of the stronger and important issues discussed within include:

Why it is important to use the proper vocabulary to express Vedic concepts.

Why all religions really are not the same, though many Hindus and gurus like to think they are. Time to wake up to reality.

The power of a united Vedic community, and how it could rapidly change things if Hindus actually became more united and worked together.

The importance of becoming a Dharmic leader and to do your part, and the danger of Hindu teachers who really do not know how to lead.

The long-term but realistic cure for the corruption in India.

The importance of Vedic temples as centers of sacred knowledge, and why temples should be open to everyone.

How and why the Vedic texts say that the knowledge within them must be shared with everyone.

The real purpose of the natural Vedic way of social arrangement, but why the present caste system in India should be changed.

An eight point action plan for how Hindus in America can best use the freedoms they have, which often exceed the decreasing freedoms in India, to cultivate their tradition to its fullest extent.

The clarity with which these and other issues are addressed make this an important book for consideration.

This book is 212 pages, $12.95, ISBN: 1466342277.

www.stephen-knapp.com
www.stephenknapp.info
http://stephenknapp.wordpress.com

Be sure to visit Stephen's web site. It provides lots of information on many spiritual aspects of Vedic and spiritual philosophy, and Indian culture for both beginners and the scholarly. You will find:

- All the descriptions and contents of Stephen's books, how to order them, and keep up with any new books or articles that he has written.
- Reviews and unsolicited letters from readers who have expressed their appreciation for his books, as well as his website.
- Free online booklets are also available for your use or distribution on meditation, why be a Hindu, how to start yoga, meditation, etc.
- Helpful prayers, mantras, gayatris, and devotional songs.
- Over a hundred enlightening articles that can help answer many questions about life, the process of spiritual development, the basics of the Vedic path, or how to broaden our spiritual awareness. Many of these are emailed among friends or posted on other web sites.
- Over 150 color photos taken by Stephen during his travels through India. There are also descriptions and 40 photos of the huge and amazing Kumbha Mela festival.
- Directories of many Krishna and Hindu temples around the world to help you locate one near you, where you can continue your experience along the Eastern path.
- Postings of the recent archeological discoveries that confirm the Vedic version of history.
- Photographic exhibit of the Vedic influence in the Taj Mahal, questioning whether it was built by Shah Jahan or a pre-existing Vedic building.
- A large list of links to additional websites to help you continue your exploration of Eastern philosophy, or provide more information and news about India, Hinduism, ancient Vedic culture, Vaishnavism, Hare Krishna sites, travel, visas, catalogs for books and paraphernalia, holy places, etc.
- A large resource for vegetarian recipes, information on its benefits, how to get started, ethnic stores, or non-meat ingredients and supplies.
- A large "Krishna Darshan Art Gallery" of photos and prints of Krishna and Vedic divinities. You can also find a large collection of previously unpublished photos of His Divine Grace A. C. Bhaktivedanta Swami.

This site is made as a practical resource for your use and is continually being updated and expanded with more articles, resources, and information. Be sure to check it out.

Printed in Great Britain
by Amazon